THE MAMMOTH BOOK OF

FIGHTER PILOTS

Also available

THE MAMMOTH BOOK OF
FIGHTER PILOTS

EDITED BY JON E. LEWIS

WITH JULIAN JENKINS

CARROLL & GRAF PUBLISHERS
New York

Carroll and Graf Publishers
An imprint of Avalon Publishing Group, Inc.
245 West 17th Street
New York, NY 10011
www.carrollandgraf.com

First published in the UK by Robinson,
an imprint of Constable & Robinson Ltd, 2002

First Carroll & Graf edition 2002

Reprinted 2004

ISBN 0-7867-1066-7

Printed and bound in the EU

This one is for Alice Jenkins,
Tristram and Freda Lewis-Stempel, all "ace" kids.

CONTENTS

ACKNOWLEDGMENTS & SOURCES

The editor has made every effort to locate all persons having rights in the selections appearing in this anthology and to secure permission for reproduction of material from the holders of such rights. In the event of any errors being inadvertently made, these will be corrected in future editions. Queries regarding the use of material should be made to the editor c/o the publishers.

"The Wings Starts to Grow" is an extract from *Wind in the Wires*, Duncan Grinnell-Milne, Mayflower Books Ltd, 1966. Copyright (C) Duncan Grinnell-Milne 1966.

"The Red Air Fighter" is an extract from *The Red Battle Flyer*, Manfred von Richthofen, trans T. Ellis Barker, McBride & Co., 1918.

"Blue Nose" is an extract from *Winged Warfare*, William A. Bishop, Pan Books Ltd., 1978. Copyright (C) Stanley M. Ulanoff 1967.

"Sagittarius Rising" is an extract from *Sagittarius Rising*, Cecil Lewis, Peter Davies Ltd, 1966 Copyright (C) Cecil Lewis 1936.

"Letters Home" by H.G. Downing, Department of Documents, Imperial War Museum, London.

"Flying Fury" is an extract from *Five Years in the Royal Flying Corps*, James McCudden, Aeroplane & General Publishing Co., 1940.

"Death Flies Faster" is an extract from *Ace of the Iron Cross*, Ernst Udet, edited by Stanley M. Ulanoff, Doubleday & Co., 1970. Trans. Richard K. Riehn. Copyright (C) Stanley M. Ulanoff 1970.

"Crashes & Cocktails" is an extract from *War Birds: Diary of an Unknown Aviator* (John McGavock Grider), John Hamilton Ltd, 1926.

"Prisoner of War" is an extract from *High Adventure*, James Norman Hall, Houghton Mifflin, 1918.

"A Regular Dog-Fight and the Strafing of a Drachen" is an extract from *Fighting the Flying Circus*, Captain Edward V. Rickenbacker, Stokes, 1919.

"Action" is an extract from *Fighter Pilot*, Paul Richey, Pan Books Ltd, 1969. Copyright (C) Paul Richey 1969.

"Battle of Britain Diary", D.H. Wissler, unpublished diary, Department of Documents, Imperial War Museum, London. Reprinted by permission of Edith Kup.

"Finest Hour" by John Beard, quoted in *Their Finest Hour*, Allan A. Michie and Walter Graebner, Harcourt Brace, & Co., 1941.

"Tally Ho!" is an extract from *Clouds of Fear*, Roger Hall, Bailey Brothers and Swinfen Ltd, 1975. Copyright (C) 1975 R.M.D. Hall.

"Shall I Live For a Ghost?" is an extract from *The Last Enemy*, Richard Hillary, Macmillan & Co., 1943.

"Night Fighter" is an extract from *Cover of Darkness*, Roderick Chisholm, Chatto & Windus, 1953.

"Dogsbody" is an extract from *Wing Leader*, "Johnnie Johnson", Goodall Publications Ltd. 1990. Copyright (C) 1956, 1974, 1990 J.E. Johnson.

"The Flying Tigers" is an extract from *Way of a Fighter*, Claire L. Chennault, Putnam, 1949. Copyright (C) Claire L. Chennault 1949.

"To Kill a Man" is an extract from *Heaven Next Stop*, Gunther Bloemertz, William Kimber & Co. Ltd., 1953. Copyright (C) William Kimber & Co. Ltd. 1953.

"The Straits of Messina" is an extract from *Straits of Messina*, Johannes Steinhoff, André Deutsch Ltd., 1973. Copyright (C) Paul List Verlag KG 1969. Translation copyright (C) André Deutsch Ltd. 1971.

"Baa Baa Black Sheep" is an extract from *Baa Baa Black Sheep*, "Pappy" Boyington, Putnam, 1958. Copyright (C) Gregory Boyington 1958.

"Heavy Babies" is an extract from *I Flew for the Führer*, Heinz Knoke, Corgi, 1956. trans John Ewing.

"Mission to Regensburg", Beirne Lay, is extracted from *Bombs Away!*, edited by Stanley M. Ulanoff, Doubleday, 1971.

"Flying High" is an extract from *Yeager*, General Chuck Yeager and Leo Janos, Century Hutchinson, 1986. Copyright (C) Yeager Inc. 1985. Reprinted by permission of Random House Group Ltd.

"Marine Crusader" is extracted from *Life on the Line*, Philip Chinnery, Arrow Books, 1990. Copyright (C) Philip Chinnery 1988.

"Night Mission on the Ho Chi Minh Trail" by Mark Berent was first published in USAF *Air Force/Space Digest*, 1971.

"Sea Harrier Over the Falklands" is an extract from *Sea Harrier Over the Falklands*, "Sharkey" Ward, Leo Cooper, 1992. Copyright (C) Commander N.D. Ward, DSC, AFC, RN, 1992. Reproduced by permission of Pen & Sword Books.

"Interrogation" is an extract from *Tornado Down*, John Peters and John Nichol, Michael Joseph, 1992. Copyright (C) John Peters and John Nichol. Reproduced by permission of Penguin UK.

"German War Birds" is an extract from *The Flying Dutchman*, Anton H.G. Fokker, Holt, Rinehart & Winston, 1931. Copyright (C) Bruce Gould 1959.

INTRODUCTION

When the Wright brothers invented the world's first practicable aircraft in 1903, they had a dream that flight would bring the world's people closer together. It didn't take long, of course, for someone to come up with the nightmare ruse of turning the airplane into a weapon. Bombs could be dropped from it. Bullets could be fired from it. Whoever first took up a gun in his tiny canvas and wood aircraft is lost to history, but by the Balkans War of 1912 the armed flying machine was in service . . . and the fighter pilot born.

Curiously, the Great War, which opened two years later was initially reluctant to embrace the fighter pilot's martial charms. At first, the belligerents used aircraft for scouting and reconnaissance alone, with pilots waving happily to enemy airmen when they passed in the sky. This state of affairs, in a situation of total war, could not and did not last long. By winter 1915 it was commonplace for the observer in a two-seater aircraft to be toting a carbine, and soon after to be wielding a machine-gun. When Antony Fokker perfected a synchronized gear that allowed a machine gun to be fired through the propeller it allowed a single man to both fly and fire. The "classic" period of the fighter pilot followed, in which one man jousted with another in a "dog-fight" over the Western

Front and "aces" (pilots with five or more kills) such as Manfred von Richthofen and James McCudden became global legends. Much romance and status attracted to the fighter pilot, who was often an officer and a gentleman from a cavalry regiment, yet it is too easy to forget that the life-expectancy of a pilot in World War I was measured in weeks. For all the daring of those magnificent men in their flimsy flying machines, they too were bullet fodder.

In the long interval of the 1920s and 30s, before World War was recommenced, the fighter pilot went somewhat out of fashion, at least in the higher circles of military thinking. Under the influence of the Italian military theorist Douhet a number of notable air forces, including Britain's RAF, became wedded to the notion that wars might be won by strategic bombing campaign. Only in the very last year of peace was the RAF persuaded to invest heavily in fighter, as opposed to bomber, production. As history has recorded, it was a wise move; for it was "The Few", the fighter pilots of the RAF, who won the air Battle of Britain in 1940 and prevented a Nazi invasion of that country.

If the First World War provided the greatest fighter pilot legends, the Second donated to posterity the most memorable fighter aircraft. The Spitfire. The Me-109. The Zero. The Mustang. This reminds us that the fighter pilot himself (and sometimes, herself) is a creature of the machine. No other warrior, not even tank crew, is so dependent on technology, on advances in technology and understanding of that technology. Invariably the pilot with the fleeter, faster and better armoured craft will triumph in an engagement. Hence the frenzied development of the fighter over the last century, a development which took a quantum leap into the air when the Luftwaffe, in the dying days of World War II, brought the jet-powered Me 262 out of the hangar. The Me 262 was produced too late to save the Third Reich but it was the writing in the sky for the future of the fighter pilot and his charge. The Korean War of 1950–3 was the last major war to see the use of propeller-driven fighter. Since then, the fighter pilot has become an ever more accomplished jet-powered technocrat. The F-16s, Tornados and Harriers which screamed over the skies of Vietnam, the Falklands and the Gulf were computerised, hitec, multi-million dollar machines that delivered death at a speed and intensity that von Richthofen would have been incapable of even imagining. Such indeed is the speed of modern jet fighters, which in the shape of the Russian Mikoyan MiG-25 "Foxbat" can top March 3, that classic dog fighting is impossible. Jet duels, instead, are high-speed passes where the missile-firing protagonists are often miles apart.

Von Richthofen would, however, recognise much of himself in the man in the contemporary cockpit. The fighter pilot of today, like his forbear, still relies on quick wits, courage, some uncanny sixth spatial sense of danger and evasion, plus the deadly hunting instinct. (The first German air units were, incidentally, called *Jagdstaffeln* or Hunting Squadrons). There is a true paradox in the heart of every fighter pilot: he flies the only truly modern weapon, yet uses the same warrior skills as an ancient *samurai*. The sheer individuality of the fighter pilot, a man alone or at most accompanied by one or two crew, also stands out in the epoch of mass, uniformed warfare. Small wonder, then, that history and culture has tended to see the fighter pilot as a knight in flying armour, jousting with opponents in a blue battlefield. The Sir Galahad of the Air, in fact

The pages which follow address the perennial question of the earth-bound: What is it like to be a fighter pilot? Twenty-seven fighter pilots, from World War I to the Gulf, answer that question in their own words, from their autobiographies, diaries and letters. There are necessarily and happily (for the armchair reader, at least) numerous accounts of aerial combat, but other aspects of the fighter pilot's active service over the last century are not forgotten: R&R in World War I, capture and interrogation by enemy forces in the Gulf, being hospitalised for burns after baling out of a flaming Spitfire in the Battle of Britain. For good measure, there is also an account by a USAAF bomb crew member, Beirne Lay, on the few joys of being on the receiving end of a fighter pilot's attention. The book follows a rough time order, to allow the reader to appreciate the changing experience, tactics and machinery of war in the air.

Scramble! It's now time to climb into the cockpit . . .

Jon E. Lewis

THE WINGS START TO GROW

DUNCAN GRINNELL-MILNE

Grinnell-Milne left the infantry in 1915 for training as a pilot in the Royal Flying Corps. The experience is recorded below.

I arrived at Shoreham after dark. On the way from London, or rather during the change of trains at Brighton, I met an officer bound for the same destination. His name was on his luggage-labels, together with the address of the particular Reserve Air Squadron which I myself was to join. As he was a subaltern and as I saw no signs of his being a qualified aviator, I was not more than usually awed by the fact that he was a Gunner. I had hoped that in aviation he would be as much of a novice as I was, but in the course of conversation he informed me that he had been at Shoreham quite a long time, that he was in fact just returning from leave which, I knew, was not usually granted until one had fully qualified. My respect for him increased.

I asked him about the Squadron. He was very willing to talk and the first impression he gave me was encouraging: few parades, no unnecessary drill, no compulsory church on Sundays, rather more liberty than in an infantry regiment – provided, of course, that one "got on well." That, to me, meant showing promise as a pilot; my head was, so to speak, already in the air. And my companion must, I thought, be something of an expert, spending most of each day off the ground, for he told me that he "simply loved the work."

But a little later he let fall that he was struggling to qualify as a Squadron Adjutant and had practically given up the idea of becoming an Active Service pilot. Also he told me that no one did much flying at Shoreham and that after a few days' trial many officers returned to their regiments. I was not quite so sure that I was going to "love the work."

At Shoreham station a Crossley tender met us – that, at any rate, was a step up from the infantry! – and took us over to the Mess in a bungalow near the sea. There, in addition to an air of comfortable informality, I found cheese, biscuits and beer.

ii

The next day was Saturday, no parades but attendance at the aerodrome. From the Mess to the aerodrome was perhaps as much as a mile; we were driven there in a Crossley tender.

In the sheds was a collection of aircraft, most of them interesting museum pieces in which we were to be instructed, and two dangerous-looking single-seaters (said to be capable of ninety miles an hour!) with which, I was glad to hear, we were to have no dealings whatsoever. There were about half a dozen of us novices and the same number of older pupils. The instructors were pre-war regular officers, of the rank of Captain; they had flown in France, had actually been fired at in the air, had survived engine failures, forced landings, rifle fire and what not. We regarded them as living evidence that the Age of Heroes had come again.

During the morning, one of the museum pieces was wheeled from its shed and set down upon the edge of the turf. With much pushing and pulling it was carefully arranged so as to face into the wind, although to us laymen the manoeuvre was a little obscure, since the bows of the aeroplane were almost identical with its stern. It had an elevator – or stabilizing surface – stuck out in front upon curving outriggers of wood, and a double set of stabilizers – or elevators – fixed to wooden spars at the stern. But for the propeller which drove the machine inexorably forward and the arrangement of the pilot's seat and controls, it might have been designed to travel in either direction. Officially it was called after its inventor: a Maurice Farman biplane; but it was better known as a "Long-horn," because of the outriggers to the forward elevator. A slightly more modern sister-ship was called the "Short-horn," because the inventor had, rather rashly we thought, done away with the outriggers and elevator; and taking them all round the *vaches mécaniques* of Monsieur Farman's breeding were pleasant beasts. But except for slowness and docility the resemblance to cows ended with the horns. To the uninitiated eye the Longhorn presented such a forest of struts and spars, with floppy white fabric drooped over all, it inevitably brought to mind a prosperous seaport in the heyday of sailing ships, whilst piano-wire was festooned everywhere to such an extent that the wrecking of a few of these machines before the lines in Flanders would have provided our troops with an impenetrable entanglement. At the sight of the craft before us, we put our heads on one side like puzzled terriers.

Presently the Longhorn's engine was started up. It was a Renault of uncertain strength, eight-cylindered, air-cooled, small but wonderfully reliable. When running slowly it made a noise like a pair of alarm-clocks ticking upon a marble mantelpiece.

One of the instructors and a senior pupil picked their way through the wire entanglements, stepped over the wooden horns where they curved to the ground to become skids, mounted upon the wheels and clambered with a good deal of difficulty into the *nacelle*. No, it was not a body, nor a fuselage, nor yet a cockpit; it was a *nacelle*. The same name is used for the things that hang beneath balloons, but this *nacelle* was not of wicker. It was smooth and fairly solid-looking. It recalled the bath in which Marat was murdered. Doubtless to remove this ominous impression it had been painted a nice cheerful blue. . . . The pilot and his passenger settled down into their elevated seats, adjusted goggles, helmets, etcetera, and took a long look round as though it might be their last. After listening awhile to the engine, the pilot waved hands, attendant mechanics removed wooden blocks from beneath the wheels, and the machine moved forward slowly, lurching slightly over the uneven ground like a cow going out to pasture. The alarm-clocks ticked much louder; the mass of shipping, the network of piano-wire, the *nacelle* with its occupants, all hanging rather mysteriously together, moved away at increasing speed. The draught from the propeller rippled the grass, rushing back to make us duck and clutch at our caps.

When I looked again the Longhorn was scurrying across the aerodrome at the most alarming speed. It seemed impossible that the various parts should still be holding together. The machine hugged the ground; the curving horns, the wheels and skids, the tail-booms were all buried in the uncut grass through which the propeller seemed to be blazing a trail, and that and the noise of the receding engine made me think of nothing so much as a harvester running amok. I watched, holding my breath. And – lo! – it began to unstick from the earth. It rose a few inches; higher; it flew! O wondrous contrivance: "Hail to thee, blithe spirit, bird thou never wert!" Shelley should have been a pilot.

iii

Nowadays such a machine in flight would seem ridiculous even to a child; but to us it was impressive enough. It was flying: that alone was sufficient. There in the sky was an aeroplane in which we could take a personal interest, in which presently we too would ascend, not as passengers but as pupils. It was very thrilling.

We watched that antiquated cage of a machine as if it were our own property. We noted the manner of its leaving the ground, followed its course in the distance, observed how it banked at the turns, held our breath as it glided in to land as lightly as any thistledown. We forbore from criticism, we did not even remark to each other how, flying into the wind, this Longhorn appeared to have solved the problem of hovering like a helicopter, so low against the breeze was its forward speed. Nor did we discuss the value of such a craft in war. No matter what its limitations, this machine was to give up to us its one priceless secret, the mystery of how to fly. With luck we might some day progress to swifter, more deadly aircraft, but in this one we would first learn to grow our wings. She (*it* for such a venerable machine is not nearly enough) – she would foster the fledgelings. And out of a hundred craft, her we should never forget. . . .

We crowded round when she came to rest in front of the sheds. The instructor got down from the *nacelle*, gave orders for the machine to be put away and strode forward with an expressionless face. A pupil braver than the rest of us made so bold as to ask: "Will there be any flying today? Instructional flying?"

The instructor chewed a piece of grass.

"No," he said curtly, "It's not good enough."

There was a thin layer of cloud at about a thousand feet from the ground; the wind speed was perhaps as much as ten miles an hour. Out to sea it was a little misty. No, it was clearly not good enough.

"You didn't get very high during your flight," another pupil remarked to the lucky one who had been passenger, a grave individual who seldom spoke to the novices because he had been a motor salesman before the war and had then taken a few lessons in piloting which placed him upon a higher level than the rest of us. He pushed his way through our crowd, looking rather grim and haughty.

"Of course we didn't get high!" he answered, and there was a rebuke in his tone, "We could hardly get off the ground. No lift in the air."

He seemed very wise as I watched him stroll away. Here, thought I, was another complexity added to the puzzling business of aviation. One had to study the air. The wind must be of a certain strength, the clouds at a given height and of known density. In addition there was something of which I as yet knew nothing. I must learn to sniff the air like an old hound, a flying hound; to judge the quality of the atmosphere from the wind upon my cheek; to feel its nature between finger and thumb. Otherwise I might some day embark upon a flight only to find that there was "no lift in the air" – whatever that might mean.

iv

"In aviation," a friend of mine was wont to say, "there is as much art as science." And there is more in this remark than is at first apparent. Pursuits there are and professions that demand science and nothing else; for instance one may suppose that splitting the atom or solving the square root of minus one calls for very little art. On the other hand certain arts have scant need of science to bring them to fruition. A poet is not necessarily a scientist, not even as much of a chemist as Keats; and that other who "shot an arrow in the air" can scarcely have been an accurate observer or he would have calculated the exact spot at which "it fell to earth" – but then perhaps he was not a very good poet. And with aeronautics, in its earlier stages, art often seemed to be marching ahead of a science that was in its infancy and waiting for the pilots whose progressive discoveries, be it said, were frequently the result of accident.

I began to glean information concerning my new calling.

To be successful, I gathered, a pilot must learn to steer a steady course between the Charybdis of "spinning," the remedy for which was not yet known, and the Scylla of diving into the hard, hard ground. "Stalling" – that was a word I heard on everyone's lips: to lose flying-speed and, in consequence, all control of the machine. There were other minor difficulties to be reckoned with, mainly those connected with the strength – or rather the weakness – of the aeroplanes of those days. At all points one encountered either the unknown, or else more or less certain structural dangers. It was, they told me, courting death to dive the majority of machines at any appreciable angle, the speed and increased strain would pull the wings off. To bank too steeply might involve a sideslip or loss of flying-speed, either of which might quickly develop into the irremediable spin. "Looping" had, of course, been done and overdone before the war, but only on machines strong enough to stand the strain. Had anyone attempted to loop a Longhorn, the poor old lady would have tied herself into knots. And since looping was of no value by itself it was neither taught nor encouraged on any type of machine.

Before coming to Shoreham I had been taken up as a passenger several times, so that I had a rudimentary knowledge of flying. But now I perceived what innumerable lessons there were to be learned, anxiously, attentively, before one could hope to become an artist worthy of the name of Air Pilot. The whole business was unpleasantly suggestive of tight-rope walking, the margins of safety were so narrow. A Longhorn – and a good many other machines for that matter – would leave the ground at under forty miles an hour, and I doubt if her top speed ever exceeded forty-six or seven whatever may have been calculated on paper. This gave one a variation of some ten miles an hour; if you went too fast something fell off or snapped; if any slower you stalled, spun, dived, slipped one way or another and ended for a certainty by breaking your neck. And then there was the question of the engine. At full power it was just enough to get one safely off the ground and to climb high enough for turning, but if you drove along at too great a speed the engine would overheat, and at the slightest loss of power the nose of the machine had to be pushed well down to maintain flying-speed. A tricky business!

In the Mess we talked a great deal of shop.

v

Eighteen is an impressionable age, especially for a budding pilot, so that it is not surprising that the first real lessons – roughly, horribly taught – should have been driven into me with such force that I never afterwards forgot them. It happened on a Sunday, my very first Sunday at Shoreham.

The day of the week did not make much difference to the routine of a Flying Corps squadron. If it were fine and there were machines available and pupils to be taught, instruction took place as usual, save that early flying was cancelled, we got up later and spent more time over breakfast. On this particular Sunday, however, the weather was not suitable. A stiff breeze came off the sea and the large masses of damp cloud everywhere would have made it far too bumpy for Longhorn work. But we strolled down to the sheds because we were all young enough to enjoy stroking our cows in the byre, even if we could not have them brought out for exercise.

At the aerodrome a treat was in store for us. A brand-new aeroplane of the most modern type had just arrived on a visit. It was being flown around the country upon a series of test flights by a well-known pilot from the Royal Aircraft Factory at Farnborough, accompanied by a civilian expert. We gathered about it in silent wonder, mindful of the pilot's request that we should not touch anything.

It was sheer joy to examine such a machine at close quarters. Those of us who had flown as passengers before coming to Shoreham had seen a good many sorts of ancient aircraft; all the greater now was our interest and admiration. The engine of this biplane was in front (like some German machines I had seen before the war), whereas most of those we knew by sight had it astern – "pushers" – and the body was long, narrow, neatly shaped. The wings were thicker than those of Maurice Farman machines; they looked solid, strong. The bracing wires were no longer cable or piano, they were of a new design: "streamline." In the pilot's cockpit was a neat dashboard with instruments. The controls were operated by a straight "stick," not "handlebars" as in the Long-horn; there was a rudder bar instead of pedals. The tanks were said to contain fuel for nearly four hours' flying, and it was evident that in addition to the passenger this aero-plane would be capable of carrying a machine-gun or bombs. An improvement upon older models of the same type, it was believed to attain no less than seventy-six miles an hour at full speed. It was known as the B.E.2c.*, its engine was the 90 horse-power "R.A.F." – the letters standing for Royal Aircraft Factory, the home of those expert minds whose latest and most immaculate concep-tion this aeroplane was.

I gazed at the pilot with envy while my imagination soared faster than the swiftest biplane. Some day I too would wear Flying Corps "Wings" upon the left breast of my tunic, I too would steer a wonderful B.E.2c. and learn to manoeuvre it with graceful ease. I would fly such a machine in France; my wings would darken the skies above the expectant battle-front, the enemy's secrets would be disclosed to me. At my approach Zeppelins would hurry home, their huge sheds leap up in flames beneath my deadly rain of bombs, Berlin would pass sleepless nights. And at the end I would make a perfect landing before the assembled heads of the Flying Corps. . . .

So much for the colourful imagination of extreme youth.

---

* Bleriot Experimental 2c, *nicknamed "The Quirk". A two-seater air-craft, equipped with two machine guns, it was used primarily as a reconnaissance aircraft on the Western Front.*

At lunch in the Mess that day we were very quiet, listening in awed silence to the instructors and the pilot from Farnborough, discussing technicalities almost entirely over our heads. It was thrilling to hear the names of famous airmen bandied familiarly about, to hear of all the different types of aeroplanes with exaggerated speeds which we might hope to fly, and particularly to hear this so experienced pilot (a test-pilot!) give his views on how to do this and that, how to turn quickly and with almost vertical banking, how to do a spiral glide, how to deal with the ever-mysterious "spinning" and so on. It was rumoured that this pilot had frequently looped, and had even looped a B.E.2c.! We listened attentively, trying to pick up what crumbs we might from his learned conversation.

There had been talk of the test-pilot staying the night at Shoreham; he had landed because of the bad weather. But during the afternoon it cleared up considerably and the wind, although still strong, showed signs of abating. He decided to leave. We hurried down to the aerodrome to watch him go.

The beautiful machine was wheeled forward, her engine started, warmed up. The test-pilot and his civilian passenger donned much leather flying clothing, climbed into their seats. The engine having been run up and found satisfactory, the wooden chocks were removed, the machine turned and taxied out to the far side of the aerodrome. A short pause, and the pilot gave the engine full throttle, taking off obliquely towards the sheds.

Against the wind the machine rose at once and began to climb steeply. The pilot waved farewell as he passed us by, about fifty feet up, heading west into the sunlight. Against the bright sky the machine was silhouetted, hard to see beyond the end of the sheds. But, as we watched, shading our eyes, there came to us suddenly the spluttering of a starved engine. The steady roar of the exhaust died down, the nose of the machine dropped. And now this too expert pilot made his great mistake.

In the course of the short flight, he had attained a height of about one hundred and fifty feet and had crossed the boundary of the aerodrome. A road, a line of telegraph wires were beneath him, ahead a series of small meadows intersected by ditches. Rough ground, but possible in an emergency, especially as the strong wind against him would make the run on landing exceptionally short. There was, strictly speaking, no alternative for a safe, a wise pilot. But this pilot was exceedingly clever, and he wanted to save his beautiful new machine from damage. Not that it would have suffered anything worse than a broken under-carriage, possibly a smashed propeller, from the forced landing; he wished to avoid even that much. And so he tried something which, in this instance, he had not one chance in a thousand of bringing off. He turned back to the aerodrome.

In the very few seconds that followed I remember feeling, in spite of my utter ignorance of piloting, an intense admiration for the brilliant way in which he handled the machine. Without a moment's hesitation he turned down wind as quickly and as flatly as possible so as not to lose the little height he had gained, held a straight course for an instant, then over the sheds began another sharp turn that, when completed, would bring him into wind with a space of fifty or sixty yards of smooth ground on which to land. Actually it was just possible of achievement, although as I see it now he was taking a terrible risk; but the whole performance was cut too fine. He failed by much more than inches.

As he came towards the sheds his speed down wind seemed terrific, yet in trying to maintain his height he had in fact lost the essential flying-speed. He was stalling even as he banked over the sheds. The nose went down with a jerk in the first turn of a spin. He missed the roof by a miracle, but within a second of the machine's disappearance behind the shed we were horrified to hear an appalling crash.

Naturally we rushed forward in spite of the first-shouted order that all pupils should stand back – the sight of a probably fatal crash, it was rightly thought, might upset some of us – we *had* to see; we ran for it. Beyond the shed the new aeroplane lay flat on the ground, a mass of wreckage. Both men sat in their smashed cockpits motionless. Unconscious or dead? We were not long in doubt for worse was to follow. As we came nearer the wreck from which mechanics were already trying to extricate pilot and passenger, there was a flicker of flame from beneath the fuselage. And all at once the mechanics sprang back as with a roar a great flame shot up from the burst petrol tank. It swept back over the passenger; when it reached the pilot he moved uneasily, seemed to shake himself, fumbled with his safety belt, then jumped out just in time, his clothing on fire.

There were cries for extinguishers, for axes to hack through the broken wings, for help to pull away the wreckage, for the ambulance – for anything and everything to save the passenger. He was still in the machine and still alive. Mercifully he did not recover consciousness – afterwards it was found that his skull had been fractured in the crash – but he kept on moving. And we were powerless. The extinguishers had no effect upon thirty gallons of blazing petrol. The strong wind blew the flames into his face. Before our very eyes he was burnt to death, roasted. It took a long time; it was ghastly. . . .

The fire died down, smouldered awhile, went out. The wind dropped; the sun set and the sky glowed with rare beauty. But we pupils walked back to the Mess in glum silence.

vi

Upon the following morning all officers were summoned to the squadron office. We expected the summons, although I do not quite know what we expected to hear. I suppose that, amongst other things, we thought to be given news of the pilot in hospital, but possibly to be complimented upon the vain efforts we had made to penetrate the barrier of fire, and upon the sang-froid we had shown afterwards. Perhaps more than anything we hoped to hear that the fire had not been so intense as our eyes had led us to believe, that the unfortunate victim had in some way been protected – by his goggles, by his flying helmet or by his leather clothing – from the devouring fury of the flames, so that there might be a chance of his recovery. Or did we hope to be told that something mysterious had gone wrong with this new aeroplane, something very startling and unusual which could not occur again, that flying was not like this, horrible, cruel?

The Squadron-commander strode into the office, flung his cap upon the table, drew a cane chair forward. Placing one foot upon the chair, he rested an elbow on his knee.

"With regard to this unfortunate and unnecessary happening," he began harshly, "the first and only thing to do is to find out the causes of the accident, to see where the pilot was to blame so as to learn what lessons we may. Now in this particularly stupid case . . ."

I thought him terribly callous.

"A pilot must never turn down wind at a low altitude when faced with the possibility of a forced landing.

"A pilot in difficulties after leaving the ground must keep straight on.

"A pilot must save himself and his passengers first, not the aeroplane. It is better to smash wheels and propeller than burn a man to death.

"A pilot must take particular care to maintain flying-speed after engine failure. . . ."

Those were the lessons. If the manner of their teaching was hard, it was also effective.

vii

It was a long time between this accident and the start of my regular training in the air. After one preliminary flight many days passed before I was again taken up. Bad weather, too few machines and instructors, too many pupils were the real causes of delay; but I began to fret and to wonder if discrimination rather than luck was not responsible for my name so seldom being called when the Longhorns stood in fantastic array upon the turf. I remembered the words heard on the evening of my arrival from the would-be adjutant: that little flying was done at Shoreham and that many pupils returned in disgust to their regiments. I had no intention of leaving the Flying Corps until I had had a fair chance of becoming a proficient pilot, but the slowness of the commencement was discouraging.

Nearly two weeks had gone by when one evening I was noticed as I stood disconsolate in front of the sheds. An instructor saw me and beckoned. We embarked in a Longhorn; I was given a flight lasting nearly half an hour. And after that things moved more quickly. Several days in succession were marked by flights either in the stillness of very early morning or in the calm of late afternoon. I began to know my way about a Longhorn. The forest of struts did not grow any thinner, but meaning and order came to it. It no longer took me minutes to thread an anxious path through the wires; I learnt to scramble quickly into my seat in the *nacelle* where the controls were at last becoming familiar. I was allowed to feel those controls while flying. After half a dozen flights I was even permitted to land and take off with only slight assistance from the instructor. In the air I could sense some connection, however vague, between the harmonium pedals working the rudder and the handlebars shaped like a pair of spectacles which gave lateral control. Presently I felt sure that I was making steady progress.

viii

One cold grey morning a few of us were gathered upon the stretch of tarmac in front of the sheds expecting to enjoy that most exquisite of amusements, the sight of another's embarrassment, agony and discomfiture. One of our number, a man who had come to Shoreham before me and who had done considerably more flying, was to go for his first solo flight. He had been warned the night before, after half an hour in the air with the senior instructor.

"You'll go solo at dawn tomorrow," he had been told briefly. And if for "go solo" the words "be shot" had been substituted he could not have been more upset.

Anxious though we were to be taken up for instruction, we hoped that first of all we should be permitted to witness the unfortunate man's departure. Secretly, I think we rather hoped that he would crash – not badly, we wished him no harm, but just enough to provide us with real entertainment. Before one's own turn comes, one is apt to be merciless – not only in aviation.

We were discussing the prospects of this little quiet fun at another's expense, when the instructors came from the office. One of them marched up to our group; as he passed I caught his eye. He stopped. Ah-ha, I thought, this is where I put in some more instructional flying. But the winged Hero was regarding me thoughtfully with something in his eye that reminded me of a hungry tiger looking at his meat.

"How much dual control have you done?" he asked.

"Three hours and twenty minutes," I answered, hopeful that so small an amount would induce him to give me more at once.

"H'm –" he muttered, still looking at me fixedly. "Do you think you could go solo?"

The question staggered me. All my past lies flashed before me, whirled in my head and merged into one huge thumping fib.

"Yes," I answered, and at once regretted it.

"Very well then –" The instructor's voice was kind now, like that of a surgeon about to announce the necessity for a major operation. "Very well, take up Longhorn Number 2965."*

* Aircraft numbers, flying times and other details are taken from the Pilot's Log Book in the Author's [D.G-M] possession.

Behind me there was a titter of mirth, but it evoked no response on my part. My hour had struck before I was prepared. I knew nothing whatever about flying, and it was far too early in the morning and it was cold and I hadn't had my breakfast or said my prayers. I was doomed and I knew it. I felt like asking for a priest. . . . Walking blindly forward, I put on my flying cap.

Against the wings and struts of Longhorn Number 2965 mechanics were idly leaning. They made no move as I approached, gave me no more than a quick glance. They knew well enough that I was a pupil, that unless I came to a machine with an instructor there was nothing doing. But when I began to clamber into the *nacelle* they stopped talking and looked at one another uneasily.

"I am taking this machine up, Flight-Sergeant," I announced boldly.

There was a nasty sort of silence during which I felt that behind my back signs were being made indicating doubt of my sanity. At length I heard a subdued voice say, "Very good, sir. Switch off?"

"Switch off," I replied, nervously settling into the front seat of that *nacelle*, which now seemed as lonely as an autocrat's throne. At my back whispering mechanics turned the propeller. "Contact?" came a voice like that of an undertaker.

For a moment I gave myself up to the wild and wonderful hope that the engine was not going to start. They had to pull it round twice. And then it clitter-clattered into life and I knew that I was "for it." Adjusting the throttle to slowest running, I stared round fearfully at the ghastly collection of struts, tail-booms and spars that had once again resolved itself into a dense forest in which I should presently be as lost as any Babe in the Wood. Through wire entanglements I caught sight of two mechanics grinning at me. Horrible ghouls, gloating over my forthcoming demise! Was there no way out? I turned my face to the morning sky where the light was still growing. Like the tenor in *Tosca* I had never loved life so much. Not a breath of wind anywhere, save the slight draught of the slowly revolving propeller. I sniffed the air, and inspiration came to me. Perhaps if I got out of the *nacelle* and strolled nonchalantly over to the sheds murmuring, "No lift in the air," I should be granted a reprieve. I looked hastily over the side. Below stood the instructor.

"Get well out across the aerodrome before you take off," he said. "And don't taxi too fast."

I nodded, speechless, and buckled up the safety-belt.

ix

In those days the newspapers still occasionally referred to an aeroplane pilot as "the intrepid rider," and upon the instant when Longhorn and I rose gently into the air I came to know that the expression referred to me. I was intrepid whether I liked it or not. And I was certainly a rider. I squatted rigidly upright upon the edge of my elevated seat, holding the handlebars delicately between forefinger and thumb, treading the rudder pedals as though I were walking upon unbroken eggs. Behind me the alarm-clocks ticked relentlessly; ahead that tea-tray of an elevator held not only my gaze but all my hopes of surviving the adventure.

Ah, that forward elevator, what a blessing it was! It gave one something to look at, something to guide one in keeping the nose of the machine at the right level. If you kept it on or just below the horizon you were safe – until the time came to make a turn. Then you put the nose down lower still. Never make a level turn, still less a climbing one – that was bound to be fatal. Before putting on any bank push the stick forward a little to increase the speed. . . . I was remembering my lessons, anxiety was diminishing. I looked quickly about me. Everything seemed to be all right. But it would not last unless I continued to be very, very careful. I glued my eyes to the front elevator.

Presently, without daring to move my head, I rolled my

eyes towards the instruments. The altimeter was recording something. I was indeed off the ground: nearly four
hundred feet! It was exhilarating at this altitude. But only
momentarily so; I had to get back. My wrist-watch
showed that I had been in the air for no less than three
minutes. Underneath the elevator, Worthing pier was
beginning to come close. Yes, I had to get back! Without
great skill this turn would be my last. . . .

Nose down; a slight movement of the handlebars; the
machine banked slowly. Softest pressure of the foot; she
began to turn. I repeated my lessons aloud: "Beware of
stalling. Beware of spinning. Don't push the nose down
too far, or you'll strain the engine or pull the wings off or
something. Gently does it!" The bungalows of Shoreham
came in sight. "Now – off rudder, off bank – steady! Level
up, watching the elevator. And watch the speed-gauge too.
Fifty-three miles an hour? Oh, that's far too much! Up
with the nose – gently – just a ve-ry lee-tle. There!" I had
completed my first turn.

The aerodrome came towards me again, passed by
directly underneath. I risked a glance over the side. There
was quite a crowd of pupils on the tarmac. They were
staring up, watching me; I was on my first solo and it was
proving to be successful! But I was not home yet and pride
comes before a fall. Hurriedly I touched wood, there was a
lot of it round me. . . . The speed indicator showed thirty-
eight. Too slow! Down with the nose – but *gently*. Unless I
was gentle as a nursing mother something dreadful would
happen. I would spin into the ground and wake up to find,
at best, wings very different from those I coveted sprout-
ing from between my shoulder-blades.

Not far from Brighton I made my second turn and
headed back into wind. Then over Shoreham town I
pushed the nose firmly down and pulled back the throttle.
Longhorn commenced to glide towards the aerodrome.
The air-speed settled down to a steady forty-two. I had
entered the last phase.

In the very early days machines used to be flown down

with the engine almost full out, a procedure considered necessary to maintain flying-speed. Of course the majority of the early aviators never had to come down from any very great height or they would have found it a tiresome business; but the first time that a pilot (whose engine, it so happened, had failed at a considerable altitude) *glided* down to his landing something new and wonderful was discovered. The French called it a *vol plané*, the British Press a "Death Dive". It was that morbid expression which I remembered as Longhorn bore me earthwards.

Not that I found, on this occasion more than on any other, that gliding itself was unpleasant. It was the prospect of landing that I dreaded. All had gone well so far. Longhorn was still intact, making a happy rustling sound as she sailed slowly through the calm air. On the green surface of the aerodrome the sun shone, the wind rippled the long grass. But what was going to happen when these two met, the aeroplane and the aerodrome? I was sure I could never bring myself – alone, unaided – to "flatten out" at just the right moment. There would not be much noise, I thought; a heavy crunch and then struts, spars, wires, white fabric would all collapse and fold themselves about me. I would remain sitting in the crushed *nacelle* until they sent a party from the sheds to liberate me; and their laughter would be restrained only if I were seriously hurt.

Meanwhile the ground seemed to be coming up in normal fashion. The broad river curving towards the sea glinted darkly, momentous as Rubicon. But Longhorn did not falter; she crossed it, and was at just the right height on passing the tall bank at the eastern side of the aerodrome. The sun still shone. I could see the daisies in the grass beneath me. Time to flatten out. With the utmost gentleness I pulled back the handlebars, treading nervously on the harmonium pedals to bring the nose dead into wind. The front elevator rose, the noise of wind in the wires died away. I stared ahead like a hypnotized rabbit. From directly underneath there came a hollow rumble, from further astern a scraping sound; the machine shook, gave a gentle lurch. Still keeping my head rigidly to the front I squinted down at the speed indicator. Nothing! At the altimeter – Zero. . . . I looked boldly over the side. The grass was very near, almost motionless, I could see each blade. Fuzz from a dandelion blew slowly past the lower plane. I had landed.

As I taxied back to the sheds two mechanics came out to guide the machine in. They were still grinning. Never have I seen smiles of such seraphic beauty.

"How did you get on?" a fellow pupil asked.

"Oh, all right," I answered carelessly. "But – not much lift in the air."

Back at the Mess I ate the heartiest breakfast of my life.

x

Not many days later a number of us were transferred at short notice to Gosport, to complete our training and to be attached to a new squadron then being formed. The transfer was something of a move up, but to me it was also very alarming. I had got the hang of things at Shoreham; I had done some half a dozen solo flights, I knew the instructors and their ways, I was at home in two different Longhorns, and I had learnt to find my way about the country within a radius of as much as three miles in the air. What was going to happen at Gosport? Would the new instructors understand me or I them? Would they fly in the same manner? Would their machines be the same? There were many different types at Gosport; would I be expected to fly them all? If I were not taken up again soon I might forget the little I had learnt. The very air might be different; it might not have as much lift as at Shoreham. It was all very disquieting.

And indeed for the first few days at the new station I was not altogether happy. The quarters were uncomfortable, my kit had not arrived, the place was overcrowded, and overcrowded not only with pupils but with a lot of people who already had their "Wings" and would scarcely speak to the novices. Worst of all when I arrived there was only one Longhorn available for training; a queue waited to fly her.

There were also, it is true, a couple of Shorthorns, but my log-book showed that I had not yet been up in one and the shortage of instructors prevented my being given the necessary dual-control flights. The trouble with a Shorthorn was that it had no nice tea-tray elevator in front with which to judge the correct flying angle, and thus the first impression to a Longhorn pilot was rather perilous, as if he were hanging head down over a balcony. I stationed myself close to the only Longhorn and pestered everyone who came by to let me take her up.

In this way I managed to get in an occasional flight, accomplished safe landings, broke nothing. But progress was distressingly slow. I began to think that perhaps I was fated to remain a Longhorn pilot all my days; at times I even hoped so, for some of the other machines at Gosport were rather terrifying. There were B.E.s of various categories – and the last B.E. I had seen had been the burning wreck at Shoreham – there were Caudrons with powerful 80 horse-power "Gnome" engines, Blériot monoplanes, Martinsyde scouts and many others. I did not know which I should have chosen for my own; they all seemed wonderfully fast, modern, powerful, and all a trifle dangerous to the eye of a novice.

One fine evening after I had completed a practice flight in the Longhorn, a friendly young instructor took me over to look at a Caudron from close quarters. She was a nice little machine with engine and propeller in front, a small boat-shaped body for two people, and wooden tail-booms running back to the elevator and rudders. She could do about sixty miles an hour when hard pressed.

The instructor climbed up, inviting me into the passenger seat in front of him. It was a bit cramped and I did not at all like the way a piece of cowling, removed to let me enter, was bolted down behind me to prevent my falling out. I was afraid that if the machine crashed that front seat would become a death-trap. But I said nothing and a moment later the engine was started.

I held my breath as we took off, but except for the engine smelling abominably and making a great deal of noise (it was the first time I had flown behind a rotary engine) I enjoyed the flight thoroughly. I was with an excellent pilot and I felt quite safe after all in the front seat. This was, for me, a new type of aeroplane, a new experience about which I would be able to talk in the Mess. All too soon it was over. I was rather surprised when we landed in the middle of the aerodrome and when, turning round, I saw the pilot getting out of his seat although the engine was still running. I unbolted the cowling at my back and started to get out too, thinking that perhaps something had gone wrong and that I could help. But by now the pilot was standing on the grass, buzzing the engine on and off by means of a switch at the side of the body. He signed to me not to get down but to climb into the pilot's seat.

"Try the controls," he said between buzzes.

I tried them. They seemed all right. Lateral control was by "warping" the wing instead of by aileron; it seemed rather stiff, but I supposed that very little would be necessary for normal bank. The rudder control was much lighter.

"She needs a bit of left rudder in the air," the pilot remarked. "And you can leave the throttle control there –" He indicated the position. "– all the time you're flying, but hold on to it. Cut it down a little when you want to glide, and use your thumb-switch. Understand?"

I nodded intelligently, thinking it all over and trying to remember some of it for future reference.

"All right," he went on, "don't stay up for more than twenty minutes. Off you go!"

"Off I go?" I repeated, unable to believe my ears.

He wagged his head cheerfully and let go of the switch. The machine began to move forward.

I cried out anxiously, but the engine was making a horrible noise and I had forgotten where the switch was. The pilot did not hear me.

"Don't forget," he shouted as he skipped out of the way of the tail-booms, "don't forget that she stalls at forty-two!"

I stared forward helplessly, hopelessly, The machine was bounding over a stretch of uneven ground, swinging wildly from side to side. Which rudder had he told me to use? Left or right? I tried each in turn, gradually discovering how to keep the nose straight while fumbling around with my left hand to find the switch. My fingers encountered the throttle lever, pushed it forward to the position the instructor had indicated. The engine roared with satisfaction. The tail came off the ground, I felt myself being lifted in my seat. Instinctively – already it was becoming an instinct! – I eased back the control stick to prevent the machine from falling on her nose. The bumping and bounding suddenly ceased – merciful heavens, I was off the ground!

My immediate reaction was one of far greater apprehension than I had experienced upon my first solo. Then, for all my ignorance, I had really been quite comfortable in a Longhorn seat. Now everything was unfamiliar. I could not see ahead; there was a flame-spitting, whirling mass of cylinders and propeller in front of the frail boat in which I squirmed. And wherever I looked there seemed to be struts or wings to obscure the view – except of the departing earth. I held the stick firmly in what I judged to be a neutral position and watched the speed gauge.

I found the switch at last, but now I deemed it wiser to go on. I had very little spare flying speed. If I tried to land I should come down like a cast-iron pancake, smashing the machine to matchwood. Besides, there was a line of trees ahead – about the only thing I could see – somehow I would have to get over them before finding safety. No use getting upset, I had to make a circuit of the aerodrome if I wanted to live to tell that young instructor what I thought of him. Clutching desperately at the throttle and stick I was borne aloft thinking upon Elijah.

Compared to a Longhorn this Caudron was speedy and climbed remarkably fast. In no more than ten minutes I had reached a height of one thousand feet. She seemed to be climbing too fast. I peered hastily at the speed gauge. It was very hard to see, for the cockpit was dark and my eyes were half blinded by the sunset (probably my last) over the Solent towards which I was flying – towards which I was being unwillingly carried. At what speed, I wondered, had that awful man told me she would stall? Was it forty-two? Anyway, I was taking no risks. Well above forty-five for me. I pushed the stick farther forward – *Trial by Jury*, slightly parodied, came into my head in tune with the engine's beat:

> "She might very well stall at forty-five,
> In the dusk with the light behind her."

The light was certainly behind the instruments; I had to guess my speed by the feel of the machine, a lesson it was just as well I should learn then and there. Dusk? Yes, that was coming; unless I hurried the light would be bad for landing, I should bounce like a tennis ball. I tried a turn. It succeeded better than I had hoped. And of a sudden I felt a new confidence coming to me. This was fine, this was real flying, better than Longhorn. I made another turn. The light was on the instruments now, I felt much happier. Height two thousand feet, speed fifty-one, revolutions per minute one thousand and fifty; everything smooth and comfortable. I looked out of the boat and down.

Fort Grange was directly underneath; the aerodrome a little to my left. Ahead the houses of Gosport; in distant Portsmouth lights were already beginning to twinkle in the streets. I throttled down, buzzing the engine to keep the propeller turning. The machine glided slowly but extraordinarily steeply, I found; it was so nearly a dive that I watched the ground over the top plane. The summer air grew pleasantly warmer as I came lower, and greatly daring I essayed a turn on the glide. It was easier than I had thought, for there was not a bump or a pocket in the air on this quiet August evening.

Above the sheds, still a good fifty feet up, I straightened out, began calculating my landing point. A sidelong glance at the tarmac showed me the young instructor looking up from among a group of other pilots. He was very tall and therefore known as "Tiny." I hoped that he was proud of his pupil. I felt angry no more. Rather I wanted to laugh and shake him by the hand. I was glad that he had had confidence enough in my abilities to send me off upon this delightful machine. . . .

The landing held all my thoughts. Shakily I buzzed the engine as though I were sending out an SOS, drew the stick back gently, gradually, guessing the distance to the ground. The rush of wind died away; the nose came up steadily; the tail sank. I looked at the air-speed: dangerously near to the fatal forty-two mark, then just under. The machine sank a little, slowing down. And but for the rumbling of the wheels and the scratch of the tail-booms over stones beneath the grass, I should not have known that I had landed.

xi

There followed a spell of exceptionally fine weather, during which I was sent up two or three times every day for short flights on the Caudron, the Longhorn, or occasionally on one of the Shorthorns. But in spite of my new confidence I was still very cautious in the air, and on the ground I found myself always listening for useful hints that might be dropped by those Winged Heroes, the fully-fledged pilots. There were plenty of minor crashes, but none so ghastly or so close to me as that first one at Shoreham, and I fancy that those of us who had survived the moral effect of that disaster were no longer much disturbed by other people's misfortunes. And yet some of the mysterious happenings to experienced aviators filled me every now and then with anxiety for the future. There was a limit it seemed to the wisdom of even the best pilots; what on earth – or in the air – could I be expected to do in circumstances with which they themselves did not know how to deal?

The newly forming squadron at Gosport was being equipped with B.E.2c. Aeroplanes. A pilot whom I knew and liked was sent to bring one from a depot near London. When he landed he became at once the centre of an admiring crowd, for the B.E. with its latest improvements and its 90 horsepower engine was a novelty and highly thought of. The pilot gave a half-humorous account of his flight.

"It was very bumpy over Winchester," he announced, "and the dirty beast tried to spin on me!"

Exclamations of interest were followed by many questions. How had it started? What was it like, how serious had it been, what had he done to correct it? His answers were calmly given, but they were not very clear. I at least could gather little or nothing from them; a spin remained something mysterious and deadly, a danger from which there was no salvation, which attacked one suddenly and for no reason in mid-air. I must watch for signs of that spin as a traveller through unexplored country might watch for a savage ambush.

The little Caudron, however, was perfectly safe; she had never been known to spin. Providing one did not stall her, she would give no trouble. She was strong, had a low landing-speed, required a comparatively short run for taking off and was more or less fool-proof in the air. Her one weakness was that whirling incinerator of an engine. But in spite of occasional trouble, I developed a great affection for the little machine. In her I made my first long cross-country flights and enjoyed my first two forced landings. I say "enjoyed" retrospectively, because I managed to bring them both off successfully, not because I was at all happy at the time they occurred.

xii

It happened one day that, when I was about to leave on a cross-country flight in the Caudron, a letter had to be delivered urgently to a senior officer at that moment inspecting the reserve Squadron at Shoreham. With some formality and many cautions not to tarry on the way, I was entrusted with the despatch.

To say that I was pleased to revisit in so smart a machine the scene of my first trembling solo would be far short of the truth. It mattered not to me that the despatch was of no real importance and that a copy was being sent by post; at being selected to perform this mission I was as elated as if I had won the Derby Sweep. It was a glorious morning, the engine sang a crackling paean of triumph; I flew via Fareham, Chichester, Arundel and Lancing. After much climbing, the Caudron reached a height of four thousand feet; below me small puffs of cloud drifted slowly astern. I felt rather reckless in thus flying above them, they gave such an impression of altitude; but I was beginning to know the look of the country from the air. I could distinguish between a railway and a river, between forests and factory chimneys.

Everything went well on the way out and I reached Shoreham in good time, looking down proudly before commencing the glide. Some of the less fortunate pupils of my day were still being taught there. I fancied I could discern one or two of them in the drooping Longhorns slowly circling the aerodrome. I switched off and dived earthwards – dived, because gliding in a Caudron, except that it was delightfully slow, resembled in angle of descent the "Death Dive" of the newspapers. Over the sheds I buzzed the engine a good deal and did one gentle turn of a spiral so as to make sure of having an audience, then straightening out, came lower and – glory be! – made a very decent landing.

To complete the impression of efficiency I taxied in very fast, and in a Caudron that meant with the tail off the ground to avoid the braking effect of the tail-booms in the grass. More by luck than by good judgment, I switched off in the nick of time, fetching up on the edge of the tarmac, my propeller almost touching a Longhorn's rudder. A few yards away a group of officers stood watching; I spied my senior officer amongst them. Wishing to complete my performance as smartly as possible, I sprang lightly from the pilot's seat, forgot the control wires which ran aft to the tail and, tripping over a cable, fell flat on my face. I began to regret that all the pupils were now assembled in front of the sheds; I could see wide grins on several familiar faces. However, picking myself up I limped clear of the Caudron with a barked shin, and hastened to deliver my despatch to the senior officer. He smiled, thanked me warmly; and when he added that I had made a very nice landing and that he hoped I had not hurt myself, I felt as proud as though I were the dying patriot reporting to the Emperor at Ratisbon.

In the Mess they treated me as if I already had my Wings. Even the No-lift-in-the-air motor salesman (*still* there) deigned to talk with me. I told him the Caudron was very apt to spin.

xiii

But upon the return journey I paid for the pride and joy of the morning. I had had a swim and an excellent lunch; had I been my own master I should also have had a short *siesta*. When at length I soared into the air, watched by a crowd of envious pupils, and set course for Gosport I felt – for the first time in my life in an aeroplane – really happy, almost drowsy. The engine no longer seemed to emit a menacing roar, but rather to hum a regular, slightly monotonous lullaby. The air had all the requisite "lift" in it, there were no bumps, it was warm even at two thousand five hundred feet and the sky was cloudless all the way to Gosport. I leaned back, very nearly at my ease.

On the way home I followed the seashore to see from the air a coast I had long known on the ground. Ahead, Hayling Island came gradually into my ken. I had done a course in machine-gunnery there before joining the Flying Corps and I thought that I would like to look more closely at so familiar a locality. After passing over it I should, of course, have to turn inland to avoid the pro-hibited area of Portsmouth; that would involve quite a long detour by Fareham. But there was plenty of time before sunset; the evening was calm, clear, and of such beauty as to make the temptation to stay up a little longer irresistible to a young airman.

Presently I was above marshes and mudflats and the arms of the quiet sea encircling the island. I began to recognize roads, lanes, cottages, clumps of trees, to see paths down which I had rushed perspiringly with weighty pieces of Vickers or Lewis guns. I smiled contentedly from the superior position to which I had advanced. . . . Perhaps it was over-confidence that did it. I don't know. At all events there was a sudden change of note in the engine's steady music, then a slowing down and much vibration. From rhythmical roaring the explosions dwindled until they were like nothing more than a faint crackling of ice in a cocktail-shaker. Then they ceased altogether. The silence seemed immense. And with it came a nasty pain in the pit of my stomach: two thousand feet up, an amateur pilot, and no engine! This must be the end. I fumbled around desperately; wiggled the throttle lever, tried the switch, buried my head in the cockpit to see if the petrol was properly turned on, fumbled some more.

When I took my head out of the cockpit I found that the noise of wind in the wings and wires had unaccountably died away. The rudder bar and control stick seemed strangely easy to move. And the nose of the machine was dropping heavily, uncontrollably . . . I was stalling – about to spin? Without thinking or hesitating I pushed the stick hard forward. The Caudron gathered speed; and within two seconds I was sighing my relief, wind had come back to the wires, feeling to the controls. I flattened to a more normal glide and began to do some quick thinking.

What were my lessons? "Keep straight on, don't lose flying-speed." Well, after a moment's panic I was doing that all right. The next step? "Make sure of the direction of the wind." At Shoreham I had been heading directly into it, how was it here? I gazed earthwards. There was a ripple of air over the cornfields, too erratic to be a sure guide. A herd of cows was obstinately refusing to obey the laws of bovine nature, for not two faced the same way. No sailing craft at sea, no flags on the houses. Ah, smoke from a cottage chimney! I had never seen household smoke so friendly. Country people should always let their chimneys smoke to help poor airmen in distress. I took the wind's bearing with precision, turned into it at once. Now? "Choose the field in which you intend to land, and choose it as early as you can." A glance at the altimeter – less than fifteen hundred feet – I hung over the side, goggling at the earth. Choose? Not so easy. There were innumerable fields, but only a few large enough. I examined those few attentively, Marshes! Or else green mud from which the tide had receded. . . . Under a thousand feet now. No time to lose. I had been told that, from long periods of sitting still in the air, an airman's chief trouble was constipation. In this business of forced landing I fancied I had found a certain cure; I wanted that field for more reasons than one.

And at last, just in time, I found it. The only smooth bit of pasture, it seemed, for miles, but not so very smooth at that. A sort of paddock, small, enclosed on three sides by trees, with a tall hedge upon my side. "Aim at the hedge on the near side," I had been taught. I did so and found that I was too high. Another lesson came back to me: "if you think you are going to overshoot make 'S'-turns so as to lose height. . . ." In the middle of the second turn the engine all at once started again. If it had happened any higher up I might have tried to continue the flight, low down it only served to remind me of one more lesson:

"Always switch off before a forced landing, to minimize the risk of fire." I knocked up the switch immediately, I might crash and crash badly, but I refused to burn. I could remember no more lessons, there was no time to think of anything else. The machine hopped over the hedge; I commenced shakily to flatten out.

The landing was not too bad, although rather fast – a better fault than stalling! – and all would have been well but for a partly filled in drainage ditch concealed by the grass. I was staring ahead, wondering whether I should be able to stop before hitting the trees on the far side of the field, when there came a heavy bump beneath the wheels. The machine swerved, listed to port, came to a sudden stop.

It took me a few moments to recover from the relaxed tension, the joy of safely landing, the surprising stillness of the summer's evening here on the ground. It seemed very wrong of me to have thus brusquely disturbed the dignified quiet of this sweet-smelling field. Then I scrambled out to inspect the damage. It was nothing much. A wheel had been broken in the ditch, a steel undercarriage strut twisted. It could all easily be repaired on the spot . . . .

Solicitous inhabitants crowded round, offering help, advice, congratulations, food and drink, shelter for the night, first-aid or a guard for the machine. I asked for a telephone. This was the first time I had broken anything since starting to fly, and now that the anguish of the descent was past I wondered ruefully whether the breaking of a wheel would not put a black mark against my name. From the nearest house I 'phoned through to Gosport.

The orderly-officer to whom I spoke was non-committal, he told me to stay where I was and that perhaps help would be forthcoming on the morrow. Then he rang off. I passed an uneasy night despite hospitable surroundings. . . .

But upon the next day, back at Gosport with the repaired Caudron, they said I had not managed so badly for a beginner – although they refused to believe that I had not got a girl hidden away on Hayling Island. No one, they said, would land there for less than that.

xiv

These ugly rumours were soon dispelled. Another and much longer cross-country flight in the same Caudron resulted in a second forced landing, this time at Winchester. And not only was it generally agreed by the pilots of Gosport that, with Portsmouth so close, no one in his senses would have a girl in Winchester, but the condition of the "Gnome" engine revealed on examination that I could not have flown another yard in any direction.

I had broken nothing on this landing and I was now considered advanced enough to pilot the famous B.E.2c. As a matter of fact I am not quite sure whether the machine I flew at Gosport was a "2c." or some other earlier category. It had a less powerful engine – an 80 horse-power Renault – cables instead of streamline wires, and wooden skids on the undercarriage. Altogether a less modern craft than the ill-fated machine I had seen burned at Shoreham, which had been of the type just coming into fashion.

But despite some preliminary nervousness due to the rumours of spinning, I soon began to like the B.E. as much and more than the other types I had flown. She was stable, easily manageable if a bit heavy on the controls, strongly built. One of the more experienced of the Gosport pilots had been known to loop his B.E. several times and no harm done, although he had not been allowed to repeat the performance in front of the novices lest we should be tempted to emulate him, which, frankly, was not very likely. After a few practice flights in this type of machine I was allowed to take up my first passengers, luckless young men who little knew into what trembling hands they had trusted their lives. Also I was allowed to fly in windy, bumpy weather that hitherto had been the signal for

machines to be securely locked in their sheds for the day.
. . . I flew over the New Forest, circling above lonely
heaths and dark glades and gypsy encampments, retracing
a hundred boyhood rides. I flew over the Solent and
peered into the secret places of that shallow sea whose
waters roll over my early dreams. I learned to fly a straight
course by compass and to make allowance for the wind; I
learned how to bank at more than 45 degrees, and how to
do a spiral glide from a height of several thousand feet.
The war? It seemed far away, but I would be in it soon
enough.

xv

On the ground, during all this time, instruction in rigging
and engine fitting went steadily on; occasionally we were
given vaguely scientific lectures upon aerodynamics. And
at length the great day arrived. A few of us who were
deemed worthy were driven off in a Crossley tender to the
Central Flying School at Upavon to be examined in our
knowledge of aeronautics.

That the tests were not entirely easy was a matter of
common knowledge. If we passed we would be qualified as
pilots, if we failed we would be set back many weeks,
perhaps months. Failure was by no means unknown. In
my own case it happened that I was a little ahead of the
customary time, but there were only two things I had
cause to dread: that I might not yet have enough flying
hours to my credit or – much worse – that I should not
have sufficiently mastered the Morse Code, a thing which
for years had tried my patience. We were required to read
messages at a fair speed, so many words a minute. My
average rate was so many minutes per word. All the way to
Upavon I practised with a portable buzzer.

The examination started as soon as we had disem-
barked, and I quickly found that it was less terrifying
than I had been led to expect. I was conducted round the
sheds by a venerable naval airman – anything over thirty

with pre-war flying experience was considered venerable –
who asked all the hard questions of which I had had
warning and who seemed surprised that I could also
answer the easy ones. Another old gentleman – his hair
was grey at the temples – took me to the repair shops and
asked me what most generally went wrong with "Gnome"
engines. From personal experience with the Caudron I
was able to tell him quite a lot of things, in the manner of
an expert, and I gathered from his friendly smile that I had
scored a good mark. Then came the Morse. In a darkened
shed a nasty little lamp flashed irritatingly before my
dazed eyes. Pencil and paper were handed to me; I made
a pretence of scrawling. And to my amazement the dots
and dashes assembled themselves in the correct order. The
letters, even the words came out right. But I must have
been helped by some guardian angel, for never again was I
able to repeat the performance.

The dreaded business was over. In the cool of the
evening we motored home, singing and occasionally stopping at a way-side pub to drink to our own success.

xvi

Before leaving Upavon I had made fairly sure that I had
qualified, but the official result was not announced at
Gosport until a day or two later. At length the news came
through. I was summoned to the squadron office to hear it.
The Squadron-commander beamed, offered congratulations. I was no more a fledgeling, he said, I was a pilot, a
member of the Corps, entitled to wear the badge and
uniform, *sic itur ad astra* and so on. But to me it meant
even more than that. I felt that I was no longer temporarily
"attached" to the Flying Corps; I was permanently devoted.

In a momentarily serious frame of mind I hurried from
the office and across the sunlit barrack square of Fort
Grange. Barely six weeks previously, at Shoreham, I had
seen a man burnt to death because of a pilot's error. Since

then I had learnt to fly. I had made no fatal errors so far, I must see to it that I made none in the future. I had been taught all the essential lessons. Now to apply them.

In the tailor's shop I watched a man sew the Wings to my tunic. When this was done I went to the sheds and had the old training machine brought out. By my orders and upon my responsibility she was started up. As soon as she was ready I took her into the air. For half an hour I flew steadily and, in a Longhorn, for the last time.

Grinnell-Milne was captured, after a forced landing, in winter 1915. He escaped from a German POW camp two and half years later, returning to active service on the Western Front in May 1918.

THE RED AIR FIGHTER

MANFRED VON RICHTHOFEN

At first in the cavalry, von Richthofen joined the German air force to become commander of the 11th Chasing Squadron ("Richthofen's Flying Circus"), where his habit of painting his aircraft red earned him the soubriquet of "The Red Baron". The victor in 80 aerial combats, and thus the highest-ranking ace of World War I, he was mortally shot down himself on the morning of 21 April 1918 during an encounter with Sopwith Camels of No 209 Squadron RAF. His brother Lothar, who survived the war, was also a fighter ace, with 40 confirmed victories. The extracts below are from Rittmeister Manfred Freiharr von Richthofen's own memoir, written in 1917.

17 September 1915

We were all at the butts trying our machine guns. On the previous day we had received our new aeroplanes and the next morning Boelcke* was to fly with us. We were all beginners. None of us had had a success so far. Conse-

---

* *Oswald Boelcke, born in 1891, one of the first pilots in the German Air Service to develop the tactics of aerial combat, and an early recipient of the coveted* Ordre Pour le Mérite (*"The Blue Max"*). *After 40 aerial victories he died on 28 October 1916. See Appendix II.*

quently everything that Boelcke told us was to us gospel truth. Every day, during the last few days, he had, as he said, shot one or two Englishmen for breakfast.

The next morning, the seventeenth of September, was a gloriously fine day. It was therefore only to be expected that the English would be very active. Before we started Boelcke repeated to us his instructions and for the first time we flew as a squadron commanded by the great man whom we followed blindly.

We had just arrived at the Front when we recognized a hostile flying squadron that was proceeding in the direction of Cambrai. Boelcke was of course the first to see it, for he saw a great deal more than ordinary mortals. Soon we understood the position and every one of us strove to follow Boelcke closely. It was clear to all of us that we should pass our first examination under the eyes of our beloved leader.

Slowly we approached the hostile squadron. It could not escape us. We had intercepted it, for we were between the Front and our opponents. If they wished to go back they had to pass us. We counted the hostile machines. They were seven in number. We were only five. All the Englishmen flew large bomb-carrying two-seaters. In a few seconds the dance would begin.

Boelcke had come very near the first English machine but he did not yet shoot. I followed. Close to me were my comrades. The Englishman nearest to me was traveling in a large boat painted with dark colors. I did not reflect very long but took my aim and shot. He also fired and so did I, and both of us missed our aim. A struggle began and the great point for me was to get to the rear of the fellow because I could only shoot forward with my gun. He was differently placed for his machine gun was movable. It could fire in all directions.

Apparently he was no beginner, for he knew exactly that his last hour had arrived at the moment when I got at the back of him. At that time I had not yet the conviction "He must fall!" which I have now on such occasions, but on the contrary, I was curious to see whether he would fall. There is a great difference between the two feelings. When one has shot down one's first, second or third opponent, then one begins to find out how the trick is done.

My Englishman twisted and turned, going criss-cross. I did not think for a moment that the hostile squadron contained other Englishmen who conceivably might come to the aid of their comrade. I was animated by a single thought: "The man in front of me must come down, whatever happens." At last a favorable moment arrived. My opponent had apparently lost sight of me. Instead of twisting and turning he flew straight along. In a fraction of a second I was at his back with my excellent machine. I give a short series of shots with my machine gun. I had gone so close that I was afraid I might dash into the Englishman. Suddenly, I nearly yelled with joy for the propeller of the enemy machine had stopped turning. I had shot his engine to pieces; the enemy was compelled to land, for it was impossible for him to reach his own lines. The English machine was curiously swinging to and fro. Probably something had happened to the pilot. The observer was no longer visible. His machine gun was apparently deserted. Obviously I had hit the observer and he had fallen from his seat.

The Englishman landed close to the flying ground of one of our squadrons. I was so excited that I landed also and my eagerness was so great that I nearly smashed up my machine. The English flying machine and my own stood close together. I rushed to the English machine and saw that a lot of soldiers were running towards my enemy. When I arrived I discovered that my assumption had been correct. I had shot the engine to pieces and both the pilot and observer were severely wounded. The observer died at once and the pilot while being transported to the nearest dressing station. I honored the fallen enemy by placing a stone on his beautiful grave.

When I came home Boelcke and my other comrades were already at breakfast. They were surprised that I had not turned up. I reported proudly that I had shot down an Englishman. All were full of joy for I was not the only victor. As usual, Boelcke had shot down an opponent for breakfast and every one of the other men also had downed an enemy for the first time.

I would mention that since that time no English squadron ventured as far as Cambrai as long as Boelcke's squadron was there.

The Battle of the Somme

During my whole life I have not found a happier hunting ground than in the course of the Somme Battle. In the morning, as soon as I had got up, the first Englishmen arrived, and the last did not disappear until long after sunset. Boelcke once said that this was the El Dorado of the flying men.

There was a time when, within two months, Boelcke's bag of machines increased from twenty to forty. We beginners had not at that time the experience of our master and we were quite satisfied when we did not get a hiding. It was an exciting period. Every time we went up we had a fight. Frequently we fought really big battles in the air. There were sometimes from forty to sixty English machines, but unfortunately the Germans were often in the minority. With them quality was more important than quantity.

Still the Englishman is a smart fellow. That we must allow. Sometimes the English came down to a very low altitude and visited Boelcke in his quarters, upon which they threw their bombs. They absolutely challenged us to battle and never refused fighting.

We had a delightful time with our chasing squadron. The spirit of our leader animated all his pupils. We trusted him blindly. There was no possibility that one of us would be left behind. Such a thought was incomprehensible to us. Animated by that spirit we gaily diminished the number of our enemies.

On the day when Boelcke fell the squadron had brought down forty opponents. By now the number has been increased by more than a hundred. Boelcke's spirit lives still among his capable successors.

Boelcke's Death, (18th October 1916)

One day we were flying, once more guided by Boelcke against the enemy. We always had a wonderful feeling of security when he was with us. After all he was the one and only. The weather was very gusty and there were many clouds. There were no aeroplanes about except fighting ones.

From a long distance we saw two impertinent Englishmen in the air who actually seemed to enjoy the terrible weather. We were six and they were two. If they had been twenty and if Boelcke had given us the signal to attack we should not have been at all surprised.

The struggle began in the usual way. Boelcke tackled the one and I the other. I had to let go because one of the German machines got in my way. I looked around and noticed Boelcke settling his victim about two hundred yards away from me. It was the usual thing. Boelcke would shoot down his opponent and I had to look on. Close to Boelcke flew a good friend of his. It was an interesting struggle. Both men were shooting. It was probable that the Englishman would fall at any moment. Suddenly I noticed an unnatural movement of the two German flying machines. Immediately I thought: Collision. I had not yet seen a collision in the air. I had imagined that it would look quite different. In reality, what happened was not a collision. The two machines merely touched one another. However, if two machines go at the tremendous pace of flying machines, the slightest contact has the effect of a violent concussion.

Boelcke drew away from his victim and descended in large curves. He did not seem to be falling, but when I saw him descending below me I noticed that part of his plane had broken off. I could not see what happened afterwards, but in the clouds he lost an entire plane. Now his machine was no longer steerable. It fell accompanied all the time by Boelcke's faithful friend.

When we reached home we found the report "Boelcke is dead!" had already arrived. We could scarcely realize it.

The greatest pain was, of course, felt by the man who had the misfortune to be involved in the accident.

It is a strange thing that everybody who met Boelcke imagined that he alone was his true friend. I have made the acquaintance of about forty men, each of whom imagined that he alone was Boelcke's intimate. Each imagined that he had the monopoly of Boelcke's affections. Men whose names were unknown to Boelcke believed that he was particularly fond of them. This is a curious phenomenon which I have never noticed in anyone else. Boelcke had not a personal enemy. He was equally polite to everybody, making no differences.

The only one who was perhaps more intimate with him than the others was the very man who had the misfortune to be in the accident which caused his death. Nothing happens without God's will. That is the only consolation which any of us can put to our souls during this war.

My Eighth Victim

In Boelcke's time eight was quite a respectable number. Those who hear nowadays of the colossal bags made by certain aviators must feel convinced that it has become easier to shoot down a machine. I can assure those who hold that opinion that the flying business is becoming more difficult from month to month and even from week to week. Of course, with the increasing number of aeroplanes one gains increased opportunities for shooting down one's enemies, but at the same time, the possibility of being shot down one's self increases. The armament of our enemies is steadily improving and their number is increasing. When Immelmann shot down his first victim he had the good fortune to find an opponent who carried not even a machine gun. Such little innocents one finds nowadays only at the training ground for beginners.

On the ninth of November, 1916, I flew towards the enemy with my little comrade Immelmann,* who then was eighteen years old. We both were in Boelcke's squadron of chasing aeroplanes. We had previously met one another and had got on very well. Comradeship is a most important thing. We went to work. I had already bagged seven enemies and Immelmann five. At that time this was quite a lot.

Soon after our arrival at the front we saw a squadron of bombing aeroplanes. They were coming along with impertinent assurance. They arrived in enormous numbers as was usual during the Somme Battle. I think there were about forty or fifty machines approaching. I cannot give the exact number. They had selected an object for their bombs not far from our aerodrome. I reached them when they had almost attained their objective. I approached the last machine. My first few shots incapacitated the hostile machine gunner. Possibly they had tickled the pilot, too. At any rate he resolved to land with his bombs. I fired a few more shots to accelerate his progress downwards. He fell close to our flying ground at Lagnicourt.

While I was fighting my opponent, Immelmann had tackled another Englishman and had brought him down in the same locality. Both of us flew quickly home in order to have a look at the machines we had downed. We jumped into a motor car, drove in the direction where our victims lay and had to run along a distance through the fields. It was very hot, therefore I unbuttoned all my garments even the collar and the shirt. I took off my jacket, left my cap in the car but took with me a big stick. My boots were miry up to the knees. I looked like a tramp. I arrived in the

* *Max Immelmann, fighter ace, born 1890, died 18 June 1916. Recipient of* Ordre Pour le Mérite. *Mostly remembered for the "Immelmann turn", a half loop, followed by a half roll.*

vicinity of my victim. In the meantime, a lot of people had of course gathered around.

At one spot there was a group of officers. I approached them, greeted them, and asked the first one whom I met whether he could tell me anything about the aspect of the aerial battle. It is always interesting to find out how a fight in the air looks to the people down below. I was told that the English machines had thrown bombs and that the aeroplane that had come down was still carrying its bombs.

The officer who gave me this information took my arm, went with me to the other officers, asked my name and introduced me to them. I did not like it, for my attire was rather disarranged. On the other hand, all the officers looked as spic and span as on parade. I was introduced to a personage who impressed me rather strangely. I noticed a General's trousers, an Order at the neck, an unusually youthful face and undefinable epaulettes. In short, the personage seemed extraordinary to me. During our conversation I buttoned my shirt and collar and adopted a somewhat military attitude.

I had no idea who the officer was. I took my leave and went home again. In the evening the telephone rang and I was told that the undefinable somebody with whom I had been talking had been His Royal Highness, the Grand-Duke of Saxe-Coburg Gotha. I was ordered to go to him. It was known that the English had intended to throw bombs on his headquarters. Apparently I had helped to keep the aggressors away from him. Therefore I was given the Saxe-Coburg Gotha medal for bravery. I always enjoy this adventure when I look at the medal.

Major Hawker

I was extremely proud when, one fine day, I was informed that the airman whom I had brought down on the twenty-third of November, 1916, was the English Immelmann.

In view of the character of our fight it was clear to me

that I had been tackling a flying champion. One day I was blithely flying to give chase when I noticed three Englishmen who also had apparently gone a-hunting. I noticed that they were ogling me and as I felt much inclination to have a fight I did not want to disappoint them.

I was flying at a lower altitude. Consequently I had to wait until one of my English friends tried to drop on me. After a short while one of the three came sailing along and attempted to tackle me in the rear. After firing five shots he had to stop for I had swerved in a sharp curve.

The Englishman tried to catch me up in the rear while I tried to get behind him. So we circled round and round like madmen after one another at an altitude of about 10,000 feet.

First we circled twenty times to the left, and then thirty times to the right. Each tried to get behind and above the other. Soon I discovered that I was not meeting a beginner. He had not the slightest intention of breaking off the fight. He was traveling in a machine which turned beautifully. However, my own was better at rising than his, and I succeeded at last in getting above and beyond my English waltzing partner.

When we had got down to about 6,000 feet without having achieved anything in particular, my opponent ought to have discovered that it was time for him to take his leave. The wind was favorable to me for it drove us more and more towards the German position. At last we were above Bapaume, about half a mile behind the German front. The impertinent fellow was full of cheek and when we had got down to about 3,000 feet he merrily waved to me as if he would say, "Well, how do you do?"

The circles which we made around one another were so narrow that their diameter was probably no more than 250 or 300 feet. I had time to take a good look at my opponent. I looked down into his carriage and could see every movement of his head. If he had not had his cap on I would have noticed what kind of a face he was making. My Englishman was a good sportsman, but by and by the thing became a little too hot for him. He had to decide whether he would land on German ground or whether he would fly back to the English lines. Of course he tried the latter, after having endeavored in vain to escape me by loopings and such like tricks. At that time his first bullets were flying around me, for hitherto neither of us had been able to do any shooting.

When he had come down to about three hundred feet he tried to escape by flying in a zig-zag course during which, as is well known, it is difficult for an observer to shoot. That was my most favorable moment. I followed him at an altitude of from two hundred and fifty feet to one hundred and fifty feet, firing all the time. The Englishman could not help falling. But the jamming of my gun nearly robbed me of my success.

My opponent fell, shot through the head, one hundred and fifty feet behind our line. His machine gun was dug out of the ground and it ornaments the entrance of my dwelling.

I Get the *Ordre Pour le Mérite*

I had brought down my sixteenth victim, and I had come to the head of the list of all the flying chasers. I had obtained the aim which I had set myself. In the previous year my friend Lynker, with whom I was training, had asked me: "What is your object? What will you obtain by flying?" I replied, jokingly, "I would like to be the first of the chasers. That must be very fine." That I should succeed in this I did not believe myself. Other people also did not expect my success. Boelcke is supposed to have said, not to me personally – I have only heard the report – when asked: "Which of the fellows is likely to become a good chaser?" – "That is the man!" pointing his finger in my direction.

Boelcke and Immelmann were given the Ordre Pour le Mérite when they had brought down their eighth aeroplane. I had downed twice that number. The question was, what would happen to me? I was very curious. It was rumored that I was to be given command of a chasing squadron.

One fine day a telegram arrived, which stated: "Lieutenant von Richthofen is appointed Commander of the Eleventh Chasing Squadron."

I must say I was annoyed. I had learnt to work so well with my comrades of Boelcke's Squadron and now I had to begin all over again working hand in hand with different people. It was a beastly nuisance. Besides I should have preferred the Ordre Pour le Mérite.

Two days later, when we were sitting sociably together, we men of Boelcke's Squadron, celebrating my departure, a telegram from Headquarters arrived. It stated that His Majesty had graciously condescended to give me the Ordre Pour le Mérite. Of course my joy was tremendous.

I had never imagined that it would be so delightful to command a chasing squadron. Even in my dreams I had not imagined that there would ever be a Richthofen's squadron of aeroplanes.

Le Petit Rouge

It occurred to me to have my packing case painted all over in staring red. The result was that everyone got to know my red bird. My opponents also seemed to have heard of the color transformation.

During a fight on quite a different section of the Front I had the good fortune to shoot into a Vickers' two-seater which peacefully photographed the German artillery position. My friend, the photographer, had not the time to defend himself. He had to make haste to get down upon firm ground for his machine began to give suspicious indications of fire. When we airmen notice that phenomenon in an enemy plane, we say: "He stinks!" As it turned out it was really so. When the machine was coming to earth it burst into flames.

I felt some human pity for my opponent and had

resolved not to cause him to fall down but merely to compel him to land. I did so particularly because I had the impression that my opponent was wounded for he did not fire a single shot.

When I had got down to an altitude of about fifteen hundred feet engine trouble compelled me to land without making any curves. The result was very comical. My enemy with his burning machine landed smoothly while I, his victor, came down next to him in the barbed wire of our trenches and my machine overturned.

The two Englishmen who were not a little surprised at my collapse, greeted me like sportsmen. As mentioned before, they had not fired a shot and they could not understand why I had landed so clumsily. They were the first two Englishmen whom I had brought down alive. Consequently, it gave me particular pleasure to talk to them. I asked them whether they had previously seen my machine in the air, and one of them replied, "Oh, yes. I know your machine very well. We call it 'Le Petit Rouge'."

English and French Flying. (February 1917)

I was trying to compete with Boelcke's squadron. Every evening we compared our bags. However, Boelcke's pupils are smart rascals. I cannot get ahead of them. The utmost one can do is to draw level with them. The Boelcke section has an advantage over my squadron of one hundred aeroplanes downed. I must not allow them to retain it. Everything depends on whether we have for opponents those French tricksters or those daring rascals, the English. I prefer the English. Frequently their daring can only be described as stupidity. In their eyes it may be pluck and daring.

The great thing in air fighting is that the decisive factor does not lie in trick flying but solely in the personal ability and energy of the aviator. A flying man may be able to loop and do all the stunts imaginable and yet he may not succeed in shooting down a single enemy. In my opinion the aggressive spirit is everything and that spirit is very strong in us Germans. Hence we shall always retain the domination of the air.

The French have a different character. They like to put traps and to attack their opponents unawares. That cannot easily be done in the air. Only a beginner can be caught and one cannot set traps because an aeroplane cannot hide itself. The invisible aeroplane has not yet been discovered. Sometimes, however, the Gaelic blood asserts itself. The Frenchmen will then attack. But the French attacking spirit is like bottled lemonade. It lacks tenacity.

The Englishmen, on the other hand, one notices that they are of Germanic blood. Sportsmen easily take to flying, and Englishmen see in flying nothing but a sport. They take a perfect delight in looping the loop, flying on their back, and indulging in other stunts for the benefit of our soldiers in the trenches. All these tricks may impress people who attend a Sports Meeting, but the public at the battle-front is not as appreciative of these things. It demands higher qualifications than trick flying. Therefore, the blood of English pilots will have to flow in streams.

I Am Shot Down. (Middle of March 1917)

I have had an experience which might perhaps be described as being shot down. At the same time, I call shot down only when one falls down. Today I got into trouble but I escaped with a whole skin.

I was flying with the squadron and noticed an opponent who also was flying in a squadron. It happened above the German artillery position in the neighborhood of Lens. I had to fly quite a distance to get there. It tickles one's nerves to fly towards the enemy, especially when one can see him from a long distance and when several minutes must elapse before one can start fighting. I imagine that at such a moment my face turns a little pale, but unfortunately I have never had a mirror with me. I like that feeling for it is a wonderful nerve stimulant. One observes the enemy from afar. One has recognized that his squadron is really an enemy formation. One counts the number of the hostile machines and considers whether the conditions are favorable or unfavorable. A factor of enormous importance is whether the wind forces me away from or towards our Front. For instance, I once shot down an Englishman. I fired the fatal shot above the English position. However, the wind was so strong that his machine came down close to the German captive balloons.

We Germans had five machines. Our opponents were three times as numerous. The English flew about like midges. It is not easy to disperse a swarm of machines which fly together in good order. It is impossible for a single machine to do it. It is extremely difficult for several aeroplanes, particularly if the difference in number is as great as it was in this case. However, one feels such a superiority over the enemy that one does not doubt of success for a moment.

The aggressive spirit, the offensive, is the chief thing everywhere in war, and the air is no exception. However, the enemy had the same idea. I noticed that at once. As soon as they observed us they turned round and attacked us. Now we five had to look sharp. If one of them should fall there might be a lot of trouble for all of us. We went closer together and allowed the foreign gentlemen to approach us.

I watched whether one of the fellows would hurriedly take leave of his colleagues. There! One of them is stupid enough to depart alone. I can reach him and I say to myself, "That man is lost." Shouting aloud, I am after him. I have come up to him or at least am getting very near him. He starts shooting prematurely, which shows that he is nervous. So I say to myself, "Go on shooting. You won't hit me." He shot with a kind of ammunition which ignites. So I could see his shots passing me. I felt as if I were sitting in front of a gigantic watering pot. The sensation was not pleasant. Still, the English usually shoot with their beastly stuff, and so we must try and get accustomed to it. One can get accustomed to anything. At the moment I think I laughed aloud. But soon I got a lesson. When I had approached the Englishman quite closely, when I had come to a distance of about three hundred feet, I got ready for firing, aimed and gave a few trial shots. The machine guns were in order. The decision would be there before long. In my mind's eye I saw my enemy dropping.

My former excitement was gone. In such a position one thinks quite calmly and collectedly and weighs the probabilities of hitting and of being hit. Altogether the fight itself is the least exciting part of the business as a rule. He who gets excited in fighting is sure to make mistakes. He will never get his enemy down. Besides calmness is, after all, a matter of habit. At any rate in this case I did not make a mistake. I approached my man up to fifty yards. Then I fired some well aimed shots and thought that I was bound to be successful. That was my idea. But suddenly I heard a tremendous bang, when I had scarcely fired ten cartridges. Presently again something hit my machine. It became clear to me that I had been hit or rather my machine. At the same time I noticed a fearful benzine stench and I observed that the motor was running slack. The Englishman noticed it, too, for he started shooting with redoubled energy while I had to stop it.

I went right down. Instinctively I switched off the engine and indeed it was high time to do this. When a pilot's benzine tank has been perforated, and when the infernal liquid is squirting around his legs, the danger of fire is very great. In front is an explosion engine of more than 150 h.p. which is red hot. If a single drop of benzine should fall on it the whole machine would be in flames.

I left in the air a thin white cloud. I knew its meaning from my enemies. Its appearance is the first sign of a coming explosion. I was at an altitude of nine thousand feet and had to travel a long distance to get down. By the kindness of Providence my engine stopped running. I have no idea with what rapidity I went downward. At any rate the speed was so great that I could not put my head out of the machine without being pressed back by the rush of air.

Soon I lost sight of my enemy. I had only time to see what my four comrades were doing while I was dropping to the ground. They were still fighting. Their machine-guns and those of their opponents could be heard. Suddenly I notice a rocket. Is it a signal of the enemy? No, it cannot be. The light is too great for a rocket. Evidently a machine is on fire. What machine? The burning machine looks exactly as if it were one of our own. No! Praise the Lord, it is one of the enemy's! Who can have shot him down? Immediately afterwards a second machine drops out and falls perpendicularly to the ground, turning, turning, turning exactly as I did, but suddenly it recovers its balance. It flies straight towards me. It also is an Albatross. No doubt it had the same experience as I had.

I had fallen to an altitude of perhaps one thousand feet and had to look out for a landing. Now such a sudden landing usually leads to breakages and as these are occasionally serious it was time to look out. I found a meadow. It was not very large but it just sufficed if I used due caution. Besides it was favorably situated on the high road near Henin-Lietard. There I meant to land.

Everything went as desired and my first thought was, "What has become of the other fellow?" He landed a few kilometers from the spot where I had come to the ground.

I had ample time to inspect the damage. My machine had been hit a number of times. The shot which caused me to give up the fight had gone through both benzine tanks. I had not a drop of benzine left and the engine itself had also been damaged by shots. It was a pity for it had worked so well.

My First Double Event

The second of April, 1917, was a very warm day for my Squadron. From my quarters I could clearly hear the drum-fire of the guns which was again particularly violent.

I was still in bed when my orderly rushed into the room and exclaimed: "Sir, the English are here!" Sleepy as I was, I looked out of the window and, really, there were my dear friends circling over the flying ground. I jumped out of my bed and into my clothes in a jiffy. My Red Bird had been pulled out and was ready for starting. My mechanics knew that I should probably not allow such a favorable moment to go by unutilized. Everything was ready. I snatched up my furs and then went off.

I was the last to start. My comrades were much nearer to the enemy. I feared that my prey would escape me, that I should have to look on from a distance while the others were fighting. Suddenly one of the impertinent fellows tried to drop down upon me. I allowed him to come near and then we started a merry quadrille. Sometimes my opponent flew on his back and sometimes he did other tricks. He had a double-seated chaser. I was his master and very soon I recognized that he could not escape me.

During an interval in the fighting I convinced myself that we were alone. It followed that the victory would accrue to him who was calmest, who shot best and who had the clearest brain in a moment of danger. After a short time I got him beneath me without seriously hurting him with my gun. We were at least two kilometers from the front. I thought he intended to land but there I had made a mistake. Suddenly, when he was only a few yards above the ground, he once more went off on a straight course. He tried to escape me.

That was too bad. I attacked him again and I went so low that I feared I should touch the roofs of the houses of the village beneath me. The Englishman defended himself up to the last moment. At the very end I felt that my engine had been hit. Still I did not let go. He had to fall. He rushed at full speed right into a block of houses.

There was little left to be done. This was once more a

case of splendid daring. He defended himself to the last. However, in my opinion he showed more foolhardiness than courage. This was one of the cases where one must differentiate between energy and idiocy. He had to come down in any case but he paid for his stupidity with his life.

I was delighted with the performance of my red machine during its morning work and returned to our quarters. My comrades were still in the air and they were very surprised, when, as we met at breakfast, I told them that I had scored my thirty-second machine. A very young Lieutenant had "bagged" his first aeroplane. We were all very merry and prepared everything for further battles. I then went and groomed myself. I had not had time to do it previously. I was visited by a dear friend, Lieutenant Voss★ of Boelcke's Squadron. We chatted. Voss had downed on the previous day his twenty-third machine. He was next to me on the list and is at present my most redoubtable competitor.

When he started to fly home I offered to accompany him part of the way. We went on a roundabout way over the Fronts. The weather had turned so bad that we could not hope to find any more game.

Beneath us there were dense clouds. Voss did not know the country and he began to feel uncomfortable. When we passed above Arras I met my brother who also is in my squadron and who had lost his way. He joined us. Of course he recognized me at once by the color of my machine.

Suddenly we saw a squadron approaching from the other side. Immediately the thought occurred to me: "Now comes number thirty-three." Although there were nine Englishmen and although they were on their own territory they preferred to avoid battle. I thought that perhaps it would be better for me to re-paint my machine. Nevertheless we caught them up. The important thing in aeroplanes is that they are speedy.

★ *Werner Voss, born 1897, fifth highest scoring German ace of WWI, with 48 victories. Killed in action on 23 September 1917. See pp 112–113.*

I was nearest to the enemy and attacked the man to the rear. To my greatest delight I noticed that he accepted battle and my pleasure was increased when I discovered that his comrades deserted him. So I had once more a single fight. It was a fight similar to the one which I had had in the morning. My opponent did not make matters easy for me. He knew the fighting business and it was particularly awkward for me that he was a good shot. To my great regret that was quite clear to me.

A favorable wind came to my aid. It drove both of us into the German lines. My opponent discovered that the matter was not so simple as he had imagined. So he plunged and disappeared in a cloud. He had nearly saved himself.

I plunged after him and dropped out of the cloud and, as luck would have it, found myself close behind him. I fired and he fired without any tangible result. At last I hit him. I noticed a ribbon of white benzine vapor. He had to land for his engine had come to a stop.

He was a stubborn fellow. He was bound to recognize that he had lost the game. If he continued shooting I could kill him, for meanwhile we had dropped to an altitude of about nine hundred feet. However, the Englishman defended himself exactly as did his countryman in the morning. He fought until he landed. When he had come to the ground I flew over him at an altitude of about thirty feet in order to ascertain whether I had killed him or not. What did the rascal do? He took his machine-gun and shot holes into my machine.

Afterwards Voss told me if that had happened to him he would have shot the airman on the ground. As a matter of fact I ought to have done so for he had not surrendered. He was one of the few fortunate fellows who escaped with their lives.

I felt very merry, flew home and celebrated my thirty-third aeroplane.

The English Attack Our Aerodrome

Nights in which the full moon is shining are most suitable for night flying. During the full moon nights of the month of April our English friends were particularly industrious. This was during the Battle of Arras. Probably they had found out that we had comfortably installed ourselves on a beautiful large flying ground at Douai.

One night when we were in the Officers' Mess the telephone started ringing and we were told: "The English are coming." There was a great hullabaloo. We had bombproof shelters. They had been got ready by our excellent Simon. Simon is our architect, surveyor and builder.

We dived down into shelter and we heard actually, at first a very gentle humming and then the noise of engines. The searchlights had apparently got notice at the same time as we, for they started getting ready. The nearest enemy was still too far away to be attacked. We were colossally merry. The only thing we feared was that the English would not succeed in finding our aerodrome. To find some fixed spot at night is by no means easy. It was particularly difficult to find us because our aerodrome was not situated on an important highway or near water or a railway, by which one can be guided during one's flight at night. The Englishmen were apparently flying at a great altitude. At first they circled around our entire establishment. We began to think that they had given up and were looking for another objective. Suddenly we noticed that the nearest one had switched off his engine. So he was coming lower. Wolff said: "Now the matter is becoming serious."

We had two carbines and began shooting at the Englishman. We could not see him. Still the noise of our shooting was a sedative to our nerves. Suddenly he was taken up by the search lights. There was shouting all over the flying ground. Our friend was sitting in a prehistoric packing case. We could clearly recognize the type. He was half a mile away from us and was flying straight towards us.

He went lower and lower. At last he had come down to an altitude of about three hundred feet. Then he started his engine again and came straight towards the spot where we were standing. Wolff thought that he took an interest in the other side of our establishment and before long the first bomb fell and it was followed by a number of other missiles.

Our friend amused us with very pretty fireworks. They could have frightened only a coward. Broadly speaking, I find that bomb-throwing at night has only a morale effect. Those who are easily frightened are strongly affected when bombs fall at night. The others don't care.

We were much amused at the Englishman's performance and thought the English would come quite often on a visit. The flying piano dropped its bombs at last from an altitude of one hundred and fifty feet. That was rather impertinent for in a moonlit night I think I can hit a wild pig at one hundred and fifty feet with a rifle. Why then should I not succeed in hitting the Englishman? It would have been a novelty to down an English airman from the ground. From above I had already had the honor of downing a number of Englishmen, but I had never tried to tackle an aviator from below.

When the Englishman had gone we went back to mess and discussed among ourselves how we should receive the English should they pay us another visit on the following night. In the course of the next day our orderlies and other fellows were made to work with great energy. They had to ram into the ground piles which were to be used as a foundation for machine guns during the coming night.

We went to the butts and tried the English machine guns which we had taken from the enemy, arranged the sights for night shooting and were very curious as to what was going to happen. I will not betray the number of our machine guns. Anyhow, they were to be sufficient for the purpose. Every one of my officers was armed with one.

We were again sitting at mess. Of course we were discussing the problem of night fliers. Suddenly an orderly rushed in shouting-: "They are there! They are there!" and disappeared in the next bombproof in his scanty attire. We all rushed to our machine guns. Some of the men who were known to be good shots, had also been given a machine gun. All the rest were provided with carbines. The whole squadron was armed to the teeth to give a warm reception to our kindly visitors. The first Englishman arrived, exactly as on the previous evening, at a very great altitude. He went then down to one hundred and fifty feet and to our greatest joy began making for the place where our barracks were. He got into the glare of the searchlight.

When he was only three hundred yards away someone fired the first shot and all the rest of us joined in. A rush of cavalry or of storming troops could not have been met more efficiently than the attack of that single impertinent individual flying at one hundred and fifty feet.

Quick firing from many guns received him. Of course he could not hear the noise of the machine guns. The roar of his motor prevented that. However, he must have seen the flashes of our guns. Therefore I thought it tremendously plucky that our man did not swerve, but continued going straight ahead in accordance with his plan. At the moment he was perpendicularly above us we jumped quickly into our bombproof. It would have been too silly for flying men to die by a rotten bomb. As soon as he had passed over our heads we rushed out again and fired after him with our machine guns and rifles. Friend Schäfer asserted that he had hit the man. Schäfer is quite a good shot. Still, in this case I did not believe him. Besides, every one of us had as good a chance at making a hit as he had.

We had achieved something, for the enemy had dropped his bombs rather aimlessly owing to our shooting. One of them, it is true, had exploded only a few yards from the "petit rouge," but had not hurt him.

During the night the fun recommenced several times. I was already in bed, fast asleep, when I heard in a dream anti-aircraft firing. I woke up and discovered that the dream was reality. One of the Englishmen flew at so low an altitude over my habitation that in my fright I pulled the blanket over my head. The next moment I heard an incredible bang just outside my window. The panes had fallen a victim to the bomb. I rushed out of my room in my shirt in order to fire a few shots after him. They were firing from everywhere. Unfortunately, I had overslept my opportunity..

The next morning we were extremely surprised and delighted to discover that we had shot down from the ground no fewer than three Englishmen. They had landed not far from our aerodrome and had been made prisoners.

As a rule we had hit the engines and had forced the airmen to come down on our side of the Front. After all, Schäfer was possibly right in his assertion. At any rate, we were very well satisfied with our success. The English were distinctly less satisfied for they preferred avoiding our base. It was a pity that they gave us a wide berth, for they gave us lots of fun. Let us hope that they come back to us next month.

BLUE NOSE

WILLIAM A. BISHOP

"Billy" Bishop was the Allies highest scoring fighter pilot (with 72 kills) after Major "Mick" Mannock (73 kills) during World War I. A Canadian, Bishop entered the war as a cavalryman and his early career as a pilot had been distinctly unpromising; he had almost been "washed out" from initial RFC training.

Dawn was due at 5.30 o'clock on Easter Monday, and that was the exact hour set for the beginning of the Battle of Arras. We were up and had our machines out of the hangars while it was still night. The beautiful weather of a few hours before had vanished. A strong, chill wind was blowing from the east and dark, menacing clouds were scudding along low overhead.

We were detailed to fly at a low altitude over the advancing infantry, firing into the enemy trenches, and dispersing any groups of men or working troops we happened to see in the vicinity of the lines. Some phases of this work are known as "contact patrols," the machines keeping track always of the infantry advance, watching points where they may be held up, and returning from time to time to report just how the battle is going. Working with the infantry in a big attack is a most exciting experience. It means flying close to the ground and constantly passing through our own shells as well as those of the enemy.

The shell fire this morning was simply indescribable. The bombardment which had been going on all night gradually died down about 5 o'clock, and the Germans must have felt that the British had finished their nightly "strafing," were tired out and going to bed. For a time almost complete silence reigned over the battlefields. All along the German lines star-shells and rocket-lights were looping through the darkness. The old Boche is always suspicious and likes to have the country around him lit up as much as possible so he can see what the enemy is about.

The wind kept growing stiffer and stiffer and there was a distinct feel of rain in the air. Precisely at the moment that all the British guns roared out their first salvo of the battle, the skies opened and the rain fell in torrents. Gunfire may or may not have anything to do with rain-making, but there was a strange coincidence between the shock of battle and the commencement of the downpour this morning. It was beastly luck, and we felt it keenly. But we carried on.

The storm had delayed the coming of day by several minutes, but as soon as there was light enough to make our presence worth while we were in the air and braving the untoward elements just as the troops were below us. Lashed by the gale, the wind cut our faces as we moved against the enemy. The ground seemed to be one mass of bursting shells. Farther back, where the guns were firing, the hot flames flashing from thousands of muzzles gave the impression of a long ribbon of incandescent light. The air seemed shaken and literally full of shells on their missions of death and destruction. Over and over again one felt a sudden jerk under a wing-tip, and the machine would heave quickly. This meant a shell had passed within a few feet of you. As the battle went on the work grew more terrifying, because reports came in that several of our machines had been hit by shells in flight and brought down. There was small wonder of this. The British barrage fire that morning was the most intense the war had ever known. There was a greater concentration of guns than at any time during the Somme. In fact, some of the German prisoners said afterward that the Somme seemed a Paradise compared to the bombardments we carried out at Arras. While the British fire was at its height the Germans set up a counter-barrage. This was not so intense, but every shell added to the shrieking chorus that filled the stormy air made the lot of the flying man just so much more difficult. Yet the risk was one we could not avoid; we had to endure it with the best spirit possible.

The waves of attacking infantry as they came out of their trenches and trudged forward behind the curtain of shells laid down by the artillery were an amazing sight. The men seemed to wander across No Man's Land, and into the enemy trenches, as if the battle was a great bore to them. From the air it looked as though they did not realize that they were at war and were taking it all entirely too quietly. That is the way with clockwork warfare. These troops had been drilled to move forward at a given pace. They had been timed over and over again in marching a certain distance, and from this timing the "creeping" or rolling barrage which moved in front of them had been mathematically worked out. And the battle, so calmly entered into, was one of the tensest, bitterest of the entire world war.

For days the battle continued, and it was hard work and no play for everybody concerned. The weather, instead of getting better, as spring weather should, gradually got worse. It was cold, windy, and wet. Every two or three hours sudden snowstorms would shut in, and flying in these squalls, which obliterated the landscape, was a very ticklish business.

On the fourth day of the battle I happened to be flying about 500 feet above the trenches an hour after dawn. It had snowed during the night and the ground was covered with a new layer of white several inches thick. No marks of the battle of the day before were to be seen; the only blemishes in the snow mantle were the marks of shells which had fallen during the last hour. No Man's Land itself, so often a filthy litter, was this morning quite clean and white.

Suddenly over the top of our parapets a thin line of infantry crawled up and commenced to stroll casually toward the enemy. To me it seemed that they must soon wake up and run; that they were altogether too slow; that they could not realize the great danger they were in. Here and there a shell would burst as the line advanced or halted for a moment. Three or four men near the burst would topple over like so many tin soldiers. Two or three other men would then come running up to the spot from the rear with a stretcher, pick up the wounded and the dying, and slowly walk back with them. I could not get the idea out of my head that it was just a game they were playing at; it all seemed so unreal. Nor could I believe that the little brown figures moving about below me were really men – men going to the glory of victory or the glory of death. I could not make myself realize the full truth or meaning of it all. It seemed that I was in an entirely different world, looking down from another sphere on this strange, uncanny puppet-show.

Suddenly I heard the deadly rattle of a nest of machine guns under me, and saw that the line of our troops at one place was growing very thin, with many figures sprawling on the ground. For three or four minutes I could not make out the concealed position of the German gunners. Our men had halted, and were lying on the ground, evidently as much puzzled as I was. Then in a corner of a German trench I saw a group of about five men operating two machine guns. They were slightly to the flank of our line, and evidently had been doing a great amount of damage. The sight of these men thoroughly woke me up to the reality of the whole scene beneath me. I dived vertically at them with a burst of rapid fire. The smoking bullets from my gun flashed into the ground, and it was an easy matter to get an accurate aim on the German automatics, one of which turned its muzzle toward me.

But in a fraction of a second I had reached a height of only 30 feet above the Huns, so low I could make out every detail of their frightened faces. With hate in my heart I fired every bullet I could into the group as I swept over it, then turned my machine away. A few minutes later I had the satisfaction of seeing our line again advancing, and before the time had come for me to return from my patrol, our men had occupied all the German positions they had set out to take. It was a wonderful sight and a wonderful experience. Although it had been so difficult to realize that men were dying and being maimed for life beneath me, I felt that at last I had seen something of that dogged determination that has carried British arms so far.

The next ten days were filled with incident. The enemy fighting machines would not come close to the lines, and there was very little doing in the way of aerial combats, especially as far as I was concerned, for I was devoting practically all of my time to flying low and helping the infantry. All of our pilots and observers were doing splendid work. Everywhere we were covering the forward movement of the infantry, keeping the troops advised of any enemy movements, and enabling the British artillery to shell every area where it appeared concentrations were taking place. Scores of counter-attacks were broken up before the Germans had fairly launched them. Our machines were everywhere behind the enemy lines. It was easy to tell when the Germans were massing for a counter-stroke. First of all our machines would fly low over the grey-clad troops, pouring machine-gun bullets into them or dropping high-explosive bombs in their midst. Then the exact location of the mobilization point would be signalled to the artillery, so that the moment the Germans moved our guns were on them. In General Orders commending the troops for their part in the battle, Field-Marshal Sir Douglas Haig declared that the work of the Flying Corps, "under the most difficult conditions," called for the highest praise.

We were acting, you might say, as air policemen.

Occasionally one of our machines would be set upon by the German gangsters – they were "careful" fighters and seldom attacked unless at odds of four to one – and naturally we suffered some casualties, just as the ordinary police force suffers casualties when it is doing patrol duty in an outlaw country. The weather was always favourable to the German methods of avoiding "open-air" combats. Even the clearer days were marked by skies filled with clouds sufficiently large and dense enough to offer protection and hiding-places to the high winging Hun machines.

I had several skirmishes, but did not succeed in bringing down another machine until April 20th, when I was fortunate enough to begin another series of extremely interesting and successful fights. I was promoted to be a Captain about this time and thought I was very happy; but the promotion was followed by another incident which really made me proud. The sergeants of my squadron had made me a round "nose" for my machine. It fitted on the propeller head and revolved with it. I had it painted a brilliant blue, and from that time on my machine was known as "Blue Nose." It was given to me, the Sergeant-Major explained, as a sign that I was an "Ace" – that I had brought down more than five machines. I was so pleased with this tribute from the men that I took old "Blue Nose" visiting to several other squadrons, where I exhibited my new mark of distinction to many of my friends and flying companions.

The machine I got on April 20th was the first I ever destroyed in flames. It is a thing that often happens, and while I have no desire to make myself appear as a bloodthirsty person, I must say that to see an enemy going down in flames is a source of great satisfaction. You know his destruction is absolutely certain. The moment you see the fire break out you know that nothing in the world can save the man, or men, in the doomed aeroplane. You know there is no "camouflage" in this, and you have no fear that the enemy is trying any kind of flying trick in the hope that he will be left alone.

I was flying over a layer of white clouds when I saw a two-seater just above me. We generally met the enemy in force during these days, but this German machine was all alone. Neither the pilot nor observer saw me. They flew along blissfully ignorant of my existence, while I carefully kept directly underneath them, climbing all the time. I was only ten yards behind the Hun when I fired directly up at him. It had been an exciting game getting into position underneath him, carefully following every move he made, waiting, hoping, and praying that he would not see me before I got into the place I wanted. I was afraid that if he did see me I would be at a distinct disadvantage below him. My hand must have been shaky, or my eye slightly out, because, although I managed to fire ten rounds, I did not hit anything vital. Even in this crucial moment the humour of the situation almost got the better of me. My machine seemed so little, carefully flying there under the big, peaceful Hun; who thought he was so safe and so far from any danger. Suddenly, from just underneath him, he heard the "tat-tat-tat-tatter-tatter" of my machine gun almost in his ear, the range was so close. Then he must have seen my smoking bullets passing all around him. Anyway, there was consternation in the camp. He turned quickly, and a regular battle in the air began between the two of us. We manœuvred every way possible, diving, rolling, stalling; he attempting to get a straight shot at me, while my one object was to get straight behind him again, or directly in front of him, so as to have a direct line of fire right into him.

Twice I dived at him and opened fire from almost point-blank range, being within two lengths of him before I touched the lever which set my gun to spouting. But there was no success. The third time I tried a new manœuvre. I dived at him from the side, firing as I came. My new tactics gave the German observer a direct shot at me from his swivel gun, and he was firing very well too, his bullets passing quite close for a moment or two. Then, however, they began to fly well beyond my wing-tips, and on seeing this I knew that his nerve was shaken. I could now see my own bullets hitting the right part of the Hun machine, and felt confident the battle soon would be over.

I pulled my machine out of its dive just in time to pass about 5 feet over the enemy. I could see the observer evidently had been hit and had stopped firing. Otherwise the Hun machine seemed perfectly all right. But just after I passed I looked back over my shoulder and saw it burst into flames. A second later it fell a burning mass, leaving a long trail of smoke behind as it disappeared through the clouds. I thought for a moment of the fate of the wounded observer and the hooded pilot into whose faces I had just been looking – but it was fair hunting, and I flew away with great contentment in my heart.

This fight seemed to have changed my luck for the better. Everywhere I went for the next few weeks enemy machines were easily found, and I had numerous combats, many of them successful. Some days I could have been accused of violating all the rules of a flying men's union (if we had had one). I would fly as much as seven and a half hours between sunrise and sunset. Far from affecting my nerves, the more I flew the more I wanted to fly, the better I seemed to feel, and each combat became more and more enjoyable. Ambition was born in my breast, and, although I still dared not entertain hope of equalling the record of the renowned Captain Ball,* who by this time had shot down over thirty-five machines, I did have vague hopes of running second to him.

Along with the new ambition there was born in me as well a distinct dislike for all two-seated German flying machines! They always seemed so placid and sort of contented with themselves. I picked a fight with the two-seaters wherever I could find one, and I searched for them high and low. Many people think of the two-seater as a superior fighting machine because of its greater gun-power. But to me they always seemed fair prey and an

* Captain Albert Ball, born 1896, British fighter ace, killed in action on 7 May 1917 See pp 82–85

easy target. One afternoon, soon after this new Hun hatred had become a part of my soul, I met a two-seater about three miles over the German lines and dived at him from a very low height. As bad luck would have it, my gun had a stoppage, and while I turned away to right it, the enemy escaped. Much disgusted, I headed away homeward, when into my delighted vision there came the familiar outlines of another Hun with two men aboard. I flew at this new enemy with great determination; but after a short battle he dived away from me, and although I did my best to catch him up, I could not. He landed in a field underneath me. To see him calmly alight there under perfect control filled me with a towering rage. I saw red things before my eyes. I vowed an eternal vendetta against all the Hun two-seaters in the world, and, the impulse suddenly seizing me, I dived right down to within a few feet of the ground, firing a stream of bullets into the machine where it was sitting. I had the satisfaction of knowing that the pilot and observer must have been hit, or nearly scared to death, for, although I hovered about for quite a long time, neither of them stepped from the silent machine.

Half an hour after this occurrence I saw one of our machines in difficulties with three of the enemy. The Huns were so engrossed with the thought that they had a single British machine at their mercy, I felt there was a good chance that I might slip up and surprise them. My scheme worked beautifully. I came up to within 15 yards of one of the Huns, and, aiming my machine at him with dead accuracy, shot him down with my first ten bullets. He probably never knew where the bullets came from, not having the slightest idea another British machine was anywhere in that part of the sky. I turned now to assist with the other two Huns, but by this time my brother-pilot had sent one of them spinning out of control, while the last remaining enemy was making good his escape as fast as his Mercédès engine could pull him through the air. It is surprising sometimes how much dead resistance there is in the air when you are in a hurry. Having nothing better to do under the circumstances, I dived down after my own victim to get a view of the crash. I was just in time. He struck the ground at the corner of a field, and what was one instant a falling machine was next a twisted bit of wreckage.

It was apparent to us by this time that the Germans were bringing their best pilots opposite the British front to meet the determined offensive we had been carrying on since April 1st. Most of the machines we met were handled in a manner far above the German average. Each night our pilots brought in exciting stories of the chase. Although they were a higher class of fighting men than we had hitherto flown against, the Germans still showed a reluctance to attack unless they outnumbered us by at least three to one. One lone German was induced to take a fatal chance against a British scout formation. By clever manœuvring, at which the hostile airman was also quite adept, we managed to entice him to attack one of our machines from behind. As he did so, a second British machine dived at him, and down he went, one of his wings breaking off as he fell.

I can best illustrate the German tactics of the time by telling the experience of one of our faithful old photographic machines, which, by the way, are not without their desperate moments and their deeds of heroism. All of which goes to show that the fighting scouts should not get all the credit for the wonders of modern warfare in the air. The old "photographer" in question was returning over the lines one day when it was set upon by no less than eleven hostile scouts. Nearly all the controls of the British machine were shot away, and the observer, seriously wounded, fell half-way out of the *nacelle*. Although still manœuvring his machine so as to escape the direct fire of the enemies on his tail, the British pilot grasped the wounded observer, held him safely in the machine, and made a safe landing in our lines. A moment later the riddled aeroplane burst into flames. Under heavy shell-fire the pilot carried the wounded observer to safety.

One of the distinguished German flying squadrons opposite us was under command of the famous Captain Baron von Richthofen. One day I had the distinction of engaging in three fights in half an hour with pilots from this squadron. Their machines were painted a brilliant scarlet from nose to tail – immense red birds, they were, with the graceful wings of their type, Albatross scouts. They were all single-seaters, and were flown by pilots of undeniable skill. There was quite a little spirit of sportsmanship in this squadron, too. The red German machines had two machine guns in fixed positions firing straight ahead, both being operated from the same control.

The first of my three fights with these newcomers in our midst occurred when I suddenly found myself mixed up with two of them. Evidently they were not very anxious for a fight at the moment, for, after a few minutes of manœuvring, both broke it off and dived away. Ten minutes later I encountered one of the red machines flying alone. I challenged him, but he wouldn't stay at all. On the contrary, he made off as fast as he could go. On my return from chasing him I met a second pair of red Huns. I had picked up company with another British machine, and the two Huns, seeing us, dived into a cloud to escape. I went in after them, and on coming out again found one directly beneath me. On to him I dived, not pulling the trigger until I was 15 yards away. Once, twice, three times I pressed the lever, but not a shot from my gun! I slipped away into another cloud and examined the faithless weapon, only to find that I had run completely out of ammunition. I returned home quite the most disgusted person in the entire British Army.

During the changeable days of the Arras offensive we had many exciting adventures with the weather. On one occasion I had gone back to the aircraft depot to bring to the front a new machine. Sunshine and snow-squalls were chasing each other in a seemingly endless procession. On the ground the wind was howling along at about fifty miles an hour. I arrived at the depot at 9 o'clock in the morning, but waited about until four in the afternoon before the weather appeared to be settling down to something like a safe and sane basis. The sunshine intervals were growing longer and the snow periods shorter, so I climbed into my machine and started off. It was only a fifteen minutes' fly to the aerodrome, but in that time a huge black cloud loomed up and came racing toward me. I was headed straight into the gale, and the way was so rough from the rush of the wind and the heavy clouds floating by that the little machine was tossed about like a piece of paper. Several times I thought I was going to be blown completely over. Occasionally, without any warning, I would be lifted a sheer hundred feet in the air. Then later I would be dropped that distance, and often more. I was perspiring freely, although it was a very cold day. It was a race against the weather to reach my destination in time.

One cannot see in a snowstorm, and I felt that if the fleecy squall struck me before I sighted the aerodrome I would have to land in a ploughed field, and to do this in such a gale would be a very ticklish proposition. Added to all this, I was flying a machine of a type I had never handled before, and naturally it was a bit strange to me. Nearer and nearer the big cloud came. But I was racing for home at top speed. About half a mile from the haven I sought, the storm struck me. The moment before the snow deluge came, however, I had recognized the road that led to the aerodrome, and coming down to 50 feet, where I could just make it out, I flew wildly on, praying all the time that the snow striking my engine would not cause it to stop. Then the awful thought came to me that perhaps I was on the wrong road. Then, even more suddenly than it had come, the snow stopped – the storm had swept right over me. There, just ahead of me, I saw the tents and hangars and the flying pennant of the aerodrome – home. This was my first experience in flying through snow, and I did not care for another.

A few days after my unsuccessful experience with the red Richthofen scouts, I got my just revenge and a little more back from the Huns. My Major had been told to have some photographs taken of a certain point behind the German lines, and by special permission he was given the privilege of taking them himself. The point to be photographed was about seven miles in German territory, and in order to make a success of the snapshotting it would be necessary to have a strong escort. The Major offered to go out and do the photographs on his own without an escort, but the Colonel would not hear of it, and so it was arranged that an offensive patrol would go out at 9 o'clock in the morning, meet the Major at a given point, and escort him over the ground he wished to cover.

My patrol was the one working at the time, and I was the leader. At 9.30 we were to meet, just east of Arras, at 6000 feet. The rendezvous came off like clockwork. I brought the patrol to the spot at 9.28, and two minutes later we spied a single Nieuport coming toward us. I fired a red signal light and the Nieuport answered. It was the Major. I then climbed slightly and led the patrol along about 1000 feet above the Nieuport in order to protect the Major and at the same time keep high enough to avoid too much danger from anti-aircraft fire. We got to the area to be photographed without any other excitement than a very heavy greeting from the "Archies." There were a number of big white clouds floating around about 6000 feet, and these made it difficult for the guns to shoot at us. But they also made it difficult for the Major to get his photographs. We went around and around in circles for what seemed an eternity. During one of these sweeping turns I suddenly saw four enemy scouts climbing between two clouds and some distance off. I knew they would see us soon, so it occurred to me it would be a brilliant idea to let the enemy think there was only one British machine on the job. Under these circumstances I knew they would be sure to attack, and then the rest of us could swoop down and surprise them. I had no intention of letting the Major in for any unnecessary risks, but it seemed such a rare chance, I could not resist it.

I led the patrol about 2000 feet higher up and there we waited. The enemy scouts did not see us at all, but they did see the Major. And they made for him. The first the Major knew of their approach, however, was when they were about 200 yards away, and one of them, somewhat prematurely, opened fire. His thoughts – he told me afterward – immediately flew to the patrol, and he glanced over his shoulder to see where we were. But we had vanished. He then wondered how much money he had in his pockets, as he did not doubt that the four Huns, surprising him as they had, would surely get him. Despite these gloomy and somewhat mercenary thoughts, the Major was fighting for his life. First he turned the nose of his machine directly toward the enemy, poured a burst of bullets toward a German at his right; then turned to the left, as the second machine approached in that direction, and let him have a taste of British gunfire as well. This frightened the first two Huns off for a moment, and, in that time, I arrived down on the scene with the rest of the patrol.

One of the Huns was firing at the Major's machine as I flashed by him, and I fired at a bare ten yards' range. Then I passed on to the second enemy machine, firing all the while, and eventually passing within 5 feet of one of his wing-tips. Turning my machine as quickly as I could, I was yet too late to catch the other two of the formation of four. They had both dived away and escaped. I had hit the two that first attacked the Major, however, and they were at the moment falling completely out of control 1000 or more feet below me, and finally went through the clouds, floundering helplessly in the air.

This little interruption ended, we all reassembled in our former positions and went on with the photographing. This was finished in about fifteen minutes, and, under a very heavy anti-aircraft fire, we returned home. The episode of the four Huns was perhaps the most successful bit of trapping I have ever seen, but it was many weeks before the squadron got through teasing me for using our commander as a decoy. I apologized to the Major, who agreed with me that the chance was too good a one to miss.

"Don't mind me," he said; "carry on."

SAGITTARIUS RISING

CECIL LEWIS

Cecil Lewis served with the RFC on the Western Front, surviving three tours to become a post-war test pilot. During World War II, he again donned uniform, this time as a flying instructor.

In 1917 co-operative tactics in single-seater fighting were rudimentary. A combat was a personal matter. In a fight no pilot has time to watch others; he is too occupied in attempting to down his own man or in avoiding an enemy intent on downing him. Tactics apart, the vital question is that of performance. A machine with better speed and climbing power must always have the advantage.

During the next ten days Offensive Patrols were carried out daily and, unfortunately, it soon became clear that, good as the SE5 was, it was still not equal to the enemy. Scrapping at high altitudes, fifteen to eighteen thousand feet, the Huns had a marked superiority in performance. This naturally tended to make us cautious, since we knew that, once we came down to their level, we should not be able to get above them again. Height, apart from its moral superiority, means added speed for the one above, who in his dive and zoom away has gravity on his side. Since machine guns in a scout are fixed, firing forward in the line of flight, it follows that the pilot aims the whole machine at his adversary. If that adversary is above him, he will be forced to pull his machine up on its tail to get him in the sights. That means loss of speed, manoeuvrability and, if carried to an extreme, a stall, and wandering about at stalling speed is asking for trouble when there are enemy guns about. This inferiority of performance was an initial difficulty. Later, when the SE5 got a larger motor, things looked up.

Single combat, a duel with another machine, was, performance apart, a question of good flying. Two machines so engaged would circle, each trying to turn inside the other and so bring his guns into play. Ability to sustain such tight vertical turns is the crucial test of a fighting pilot. Once the balance of the controls is lost, the machine will slip, lose height, and the enemy will rush in. Then, by all the rules of the game, you are a dead man.

But when a number of machines had closed and were engaged in a "dog-fight", it was more a question of catch as catch can. A pilot would go down on the tail of a Hun, hoping to get him in the first burst; but he would not be wise to stay there, for another Hun would almost certainly be on *his* tail hoping to get him in the same way. Such fights were really a series of rushes, with momentary pauses to select the next opportunity – to catch the enemy at a disadvantage, or separated from his friends.

But apart from fighting, when twenty or thirty scouts were engaged, there was always a grave risk of collision. Machines would hurtle by, intent on their private battles, missing each other by feet. So such fighting demanded iron nerves, lightning reactions, snap decisions, a cool head, and eyes like a bluebottle, for it all took place at high speed and was three dimensional.

At this sort of sharpshooting some pilots excelled others; but in all air fighting (and indeed in every branch of aerial warfare) there is an essential in which it differs from the war on the ground: its absolute coldbloodedness. You cannot lose your temper with an aeroplane. You cannot "see red", as a man in a bayonet fight. You certainly cannot resort to "Dutch" courage. Any of these may fog your judgment – and that spells death.

Often at high altitudes we flew in air well below freezing point. Then the need to clear a jam or change a drum meant putting an arm out into an icy 100 m.p.h. wind. If you happened to have bad circulation (as I had), it left the hand numb, and since you could not stamp your feet, swing your arms, or indeed move at all, the numbness would spread to the other hand and sometimes to the feet as well. In this condition we often went into a scrap with the odds against us – they usually were against us, for it was our job to be "offensive" and go over into enemy country looking for trouble – coldbloodedly in the literal sense; but none the less we had to summon every faculty of judgment and skill to down our man or, at the worst, to come out of it alive ourselves. So, like duelling, air fighting required a set steely courage, drained of all emotion, fined down to a tense and deadly effort of will. The Angel of Death is less callous, aloof and implacable than a fighting pilot when he dives.

There were, of course, emergency methods, such as standing the machine on its tail and holding it there just long enough to get one good burst into the enemy above you; but nobody would fight that way if he could help it, though, actually, an SE5 pilot could do the same thing by pulling his top gun down the quadrant. He could then fire it vertically upward while still flying level.

This was how Beery Bowman once got away from an ugly situation. He had been scrapping a couple of Huns well over the other side of the lines. He managed to crash one of them, but in so doing exhausted the ammunition of his Vickers gun: his Lewis was jammed. The other Hun pursued him and forced him right down on to the "carpet" – about a hundred feet from the ground. There was nothing to do but to beat it home. The Hun, out to avenge the death of his friend, and having the advantage of speed and height over Beery, chivvied him back to the lines, diving after him, bursting his gun, zooming straight up again, hanging there for a moment in a stall, and falling to dive again. He repeated this several times (he must have been a rotten shot) while Beery, with extraordinary coolness and presence of mind, pulled down his Lewis gun and managed to clear the jam. The next time the Hun zoomed, Beery throttled right down and pulled back to stalling speed. The result was that when the Hun fell out of his zoom, Beery was not ahead of him as before, but beneath him. As the Hun dropped into his dive Beery opened fire with his Lewis gun, raking the body above him with a long burst. The Hun turned over on his back, dived, and struck the ground, bursting into flames. Beery laconically continued his way home. He was awarded the D.S.O.

With the exception of Ball,* most crack fighters did not get their Huns in dog-fights. They preferred safer means. They would spend hours synchronizing their guns and telescopic sights so that they could do accurate shooting at, say, two or three hundred yards. They would then set out on patrol, alone, spot their quarry (in such cases usually a two-seater doing reconnaissance or photography), and carefully manoeuvre for position, taking great pains to remain where they could not be seen, *i.e.* below and behind the tail of the enemy. From here, even if the Hun observer did spot them, he could not bring his gun to bear without the risk of shooting away his own tail plane or rudder. The stalker would not hurry after his quarry, but keep a wary eye to see he was not about to be attacked himself. He would gradually draw nearer, always in the blind spot, sight his guns very carefully, and then one long deadly burst would do the trick.

Such tactics as those were employed by Captain McCudden, V.C., D.S.O., and also by the French ace, Guynemer. Both of them, of course, were superb if they got into a dog-fight; but it was in such fighting that they were both ultimately killed.

* * *

* *Captain Albert Ball, born 1896, gained RFC "wings" on 22 January 1916*

Typical logbook entries:

"5/5/17. Offensive patrol: twelve thousand feet. Hoidge, Melville and self on voluntary patrol. Bad Archie over Douai. Lost Melville in cloud and afterwards attacked five red scouts. Sheered off when seven others came to their assistance. Two against twelve 'no bon'. We climbed west and they east, afterwards attacked them again, being joined by five Tripehounds, making the odds seven to twelve. Think I did in one, and Hoidge also did in one. Both granted by Wing."

"7/5/17. Ran into three scouts east of Cambrai. Brought one down. Meintjies dived, but his gun jammed, so I carried on and finished him. Next fired on two-seater this side lines, but could not climb up to him. Went up to Lens, saw a two-seater over Douai, dived and the others followed. Fixed him up. Afterwards this confirmed by an FE2d, who saw burst into flames. Tackled three two-seaters who beat it east and came home. Good day!"

The squadron was doing well in Huns. Ball came back every day with a bag of one or more. Besides his SE5 he had a Nieuport scout, the machine in which he had done so well the previous year. He had a roving commission and, with two machines, was four hours a day in the air. Of the great fighting pilots his tactics were the least cunning. Absolutely fearless, the odds made no difference to him. He would always attack, single out his man, and close. On several occasions he almost rammed the enemy, and often came back with his machine shot to pieces.

One morning, before the rest of us had gone out on patrol, we saw him coming in rather clumsily to land. He was not a stunt pilot, but flew very safely and accurately, so that, watching him, we could not understand his awkward floating landing. But when he taxied up to the sheds we saw his elevators were flapping loose – controls had been completely shot away! He had flown back from the lines and made his landing entirely by winding his adjustable tail up and down! It was incredible he had not crashed. His oil tank had been riddled, and his face and the whole nose of the machine were running with black castor oil. He was so angry at being shot up like this that he walked straight to the sheds, wiped the oil off his shoulders and face with a rag, ordered out his Nieuport, and within two hours was back with yet another Hun to his credit!

Ball was a quiet, simple little man. His one relaxation was the violin, and his favourite after-dinner amusement to light a red magnesium flare outside his hut and walk round it in his pyjamas, fiddling! He was meticulous in the care of his machines, guns, and in the examination of his ammunition. He never flew for amusement. The only trips he took, apart from offensive patrols, were the minimum requisite to test his engines or fire at the ground target sighting his guns. He never boasted or criticized, but his example was tremendous.

The squadron sets out eleven strong on the evening patrol. Eleven chocolate-coloured, lean, noisy bullets, lifting, swaying, turning, rising into formation – two fours and a three – circling and climbing away steadily towards the lines. They are off to deal with Richthofen and his circus of Red Albatrosses.

The May evening is heaving with threatening masses of cumulus cloud, majestic skyscapes, solid-looking as snow mountains, fraught with caves and valleys, rifts and ravines – strange and secret pathways in the chartless continents of the sky. Below, the land becomes an ordnance map, dim green and yellow, and across it go the Lines, drawn anyhow, as a child might scrawl with a double pencil. The grim dividing Lines! From the air robbed of all significance.

Steadily, the body of scouts rises higher and higher, threading its way between the cloud precipices. Sometimes, below, the streets of a village, the corner of a wood, a few dark figures moving, glide into view like a slide into a lantern and then are hidden again.

But the fighting pilot's eyes are not on the ground, but

roving endlessly through the lower and higher reaches of the sky, peering anxiously through fur-goggles to spot those black slow-moving specks against land or cloud which mean full throttle, tense muscles, held breath, and the headlong plunge with screaming wires – a Hun in the sights, and the tracers flashing.

A red light curls up from the leader's cockpit and falls away. Action! He alters direction slightly, and the patrol, shifting throttle and rudder, keep close like a pack of hounds on the scent. He has seen, and they see soon, six scouts three thousand feet below. Black crosses! It seems interminable till the eleven come within diving distance. The pilots nurse their engines, hard-minded and set, test their guns and watch their indicators. At last the leader sways sideways, as a signal that each should take his man, and suddenly drops.

Machines fall scattering, the earth races up, the enemy patrol, startled, wheels and breaks. Each his man! The chocolate thunderbolts take sights, steady their screaming planes, and fire. A burst, fifty rounds – it is over. They have overshot, and the enemy, hit or missed, is lost for the moment. The pilot steadies his stampeding mount, pulls her out with a firm hand, twisting his head right and left, trying to follow his man, to sight another, to back up a friend in danger, to note another in flames.

But the squadron plunging into action had not seen, far off, approaching from the east, the rescue flight of Red Albatrosses patrolling above the body of machines on which they had dived, to guard their tails and second them in the battle. These, seeing the maze of wheeling machines, plunge down to join them. The British scouts, engaging and disengaging like flies circling at midday in a summer room, soon find the newcomers upon them. Then, as if attracted by some mysterious power, as vultures will draw to a corpse in the desert, other bodies of machines swoop down from the peaks of the cloud mountains. More enemy scouts, and, by good fortune, a flight of Naval Triplanes.

But, nevertheless, the enemy, double in number, greater in power and fighting with skill and courage, gradually overpower the British, whose machines scatter, driven down beneath the scarlet German fighters.

It would be impossible to describe the action of such a battle. A pilot, in the second between his own engagements, might see a Hun diving vertically, an SE5 on his tail, on the tail of the SE another Hun, and above him again another British scout. These four, plunging headlong at two hundred miles an hour, guns crackling, tracers streaming, suddenly break up. The lowest Hun plunges flaming to his death, if death has not taken him already. His victor seems to stagger, suddenly pulls out in a great leap, as a trout leaps on the end of a line, and then, turning over on his belly, swoops and spins in a dizzy falling spiral with the earth to end it. The third German zooms veering, and the last of that meteoric quartet follows bursting. . . . But such a glimpse, lasting perhaps ten seconds, is broken by the sharp rattle of another attack. Two machines approach head-on at breakneck speed, firing at each other, tracers whistling through each other's planes, each slipping sideways on his rudder to trick the other's gun fire. Who will hold longest? Two hundred yards, a hundred, fifty, and then, neither hit, with one accord they fling their machines sideways, bank and circle, each striving to bring his gun on to the other's tail, each glaring through goggle eyes, calculating, straining, wheeling, grim, bent only on death or dying.

But, from above, this strange tormented circling is seen by another Hun. He drops. His gun speaks. The British machine, distracted by the sudden unseen enemy, pulls up, takes a burst through the engine, tank and body, and falls bottom uppermost down through the clouds and the deep unending desolation of the twilight sky.

The game of noughts and crosses, starting at fifteen thousand feet above the clouds, drops in altitude engagement by engagement. Friends and foes are scattered. A last SE, pressed by two Huns, plunges and wheels, gun-jammed, like a snipe over marshes, darts lower, finds refuge in the ground mist, and disappears.

Now lowering clouds darken the evening. Below, flashes of gun fire stab the veil of the gathering dusk. The fight is over! The battlefield shows no sign. In the pellucid sky, serene cloud mountains mass and move unceasingly. Here where guns rattled and death plucked the spirits of the valiant, this thing is now as if it had never been! The sky is busy with night, passive, superb, unheeding.

Of the eleven scouts that went out that evening, the 7th of May, only five of us returned to the aerodrome.

The mess was very quiet that night. The Adjutant remained in his office, hoping against hope to have news of the six missing pilots and, later, news did come through that two had been forced down, shot in the engine, and that two others had been wounded.

But Ball never returned. I believe I was the last to see him in his red-nosed SE going east at eight thousand feet. He flew straight into the white face of an enormous cloud. I followed. But when I came out on the other side, he was nowhere to be seen. All next day a feeling of depression hung over the squadron. We mooned about the sheds, still hoping for news. The day after that hope was given up. I flew his Nieuport back to the Aircraft Depot.

It was decided to go over to Douai and drop message-bags containing requests, written in German, for news of his fate. We crossed the lines at thirteen thousand feet. Douai was renowned for its anti-aircraft. They were not to know the squadron was in mourning, and made it hot for us. The flying splinters ripped the planes. Over the town the message-bags were dropped, and the formation returned without encountering a single enemy machine.

Ball was awarded a posthumous Victoria Cross. He had been the victor in 47 aerial combats.

LETTERS HOME

H.G. DOWNING

Second Lieutenant Downing served with the Royal Flying Corps in World War I. The two letters below are written to his family.

> Castle Bromwich.
> Near Birmingham
> July 24 1917

Dearest All,

I suppose I am exceeding the speed limit in letter writing, but daresay an extra letter will meet with your approval. I have been leading a most strenuous existence lately, and put in a tremendous amount of flying. Of course, unfortunately perhaps, it means going out to France sooner than expected but suppose pilots are wanted fairly badly.

I went on a cross country to a neighbouring aerodrome about 30 miles away this evening and had tea there. On my return journey I ran into a rain storm and got lost. When I came out I found I had wandered in a circle and was back at my original starting place. I thought I had just enough petrol, so continued my journey. When about 4 miles from this aerodrome, the engine started to misfire and finally stopped. I was a fair height up, about 1000 feet and just managed to make the aerodrome, missing some telegraph wires by a few inches, and finally stopping right in front of our mess door, without breaking anything. As you may guess it caused great excitement and everybody seems to think it is a good effort.

Ah! Well we don't get much money, but we do see life. I shall be going to Turnberry in Scotland for a aerial course on the 1st of August, for a fortnight. After that I shall be able to put up my wings if I do alright. In the meanwhile I had a very nice time last Saturday. Two charming members of the fair sex helped to look after this bashful young man and have now an invitation to the house, which I might say is *some* place. Oh! it is quite alright. I went and stunted over their house yesterday, and was pretty bucked to see an answering flutter of cambrio from the ground. Quite romantic. What! Well I suppose that is about all the news. Cheer oh! everybody.

BEF [France]
October 20, 1917

My dearest all,

I have been hoping for a letter, but so far the weekly budget has not turned up. I expect it takes some time nowadays.

Well, I am still in the land of the living and am enjoying myself no end. It is quite like old times. I had an exciting experience a day or two ago. You know how misty the weather is nowadays. Well we were flying about over the line, when a fellow and myself lost the rest of the patrol in a fog and we had not a bit of an idea where we were, so we came down to a few hundred feet from the ground. Presently we came to a large Town, which puzzled me immensely, and I circled round quite comically trying to locate it on the map. I thought, and so did the other fellow, that we were on our side of the lines. Imagine my amazement when I discovered it to be about 12 miles in Hun land. We were soon greeted with shells and machine gun fire. So of course we frightened everything we met on the roads, diving quite close to the ground and on to motor lorries etc and I bet we scared Huns out of their lives. When we eventually came home we noticed all the roads quite clear of men and lorries etc . . . so we were immensely bucked with ourselves and enjoyed a jolly good breakfast . . . Tonight I am dining with another squadron. I know a few fellows there and expect to have quite a cheery evening. Oh! Yes! I shall be quite good.

By the way I unfortunately smashed a machine the other day. I landed on my nose by mistake in the middle of the aerodrome. I didn't hurt myself though and my CO only laughed and suggested mildly that I should land on my wheels another time.

It was very funny because four more did exactly the same thing five minutes later. Well cheery oh! everybody

George Downing went missing in action in November 1917.

FLYING FURY

JAMES McCUDDEN VC

James McCudden entered World War I as an engine-fitter in the newly formed Royal Flying Corps. By early 1916 he had become an observer. In May 1916 he gained his "wings", making him one of the few NCO fighter pilots in the RFC. On 1 January 1917 he was commissioned and in August 1917 was made flight commander with 56 Squadron (which was equipped with SE5A single-seater fighters). By the end of that year his tally of victories stood at 37. In March 1918 McCudden was awarded the Victoria Cross in recognition of his long run of successful and courgeous actions against the enemy. He died on 9 July 1918 after an engine malfunction during a routine take-off at Auxi-le-Chateau, France. James McCudden VC, DSO & Bar, MC & Bar, MM, CdG was 23. He had shot down 57 German aircraft over the skies of Flanders. The extract below from his memoirs, which he completed only days before his death, covers the latter period of 1917 and is notable for its account of Rhys-David's downing of German ace Werner Voss, argually the classic dog-fight of air war over the Western Front.

Orders were to report to Mason's Yard at 9 a.m. on the 14th of August. I reported in good time after having packed my kit and said good-bye to my people and friends, and left Victoria at 9.30, arriving at Folkestone in time to catch the midday boat. I arrived in Boulogne again on the good ship "Victoria" at about 2 p.m. and telephoned the Adjutant of No. 56 Squadron of my arrival, who very kindly sent a tender for me. The tender arrived in due course, and I arrived at No. 56 Squadron at 7.30 p.m. on August 15th. I at once reported to Major Blomfield, and I don't think I have often experienced such pleasure as when I was able to call myself a Flight-Commander in No. 56 Squadron.

When I arrived at the Squadron I was just in time to meet the pilots landing after the evening patrol, during which the patrol had got four Huns. We adjourned to the mess and had dinner, which was enjoyed to the accompaniment of the Squadron orchestra. I sat on the C.O.'s left, Bowman on his right, and Maxwell, the other Flight-Commander, on the right of Bowman. I was to command "B" Flight, and my brother pilots were Lieutenants Barlow, Rhys-Davids, Muspratt, Coote and Cronyn, as splendid a lot of fellows as ever set foot in France.

The next morning I inspected and took over the Flight, and then had my machine fitted to my liking. The machine was No. B/519, a Vickers-built S.E.5. On the next day I led my first patrol in No. 56 Squadron, and flew over the area, Menin, Zonnebeke, at 15,000 ft. for two hours, but the only Hun we saw was one who was well above us, far too high for any of us to climb to.

On the 18th of August I led my patrol over the lines at Houthem at 14,000 ft., and we at once sighted some Huns just west of Menin; we all dived and, when we got near, saw that they were two-seaters. I tackled the nearest one, but both guns jammed immediately so badly that I landed at the nearest aerodrome at once, and after clearing the stoppages crossed the lines again over Gheluvelt, where I at once met Barlow at 8,000 ft. Very soon we saw a two-seater down below us, apparently ranging his artillery. We at once went down on him, and got in a good burst from

100 yards' range from directly behind. The fat old Hun dived, pursued by Barlow, who caused it to land near Passchendaele, but the occupants scrambled out and ran away.

Barlow now rejoined me and we flew south towards Houthem, where we saw eight of the enemy in good formation. Barlow now was above and dived into the middle of them, and caused one Albatros to dive under his formation and come towards me. I opened fire at this Hun at 100 yards and fired a good burst until we nearly collided nose on. At once the Hun's nose went down and he carried on downwards in a very steep spiral with his nose vertically down, and in this position I last saw him at about 4,000 feet, but I was unable to watch him farther as there was too much else to occupy my attention.

Barlow was meanwhile doing great execution and had got one Hun already crashed, and I was just in time to see his second go down out of control, because we were now directly underneath about eight V-strutters, who were swearing vengeance for their falling comrades.

We had to run for it like anything, and owing to our superior speed we soon out-distanced the Huns and went home for breakfast. It was very fine to be on a machine that was faster than the Huns, and I may say that it increased one's confidence enormously to know that one could run away just as soon as things became too hot for one. While at breakfast we discussed our flights, and my comrades in 56 expressed the wish that my first Hun in 56, which I obtained that morning, would be the first of fifty. I hoped so.

The S.E.5 which I was now flying was a most efficient fighting machine, far and away superior to the enemy machines of that period. It had a Vickers gun, shooting forward through the propeller, and a Lewis gun shooting forward over the top plane, parallel to the Vickers, but above the propeller. The pilot could also incline the Lewis gun upwards in such a way that he could shoot vertically upwards at a target that presented itself. As a matter of fact, these guns were rarely used in this manner, as it was quite a work of art to pull this gun down and shoot upwards, and at the same time manage one's machine accurately. The idea of using a Lewis gun on the top plane of an S.E. was first put forward by the late Captain Ball, who used his top gun with such excellent success in another Squadron whilst flying Nieuports.

However, the modern machine has nowadays such a climb and reserve of power that it is quite usual for a machine to get some speed first and then do a vertical zoom towards an opponent who is above and get in a burst of fire before losing all its speed and falling down in a stalled condition. Other good points of the S.E.5 were its great strength, its diving and zooming powers, and its splendid view. Apart from this, it was a most warm, comfortable and easy machine to fly.

A lot of my time during my first few days with No. 56 Squadron was taken up with testing my guns and aligning my sights, for I am a stickler for detail in every respect, for in aerial fighting I am sure it is the detail that counts more than the actual main fighting points. It is more easy to find a Hun and attack him from a good position than it is to do the actual accurate shooting. It may sound absurd, but such a thing as having dirty goggles makes all the difference between getting or not getting a Hun.

On the 19th of August I led a patrol of four machines over the line east of Zonnebeke, when we were immediately attacked from above by five Albatros Scouts. We manœuvred for a while, during which time Maxwell drove a Hun down, but did not get him. The Huns all now went off and nothing of much further interest occurred until towards the end of the patrol, I saw a Sopwith triplane diving away from two V-strutters over Langemarck. I fired at the nearest one, who at once left the triplane and went off east.

We now saw a formation of six Albatros Scouts coming north over Gheluvelt at about 19,000 feet. I climbed above the Huns and dived on a V-strutter painted all red with yellow stripes round him, and after firing a good burst from both my guns, the Hun went down out of control in a spin, and I watched him for a long time, but lost sight of him near the ground, as the other Huns were becoming annoyed. I had now finished my Lewis ammunition, and the trigger of my Vickers had broken, so I was forced to return home. Turnball, one of my comrades, had seen my Hun going down and had also lost sight of him near the ground.

The next evening at 6.50 p.m., whilst leading my blood-thirsty little band of six pilots over Poelcappelle, at about 11,000 feet I saw an enemy scout formation coming north from over Zandvoorde. They had apparently not yet seen us, so I throttled down my engine and, signalling to my comrades, I flew round east of the Huns and attacked them from the south. I selected the leader, and opened fire on him with my Vickers at 150 yards' range and, closing to 50 yards, fired a short burst with both guns.

At once a little trickle of flame came out of his fuselage, which became larger and larger until the whole fuselage and tailplane was enveloped in flames. The Albatros at once went down in a vertical dive, and I zoomed upwards and felt quite sick. I don't think I have ever been so conscience-stricken as at that time, and I watched the V-strutter until he hit the ground in a smother of flame in a small copse north-east of Polygon Wood, and caused a fire which was still burning when we flew home.

As soon as this Hun went down in flames, the remainder of the Hun formation all scuttled off down east as fast as possible, and so I now re-formed my patrol and looked for some more Huns, and for the remainder of the flight I was very uneasy indeed, and kept glancing behind me to look for the avenging German machines, which I felt sure would dive on me any moment.

That was my first Hun in flames. As soon as I saw it I thought "poor devil," and really felt sick. It was at that time very revolting to see any machine go down in flames, especially when it was done by my own hands. One seems to feel it more than sending a Hun to Hell out of control or crashed or in pieces. However, I had to live down my better feelings.

Later in that same patrol, whilst manœuvring for position with several Albatros Scouts over Polygon Wood, I saw one of my comrades (Johnson) being closely engaged by two V-strutters. I drove one off at 200 yards by firing some shots at him, and closed to 30 yards on the second Hun and, getting a favourable sight, opened fire with both guns. The Albatros at once went down vertically and, after flattening out, zoomed upwards. I followed, and zooming also, caught up with the Hun at the top of his zoom, opened fire, and continued doing so until I nearly crashed into his tail. By Jove! It was close.

The Hun turned upside down, and fell for about two hundred feet in this position, and then came out in a dive, after which he went down in a steep side-slipping dive, but I could not watch him till he crashed, as it was rather hazy, and it was nearly dusk.

All the remainder of the Huns having been dispersed by my comrades, and Rhys-Davids having crashed one, we flew home, having that evening "waged much war with great cunning," as my friend Meintjes invariably says. On landing at our aerodrome all were waiting eagerly to hear of any success that we had to report. It was very amusing to hear one mechanic bragging that his pilot had got a Hun while so-and-so hadn't, and all that sort of chaff.

After we had landed we made out our combat reports, and then adjourned to the mess for our dinner, to which we "hired assassins" did full justice, but for the remainder of the evening the thought of that Albatros going down in flames, I confess, made me quite miserable. However, I finally got over that feeling, for I had to if I was to make a success of my work.

The next evening we were up over the usual area at the same time, and saw the same patrol that we had engaged the previous evening coming up, but one does not usually catch the same patrol of Huns a second time so easily.

However, we went down on these Huns a long way east of the lines and drove them down east of the Menin-Roulers road, and I had a very anxious time firing recall signals for the benefit of Barlow and Rhys-Davids, who would have chased the Huns over to the Russian front if I had let them. We re-formed and were then chased back to our lines by about fifteen Huns, who were above us and at an advantage, so we simply had to run. For the remainder of that patrol there was not much activity and so we returned at the termination of our time without having downed a Hun.

The next morning early we were to escort some D.H.4's, who were going over to bomb the junction of Ascq, which lies just east of Lille. We met the D.H.4's over our aerodrome at 10,000 feet, as arranged, and after climbing in company with them for an hour, we crossed the lines over Armentières at 16,500 feet. By the time we reached Lille at 17,000 feet, my machine was about up against its ceiling, that is, it was as high as it would go. The D.H.4's had just unshipped their eggs when we saw a few V-strutters coming from the north and slightly below us. I picked out one fellow and got on to his tail and, pressing the triggers of both guns, nothing happened. The Hun lost no time at all in making good his escape.

Now there was another Hun whom I missed through sheer carelessness, and he was a dud Hun too, for he just dived away straight. I will explain how.

As soon as I crossed the lines, usually I at once fired both guns to see that they were all right, but on this occasion I had neglected to do so, and the episode I have mentioned was the outcome. As soon as I reloaded each gun they went splendidly, and the reason they did not go at first was because they were too cold, and stopped after the first shot, but as soon as they had each fired a few shots and got warm they were all right. The other Huns had made a very poor attempt to attack the bombers, but were at once dispersed by my comrades, and very soon we saw our charges safely west of the lines.

Still having some petrol remaining, we went back over the lines and saw some Albatros Scouts attacking some F.E.'s of another squadron. "Now then, chaps! the Squadron to the rescue," we felt, and after the Huns' blood we rushed.

One Hun pilot had become so engrossed fighting an F.E. that he got below and west of me before he saw me. As I went down on him I saw that he was painted black and purple, a fellow whom I had noticed before. I got behind him at fair range, and he immediately dived and then zoomed. I did the same and, firing both guns whilst zooming, saw my tracers passing to the right of his fuselage. He now half-rolled and I followed and, passing a few feet above him, saw the German pilot look upwards; and it struck me that he did not seem the least perturbed, as I should have expected him to be.

I came to the conclusion that this Hun was very good, and that it would be most difficult to shoot him, so I turned away, just in time to see four others coming down to aid him. I had not turned away a second too soon.

That Hun was a good one, for every time I got behind him he turned upside down and passed out underneath me. I well remember looking at him too. He seemed only a boy.

It seems all very strange to me, but whilst fighting Germans I have always looked upon a German aeroplane as a machine that has got to be destroyed, and at times when I have passed quite close to a Hun machine and have had a good look at the occupant, the thought has often struck me: "By Jove! there is a man in it." This may sound queer, but it is quite true, for at times I have fought a Hun and, on passing at close range, have seen the pilot in it, and I have been quite surprised.

On the evening of the 22nd, I again led my patrol over the lines, and very soon saw four Huns flying west over Zandvoorde, so, as we were north of them, we soon got between them and their lines, and then we attacked them over Ypres. They turned out to be all D.F.W.'s, apparently doing a formation reconnaissance.

We each picked out our man and commenced shooting. I shot an awful lot at my man, who finally went down in a steep, jerky dive towards the east. I then turned away and saw Muspratt finish off his opponent in great style. This Hun went into a very flat spin, which lasted from 14,000 feet to the ground, and I watched him the whole way until he crashed in our lines near St. Julien. I never have seen anything so funny for a long time as that old Hun going round and round for over two minutes. I bet the pilot and observer had a sick headache after that.

Meanwhile, Cronyn had finished off another, who also fell in our lines, so between us we made that two-seater formation sorry that it ever crossed our lines that evening. That was the end of activity that evening, so we flew home, all very happy.

On the evening of September 3rd I had been out alone looking for stray Huns, and not having seen any, I went up to the Salient, when Potts and Jeffs, of "A" Flight, quietly attached themselves to me, having lost Maxwell in the heat of a fight. We saw three V-strutters going north over Poel-cappelle, and so down we went, and just before I got to the rear Hun, my engine chocked, and I got vertically below the last Hun, whom I saw looking over the side of his fuselage at me.

The next thing I saw was tracers passing this Hun, who immediately burst into flames and fell instantly. So quickly did he fall that I did not have time to dodge, and the Albatros, a flaming mass, fell about fifty feet away from me. I distinctly heard the roar of it as it passed me, for my engine was not making much noise, and was throttled down. I now got my engine going, and chased one of the remaining Huns, who at once went down in an awfully obvious funk, having seen his comrade go down in flames, but I could not shoot this fellow, for he knew how to manœuvre in defence.

On September 4th, 1917, I led my patrol up to 14,000 feet over Ypres, and then we crossed the lines to meet a formation of D.H.4's on their return from bombing

Audenarde. My orders were to meet them over Courtrai at 2.10 p.m. at 15,000 feet, and punctually to the minute we saw the big British two-seaters coming towards us amid a cloud of black Archies.

We turned, and whilst escorting them back to the line, we saw several Albatros climbing up north of Lille. We took the D.H.4's west of the lines and then went back to look for the Huns we had seen. We found them at 16,000 feet near Lille, but they were going east, and by the time we would have got to them, we would have been too far east of the lines. However, young Rhys-Davids kept calling my attention to them, for he was all for chasing the Huns out of the sky altogether, and I had some difficulty in making him realise that bravery should not be carried to the extent of foolhardiness.

The Huns soon returned, and we met them at 17,500 feet over Baccelaere. I singled out my Teuton partner, and we circled around each other until I at last managed to get on his tail. He at once went down in a spiral. It is the most difficult thing imaginable to shoot an opponent who is spiralling, so after chasing him down to 8,000 feet and firing a lot of ammunition to little effect, I turned away just in time to see Coote chase a Hun away who had been following me down. By this time I had reformed the patrol; we found it was time to go home, so I fired the "washout" signal.

As the visibility was good I thought I would save my height as much as possible until I got over my aerodrome, in the hope of running into a two-seater over our lines, so I crossed our lines homeward bound at about 16,000 feet, and I then saw a Hun two-seater above me near Armentières. As he was 500 feet above me, I pulled my top gun down and fired a drum of Lewis at him, but it did not take much effect, for it is rather difficult to fire at a machine that is vertically above one and fly straight at the same time, so this old Hun got away east of the lines.

I resumed my homeward journey at 17,000 feet and very soon saw a Hun two-seater, a D.F.W., coming towards me from the S.W. over Estaires. I intercepted him, and took up a position to shoot at him in such a way that he could not shoot at me, as I had been practising this method of attack for a long time. My Vickers gun was out of action, but the Lewis was working, and so I opened fire at two hundred yards. I fired a whole drum, and the Hun commenced to shy, so I quickly changed a drum, and whilst doing so, I exposed myself to the Hun's fire, whose bullets I felt hit my machine.

"Never mind," I thought, so I closed again, and fired my last drum, which caused the old D.F.W. to wobble and pitch like anything, and then the observer disappeared into the cockpit apparently disabled, and the Hun went sliding down over Quesnoy under control. I had hard luck with this fellow, for if I had had another drum, I could have concentrated on my shooting without troubling about the gunner. However, this was all good practice for me.

I returned to my aerodrome, and after landing found that I should require a new machine, as the Hun had put an incendiary bullet into one of my longerons just at my feet, and this meant the machine going into the repair-section for a while. Lieutenant Sloley went to St. Omer for me to get another machine, and brought back a Factory-built S.E.5 No. A/4863. This S.E. was destined to give me a lot of trouble before I got it going well finally.

The weather during this time was simply glorious, and we always had plenty of spare time, so we thoroughly enjoyed it. Our usual patrol time was about six p.m. during the late summer, and as a rule we were not sent up unless there was pronounced enemy aerial activity. We spent our spare time in various ways.

We had a wonderful game called "Bumple-puppy," which one played with tennis rackets. A ball is tied by a length of string to the top of a pole and the two players stand opposite each other with the pole between. They both try to hit the ball opposite ways until either of them has wound the ball up to the fullest extent on the pole, and the player who succeeds in doing this first wins. This does not sound very exciting, but it is when two good players get going.

In the hot afternoons we all bathed in a little stream a few miles from the aerodrome, and all went very well until one day we went down there to find a lot of Portuguese soldiers in possession of our bathing place. Needless to say, the water in that place never recovered its pristine clearness, nor odour.

When the days were dull or wet, we had tenders in which to go up to the trenches or to go to St. Omer to see the fair maids of France. Most fellows had an attraction of some sort in St. Omer, and the teashops, where was usually to be had wonderful French pastry, were always full. In the mess we had many games, ping-pong being easily the most popular. Then we had the inevitable cards, gramophone, and piano, which several fellows could play nicely.

One dud day Barlow and I set off to visit Vimy Ridge. On our way we called in at another Squadron to visit my young brother, who was a Sergeant-pilot, flying D.H.4's. We resumed our journey and then visited some friends of Barlow's at an Artillery Group Headquarters. I think Barlow had a cousin there. After lunch we went by tender through the valley of Notre Dame de Lorette, and through Carency and Souchez, in which valley so many gallant Frenchmen gave their lives in the intense fighting of early 1915.

Souchez and Carency were merely a pile of rubbish, and on our left towered the height of Vimy Ridge. After thoroughly viewing this natural fortress, which was held by the Germans in 1914, '15, '16 and part of '17, I was amazed to think that it fell to a direct frontal attack such as it did in April, 1917, when the Huns were completely routed for some miles by the Canadians.

We drove over the Vimy Ridge on a plank roadway constructed by the Sappers, and sheltered the car on the eastern slopes of the ridge. We then walked to an observation post which was near, and viewed the trenches from this vantage point. The visibility was poor, so we could not see too much, but we could, with the aid of glasses, see the clock-face on the church tower of Haines, a small village some way behind the enemy lines, and we could also see the Wingles Tower, a large steel structure that the enemy uses for his observation post.

After we had had a good look round we went to find some souvenirs off the Vimy battlefield. We could have taken away heaps of souvenirs had we the room for them. We saw some huge mine craters about 100 yards across. One of the largest is known as Winnipeg Crater, I think. War material of every description littered the ground: rifles, grenades, both British and Boche, trench mortars and shells of all calibres. I got a very good German rifle, and we had some fun pulling the string of the German bombs, known amongst our Tommies as potato mashers, and then throwing them down a crater to burst. We spent some time examining the graves of fallen German soldiers which bore crosses with many forms of German inscriptions. After which we walked to our tender and then came away.

We had spent a most interesting and instructive afternoon and we were only sorry that we had not seen German machines up over the trenches, for we had been within a mile of our front line the whole afternoon.

On our way from Vimy we decided to have tea in Béthune, so we went to a little teashop that is on the main road to Lillers, and is a stone's throw from Béthune church tower, and here was the same dainty little Madeline who had given us tea when I was a Corporal, and passed through Béthune a lot in late 1914. Madeline was very grieved when I last saw her, for her fiancé, a Lieutenant in the French infantry, had been killed at Verdun. I expressed my sympathy, as well as I could, in my not too perfect French, which elicited the remark: "Ah, M'sieu! c'est la Guerre!"

We had a very nice tea, and then walked round Béthune

to make a few purchases. Béthune, since I had seen it last in 1915, had not been shelled much, although the square had been damaged a lot, but it is remarkable how well the French people take it as a rule. Many who read this book will remember the dainty little Ma'm'selle in the "patisserie" in the main Rue to Chocques and Lillers.

Whilst passing a shop window I noticed a certain quality of brilliantine of which I had last purchased a quantity at Avesnes-le-Compte in 1916, and since then I had tried everywhere to find this same quality. I went into the shop and bought up the entire stock of that grade, and the tradesman must have thought that I was going to start a barber's shop. I think the total cost was something over thirty francs, and it was only recently that I finished my last bottle.

After this, Barlow and I resumed our journey, and arrived back at our aerodrome just in time for dinner. Some of the fellows had been to Calais, some to Ypres, and some to St. Omer.

On September 6th, the anniversary of shooting down my first Hun, I went up on my new S.E.5 at the head of my trusty Flight, and after getting up to 13,000 feet we crossed the lines about Bixschoote. Immediately after crossing the lines, we saw some enemy scouts over the Houthoulst Forest, and we flew to the attack. We got closer, and I saw two new types of enemy scouts. One was a triplane, and was not very unlike the Sopwith of that type. The other one was a machine with very obliquely cut wing tips and tailplane. These two machines, I afterwards found, were the Fokker triplane and the Pfalz scout.

We manœuvred around for a while, and the Huns did most of the shooting, for they were above and had the initial advantage on their side, but finally there was no advantage to either side, and after some time the Huns withdrew. My Vickers was now out of action owing to a fault in my interrupter gear, and so I only had my Lewis.

On sighting two Albatros Scouts over Passchendaele I dived and, getting to close range of one, my Lewis fired one shot and stopped. The Boche at once spun and got away, but the other, after having been engaged by Jeffs of "A" Flight, crashed near Poelcappelle Station.

We now reformed, and then dived on three two-seaters over Houthem, who were about 4,000 feet high. I opened fire on one at once and fired sixty rounds at him, and he then put his nose down east and flew off into a fringe of mist as though he was all right. Nothing happened of further interest, so we flew back to our aerodrome, and, after having breakfast, I had to give a full description of the two new German types that I had seen.

After that I spent the remainder of the morning working on my Constantinesco interrupter gear, which was giving a lot of trouble on my new machine, for up till now I had hardly fired my Vickers guns at all.

Whilst on the aerodrome Bowman landed, and after taxiing up to where I stood, started to get out of his machine, and I spoke to him about something. While listening to me he put the back of his leg, just behind the knee, on his red-hot exhaust pipe. As he was wearing shorts that finish above the knee, he rested his bare flesh on the very, very hot metal.

There was immediately a hell of a yell, and a sizzling sound as Bowman leapt about four feet into the air, shouting most angry profanity. I very quickly made myself scarce, for, as I said to Bowman afterwards, the smell of roast pork was most appetizing. Poor old Bowman's leg was tied up for weeks afterwards.

For two whole days I tested my guns, and could not get them to my liking. All my comrades and "Grandpa," our dear old Recording Officer, simply chaffed me to death, and suggested that why my guns did not go when I got into the air was because I wore them out first on the ground. By Jove! How those fellows chaffed me. But for a gun to fire forty rounds of ammunition and then stop was not good enough for me. I wanted my guns to fire every round I carried without stoppage, as good guns ought, and I was not going to give up until they would do so.

Rhys-Davids got two German scouts on the 9th of September just south of Houthoulst Forest, and Maybery got two the next day near Zonnebeke whilst I sat on the aerodrome, working like the proverbial nigger on my machine.

The next day I led my patrol over the lines early in the morning over Bixschoote at 13,000 feet. We flew east to Roulers and then turned south to Menin, whence we turned north-west again. I now saw a patrol of Albatros Scouts west of us, over Baccelaere at about the same height.

I led my artists into the sun, and then we pounced on the Huns who were fast asleep, and looking no doubt towards the west, as they usually do. I picked out my prize as I thought, got 50 yards behind him, took very careful aim, pressed both triggers and nothing happened. I chased this Hun down to 9,000 feet, rectifying my Vickers on the way, but the damned Hun got away, and was very lucky, for he was very dud. My word! You cannot realise what it is to get on Hun's tails time after time, and then have your guns let you down.

During the first fortnight in September I had the most rotten luck that I think it is possible for a fighting pilot to experience. I can count up at least six scouts which I very likely would have shot down in the early part of September alone.

Later on this patrol I saw an S.E. down very low, being driven down by a skilful Albatros pilot. Rhys-Davids and I dived to the rescue, and drove the Hun away, and I continued pursuing him. I drove him off east of Zonnebeke at 500 feet, but although I did a lot of shooting at him, I did not bring him down, and as I was now well east of the lines I returned. By this time petrol was low, so I fired the "washout" signal, and we all flew home to breakfast.

At this period up on the Ypres sector, the German Scout pilots as a rule were undoubtedly good, and one met a larger proportion of skilful pilots up there than I have ever come across elsewhere on the front from La Fère to the sea. Of course, the Albatros Scout, type D.5, was undoubtedly good, but at the same time prisoners said that the German pilots considered the S.E.5 a most formidable fighting machine.

On the evening of the 14th of September we had some fine sport on the evening patrol. I led my flight over the lines at 14,000 feet over Bixschoote at six p.m., and flew towards Roulers, where we saw seven Albatroses on whom we at once dived. I picked out my target, fired a burst from my Lewis, after which the Hun went down in a spiral, his whole machine vibrating most violently as though some of the bullets had perforated his cylinders, and caused his engine partially to seize. I watched this Hun in a spiral down to about 4,000 feet over Ledeghem, but after that I lost sight of him as he was so low.

I turned round west, and then saw two Huns north-east of Houthoulst Forest, a good deal lower. I had now lost my patrol, and so dived down alone, and when I got closer saw that they were two-seaters, one of whom was painted a bright red. I fired at this fellow at very close range, and only just had enough time to zoom above him to save myself from running into his tail.

On looking round very soon afterwards I saw a whole patrol of Albatros Scouts between myself and the lines. Immediately I did the best thing possible; I opened out my engine full, and charged right through the middle of them, firing both guns and pulling my controls about all over the place in order to spray my bullets about as much as possible, and the old Huns seemed to scratch their heads and say, "What the devil next?" I very soon out-distanced them owing to my superior speed, for the S.E. with engine full on and dropping a little height is very fast indeed.

Three of the Huns did some shooting at me, but not close enough to worry me. I then flew south over the Houthoulst Forest and met Rhys-Davids over Polygon Wood, and so we flew down to Gheluwe, where we saw over a dozen Huns all above us, so we circled around underneath them so as to make them pursue us west, in order to get them nearer to the line. This we did, and by the time we were farther west over Gheluvelt, we were reinforced by several more S.E.'s of our Squadron. A general mêlée began, and very soon everyone was circling round shooting at something, but in the scrap I saw Rhys-Davids fighting a very skilful Hun, whose Albatros was painted with a red nose, a green fuselage and a silver tail.

It was now very cloudy, and I could not quite see where we were, but I knew we were in the vicinity of Menin. I had just finished chasing a Hun around when I saw an S.E. hurtle by in a streaming cloud of white vapour, apparently hot water or petrol. I now had a look round, and could see no sign of an Allied machine anywhere, so I went down into the clouds, and on coming out of the clouds at about 9,000 feet saw another layer of cloud below me and an Albatros Scout flying south in between two large banks of clouds.

"By Jove!" I thought, "here's a sitter!" so down I went. I had almost fired when "cack, cack, cack, cack," came from behind, and I looked over my shoulder and saw three red noses coming for me. I at once dived through the clouds and saw I was just east of Menin, and a very strong west wind was blowing. I very quickly got free from close range, and by the time I crossed our lines over Frelinghien, near Armentières, at 3,000 feet, the Huns were a good mile behind, so in about eight miles straight flight I had increased my lead from one hundred yards to a mile.

I flew home to the aerodrome and landed when it was quite dusk, and found that Rhys-Davids was still out. However, he telephoned up an hour later to say he was at a rather distant aerodrome, and had been shot in the tank and centre section by the Hun with the silver tail.

It was Rhys-Davids whom I had seen go into a cloud, emitting volumes of petrol vapour, and he was very lucky not to have been set on fire by the flame from his exhaust.

The next evening my patrol and I were over Baccelaere

at 13,000 feet when we saw some Huns engaging Bowman's formation, who were north-west of us, so we got up to the Huns without being observed. I saw an Albatros dive on Maybery, so I tackled this Hun, who executed some very weird manœuvres. I could not sit on his tail at all, and after getting very close to him, I lost sight of him under my wing, so I turned to the left, and the next thing I saw was the Hun's nose directly behind me, at very close range, but apparently he had not seen me, for he was looking over his shoulder, wondering where I had got to. He completed his turn and then flew away east.

At 6.30 p.m., whilst at 12,000 feet over Gheluvelt, we saw some S.E.'s of another squadron being engaged by some Huns over Houthem. We dived and attacked the Huns from the rear, and although I got to close range of one, I choked my engine at the critical moment and the Hun got away.

While getting my engine right, I saw Barlow finish off a V-strutter in great style, and the Albatros went down in a very fast spin, and crashed near Wervicq. We afterwards flew back to the aerodrome, and everyone seemed pleased with life except myself, for I was still having trouble with my gear and guns.

On the 19th of September I went up by myself to look for two-seaters. I climbed to 18,000 feet and flew north from Lens. The wind was very strong westerly, and there were a few clouds about lower down. I was flying over the Bois de Biez and was looking at a Hun two-seater who was east of me and had not seen me, when I looked down and saw a D.F.W. passing underneath me not 400 feet below. I closed my throttle and went down after him, but he saw me at the last moment and then turned off east. I fired a good burst at him at 200 yards range, and then the pilot pushed his nose down with such a jerk that a lot of loose material resembling small black bones, probably photographic plates, fell out in a shower. I fought this artist down to 9,000 feet, over Quesnoy, and then left him without a decision, and returned to the lines, climbing.

About half an hour later I saw a Hun cross our lines just south of Armentières at about 14,000 feet, and, as he had not seen me, I let him get well west of me before attacking him. Very soon I followed and got within range of him over Estaires. He had now seen me, but I managed to secure my two-seater firing position and fired a good burst at him with my Vickers, for the Lewis had previously gone out of action. The D.F.W.'s engine now stopped, and he went down in a spiral. I followed, shooting as opportunity offered, and he was quite hard to hit, as he was spiralling. The enemy gunner had got in a short burst at me, but now he was not to be seen, so I conjectured that I had wounded him.

Now, all the time he was spiralling the wind was blowing him near the German lines, for it was a very strong westerly wind, and we got down to 3,000 feet before I could make any definite impression on him. I fired a final burst, and then he went into a steep dive and crashed about a mile behind the German lines near Radinghem, which is south of Quesnoy.

Whilst firing at this Hun I had once passed a few feet above him, and on looking down saw the enemy gunner reclining in leisurely way on the floor of his cockpit, taking not the slightest interest in the proceedings at all.

Owing to the very strong westerly wind that was blowing, although the Hun was miles over our lines when I first shot him, owing to the wind he had fallen in the German lines. However, I was very pleased that I had got a Hun, for it was quite a long time since I had destroyed anything. I returned to my aerodrome and joyfully made out my combat report.

On the next day Maxwell and Sloley each shot down a German.

On the 21st I left the ground about midday with Barlow, as two-seater activity was reported over the Salient. On our way to the lines we had a race, as before we went up Barlow asserted that his machine was as fast as mine. We tried it, and I was faster. We arrived at the line and at once saw a two-seater coming towards us from south-east of Houthem. I attacked him from the east and Barlow from the west. The Hun went down damaged, and we last saw him gliding down very low over Gheluwe, apparently in trouble.

We now saw three Huns above us, so we climbed up to their level, and found two two-seaters and an Albatros with two bays to each wing, instead of the usual one. This machine was known as the double V-strutter, and was supposed to be flown by Baron von Richthofen. We skirmished for a while, and then the Hun went off, and seeing no more activity we went back to our aerodrome and landed.

On the evening of the 23rd I led my patrol from the aerodrome and crossed the lines at Bixschoote at 8,000 feet as there was a very thick wall of clouds up at 9,000 feet. As soon as we crossed over Hunland I noted abnormal enemy activity, and indeed there seemed to be a great many machines of both sides about. This was because every machine that was up was between 9,000 feet and the ground instead of as usual from 20,000 feet downwards.

We flew south from Houthoulst Forest, and although there were many Huns about they were all well over. Archie was at his best this evening, for he had us all silhouetted against a leaden sky, and we were flying mostly at 7,000 feet. When over Gheluvelt, I saw a two-seater coming north near Houthem. I dived, followed by my patrol, and opened fire from above and behind the D.F.W., whose occupants had not seen me, having been engrossed in artillery registration. I fired a good burst from both guns, a stream of water came from the D.F.W.'s centre-section, and then the machine went down in a vertical dive and crashed to nothing, north-east of Houthem.

We went north, climbing at about 6,000 feet. A heavy layer of grey clouds hung at 9,000 feet, and although the visibility was poor for observation, the atmosphere was fairly clear in a horizontal direction. Away to the east one could see clusters of little black specks, all moving swiftly, first in one direction and then another. Farther north we could see formations of our own machines, Camels, Pups, S.E.'s, Spads and Bristols, and lower down in the haze our artillery R.E.8's.

We were just on the point of engaging six Albatros Scouts away to our right, when we saw ahead of us, just above Poelcappelle, an S.E. half spinning down closely pursued by a silvery blue German triplane at very close range. The S.E. certainly looked very unhappy, so we changed our minds about attacking the six V-strutters, and went to the rescue of the unfortunate S.E.

The Hun triplane was practically underneath our formation now, and so down we dived at a colossal speed. I went to the right, Rhys-Davids to the left, and we got behind the triplane together. The German pilot saw us and turned in a most disconcertingly quick manner, not a climbing nor Immelmann turn, but a sort of flat half spin. By now the German triplane was in the middle of our formation, and its handling was wonderful to behold. The pilot seemed to be firing at all of us simultaneously, and although I got behind him a second time, I could hardly stay there for a second. His movements were so quick and uncertain that none of us could hold him in sight at all for any decisive time.

I now got a good opportunity as he was coming towards me nose on, and slightly underneath, and had apparently not seen me. I dropped my nose, got him well in my sight, and pressed both triggers. As soon as I fired up came his nose at me, and I heard clack-clack-clack-clack, as his bullets passed close to me and through my wings. I distinctly noticed the red-yellow flashes from his parallel Spandau guns. As he flashed by me I caught a glimpse of a black head in the triplane with no hat on at all.

By this time a red-nosed Albatros Scout had arrived, and was apparently doing its best to guard the triplane's tail, and it was well handled too. The formation of six Albatros Scouts which we were going to attack at first stayed above us, and were prevented from diving on us by the arrival of a formation of Spads, whose leader apparently appreciated our position, and kept the six Albatroses otherwise engaged.

The triplane was still circling round in the midst of six S.E.'s, who were all firing at it as opportunity offered, and at one time I noted the triplane in the apex of a cone of tracer bullets from at least five machines simultaneously, and each machine had two guns. By now the fighting was very low, and the red-nosed Albatros had gone down and out, but the triplane still remained. I had temporarily lost sight of the triplane whilst changing a drum of my Lewis gun, and when I next saw him he was very low, still being engaged by an S.E. marked I, the pilot being Rhys-Davids. I noticed that the triplane's movements were very erratic, and then I saw him go into a fairly steep dive and so I continued to watch, and then saw the triplane hit the ground and disappear into a thousand fragments, for it seemed to me that it literally went to powder.

Strange to say, I was the only pilot who witnessed the triplane crash, for even Rhys-Davids, who finally shot it down, did not see its end.

It was now quite late, so we flew home to the aerodrome, and as long as I live I shall never forget my admiration for that German pilot, who single-handed fought seven of us for ten minutes, and also put some bullets through all of our machines. His flying was wonderful, his courage magnificent, and in my opinion he is the bravest German airman whom it has been my privilege to see fight.

We arrived back at the mess, and at dinner the main topic was the wonderful fight. We all conjectured that the enemy pilot must be one of the enemy's best, and we debated as to whether it was Richthofen or Wolff or Voss. The tri-plane fell in our lines, and the next morning we had a wire from the Wing saying that the dead pilot was found wearing the Boelcke collar and his name was Werner Voss. He had the "Ordre Pour le Mérite."

Rhys-Davids came in for a shower of congratulations,

and no one deserved them better, but as the boy himself said to me, "Oh, if I could only have brought him down alive," and his remark was in agreement with my own thoughts.

The next evening Barlow and Rhys-Davids each crashed a two-seater near Houthoulst Forest.

During the period from the end of July to the time of which I write, there was colossal fighting on the ground, for we had pushed the Huns back from their very strongly-held positions on the high ground east of Ypres.

An account of the ground and the state it was in at this time baffles description. Imagine yourself standing on the roof of a farm-house, and inside the yard a stretch of soft clay mud that has been trodden by hundreds of cattle, and the whole ground marked by thousands of little imprints. That was the look of the earth up in the Ypres Salient at the end of September.

On September the 25th, Barlow did the hat-trick. He went up from the aerodrome to chase a two-seater who was over St. Omer, but having lost him wandered to the Salient in search of prey. When he crossed the lines west of Houthoulst he saw a patrol of four Hun scouts coming towards him slightly below, so down went his nose and, after firing, the first Hun went down in a steep spiral, so Barlow fired at the next Hun nose on, who promptly fell to pieces in the air. The remaining two now tootled off east, so Barlow engaged the nearest one and shot him down in flames, whilst the first Hun, who went down in a spiral, was seen to crash by Bowman, who was with his patrol in the vicinity. We all congratulated Barlow, who received that evening a congratulation from General Trenchard. Everyone was very pleased with Barlow's effort, for he got all three in as many minutes.

Nothing happened of interest that I am able to recall until the 27th, when I brought down my first German machine in our lines. I left the ground soon after lunch, and very soon saw a Hun two-seater flying round over Houthoulst Forest, apparently ranging. Whilst waiting for a favourable opportunity I saw a Spad attack this Hun, and I saw the Hun twisting and swerving about with the French Spad in pursuit, and then suddenly the Spad appeared to be hit, and went down out of control. The Hun went off east a little and then came back, apparently very pleased at having shot the Spad down.

He now came to within reasonable distance of where I was waiting, and after him I went. When I got to my two-seater position, the Hun was going due east, and I fired a good burst from both guns until I had to turn sharply to the right to avoid colliding with the Hun. As I turned I saw the Hun gunner at a range of twenty yards with his gun central to the rear waiting to see which way I would turn, for he had seen me overtaking him too fast, and knew that I should have to turn, and as I did turn I saw him turn his gun and fire just four shots, each "cack, cack, cack, cack," two bullets of which I distinctly felt hit my machine. I half rolled, and got clear of him, and glanced round to see where he was.

When I did see him he was in flames going down in a vertical dive, after which he went past the vertical, and then on to his back, so that he was now falling towards our lines, into which he fell near St. Julien, although when I had shot him he was flying east.

When the machine went beyond the vertical and on to its back, the enemy gunner either jumped or fell out, and I saw him following the machine down, twirling round and round, all arms and legs, truly a ghastly sight. A queer thing happened, the enemy gunner fell into his own lines, and the machine and the pilot in our lines.

I flew back to my aerodrome very pleased, for it is the wish of most pilots to bring Germans down in our lines, so as to get souvenirs from the machine.

The next morning, September 28th, I led my patrol over the lines at 11,000 feet over Boessinghe, and before crossing the lines I saw a patrol of Albatroses going south over the Houthoulst Forest. I signalled to my patrol, who understood what I wanted, and down went our noses, and although I thought I was going down fairly slowly, my comrades afterwards said they were recording 180 m.p.h. to keep up with me. I picked out the Albatros who was on the east of this formation and, opening fire at 200 yards, released my triggers about 50 yards short of the Albatros, whose left wings at once fell off, and then the whole machine fell to pieces at about 9,000 feet. The enemy pilot also fell out and went down much quicker than the machine.

I then flew on the leader, who was still in front of me, and having apparently seen me shoot his comrade he was very wide awake. Before I got to close range he had turned round, and we now started to do the usual circling, each trying to get behind the other: Meanwhile, all my comrades were also busily engaged with their partners.

My opponent and I continued to circle round from 8,000 feet down to 4,000 feet, when, as the German passed directly below me in the opposite direction, I did a steep Immelmann turn to get on his tail, but in doing so I lost a good deal of height and now I found the German above me. I continued to circle, but at last the German got behind me and commenced to shoot.

We were now 2,000 feet over the Forest of Houthoulst, and things for me did not look very cheerful, for I had been out-manœuvred by the German pilot, and was now over a mile behind his lines. I continued to manœuvre to prevent the Hun from shooting at an easy target, and when we were down to about 1,000 feet I dived with engine on almost to the ground, intending to contour-chase back at a few feet when the silly old Hun turned off east and flew away just at a time when things were looking rather black for me.

I heaved a sigh of relief as I recrossed the lines, and then I went up to my rendezvous, to reform my patrol, but could not find them. So, after climbing up to 10,000 feet, I flew towards Menin, and found Barlow leading them miles east of the lines, with dozens of Huns west of them. I flew towards them and fired two recall signals, and then they rejoined me, but there was nothing more that happened of interest to relate.

This is peculiar. While the Hun who had out-manœuvred me was engaging me, at about 2,000 feet, I happened to see one wing of the Hun whom I had shot to pieces floating down like a leaf quite near me, three minutes later.

Our patrol time being over we flew back to our aerodrome and had breakfast, and Maybery, who was also having breakfast when we trooped in, remarked that I was becoming expert at turning Huns out of their aeroplanes. We chatted over breakfast and found that Rhys-Davids and Barlow had each got a Hun out of the first formation whom we attacked, so out of the five only two went home.

The Hun who out-manœuvred me was very good indeed, but I never have understood why he left me at a time when he could have most likely shot me down.

After breakfast I played Maybery for the ping-pong championship of No. 56 Squadron, and after a long tussle Maybery won. I believe there was keener competition in the Squadron to be ping-pong champion than to be the star turn Hun-strafer. Maxwell and Maybery were our ping-pong experts, and put up a wonderful game every time.

On the evening patrol Bowman and Hoidge each shot an Albatros to pieces in the air. They were over the lines some way, and above the clouds when up through the gap came two wily Huns, possibly to report on the weather. The next instant they departed in pieces, and no doubt reported that it was raining lead.

At dinner on the 29th there was some argument as to which flight should do the first patrol in the morning, as our Hun total was 198, and we only wanted two to bring our total up to 200 in five and a half months which the Squadron had spent in France. This, of course, beat easily the record of Captain von Richthofen's 11th Jagdstäffel of 200 Allied machines in seven months, but we must not forget that the enemy stäffel had twelve pilots against eighteen in each of our squadrons.

It was my flight's turn to do the first patrol, but every-one in the Squadron wanted to do it, so as to shoot down the 2ooth Hun. However, after much arguing my flight did the early patrol. We were cursed by bad luck, for although we spent two hours miles over Hunland we did not see a single Hun, as the ground was mostly obscured by mist. The evening patrol went out, and Maybery got the 199th and Maxwell got the 200th.

As soon as they returned and made out their combat reports it was nearly dark, and so all the Squadron as-sembled outside the sheds armed with all the Véry light pistols in the station, and all the Squadron's stock of Véry lights, and on the word from the Major up went forty red, white and green lights simultaneously, and the whole countryside was lit up by the brilliance for a big distance around.

After we had used up all our lights we adjourned to the mess, where we had a topping dinner to the strains of our wonderful orchestra. After dinner there was much speech-making and some ragging in the ante-room, and then bed.

There was always keen competition between the flights in getting the most Huns, and when I joined the Squadron things were more or less equal, as the leading flight, which was then "A" Flight, were two ahead of the others. By now, however, each flight was well on to the seventies, and the C.O. was going to make it worth while for the first flight who totalled 100 Huns.

During this period we had a series of very clear nights, and as soon as it got dark over came the Huns every evening at 9 p.m. to bomb Eisberg, a large ore foundry near Aire. This place was only a few miles from our aerodrome, and after dinner was half over we were always disturbed every evening by the "woof, woof" of our Archies, and then the "crump, crump" of the falling Hun bombs. We used to stay looking at the shell-bursts above Aire for some time until it became a nightly occur-rence, and then we took it for granted.

A night bombing squadron of ours was stationed near

Aire, and they went bombing nearly every evening. It sounded rather funny to hear the old F.E.'s overhead droning their way towards the lines loaded with bombs and making that peculiar noise like a church organ, which the note made by the F.E.'s sounds so like.

It was about this time I saw Captain von Richthofen's machine in the air. I will explain how. About the end of September I was flying north alone over Langemarck, and happening to look round to my right saw a Sopwith scout about a mile away fighting a V-strutter, so I flew off east to be of some assistance, but long before I got there the Pup was going down out of control just like a leaf, with the V-strutter circling around it following. By the time I arrived the Pup was near the ground, a long way off east low down. When I got back to my aerodrome I found that one squadron had a pilot named Bacon missing in a Sopwith, so it must have been he.

This machine was the only British one missing on that day, and the next day the German wireless announced that "Captain von Richthofen had shot down his 60th opponent in aerial battle," so I think it is very likely that the Albatros which I saw was flown by our most redoubtable opponent.

Flying in the early morning was now becoming very chilly indeed.

On the 1st of October I went up by myself soon after lunch to look for enemy machines over our lines, and whilst over Béthune at 12,000 feet I saw a German machine, 5,000 feet higher going north-west, so I followed, climbing steadily. The Hun flew over Estaires and then turned west, and by the time he was over Hazebrouck at 19,000 feet I was up at 16,000 feet and could now see that the German machine was a Rumpler, such as the enemy use specially for long photographic reconnaissances over our lines. The Hun flew towards St. Omer, and a Nieuport now joined in the pursuit. This, I ascertained afterwards, was flown by Capt. A. W. Keen. Just short of St. Omer the Rumpler turned and flew south-east over Aire at 21,000 feet, whilst I had just got to my limit of 19,000 feet. The Nieuport got a little higher, but not so high as the Hun.

After pursuing the Rumpler for the best part of an hour we lost him, for he recrossed his lines at an altitude of 22,000 feet over La Bassée. I now turned away west at 19,000 feet, and then saw another Rumpler farther west and a little lower, so after him I went. At this time I had not fully developed my stalking art, and so attacked my photographic friend prematurely. He turned east as I secured my firing position. After firing some good few shots from both guns the Hun gunner gracefully subsided on the floor of his cockpit, but I had now got a bad No. 3 stoppage in my Vickers gun which I could not rectify in the air.

Anyhow, the Lewis was going well, so I put in a new drum and closed again to effective range. I fired the whole drum at him, and thought that I had him in flames, for a large cloud of black smoke answered my burst. Meanwhile, the Hun pilot was flying along straight, not attempting to dodge or swerve at all, and so I put on my third and last drum, and fired again but to no good effect, for the Hun still went on, and at last I left him, miles over the German lines going down in a very flat glide with his propeller stopped.

That Hun gunner must have been full of lead, but I know why I missed the machine. I had just resighted my guns before I went up and made a little error, which became apparent to me whilst engaging this Rumpler, but now that the error had become apparent, it was all to my future guidance and instruction. I returned from that height flight not disheartened, but with a very bad headache owing to high flying for so long a time at such a height without oxygen.

That evening I took my patrol over the lines at 10,000 feet east of Armentières, and then flew north. Very soon we spotted some two-seaters below us, working up and down the Menin road at 8,000 feet. Down we went and tackled them, but they were all three very good two-seaters, and any good two-seater is a most difficult fellow to attack. We chased them right down low, and when I looked round I only had Rhys-Davids with me, so we flew north together, and very soon saw some black and white Albatroses over Westroosebeke, at about 10,000 feet. We waited under these Huns until the other formation which our Squadron had out also came down from the north led by Maxwell.

Very soon the Huns came down on Rhys-Davids and me, and then Maxwell's patrol came down on the Huns, and now we were all mixed up in a real dog-fight. Just then I saw out of the corner of my eye an S.E. circling inside four Albatros Scouts, and as I glanced I saw a Hun, who was turning inside the S.E. at 25 yards range, shoot the S.E.'s left wings off and the British machine went down in a spin, with one pair of wings left. It was poor Sloley, who was, as usual, where the Huns were thickest.

This incident happened in the space of a few seconds, and as I looked round again I saw another S.E. in amongst four black and white Albatroses. This S.E. was fighting magnificently, and simply could be none other than Rhys-Davids, for if one was ever over the Salient in the autumn of 1917 and saw an S.E.5 fighting like Hell amidst a heap of Huns, one would find nine times out of ten that the S.E. was flown by Rhys-Davids. I dived down, and Maxwell joined us, and for the next few minutes we fought like anything, but the Huns were all very good, and had not Maxwell and I gone to Rhys-Davids' assistance when we did, I think the boy would have had a rather thin time.

By now the Huns, having other fish to fry, had gone off, and so Rhys-Davids and I flew away south and then went down on two two-seaters who were flying round low over and east of Zonnebeke. I fired a good burst at the nearest one, and then zoomed away, and Rhys-Davids also fired a long burst at the same Hun, who flew off east at about 2,000 feet. We returned west a little and then saw a Hun two-seater at about 200 feet over Polygon Wood. I had a good shot at him, but he took not the slightest notice, and after that Rhys-Davids had a go, and I could see his tracers splashing all over the Hun, who just flew on straight and took no notice. I believe the brute was armoured.

It was now getting dusk, and as we had been out over two hours, Rhys-Davids and I flew home abreast, a few yards apart, the exhaust from our engines roaring in a glare of flame along the sides of our fuselages in the evening darkness. We landed in the dark, and after taxi-ing into our sheds, Rhys-Davids' machine was found full of holes as usual, whilst I had only a few. We now found out that a Hun had gone down out of control during the first fight during which poor Sloley went down, but as no individual claimed it, it went down to the "A" Flight formation.

On the 3rd of October a wire came from the Wing announcing the award of the D.S.O. to Rhys-Davids, a second bar to the M.C. of Barlow, and a bar to my own M.C. It was decided to hold a very large dinner that evening to celebrate it, for the weather was bad, and there had been no flying all day. At 8.30 we marched into dinner to the accompaniment of "Old Comrades" by the Squadron orchestra, and after dinner we had to make speeches.

I cannot recall Rhys-Davids' speech, but the gist of what he said was that he was very much honoured to receive the D.S.O., and was very pleased indeed, but he would very much like to express his appreciation of the enemy whom we had daily fought, and who as a rule put up such fine examples of bravery and courage, and he felt that he was perhaps doing an unprecedented thing when he asked us all to rise to drink to "Von Richthofen, our most worthy enemy," which toast we all drank with the exception of one non-flying officer who remained seated, and said, "No, I won't drink to the health of that devil." Barlow then made an appropriate speech, and I hope I did likewise, and after that we adjourned to the ante-room.

In the mess above the C.O.'s head was the Squadron Honours Board, on which appeared the name in black and gold letters of each officer as he was awarded a decoration. At the head of the board was Captain Ball, Victoria Cross, and then under that Captain Ball, Légion d'Honneur, these two honours being posthumous awards for his service whilst with No. 56 Squadron. When he went his wonderful offensive spirit was preserved by the Squadron, and in Rhys-Davids we had a second Ball, for neither of them knew the word fear, and it was largely the splendid example which they set that made the Squadron do so extraordinarily well at a time when, taken collectively, the German *morale* was at its very zenith.

On about October 4th, the morning dawned dull and cloudy, and the O.C. insisted on us all leaving the camp for the day by way of a change, and so, having got his permission to use a motor cycle, I set off to look for the remains of the L.V.G., which I shot down in our lines at St. Julien on the 27th of September. I rode through Aire and up to Hazebrouck, and then on to Poperinghe via Steenvoorde.

By the time I arrived at Poperinghe it was lunch time, so my old squadron being quite near, I wended my way there for lunch and afterwards had a chat with Sergeant-Major Harrison and the many people I knew. Then I went on towards Ypres, where I made slower progress, for a lot of heavy fighting was still in progress, and the roads were blocked with traffic of all sorts. After passing through Ypres, St. Jean and Weiltje, I finally reached St. Julien, where a number of derelict tanks littered the place. I could not make further progress with the motor cycle, and I was rather fortunate in coming so far with it, for the ground was full of shell holes, and it was very difficult to trace the road from the ground around. I placed my motor cycle under the lee of a tank, and made my way on foot to Von Tirpitz Farm, which is half a mile east of St. Julien.

Long before I had reached the farm I had to stop and decide whether it was worth going on, for the enemy were shelling the ridge on which the farm lay very heavily, and although I could see the tail of the Hun sticking up in the air, which greatly bucked me up, I had at last to give up the idea of getting to the machine, for the Boches were dropping "crumps" all round it, and so I turned back and reached St. Julien just as the rain commenced to fall heavily.

It was now about 4 p.m., and there was a constant trickle of German prisoners on their way towards Ypres, some of them being used to carry our wounded. The prisoners' faces as a rule gave no hint of their feelings.

I now managed to start my motor cycle; but after going a hundred yards found it impossible to make progress as the sticky mud jambed between the mudguards and wheels and so locked them. I was now in a sorry state, for I was covered in mud, wet through and very fed up. To make progress I had to push the motor cycle about fifty yards with the back wheel locked, and then stop to have a rest. It was exhausting work, as I had only a thin pair of shoes on, and I slipped at every step.

I was now also on a small side-road that led uphill to Weiltje, and no traffic was passing me at all. I longed to see a cart come along so that I could put the motor cycle aboard until I came to some *pavé* where the wheels would clog no more. Once when I stopped to rest there was a field battery just each side of me. They were both banging away to their heart's content, and nearly deafened me.

All this gave me a taste of what the ground peoples' job must be like up in the trenches all the year round, and then my thoughts wandered to my clean S.E. and the very gentlemanly way in which we fought aloft. I fully appreciate the thankless lot that the infantryman's life must be and I am surprised that they carry on so well and so cheerfully through it all.

Presently I got on to the wider road at Weiltje and put my motor cycle on a G.S. wagon that was passing, but this only went for a few hundred yards before the driver said he was not going any further, so I took the machine off again and re-commenced pushing it. For at least another mile I pushed it until I came to some *pavé*, so here I stopped to clear the wheels from the mud and, having completed the job, got the motor cycle to go, with the aid of two Tommies, who gave me a good push off to start the cold engine. I now rode through St. Jean and Ypres.

On the other side of Ypres I passed about 100 German prisoners, who had just come down from the trenches, headed by an enormous officer, who looked a very fine specimen. I still remember the expression on his face as I passed by. He seemed to say: "Well, never mind; I've done my share, and I'm proud I'm German."

Thence I passed on through great mud puddles, being splashed from head to foot by the water from the wheels of an endless chain of motor lorries wending their way trenchwards. By the time I reached Hazebrouck it was dark, and I still had a long journey to do. Before reaching Aire my lamp generator fell off and I could not find it; likewise I lost a German shrapnel helmet that I had collected. However, one of our tenders was just leaving Aire, and so I rode a few yards behind it, following the glare of its lamps, and about 7 o'clock I arrived back at the camp, wet through, cold and very fed up. I remember saying that it would be a damned long time before I rode another motor cycle up to the trenches again, and so it was too.

Nothing much happened of further interest to relate until October 17th, when I shot down another Hun two-seater within our lines. We left the ground at about 10 a.m. to do a patrol over our lines, as the wind was so strong from the west that I was given orders not to cross the lines. As we got our height over the Nieppe Forest, I saw that the visibility was very good, and so I thought that we should have some Huns over our lines.

Very soon a Hun came over Armentières and then turned south, but it was no use our chasing him, for we had not yet sufficient height, so we flew on up the line towards Ypres, and on our way I watched a Hun two-seater who was over Commines, apparently waiting to cross the lines as soon as we passed, so I went on as far as Ypres, over which we arrived at 14,000 feet.

Presently we saw a German two-seater scuttling towards Neuve Eglise, so very soon we were between him and his lines. The Hun was slightly higher than we were, and as we went towards him another Hun passed over us, whom some of my patrol turned to engage. However, now that the first Hun had seen us he came east towards us and then turned away west again, no doubt with the intention of trying to out-climb us, but I am sure he did not fully appreciate the performance of a well-tuned S.E.5.

Very soon I got to my position, and fired a good burst from my Vickers, when the L.V.G. at once burst into flames which issued from the centre section. While the Hun was turning to the left I could see the unfortunate observer standing up in an attitude of abject dejection. As he turned I saw that the flame, which had burnt the fabric off his rudder, had gone out, for apparently there was not much petrol in the tank in the centre section to burn for long. By now the Hun was gliding down towards the North, and as he had no means of turning either way I was interested in following him down until he landed in our lines, for we were now over Vlammertinghe, which was fifteen miles from the trenches. But now another member of the patrol arrived and at once commenced shooting at the poor unfortunate Hun, who went down in a dive and then broke to pieces, no doubt because of the weakening of the centre section of his wings by the fire. I followed the wreckage down till the Hun crashed and then landed alongside on some good stubble in order to put a guard on the Hun.

I left my engine ticking over while I went to look at the Hun, and I found two groups of Australian infantry. I pushed my way into the middle of the first group and found that the attraction was the observer, who had fallen from the machine at about 5,000 feet. He was a huge man named Ernst Hadrich, and seeing that he was dead I went over to the other group of men, about a hundred yards away, and here found the remains of the machine and the pilot.

Everything of any value in the way of souvenirs on the machine had already gone, for although I landed a very short time after the Hun came down, the Tommies had already taken what was worth taking, and the way they behaved around the machine was not very edifying from the disciplined point of view in which I had always been brought up.

Seeing that I could not do anything more, I went to have some lunch with a Sapper officer at an artillery group headquarters, where they were very good to me and gave me a good time. After lunch I re-started my engine and flew back to my aerodrome with my machine laden with various interesting fittings from the Hun machine, which was a new type of L.V.G. with all controls "balanced," and for motive power a 200 h.p. Benz engine. To this day I have a very nice cigarette box made out of the propeller of that Hun.

When I got back to the aerodrome everyone was very pleased that I had got another Hun in our lines, and as all the patrol had seen it fall they were all very bucked about it.

On October 11th I led my patrol over the lines at 12,000 feet over Langemarck, and it was intensely cold, so cold in fact that I could hardly keep the water in my radiator warm enough. Soon after crossing the lines I saw a formation of Pfalz scouts over Westroosebeke just below us.

These scouts were new to us then, and we had not fought them much. As soon as we were near enough we dived to the attack, and each of us picked a man. The Hun I chose was very dud indeed, and at once stopped his engine and started to go down. I fired a very short burst at him, but both guns at once stopped owing to the intense cold, and I could not for the time being get them to work again, so having a red light in my Véry pistol I chased the Hun until he passed a few feet below me, and then I fired the light, but I did not allow enough for deflection, for the light fell short of him.

Eight Albatros scouts had now arrived, but we were also reinforced by some more S.E.'s, and very soon the scrap assumed the proportion of a large dog fight. I caught a glimpse of Rhys-Davids as usual in the middle of three or four Huns, slewing round like anything, and now I saw Cunningham, a new pilot in my flight, with an Albatros on his tail shooting like anything, so I at once shot at this Hun, and so did Muspratt as well. The Hun promptly did two complete rolls and a spin, and came out and zoomed almost to our level again. He was certainly a good Hun that fellow.

We continued to circle round until we were east of Menin, and now I fired a recall signal, and then every S.E. obediently turned its nose and flew westwards.

Soon after landing we found that Cunningham had been severely wounded and had landed near Armentières. He died a few days later, poor fellow. He was the second casualty in my flight from August 15th, the other being Craine, who one day was missing and none of us saw the going of him.

We all landed from this patrol absolutely perished, for it had been bitterly cold, and we were all very glad to be down again. Rhys-Davids had again managed to push a Hun down, which was the last that he got, unless he downed one, or even two, in his last fight, of which we never learned any details.

The cold weather now coming on, we began to make our quarters and Mess more comfortable. Hoidge, who was before the war an architect, designed a wonderful brick fire-place, for which we had to enlarge the Mess specially, and the fireplace took weeks to build. Eventually, shortly after it was completed, we, needless to say, received orders to move.

On October 21st a report came from the Wing to say that three German machines were coming south from Calais, and Rhys-Davids, Muspratt and I went up in pursuit and climbed towards St. Omer, over which we arrived at 12,000 feet. Just previous to leaving the ground we had seen Maxwell and Barlow off in the squadron car, for they were going home for a well-earned rest.

After going up towards Calais I saw a de Havilland type 4 which I had a look at, and then turned away. I continued to climb, and Rhys-Davids and Muspratt went down and told "Grandpa," our Recording Officer, that they had left me over St. Omer, carefully stalking a D.H.4.

I now flew east-south-east at 16,000 feet, and over Béthune saw a German two-seater coming west over Givenchy, slightly higher than myself. As I approached him he turned off south-east and I could not catch him, so I just saw him go off well behind his lines.

Now I knew the Hun was a Rumpler, and that he was probably coming over our lines on a long job, and knowing that the Rumpler also carried four hours' petrol, I thought it would be worth while to continue climbing, so off I went up north to Armentières, and although my engine was not going well I was carefully hoarding height. Whilst over Armentières I looked towards the south-east, and just caught sight of a very small speck against the herring-bone sky, in the direction of Don, which is some miles east of the place where I first spotted the Hun. I now flew east to over Haubourdin, where I arrived at 17,500 feet, and I then turned south, whilst the little speck, which I thought was my photographic Rumpler, still went west.

Having arrived over Don, due east of the Hun, I turned to the west, following him until, by the time I was passing La Bassée, the Hun was well along the canal, no doubt having seen me by now but mistaking me for another German machine, for I came from so far over his lines. I got quite close to him over Béthune at 18,000 feet, and he now saw his mistake and tried to out-distance me towards Lens.

Very soon I caught up with him and got into position and fired a long burst from both guns, which went beautifully. The Rumpler at once went down in a steep righthand spin, emitting clouds of steam. I followed quickly, thinking that the pilot was all right, but I could see that the Hun's spiral was very steep, fast and regular. I went down at 200 m.p.h., and by the time I had got down to 6,000 feet the Rumpler had hit the ground at Fosse 10, near Mazingarbe, and was completely wrecked.

Immediately I landed alongside and ran over to the machine, round which were collecting French people and Tommies. I found the observer shot dead, but the pilot was still breathing, and so I got some Tommies to find a stretcher in order to take him to hospital, but the poor fellow died in a few minutes, for he was badly shot too. I felt very sorry indeed, for shooting a man down in Hunland is a different thing from doing it in your own lines, where you can see the results of your work. Shooting Huns is very good fun while we have to do it, but at the same time it makes one think, as I say, when one views such an object as I was doing then.

I put a guard on the machine and then took off, and flew back to the aerodrome, where I met Major Blomfield, who was very pleased and promised to go out at once to look at the Rumpler. I went to "Grandpa" to report, and he laughed like anything as he told me that the other two pilots had come down and reported me stalking a D.H.4. I stalked this Rumpler for nearly an hour before I finally engaged him where I wanted to do so, over our lines, and I think that this was one of the best stalks that I have ever had. I cannot describe the satisfaction which one experiences after bringing a good stalk to a successful conclusion.

After eating a hurried lunch the O.C. and I set off to view the Hun, who was only a few miles away, and arrived there in less than an hour, passing through dear old Béthune on the way. We arrived at the spot where the Rumpler lay, and the officer who found the guard, a sapper named Creeth, whom I knew, presented me with a beautiful silk cap which belonged to the pilot, who had papers on him from which we gathered he had been on leave in Berlin. This silk cap took my fancy so much and fitted me so well that I had it copied in silk khaki and wore it in France for months, and it certainly was unique.

We stayed by the Hun for some time, and the O.C. said that it was a pity we could not down Huns without this happening – alluding to the dead occupants – and I agreed, but I suppose I am getting too sentimental, and one cannot afford to be so when one has to do one's job of killing and going on killing.

The Major collected what parts of the machine he wanted and we then came away, as it was getting late. Just as we were leaving a shell dropped a hundred yards from the machine, but I think it was by accident, although the machine lay in full view of Wingles Tower, from which the Germans observe.

We arrived back at the squadron and had tea, for which we had an immense appetite. I was very pleased with life altogether, for I had brought down three two-seaters in our lines in ten days, and to bring a Hun down in our lines was an exception to the rule.

For the last fortnight my guns and machine had been going splendidly, and my machine now left nothing to be desired, in fact it was all it should be.

On the 23rd October I went to England on a fortnight's leave, and Rhys-Davids, being the next senior, took command of my flight in my absence. The day after I left he took my patrol over the lines and never came back himself, and no one knew what happened except perhaps the Germans. On the patrol he was last seen flying east towards some Huns, but that is all that was known.

On the 25th I met an officer from my squadron in London who told me that Rhys-Davids was missing. It only seemed a few hours since I had seen him, and of course it was all the harder luck because Rhys-Davids was already due for a rest.

I had a topping fortnight's leave, during which time I think I saw nearly every show in town, and one evening coming away from seeing "Arlette" I met an officer of another squadron who told me that my machine had been crashed. I was very fed up, and asked him if he was certain, and he said, "Yes, because I heard one of the 56 fellows say, 'Won't McCudden be mad when he comes off leave to find his pet machine crashed.'" And so I was.

On November 5th I went to Hendon with Captain Clive Collett to fly a V-strutter Albatros which he had for demonstration purposes, and I had a nice ride in it, but I could not think how the German pilots could manœuvre them so well, for they were certainly not easy to handle. The Albatros which Collett flew was the one that was flown by the Hun Sergeant-Major when he was driven down in our lines by three Spads of No. 23 Squadron.

That afternoon I flew as passenger with Collett on a D.H. up to Martlesham. All the way I was experimenting to see how I could best repel the scouts' attack from the two-seater gunner's point of view, with the idea of teaching myself some of the many disadvantages against which the two-seater gunner has to work when being attacked by a scout or scouts. We landed at Martlesham, when I met Cronyn, who was a member of "B" Flight during the summer, and I also saw Reggie Carr again, with whom I served in a squadron in earlier days.

After tea Collett and I went back to town by train and had a talk about many things, for Collett was in the "Camel" squadron on the same aerodrome and he used to come back shot to ribbons nearly every time he went out. One day he drove a German machine down to the ground behind the German lines, and then to make quite sure he fired at it on the ground until it burst into flames. Collett was always for downing the Hun, whenever and wherever he could find him.

On the 9th of October leave was up, so I flew a Bristol fighter out to a certain Depôt, where I flew an R.E.8 to an "issue park," which was not far from our aerodrome, and having left Folkestone at 12.30, arrived at my Squadron at 3 p.m., having had lunch on my way. The same evening I flew over the German lines, but did not have a fight.

The new Commanding Officer, who had relieved Major Blomfield whilst I was on leave, was Major H. Balcombe-Brown, M.C. He told me that my pet machine had been crashed, but that I had a new one just as good. My new machine was a Martinsyde-built machine No. B/35, and it was very fast, I soon found out.

It appears that my machine had been flown in combat by Maybery, who had got it shot about, and landing at Bailleul left it for another pilot to bring back to our aerodrome. The pilot who did eventually bring it back had about as much judgment as my little toe, for he left the ground in the dark to fly twenty miles across France to our aerodrome, and as soon as he was off the ground he flew through the side of a house. The only thing that was undamaged was himself.

The Squadron was now actively engaged in packing up, for we had orders to move down south, and on the 12th of November the machines left for our new aerodrome near Albert. It was a very misty day, and we were to land at Le Hameau, and inquire whether the weather was fit to go on or not. We lunched at Le Hameau and then resumed our journey. My flight landed at the new aerodrome about 3 p.m. The transport arrived about 4 p.m., and we set about unloading our goods and chattels.

We were lucky in a way, for we had arrived at an aerodrome that had been used before, and consequently it had good accommodation already provided.

The squadron office was on the corner of the aerodrome, and one of the last pilots in landing came in too fast, and putting his engine on at the last minute charged the office at 60 m.p.h. and completely wrecked the show, but was himself unhurt.

We soon settled down and made ourselves at home in our new surroundings, and our machines were better off, for we left canvas hangars and we were now using permanent iron ones. The weather at this time, being mid-November, left much to be desired, and when we first arrived it was misty for days. We had now joined the Wing in which I had been previously when in my old Squadron. We spent several days flying around the aerodrome in order to let the younger pilots learn the local landmarks well; as for myself I already knew the country, for I had flown over the same area the year previously when I was on the 3rd Army Front.

We began war flying again on the 18th November, when we flew from Albert up the main road to Bapaume, thence over the trenches north of Havrincourt, where we turned south. The weather was dull and the clouds were at 2,000 feet, but it was good enough for our present work, namely, to learn the trenches.

We flew down the trenches as far as Ronsoy, when I saw a D.F.W. on my left front, so I at once gave chase, and although we had orders not to cross the line, I felt sure that that Hun was a dud one, for up to now we had not had any modern fighting machines on this part and consequently the Huns used to do very much as they liked. I very soon got a good position, and fired a long burst from both guns, which went very well, and the Hun at once went down damaged, but under control. However, he landed downwind very fast and ran into a trench at high speed, where the machine completely wrecked itself amid a shower of chalky earth.

After seeing the Hun crash from 1,000 feet I fired a recall signal and led the patrol back to the lines at once, for the Hun had crashed at Bellicourt, about four miles over, and we had quite a warm time from Archie on our way back to the trenches. After that we flew back to our aerodrome, and everyone was pleased that we had got a Hun on our first show on the new front.

We now began to hear rumours of a new offensive, in which were going to operate 300 tanks. This sounded very interesting, and the push was going to take place almost immediately. We were told that the push was going to be a novel one, in that there would be a complete absence of artillery preparation, which usually gives the show away all too early.

On the 20th of November our attack was launched at 5.30 a.m., just as dawn was breaking, and we felt the reverberation of the guns right back where we were, twenty miles behind the trenches. About 7 a.m. we were standing on the ground, and it was threatening rain. About 8.30 we left the ground, and flew along the Bapaume-Cambrai road at 300 feet, as the heavy clouds were down at this height. We arrived at Havrincourt Wood and saw smoke and gun flashes everywhere.

From 200 feet we could see our tanks well past the famous Hindenburg line, and they looked very peculiar nosing their way around different clumps of trees, houses, etc. We flew up and down the line for an hour, but no sign of any Hun machines about, although the air was crowded with our own. Very soon the clouds were altogether too low, and there was nothing else to do except go home, so I did. By now I had only one follower, Coote, who landed with me at our advanced landing ground near Bapaume, as it was too bad to fly back to our own aerodrome. Here we found a lot of our machines and pilots who had made this aerodrome their home during the present operations.

The machines were mostly D.H.5's, which were employed in low bombing and ground strafing. It was really wonderful to see these fellows come back from a show all shot about, load up with some more bombs and ammunition, and then go off again to strafe the Hun. There was quite a fair percentage coming in wounded too, which was to be expected under the circumstances.

This aerodrome at Bapaume was the saving of a lot of our machines from crashing, for it was quite close to the trenches, and if a pilot's machine was hit he could usually glide there without the use of his engine from well over the line. Also we could always get petrol and oil from here to take us over the treacherous belt of shelled and devastated country between Bapaume and Albert, which was about ten miles across, for while on patrol it was difficult to know how much petrol one had in one's machine, and so if one had been out a long time and was doubtful if one's petrol would last out to good landing country west of Albert, all one had to do was to land at Bapaume and fill up with the necessities.

About 11 o'clock the clouds lifted a little, so Coote and I flew along the Bapaume-Albert road at ten feet in places, for the mist was really awful. We arrived back at our aerodrome, and the weather was so bad that we could not get up again until the 23rd. Of course all this time infantry and artillery were deprived of the assistance of our aeroplanes, but up to now they had done remarkably well, though the advance was hung up at Flesquières by a Hun anti-tank gun which stopped a certain part of our line for twenty-four hours.

When the anti-tank gunner was killed we were able to advance again. This gunner was found to be an officer, who, having had all his gun crew killed, worked the gun himself and knocked out fourteen tanks. One of our tank officers spoke very highly of the courage of this German officer. Of course, if the weather had been fine the anti-tank gun would have been spotted at once and knocked out by our low bombers, but the weather prevented the R.F.C. from taking a part in the proceedings and greatly hampered our advance.

About 10 a.m. on the 23rd my patrol left the ground and we flew at once towards Cambrai at 3,000 feet, for we could not get any higher owing to the clouds. We crossed the lines south of Bourlon Wood and very soon saw four Albatroses over Cambrai. We got close enough to open fire, and I engaged an Albatros, who was painted with a red nose, a yellow fuselage, and a green tail. He also had the letter K on his top plane. This Hun was destined to be always fighting my patrol somehow, and for the next three months we were continually meeting him.

After I had fired a short burst at this machine he spun down a little, but at once came up again.

These four Huns now being driven down without a decision, we turned round and went west again, for there were now plenty of Huns about, and the clouds being only at

3,000 feet, every machine was under this height and also over a comparatively small area around Bourlon Wood, which by now was three parts surrounded by British troops.

I now saw a D.F.W. coming west over Cantaing at 2,500 feet, so we at once gave chase. I got my position and fired a burst into him, whereupon he at once turned east and fired his white light, which on bursting spread into many small white lights. I had seen many Hun two-seaters do this, so I suppose that is a signal, "Jagdstäffeln – to the rescue!" This Hun went down in a devil of a hurry, but I did not finally get him.

By now most of my patrol had dwindled away, and I only had Fielding-Johnson with me. We sighted two Albatros scouts attacking a Bristol Fighter over Marcoing, so at once we went to the rescue. The Bristol, seeing us coming, skilfully drew one of them after him. The remaining one, who was just about my level, saw me and fairly stood on his tall endeavouring to scrape up a foot more height than my machine.

By the time I got to him and zoomed, the S.E. just went up a little higher. Then we both turned inwards and, the Hun losing height, I at once did a quicker turn and got behind him. After a short burst from my Vickers, the Hun's hat fell out of his machine, for apparently he was wearing an ordinary service cap; and after that the V-strutter went down and hit the ground, in a vertical dive with the engine on, a fearful whack. I looked where the Hun had crashed and found it was near Rumilly.

Fielding-Johnson and I now returned to Bourlon Wood, where we saw a big formation of Albatroses near our lines, so we went down on them, and I attacked the rear machine but overshot him and missed him. That Hun must have been on his first solo, for he hadn't the foggiest notion what to do, and was looking around him in an apparent state of bewilderment, but, by the time I had turned behind him again he was in the middle of his formation, and so I had to come back. By Jove! that Hun was as dud as they make them.

By now there were some Albatroses above us, and amongst them I saw "green-tail" taking a prominent part. We revved round for a while, and then I saw Maybery tackling a big A.E.G. bomber, which had apparently been pushed up by the Huns to distract some of our attention from their two-seaters, who were on the whole having a bad time. By now it was time to go home, and we arrived back at the squadron after a morning's fine fun.

The Major had been out too, and having tackled a two-seater turned the wrong way at the critical moment, came under the fire of the two-seater's gunner at very close range, had been pipped through the petrol tank, and was nearly blinded by petrol. So he went right down to the ground before switching on his engine again, for fear of igniting the escaping petrol from the flames from his exhaust pipes, which on the S.E. are in close proximity to the petrol tank. He got safely down, and came back saying that to tackle a two-seater successfully was harder than it looked.

During the morning of the 23rd the whole squadron had been up, and Bowman and Harmon had each got a Hun also. The Albatros which I shot down near Rumilly was my 20th victim.

That evening being very dull, most of us visited Amiens, which was only 20 minutes' run from our Camp, and on arrival at Amiens we adjourned to Charlie's Bar, where we consumed large quantities of oysters and, having had our fill of them, wandered round the town to make small purchases.

Amiens is a large town and there are a lot of nice shops. One can buy almost anything there, for it is not far from Paris or the Channel ports. The last time I had been to Amiens was when I came up to Béthune from Paris in January, 1915, on the conclusion of a ten days' course at the Le Rhône works. We had a very good dinner in Amiens and returned to the Squadron about 10 p.m.

The days after our attack were not marked by much enemy aerial activity, for apparently they had been so taken by surprise that they had not yet reinforced their aerial strength on the Cambrai battle front.

Early on the morning of the 29th, I led my patrol towards St. Quentin at 12,000 feet. We crossed the lines at 12,500 feet over St. Quentin and flew north with the sun on our right-rear, and very soon I saw a two-seater coming towards me from the north-east. I signalled to my patrol and down we went. The D.F.W. tried to run for it, which is the usual procedure adopted by the Hun two-seater pilots, who nearly always rely entirely on the good shooting of their gunner.

After receiving a good burst from both my guns, the D.F.W. literally fell to a thousand pieces, the wreckage of the wings fluttering down like so many small pieces of paper, while the fuselage with its heavy engine went twirling down like a misdirected arrow, towards the south of Bellicourt, where it hit the ground. I had by now zoomed up and, on looking round, saw Fielding-Johnson going off towards the lines. One could see that he was in trouble of some sort, so after seeing him safely as far as the lines, I again flew over the lines, followed by Walkerdine and Truscott, who were both new members of my flight.

When we got as far as Cambrai, we dived down on a formation of Albatroses whom I had just seen going down on Maybery's formation, who were very low over Cambrai, and for the next few minutes we had a regular dog-fight, in which Maybery lost a good fellow named Dodds. We eventually had to run for it, and again the S.E.'s wonderful good speed stood us in good stead and enabled us to get clear. After this, we flew home.

On landing I found that when Fielding-Johnson dived with me on the D.F.W., soon after leaving St. Quentin, his stabilising fin had broken, and as it broke had turned him upside down. Poor old Fielding-Johnson, his face was mournful to behold as I got out of my machine and spoke to him.

The same morning about midday I left the aerodrome, leading three other pilots. We went out as far as Bourlon, where we turned. North-east of us we could see several Albatroses playing in the clouds east of Bourlon, the clouds being at only 2,000 feet. The Hun is an adept at using clouds to his advantage, and I always think that Hun scouts fairly revel in a cloudy day.

We continued flying north, and by the time we had arrived east of Arras I saw three German machines coming west from the direction of Douai over the Sensée river. They came quite close to the lines, and then turned north.

I waited for a good opportunity and then signalled attack. I tackled the first D.F.W., for the Hun had proved to be this type, and fired a good burst at him from both guns, and the Hun at once started to glide down. I glanced round and saw Walkerdine tackling his D.F.W. in great style. I now rectified two stoppages, one in each gun, and went down to attack my Hun again, who was now very near the ground about a mile over the German lines.

By the time I got well within range the Hun was only about a hundred feet above the ground, and still gliding down. I fired another burst at him from close range, whereupon he did a terrific zoom, and then his two top wings met above the fuselage as all the four wings dropped off. The wreckage fell to the ground like a stone, and I saw the engine roll several yards away from the machine.

I was myself now very low, and on pushing the throttle open the engine only just spluttered. A glance at my pressure gauge showed that it was registering almost nil, so I grabbed my hand-pump and pumped like anything with one hand, while with the other I was holding the machine's nose up as much as possible. By the time I was only a few feet from the ground in a semi-stalled condition the good old Hispano started again with a roar that was very welcome music to my ears.

Being now so low I could not locate my position. So I flew by the sun. While passing over a battery position at a height of a few feet I saw a German N.C.O. walk into a gun pit after glancing at me as though he saw British machines over his battery a few feet up every hour of the day. That Hun N.C.O. either did not recognise me as a British machine or else he was a very cool card, for I went straight towards him, and my slip stream must have blown his cap off as I passed over him with a few feet to spare, and he did no more than glance up at me.

Very soon I passed over the enemy trenches, where they fired a lot at me; and then in the middle of No Man's Land, which at that part was several hundred yards wide, I saw a derelict Sopwith "Camel" which had apparently been shot down several weeks previously. I saw British Tommies waving from a trench to me, and I felt much braver than I did a few minutes before, for I felt that had I been forced to land alongside the German machine that I had shot down in pieces, I should have been given a very thin time by the Fritzes.

After climbing a bit I found Walkerdine and Truscott above Arras. We flew back to our aerodrome, and after landing Walkerdine said that the D.F.W. which he had tackled went down in a dive, but he did not see it crash. A few minutes afterwards Archie rang up confirming both machines down – Walkerdine's at Neuvireuil and mine at Rouvroy, S.E. of Lens.

After I had eaten lunch I went out alone for the third time that day, but the visibility was poor and there was very little enemy activity, so I very soon returned to the aerodrome.

The next day, November 30th, I led my patrol over the lines at Bourlon Wood and at once commenced fighting with several Albatroses. Down in Bourlon Wood itself the enemy were absolutely raining gas shells. We gained no decision with the enemy over Bourlon Wood, and I now saw seven two-seater machines coming west over Cantaing, so we flew to the attack, and I settled my opponent at once, for he started gliding down emitting clouds of steam.

I now flew east of him and turned him off west, and he then landed in our lines intact near Havrincourt. While I had been tackling him the enemy gunner had hit my radiator with an explosive bullet which knocked a big hole in it, so, having to go down in any case, I landed alongside the Hun. Just as I had almost stopped my wheels ran into a small shell-hole and my machine stood gracefully on its nose. I got out and, after having pulled the tail down, ran over to where the Hun was and found the pilot having a tourniquet put on his arm, for he was badly shot, whilst the German gunner, a weedy-looking specimen, looked on very disconsolately. The pilot died on the way to hospital, and the gunner, a Corporal, was marched off.

I had a look at the machine, which was an L.V.G. and was brand new, and then telephoned my squadron for a new radiator and propeller for my machine and a breakdown party to collect the Hun's.

While waiting I was talking to an infantry Colonel, who asked me what things looked like from the air, as the Germans had reported as having broken into our line. I told him I had not seen much of the activity on the ground, because all my attention was centred on the aerial aspect. I had just had lunch with him and was just leaving his dugout when "crack, crack, crack, crack," came from above, and looking up we saw a Pfalz firing at one of our advanced balloons, which at once burst into flames and commenced to fall. The occupants at once both jumped out, and their parachutes opened at once, so they came down quite safely in our lines, for there was not much wind. I noticed that one man came down much quicker than the other, so I suppose that he was much fatter.

Thereafter I began to feel annoyed, as there were dozens of Huns up, and our pilots, I could see from the ground, had their hands fairly full. So I decided to get back to our advanced landing ground, so as to borrow a machine and get up again while activity was about normal. I tried to borrow a car at Artillery Headquarters, but they were not having any, so I made up my mind to walk. I was in a pair of long heavy thigh boots, more vulgarly known by pilots as "fug boots," and that afternoon I walked six miles in those boots through mud and slush and all manner of things, to a railhead near Velu, where I was told that I could board a train for Bapaume. Whilst on my way to Velu I saw a German two-seater come miles over our lines unmolested, apparently on an urgent reconnaissance, for he was very low, not more than 3,000 feet, and his six-cylinder engine made a very loud roar.

By Jove! I was fed up to be sitting on the ground and seeing that insolent Hun come over getting just what information he wanted. I watched him till he flew back over his own lines, and then I resumed my walk. I boarded the train at Velu about 5 p.m., and was given some tea by some Canadian railway engineers who had constructed the railroad on which we were.

We waited for some time and then started. On the way we discussed the German push, and I remember they were not too optimistic, for they had been told to get as many of their trucks back as possible.

We passed the landing ground about 6 p.m., and I jumped off and made my way to the aerodrome, where I boarded a tender that was going to Albert immediately, where I arrived very soon, and then got back to my Squadron, after having a very exciting day's work. That night the breakdown party arrived out where my machine and the Hun were. They fitted a new propeller to my machine and burnt my perfectly priceless brand-new Hun.

Their explanation was that the Huns were advancing and they did not know whether they would be cut off or not, so they fixed my machine up, and having burnt my Hun, skedaddled for Albert, home and beauty. Needless to say I was very much annoyed, for the Huns never did come anywhere near Havrincourt, where the burnt L.V.G. lay for months.

The next day I left camp in a tender with Corporal Rogers, my Scottish mechanic, who hailed "fra Glasgae," at about 7 a.m., armed with a tool box and several bars of soap. We had a devil of a job getting near to my machine, as the roads were very congested, and at last we could get no further than Trescault, where we left the car and walked the remainder of the way to my machine, which was about half a mile away.

We got to the machine and ran the engine for a little while to warm it thoroughly, and then we stuffed two bars of soap into the large hole made by the Hun's explosive bullet. Having done that we filled the radiators with water, and I at once took off. The water was pouring out, but I wanted at least to get the machine to a place farther away from the Hun shells, which were dropping around in generous quantities, so that we could fit a radiator in peace and quietness. So with my topping old S.E., with its radiator crammed full of soap, I flew as far as our advanced landing ground, where I landed without a drop of water. It had not hurt the engine at all, for it went well for weeks after that.

At the advanced landing ground the men very quickly fitted a new radiator, and that afternoon I arrived back at the camp, where I found that the party who went out to salve the L.V.G. had brought back its propeller and "spinner," and its rudder and several odds and ends, also the black crosses off the wings, which always make very good screens in the mess.

After this I made a vow not to land alongside German machines again if I could possibly help it, for I am all against walking six miles through thick mud in large fugboots.

On the 3rd of December a new Factory-built S.E.5 came to my flight and I at once took it over. I gave my Martinsyde-built S.E. to the youngest member of the flight, for it was a very good one. Truscott was quite happy with the Martinsyde, so everything was well. My new S.E. was numbered A/4891, and was fitted with elevators with a narrow chord, which was an improvement, and it also had a new type of undercarriage which was much stronger than the others. (No doubt they knew that Factory machine would come to me.)

I set to work and very soon had my special gadgets fitted

on, and got my guns and Constantinesco gear working, and by the 4th I was again ready for the Great War.

On December 5th, the visibility being good, I went up looking for photographic Rumplers, and had been up about an hour and was at 19,000 feet when I saw a Hun over Bourlon Wood coming west at about my height. I at once sneaked into the sun, and waited until the Hun was west of me, and then I flew north and cut him off from his lines. I very quickly secured a good firing position, and after firing a good burst from both guns the Rumpler went down in a vertical dive and all its wings fell off at 16,000 feet and the wreckage fell in our lines near Hermies. I went back to my aerodrome, landed, and after having had lunch took my patrol out for the afternoon sports.

We found several two-seaters over the Canal at Vendhuille, and after having sent them about their business we returned home at the end of our patrol, for the enemy activity was very slight.

The next day, December 6th, my patrol went over the lines at 10 a.m., and after being out an hour, and having some indecisive fighting, I saw a two-seater crossing our lines north of St. Quentin, so waited until he was getting to his business taking photographs. Then I appeared from the east and bore down on the Hun like an enraged farmer after a boy who was in his orchard stealing apples. I very soon put paid to the photographic D.F.W.'s bill, and he also fell to pieces, the wreckage falling in our lines near the Holnon Wood.

I now saw an L.V.G. coming north from over St. Quentin, but by the time I caught up with him he was a little too high to engage successfully, so I returned to my aerodrome and had lunch.

Afterwards my flight went off and got our height towards Havrincourt Wood, and about 3 p.m. crossed the lines at 12,000 feet over Gouzaucourt. Flying west we espied a patrol of Albatros scouts flying west over Bourlon Wood. They were slightly below us, and so I led my patrol north and then turned west behind the six V-strutters, who still flew on looking to the west. We closed on them, and I gave every one of my men time to pick a Hun before I fired and drew their attention.

It seemed to me very funny that six of us should be able to surprise six Huns so completely as to get within range before being seen. I closed on the Hun I had selected, and fired a short burst at him, after which he went down vertically with a stream of escaping petrol following him. I noticed he had a tail painted light blue.

By now I was in the middle of these Albatroses and saw that they were a patrol of good Huns whom we had fought before. They all had red noses and yellow fuselages, but each had a different coloured tail. There was a red, light blue – whom I sent to the sports – black, yellow, black and white striped, and our dear old "green-tail." By Jove! They were a tough lot. We continued scrapping with them for half an hour, and they would not go down although we were above them most of the time.

This particular Albatros patrol were different from most Huns whom we met in that they would stay and fight, even when at a disadvantage, in a way that was disconcerting to behold. During the afore-mentioned fight, blue tail was the only Hun that went down, and eventually both patrols went away without any ammunition, for apparently the Huns had run out of ammunition at the same time as we had. It was awfully difficult for two good patrols to gain a decision, although one may fire all one's bullets, for each individual is so good at manœuvring in defence that his opponent wastes a lot of bullets on empty air. We flew home that evening and at tea and toast discussed the afternoon's sport, and were all agreed that the Huns whom we had fought that afternoon had been at the game for some time.

On this date I engaged a two-seater over Bourlon Wood and drove it down damaged. This machine had a biplane tail, and is now known as the Hannover. I mention this because the description of this new machine first appeared in February, 1918, about three months after I had first encountered it.

On December 10th I was leading my patrol above Bowman's formation, and after chasing a two-seater east of St. Quentin we returned north, climbing, and then we saw some Albatroses over Le Câtelet, so we went over to wish them good-day. I went down on the rear Hun, who did not see me, and fired a short burst at him, but I was closing on him too fast, and I had to zoom up to avoid running into him. However, he went down emitting steam, and I hope his mechanics had to work all night fitting a new radiator.

We circled round the other V-strutters for a time and then came away, as they were too far east. I now missed Bowman's patrol, who had flown up north, and at the end of my patrol flew back to our aerodrome. Here I found Bowman wandering gloomily round his machine, which had three main spars broken at the interplane struts. It happened like this: Bowman had seen my patrol tackling the Albatroses over Le Câtelet and so went up farther north in search of prey. Seeing a nice fat balloon down over the Bois de Vaucelles, he decided that it was insolent looking and should be reproved immediately. So Bowman "dived like Hell," as he afterwards put it, with his adjustable tail fully forward to facilitate steep diving, and his bloodthirsty lads behind him. When a few hundred feet above the balloon, Bowman saw some Huns coming down on top of him, so he said, "That is no place for me," and hoicked out of the dive with such vim that three wing-tips at once collapsed. He then said he looked at the wing-tips wobbling about like a jelly, and he was quite surprised when they did not break off. After falling some way out of control Bowman decided that life after all was worth living, so he resumed control and flew all the way back to the aerodrome at a speed not exceeding 65 m.p.h. so as not to impose too great a strain on his weakened wings. What had happened was that the spars of three out of four main planes had broken just outside the struts.

I should think that most people, after an experience like that, would have stopped flying for a while; but not so Bowman, for he was up the very next day. Bowman now tells me that he has finished with balloons and does not like them, and he has good cause, too. You will remember his first experience with a balloon on Mount Kemmel in the autumn of 1916, when we were both in the same squadron.

On December 12th my patrol went over the lines near Vendhuille, where there was much enemy activity, and very soon we were fighting over Bourlon Wood, but, gaining no decision, went south and engaged some Pfalz and Albatros scouts who were firing into our trenches near Villers.

We dispersed these Huns and went north to Cantaing and, on looking west, I saw a Hun two-seater just below the clouds at 4,000 feet over Hermies, about four miles west of our lines, so I led the patrol towards him. I knew if I stayed below the clouds he would go into them, so just before I got to him nose on, I went into the clouds to get above, and as soon as my patrol were above the clouds I dived down below them, so now the Hun was for it, whatever way he went. As I dived down I went quite close to the Hun and opened fire with my Vickers, for my Lewis was out of action. For the next five minutes I fought that D.F.W. from 4,000 to 500 feet over our lines, and at last I broke off the combat, for the Hun was too good for me and had shot me about a lot. Had I persisted he certainly would have got me, for there was not a trick he did not know, and so I gave that liver-coloured D.F.W. best.

On December 15th I left the ground at 10 a.m. to pursue German machines alone. I climbed steadily and very soon got up to 18,000 feet, when I saw a German machine in the distance coming towards our lines. I waited in the sun until he came quite close, but he turned north and, being just above the line, I would not attack him yet, for I wanted him to fall in our lines. Also there was a very strong westerly wind high up, which was against my tactics. I followed behind him for some time until I realised that he was not going far over our lines, so I then dived on him from 19,800 feet, for the Hun was at 19,000 feet. I closed on him and opened fire, but I had misjudged my speed and was over-shooting him, so I had to do a turn to avoid running into him.

The next I saw of him he was diving steeply away to the east. I caught him up again, but could not defeat him, for the pilot was good and gave his gunner every opportunity, and I had to leave him very soon, for the wind being strong from the west I was now miles over Hunland, so I returned west.

By the time I had got to our lines the whole sky seemed alive with Hun two-seaters, and so I at once engaged another Rumpler over Villers. He at once ran away, but I overhauled him slowly and finally fired a long burst at 400 yards range, after which the Rumpler got into a steep right-hand spiral. Then he came out of it and went down in a straight dive, finally crashing just east of the Bois de Vaucelles. Having no more petrol with me for any length of time I flew back to my aerodrome.

On this day I was awarded the Distinguished Service Order, and also received a telegram of congratulation from the G.O.C., R.F.C., General Trenchard, C.B., D.S.O.*

On December 19th we lost Maybery, the "A" Flight Commander. His and my formation were working in conjunction with each other, and he was below me. We crossed the lines over Ribecourt and flew towards Cambrai, and very soon saw eight V-strutters about our own height. They were not offensively inclined, so very soon Captain Maybery, followed by his formation, dived on some Huns over Bourlon Wood at about 6,000 feet. As I went down to follow, the eight Huns from north of Cambrai came towards us, and I had to pull out of the dive and fight these Albatroses. We fought them until they dispersed, but did not gain any decisive result.

* *Later Chief of the Air Staff and Marshal of the RAF. Created a Baron in 1930.*

I could now see Maybery's formation very low going towards the lines, as though to reform, and so I flew down south towards Vaucelles Wood, over which I saw three Albatroses, on whom we leapt with great vigour. We fought these three Huns for a time, but they eventually went down east quite all right. We now flew up towards Bourlon Wood, where we encountered "green-tail" and a brown Pfalz. We scrapped these two for over half an hour, and with no result, for they co-operated wonderfully, and put up a magnificent show, for we could not attack either of them without having the other after us. There were now only three of us, and we did our very best to get one of them, but to no avail. After a time they both went down, apparently for some more petrol or ammunition, and we flew home.

At tea-time no Maybery appeared, and late that night he was reported missing. Woodman, of his formation, said they dived on some Huns over Bourlon, and Maybery got his in flames at once, but whilst firing at it he was leapt on by the "green-tail" Albatros. Then Woodman saw Maybery's machine going down out of control. Maybery's last victim was his twentieth. A few weeks later the Huns dropped a note to say that Maybery was dead.

Maybery had served some time in the cavalry, the 21st Lancers, and he was all for cavalry tactics in the air. He said that whenever Huns were seen they should at once be attacked, and we always argued as to the best way of fighting the Hun in the air. My system was to always attack the Hun at his disadvantage if possible, and if I were attacked at my disadvantage I usually broke off the combat, for in my opinion the Hun in the air must be beaten at his own game, which is cunning. I think that the correct way to wage war is to down as many as possible of the enemy at the least risk, expense and casualties to one's own side. At the same time, when one is taken at his advantage and one has to fight, one always has enough common sense to fight him like anything, for, as far as fighting the Hun in the air is concerned, nothing succeeds like boldness, and the Hun is usually taken aback when boldness is displayed.

On December 22nd I flew from our aerodrome down to St. Quentin, and arrived by myself west of that town at about 15,000 feet. The visibility was good, and I knew I should not have to wait long before an enemy came over our line barefaced to take photos. The Huns usually take the photos about the hours of eleven and twelve, for the sun is then at its brightest and the ground shadows are small. Very soon I was up to 17,000 feet, and then two D.F.W.'s came directly underneath me over Holnon Wood.

I went down at once and, selecting one very quickly, disabled him, and he started to go down, so I left him to glide down in our lines while I tackled the second one. The second one had seen me get the first, for they were both close together, and he fought as though for his life, but I maintained my firing position and shot him about a lot all the way back to the lines. Then I looked over my shoulder and saw that the first Hun was gliding east, so I left the second Hun, who could have easily interfered with me, and again attacked the disabled one. But the second one was not made of that kind of stuff, for he flew off east as hard as he could and absolutely deserted his charge.

On approaching the first Hun again I could not see the gunner – he was most likely playing poker on the floor of his cockpit – and the pilot was gliding straight. I tried to head him west but he would not go, so I was forced to fire a lot more ammunition at him, after which he went into a flat spiral glide, and then crashed in our lines just south-west of St. Quentin.

Then as I zoomed away I saw that my windscreen was covered with blood. At first I thought my nose was bleeding but soon assured myself that it was not. Then I saw that the blood was on the outside of my screen.

Not having much more petrol I flew back to the aerodrome and landed, after which I walked around my machine and found it covered with blood from the Hun two-seater. This is absolutely true, for I have a dozen different people who will vouch for it. I was very surprised, for I have never known of a parallel case. I remember that I flew for a long time directly under him, and he did not turn, so I concluded that I got the blood from him then.

The next day, the 23rd of December, I brought down four German two-seater machines, three of which fell in our lines. I left the ground at 10.30 and flew down to my happy hunting ground west of St. Quentin; and very soon saw an L.V.G. come west from St. Quentin at 17,000 feet, so I waited until he was well west of the lines and then I attacked him. I got into position and, after firing a short burst at him, he started gliding down, emitting steam and water. I could see that he was disabled, and so I tried to head him off west, as he was going south-east towards La Fère. At first he turned a little, and the observer stood up holding on with one hand and waving at me with the other, apparently in token of surrender, but the pilot was still flying south-east and by this time was very near his lines, so I was forced to fire another burst into the L.V.G., which went down in a steep dive and crashed on the canal bank at Anguilcourt, which is in the enemy lines a little north-east of La Fère.

Then I turned away and flew up north, and on my way was joined by a French Spad, who apparently came to see why I was bringing Huns down in his sector. I always was a poacher out in France, for although my area was from Arras to just south of Cambrai, I would get a Hun one day at Lens and the next at La Fère, fifty miles south.

I flew north climbing, for I had finished the L.V.G. off at about 6,000 feet, and very soon was up to 14,000 feet. There the French Spad left me, deciding that it was too cold, for at this period the weather was bitter, with a biting easterly wind.

At 17,000 feet, on looking west I saw a Hun very high over Péronne, and so I remained east of him, climbing steadily. After 15 minutes I got up to his level at 18,200 feet over Péronne. He now saw me and climbed for a little while trying to outclimb me, but he could not, for my machine was still going up well; but had we both been at 19,000 feet instead of 18,000 he could have outclimbed me, for the Rumplers at 20,000 are extremely efficient with their heavily-cambered wing, whereas the S.E. at that height, although it is fast, has not much climb on account of its flat wing section. However, I was now up at the Rumpler's height, and he tried to run for it.

I soon got into position but found that he was every bit as fast as I was, although I was able to keep up with him, because as he swerved to allow his gunner to fire at me, he lost a certain amount of speed. I fought him down from 18,000 to 8,000 feet and he tried hard to save his life, but after a final burst from both my machine-guns his right-hand wings fell off and I very nearly flew into them.

The Rumpler's wreckage fell in our lines at Contescourt, west of St. Quentin. Now Sergeant-Major Cox was out with a lorry salving the D.F.W. which I shot down on the previous day, and as he was in the locality he saw this Rumpler hurtle down. He decided to collect it as well, and he was not surprised when he got back to the Squadron and found that it was mine as well. This Rumpler was my thirtieth victim.

Next I flew north, climbing, and arrived over Havrincourt Wood, familiarly known as "Mossy-face," and very soon saw two L.V.G.'s east of me over Gouzaucourt at about 17,000 feet. I at once gave chase, and they turned east. I fought them for about five minutes, but could not gain a decision for they both co-operated well, and very soon I left them for I hadn't much more petrol. Whilst I was fighting these two, they were both using their front guns as well as the rear, and so I had a fairly warm time.

On returning to the aerodrome I was very pleased with things, so after having had lunch I led my patrol towards the lines at about 2 p.m. Whilst on the way at 14,000 feet over Fins, I saw a Rumpler coming towards us from the lines. He did not see us until too late, and then turned away. I caught up with him, got my firing position, and fired a good long burst from both guns, after which the Hun went down in a steep right-hand spiral, and crashed in our lines near Gouzaucourt.

By this time I was down to 6,000 feet, so after reforming my patrol we flew north. There we saw our friends of the varied-coloured tails above us over Bourlon Wood, so I led the patrol south; and after climbing for twenty minutes we got above the Albatros scouts, in a position to attack, and we dived on them just south of Bourlon Wood at about 13,000 feet.

At once "green tail" did his usual trick, which was, as soon as we attacked his patrol, to fly off east and, being alone, to climb above the dog fight, and then, coming back much higher, to pick off any of my men who were not looking. I had seen him do this several times, but this time, when he came back above the fight, he found one above him, so he went off at once.

Meanwhile my patrol were having a fine time, for the Huns, although at a disadvantage, continued fighting us from underneath, and kept standing on their tails shooting up at us. This lasted until we got down fairly low over Bourlon Wood, so I then fired a recall signal, and the patrol came back to reform.

We went west climbing, and then, seeing a British Archie bursting to the south of us, and flying in that direction, I soon saw an L.V.G. over Trescault at about 12,000 feet, apparently doing a reconnaissance.

I signed for Archie to stop, which he did, and after firing a burst from both my guns, I saw the L.V.G. heel over on its wing-tip. It flew along with its wings vertical and with the gunner hanging on to the cabane leaning into the pilot's cockpit. The L.V.G. then stalled and spun, and after that went down just like a leaf, and took at least three minutes to crash. It landed on a light gauge train in a vertical dive and knocked some trucks off the line.

After that I went down quite low, and saw thousands of our Tommies rushing from everywhere to look at the fallen Hun. Having circled round for a while I flew back to the aerodrome feeling very satisfied, having totally destroyed four enemy two-seaters that day.

When I landed the O.C. asked me if I was the culprit, for three Huns had already been reported brought down in our lines by an S.E.5, so I replied that I was. That evening a lot of us went into Amiens and had a dinner to celebrate the event. The weekly R.F.C. communiqué, referring to the event, stated that this was the first time four enemy machines had been totally destroyed in one day by one pilot. I also received a telegram of congratulation from General Trenchard and from several other senior officers of the R.F.C.

The weather at this time was bitterly cold, with the winter's prevailing easterly wind. At this time of the year I used to go up day after day waiting at 17,000 up to 20,000 feet for the German two-seaters, who were always over our lines during the clear visibility.

I expect some of those Huns got a shock when they came over at 18,000 feet and were dived on by an S.E. from above, for in the winter it was an exception to the rule to see an S.E. above 17,000 feet, which was the ceiling of the average 200 h.p. S.E. with its war load. My machine had so many little things done to it that I could always go up to 20,000 feet whenever I liked, and it was mainly the interest which I took in my machine which enabled me to get up so high.

By getting high I had many more fights over our lines than most people, because they could not get up to the Rumplers' height, and so could not engage them successfully.

On Xmas Day I went up for a while but the atmosphere not being clear enough for the enemy to work successfully, I soon came down again. We had a very quiet Xmas, for Bowman, our star turn in the mess, was in England on leave, having a thorough good time.

On December 28th I left the ground about 10.15 a.m. in a strong north-easterly wind, which is always very favourable to my method of fighting. It was a beautiful morning, clear, frosty and intensely cold, for on the ground the glass was registering twenty degrees of frost. I liked nothing better than these mornings, when I could go up high, with my engine, guns, and machine going perfectly, and stalk the Hun two-seaters who came over to take photographs daily.

I got up to 17,000 feet in half an hour, and very soon saw a Rumpler coming towards me, slightly lower, from the direction of Bourlon Wood. We were very close, and, getting into position quickly, I fired a short burst from both guns, and the Rumpler went into a right-hand spiral dive. Then his right-hand wings fell off at about 16,000 feet, and the wreckage fell in our lines north of Velu Wood. I watched the wreckage fluttering down like so much waste paper, and saw the fuselage and engine going down at a terrific speed, leaving a trail of blue smoke behind it.

After a look round, I soon saw another Rumpler west of me towards Bapaume, slightly below me. I went over to him and, having got into position, fired a burst from both guns. Flames at once issued from his fuselage, and he went into a spin at 17,000 feet and took about two minutes to reach the ground, on which he crashed near Flers, which, at that time, was about twenty miles west of the lines. I saw the poor devil strike the ground in a smother of flame.

Then I had a look round and at once saw a German being shelled by British A.A. guns over Havrincourt Wood. I flew all out, and soon overhauled the L.V.G., which at 16,000 feet was much slower than my machine. Whilst I was overtaking him I had to fly through our Archie bursts, as they had not yet seen me, and some of them were unpleasantly close.

As soon as I got within range and opened fire the Hun at once dived for his lines. By the time he had got down to 9,000 feet, diving at 200 miles per hour, I opened fire a second time into him, whereupon he burst into flames, after which the whole machine fell to pieces owing to the speed at which it was going, for I had most likely shot some of his main flying wire, too. This L.V.G. went down in a shower of flaming pieces, and the wreckage finally fell in our lines at Havrincourt village.

I now started climbing again, and having got up to 18,000 feet, again saw an L.V.G. coming south over Lagnicourt. I dived down, but he saw me and ran for it. However, I was much faster, and having got into position, fired a burst from my Lewis, as the Vickers at once stopped. A small flicker of flame came from the L.V.G., but it went out immediately.

By this time I was well over the Hun lines, so I had to return. I last saw the Hun gliding down over Marquion, under control, but certainly damaged, for steam was issuing from his radiator, and the pilot was very energetically kicking his rudder from side to side like wildfire.

Whilst the Hun was going down fast I noticed the observer frantically shouting and waving to the pilot over the left-hand side of the fuselage. I expect he was annoyed, because he was having a hot shower-bath from the damaged radiator. Anyhow, I hope the water froze over him solid and gave him frost-bite.

After that I pulled up away from him and returned to my aerodrome, for I had very little petrol left, and on my way back I felt very disappointed at having missed the last Hun, for if my Vickers had not stopped at the crucial moment, I think I should have dispatched him with much celerity.

When I landed, the Major said that our Archie gunners had reported Huns falling out of the sky in pieces everywhere. The O.C. was very pleased, and so was I, for I had accounted for three two-seaters in thirty minutes.

That afternoon the O.C. and I went out to see the remains of the Rumpler who went down in flames at Flers, and when we arrived we saw nothing but a charred mass of wreckage. It was a nasty sight, and it brought home to me more than ever the sterner aspect of aerial fighting.

The next day I took my flight over the lines at Bantou-zelle, and at once saw three enemy two-seaters coming towards me from Vaucelles Wood. I signalled to attack, and we lessened our altitude. I got behind the L.V.G. and fired a burst, and the Hun started to go down, with me after him. I headed him over our trenches, and as he went down low, as if to land in our lines, I followed closely, and saw him flatten out to land, but he put his engine on to miss a trench, and that must have given him an idea of making a further bid for Hunland. Thereupon he flew north, towards Havrincourt, at about 10 feet, and the pilot seeming to want to get back, while the observer was just standing in his cockpit looking at me, but not firing at all.

At Havrincourt the pilot turned east, still at about 10 feet high, and I saw that he would soon cross the trenches, so I fired another burst into him at close range. He immediately spun and crashed in our lines, not a hundred yards from the L.V.G. which the salvage party burnt after I had driven it down intact at Havrincourt village.

As I circled round I saw our Tommies assisting the occupants out of the wreck. I afterwards learned that the pilot was mortally wounded but that the observer was unscratched. How he escaped my fire I do not know, for when I fired my last burst I was directly behind the machine and the gunner was directly between my nose and the Hun pilot. I expect a bullet or two passed between his legs.

After climbing again, I found some of my patrol, and then we attacked some V-strutters over Vaucelles Wood. We drove them down, and, that accomplished, we flew home to our aerodrome.

At midday I went up alone, as the visibility was good, but I remained at 18,000 feet for nearly two hours before I saw an L.V.G. crossing our lines near Bantouzelle. I went down on him, but he saw me at once and turned for the lines. I was much faster and soon caught him, and as soon as I got into position he commenced circling. "Hallo!" I thought; "this artist has seen me at work before," and I let him circle, for there was an easterly wind and I knew that he would go straight before long, so as to get back to his lines.

I did not wait for long, for he suddenly dived away straight towards his lines, and I then got my sight on him and fired until he first of all fell to pieces and then burst into flames. As I watched the wreckage go down floating in our lines, I felt that my two hours' vigil at 18,000 feet, when the glass on the ground was reading 20° of frost, had not been wasted. I flew home, and had a generous dinner, after which we listened to the gramophone for half an hour, and life again seemed full of cheer.

That afternoon the Major and I walked to the neighbouring village of Heilly to see some infantry officers whom we knew there. It was a typical winter afternoon, snow under foot, frosty and a blue sky above. We returned about 5 p.m., and having walked eight miles in thick snow sat down and consumed immense quantities of toast and jam (not Tickler's!).

That evening was brightened by our own orchestra at dinner. They played all sorts of music, from "Poète et Paysan" to "Dixieland," and after the dinner we adjourned to our ante-room to dance and listen to the music, for the orchestra was really wonderful. It is extraordinary what a different feeling a good hour's music gives to a squadron, and I think that every squadron in France ought to have its own orchestra, for I think that good pleasant music certainly tones up a squadron's *morale* to no little extent. I am digressing, for which I most humbly ask forgiveness.

DEATH FLIES FASTER

ERNST UDET

Udet was the leading surviving ace of the Imperial German Military Service in World War I, scoring 62 victories (against the fallen Richthofen's 80). Originally flying as an NCO, he painted the taunting message on his Fokker DVII's tailplane "Definitely not you!" – but someone did, and Udet only survived the downing by baling out with his parachute. (A luxury not permitted Allied flyers, incidentally, who forwent the benefits of silk). Flying a new, and message-less, aircraft Udet was commissioned and became commander of Jasta 37 *(Fighter Squadron 37). By the end of the war, the 22-year-old Udet commanded a fighter squadron in von Richthofen's* Jagdgeschwader I *(Fighter Group I) and had been awarded the* Pour le Mérite. *In peacetime Udet became a stunt pilot in the movies, before appointment as general in the Luftwaffe in World War II. However, disagreements with his old cohort from* Jagdgeschwader I, *Herman Goering, forced Udet's suicide in 1941.*

In the extracts from his memoirs below, taken from the years 1917 and 1918, Udet describes his memorable fight with the French ace Georges Guynemer, his transfer to Richthofen's Jagdgeschwader I, *and a subsequent convalescent leave in Munich.*

Jasta 15, which grew out of the old Single-Seater Combat Command Habsheim, has now only four aircraft, three sergeants, and myself as their leader. Almost always we fly alone. Only in this way can we fulfill our assigned duties.

Much is happening on the front. It is said the other side is preparing an offensive. The balloons are up every day, hanging in long rows in the summer sky, like a garland of fat-bellied clouds. It would be good if one of them were to burst. It would be a good warning to the others in addition, on just plain general principles.

I start early in the morning, so that I can have the sun at my back to stab down at the balloon. I fly higher than ever before. The altimeter shows five thousand meters. The air is thin and icy. The world below me looks like a gigantic aquarium. Above Lierval, where Reinhold fell, an enemy pusher type is cruising around. Like a tiny water flea, he shovels his way through the air.

From the west, a small dot approaches fast. At first, small and black, it grows quickly as it approaches. A Spad, an enemy fighter. A loner like me, up here, looking for prey. I settle myself into my seat. There's going to be a fight.

At the same height, we go for each other, passing at a hair's breadth. We bank into a left turn. The other's aircraft shines light brown in the sun. Then begins the circling. From below, it might appear as though two large birds of prey were courting one another. But up here it's a game of death. He who gets the enemy at his back first is lost, because the single-seater with his fixed machine guns can only shoot straight ahead. His back is defenseless.

Sometimes we pass so closely I can clearly recognize a narrow, pale face under the leather helmet. On the fuselage, between the wings, there is a word in black letters. As he passes me for the fifth time, so close that his propwash shakes me back and forth, I can make it out: "*Vieux*" it says there – *vieux* – the old one. That's Guynemer's sign.★

★ *The full inscription on Guynemer's Spad read "Vieux Charles" – "Old Charlie."*

Yes, only one man flies like this on our front. Guyne-mer, who has brought down thirty Germans. Guynemer, who always hunts alone, like all dangerous predators, who swoops out of the sun, downs his opponents in seconds, and disappears. Thus he got Puz away from me. I know it will be a fight where life and death hang in the balance.

I do a half loop in order to come down on him from above. He understands at once and also starts a loop. I try a turn, and Guynemer follows me. Once out of the turn, he can get me into his sights for a moment. Metallic hail rattles through my right wing plane and rings out as it strikes the struts.

I try anything I can, tightest banks, turns, side slips, but with lightning speed he anticipates all my moves and reacts at once. Slowly I realize his superiority. His aircraft is better, he can do more than I, but I continue to fight. Another curve. For a moment he comes into my sights. I push the button on the stick . . . the machine gun remains silent . . . stoppage!

With my left hand clutched around the stick, my right attempts to pull a round through. No use – the stoppage can't be cleared. For a moment I think of diving away. But with such an opponent this would be useless. He would be on my neck at once and shoot me up.

We continue to twist and turn. Beautiful flying if the stakes weren't so high. I never had such a tactically agile opponent. For seconds, I forget that the man across from me is Guynemer, my enemy. It seems as though I were sparring with an older comrade over our own airfield. But this illusion lasts only for seconds.

For eight minutes we circle around each other. The longest eight minutes of my life. Now, lying on his back, he races over me. For a moment I have let go of the stick and hammer the receiver with both fists. A primitive expedient, but it helps sometimes.

Guynemer has observed this from above, he must have seen it, and now he knows what gives with me. He knows I'm helpless prey.

Again he skims over me, almost on his back. Then it happens: He sticks out his hand and waves to me, waves lightly, and dives to the west in the direction of his lines.

I fly home. I'm numb.

There are people who claim Guynemer had a stoppage himself then. Others claim he feared I might ram him in desperation. But I don't believe any of them. I still believe to this day that a bit of chivalry from the past has continued to survive. For this reason I lay this belated wreath on Guynemer's unknown grave.

For the past six weeks I am the C.O. of Jasta 37. We are based in Wynghene, a small town in the middle of the Flanders marshes. The terrain is difficult, broken up by ground folds and water ditches. Here, every emergency landing means a crack-up. When one climbs high enough, one can see across to Ostende and the sea. Gray-green and endless, it stretches to the horizon.

Many were surprised at Grashoff leaving me in command when he was transferred to Macedonia. There are men here senior both in years and rank. But, back in the fall, when I brought down the three Englishmen over Lens, he had promised it to me. It was a surprise success in Guynemer's style. I came down out of the sun and attacked the last one on the outside left, finishing him with five rounds. Then the next one and, finally, the leader. The other two were so surprised, they didn't get a shot off. The whole thing didn't last more than twenty seconds, just as it was with Guynemer back then. In war, one must learn the trade of fighter piloting or get knocked off. There is no alternative.

When I landed, Grashoff knew all about it. "When I leave here some day, Knaegges, you will inherit the *staffel*," he said. Thus I became the C.O. of Jasta 37.

Across from us are the English. Young, sharp boys, they take on anybody and usually hold out until the final decision. But we are their equals. The depressing feeling of inferiority, giving us all the doldrums at Boncourt, has disappeared. The *staffel* has a long string of victories behind it, and I myself have, up to now, nineteen confirmed.

As the winter deepens, air traffic slows down. There is much rain and snow. Even on dry days the heavy clouds drift so low that no takeoffs are ordered. We sit around in our rooms. I am quartered in the country house of a lace manufacturer. Sometimes, when I sit at the window, I see the home workers bringing up their wares. They are bent, ragged shapes, stamping through the snow.

The son of the house has entered the Royal Flying Corps on the other side. But the people don't make me ill at ease over it. "He does his duty, I do mine," is their point of view, reasonable and clear.

In the spring of 1918 a restlessness runs along the German front, from Flanders up into the Vosges. This is certainly not the spring alone. Everywhere, among the officers and men, they are speaking of the great offensive, which is supposed to be imminent. But no one knows anything for certain. On March 15, the *staffel* is ordered to load up its personnel and aircraft at once. Destination unknown. We all know this is the beginning of the offensive.

Along the highway to Le Cateau we set up our aircraft tents. The rain comes down in a fine spray, which slowly turns everything – trees, houses, and people – into the same gray mush. I have put on my leather jacket and help the mechanics drive the tent pegs into the ground.

A car comes rattling along the road. Many cars pass this way, so we have ceased paying any attention to them. We continue to work in grim silence. Someone pats me on the back, and I jump around.

Richthofen. The rain is seeping down from his cap, running into his face.

"Hello, Udet," says the captain, and he tips his cap. "Nice rotten weather today."

I salute in silence and look at him. A quiet, self-controlled face, large, cold eyes, half covered by heavy lids.

This is the man who has already brought down sixty-seven, the best of us all. His car stands on the highway below. He has clambered up the slope through the rain. I am waiting.

"How many have you brought down, Udet?"

"Nineteen confirmed, one pending," I answer.

His cane pokes around in the wet leaves.

"Hm, twenty then," he repeats. He looks up and gives me a searching glance.

"Then you would actually seem ripe for us. Would you like to?"

Would I like to? I most certainly would! If I had my way, I would pack up right now and go along with him. There are many good squadrons in the Army, and Jasta 37 is far from the worst. But there is only one Richthofen group.

"Yes, *Herr Rittmeister*," I reply, and we shake hands.

I look after him as his spare and slender shape clambers down the slope, climbs into the car, and disappears around the next bend behind a curtain of rain.

"Well, you could say we have made it now," says Behrend as I bend down beside him to continue driving the tent pegs into the ground.

There are many good squadrons on the front, but there is only one Richthofen group. And now I see the secret of their success unfold.

Other squadrons live in castles or small towns, twenty to thirty kilometers behind the front lines. The Richthofen group dwells in corrugated shacks that can be erected and broken down in a matter of hours. They are rarely more than twenty kilometers behind the foremost outposts. Other squadrons go up two or three times a day. Richthofen and his men fly five times a day. Others close down operations in bad weather; here they fly under almost any condition.

However, the biggest surprise for me is the forward combat airstrips. This was an invention of Boelcke, the senior master of the German air service. Richthofen, his most gifted pupil, has taken this practice over.

Just a few kilometers behind the lines, often within range of the enemy artillery, we are on fully dressed standby, lounging in reclining chairs in an open field. Our aircraft, gassed up and ready to go, are right alongside. As soon as an opponent appears on the horizon, we go up – one, two, or an entire *staffel*. Immediately after the fight we land, stretch out in our reclining chairs, and scour the sky with binoculars, waiting for the next opponent. Standing patrols are not flown. Richthofen doesn't believe in them. He'll allow only patrols into the enemy's rear areas. "This business of standing sentry duty in the air weakens the pilots' will to fight," he maintains. Thus we only go up to fight.

I arrive at the group at ten o'clock, and at twelve I'm already off on my first sortie with Jasta 11. In addition, Jastas 4, 6, and 10 make up the group.* Richthofen himself leads Jasta 11. He puts great store in personally trying out each new man. There are five of us, the captain in the lead. Behind him are Just and Gussmann. Scholtz and I bring up the rear. For the first time I fly the Fokker triplane. We skim over the pockmarked landscape at about five hundred meters altitude.

Above the ruins of Albert, just below the clouds, hangs an RE, a British artillery spotter. Probably ranging his batteries. We are a bit lower than he, but he apparently hasn't noticed us, because he quietly continues to circle. I exchange a quick look with Scholtz; he nods. I separate from the *staffel* and race for the "Tommy."

I take him from the front. From below I dart for him like a shark and fire at short range. His engine is riddled like a sieve. He tilts over at once and disintegrates right after. The burning fragments fall close to Albert.

In another minute, I am back with the formation and continue on in the direction of the enemy. Scholtz nods at

* *i.e. Jagdgeschwader 1*

me again, quickly and happily. But the captain has noticed. He seems to have eyes everywhere. His head whips around, and he waves at me.

Below to our right is the Roman road. The trees are still bare, and through them one can see columns move. They are moving westward. British retreating before our offensive.

Just above the treetops skims a flight of Sopwith Camels. They are probably there to protect the Roman road, one of the main arteries of the British withdrawal. I hardly have time to take in the picture when Richthofen's red Fokker dives down, all of us following. The Sopwith Camels scatter like a gaggle of chickens when the hawk stabs. Only one can't get away, the one the captain has in his gunsights.

It happens so quickly, one can hardly speak of a fight. For a moment one thinks the captain might ram him, he is that close. I estimate no more than ten meters. Then the Sopwith is shaken by a blow. His nose is pushed down, a white gasoline trail appears, and he crashes in the field alongside the road in smoke and flames.

Richthofen, the steel point of our wedge formation, continues on in a steep glide toward the Roman road. At a height of about ten meters he races along the ground, both machine guns firing without letup into the marching columns on the road. We stay behind him and pour out more fire.

A paralyzing terror seems to have seized the troops; only a few make for the ditches. Most fall where they walk or stand. At the end of the road, the captain makes a tight turn and proceeds with another pass along the treetops. Now we can clearly observe the effect of our first strafing run: bolting horse teams, abandoned guns which, like breakwaters, stem the oncoming human flood.

This time we receive some return fire from below. Infantrymen stand there, rifles pressed to the cheek, and from the ditch a machine gun barks up to us. But the captain does not come up one single meter because of this, even though his wing planes are taking bullet holes. We are flying and firing close behind him. The entire *staffel* is a body subject to his will. And this is as it should be.

He leaves off the road and begins to climb. We follow. At five hundred meters we head home and land at about one o'clock. It was Richthofen's third sortie of the morning.

As my machine touches down, he is already standing on the airstrip. He comes toward me with a smile playing around his thin lips.

"Do you always bring them down with frontal attacks, Udet?" he asks. There is a hint of approval in his tone.

"I have had repeated success that way," I say as offhandedly as I can manage.

He grins again and turns to go. "By the way, you can take charge of Jasta 11 starting tomorrow," he says over his shoulder.

I already knew that I was to receive command of a *staffel* but the form of the announcement comes as somewhat of a surprise. Scholtz slaps me on the back. "Boy, are you in with the *Rittmeister*."

"You couldn't prove it by me," I reply a bit grumbly.

But this is the way it is. One must get used to the fact that his approval will always come in an objective manner without the least trace of sentiment. He serves the idea of the Fatherland with every fiber of his being and expects nothing less from all his fliers. He judges a man by what he accomplishes to that end and also, perhaps, by his qualities as a comrade. He who passes this judgment, he backs all the way. Whoever fails, he drops without batting an eyelash. Whoever shows lukewarm on a sortie has to leave the group – on the same day.

Richthofen certainly eats, drinks, and sleeps like everyone else. But he does so only to fight. When food supplies run short, he sends Bodenschatz, the very model of an adjutant, to the rear in a squadron hack to requisition what is needed. On these occasions, Bodenschatz takes along an entire collection of autographed photos of Richthofen. "Dedicated to my esteemed fighting companion," read the inscriptions. In the rear area supply rooms these photos are highly valued. At home, in the taverns, they can reduce an entire table round to respectful silence. At the group, however, sausage and ham never run out.

A few delegates from the Reichstag* have announced that they are coming for a visit. Toward evening they arrive in a large limousine. They proceed with great ceremony, filled with the gravity of the moment. One of them even wears tails, and when he bows, they wave like the back feathers of a wagtail. At the supper table they talk so much that a flier can get a toothache.

"When you sit in your machine, flying out to meet the enemy, *Herr Baron . . .*" begins one of them. Richthofen sits there listening with a stony face.

After a bottle of wine they speak of heroic youth and Fatherland. We sit around the table with downcast eyes. Without finding the words, we feel that such things should not be overly much talked about. Then the gentlemen are shown to their sleeping quarters. They sleep in the small, corrugated shacks, just like the rest of us. In this way they'll be able to report their impressions from up front back home.

We stand around in groups until the lights are dimmed behind the small windows. "Actually," says Maushacke, called "Mousetooth," "we should give them an opportunity to experience a little more of the war, since they're only going to be here until tomorrow." Scholtz winks with his right eye and says laconically: "Air raid," nothing else. We understand at once.

A ladder is brought and carefully placed against the hut in which the delegates are sleeping. Silent as a cat, Wolff clambers up to the chimney with Very pistols and blank detonating ammunition, called fliers' fards.

* *German parliament*

From the interior of the hut comes a rattling, crackling, and the hollow bang of a detonation. Immediately after, a lot of shouting. The moon is full. We stand in the dark shade of the other huts as the door opens and three shapes in flapping white nightshirts emerge. The captain laughs until tears run down his cheeks. "Aerial attack! Back into the huts," thunders a stentorian voice out of the night, and the three shapes disappear behind the door again at a dead run.

Next morning, they are in a hurry to go on. They aren't even having breakfast with us. We continue to laugh for a long time. Fun is thinly sown out here, and once a prank hits the bull's-eye, we continue to laugh for a long time. Even later, near the end of the war, when we fought like drowning swimmers, this did not change.

I think of our prisoner in Bernes. Lothar von Richthofen, the captain's brother, has brought down another one. He's an English major, and he came down just alongside our encampment. There is no infantry near, so we keep the prisoner with us.

At supper, he appears at the casino with Richthofen and is presented to everyone. He's a long drink of water, a bit fancy, but sporting in appearance. He affects a courteous reserve; in short, a gentleman. We talk about horses, dogs, and airplanes. We don't talk of the war. The Englishman is our guest, and we don't want to give him the impression that he is being pumped for information.

In the middle of the conversation he whispers to his neighbor, then he rises and walks out.

Lothar looks after him, a bit worried.

"Where is he going?"

" 'I beg your pardon, where is the W.C.?' he asked," replies Mousetooth.

For a moment there is an embarrassed silence. The little hut in question is almost three minutes distant at the end of the ravine in which the camp is located. Beyond it are the woods. It will not be difficult for an athlete to reach freedom from there.

There are conflicting opinions. Maushacke, the well-fed Brunswicker, is the most enterprising. He wants to go out and stand alongside the Englishman. This could be done without too much ado. But Lothar disagrees. "We have treated the man as a guest thus far and he has done nothing to cast doubt on his good manners." But the tension remains. After all, we are responsible for the prisoner. If he gets away, there'll be hell to pay.

Someone steps to the window to look after the Englishman. In seconds six or eight are grouped around him. I'm there too. The Englishman walks across the open ground in long strides. He stops, lights a cigarette, and looks around. All of us immediately sink into a deep knee bend. Our hospitality is sacred, and our suspicion might offend him.

He disappears behind the pineboards of the outhouse. The boards don't reach to the ground, and we can see his brown boots. This is reassuring.

But Mauschacke's suspicions are awakened.

"Boys," he yaps almost breathlessly, "he no longer stands in his boots. He has gone over the rear wall in his stocking feet and is off and gone. The boots couldn't stand like this at all, if . . ."

He demonstrates to how the boots should be deployed during this kind of business.

The Englishman reappears from behind the wall. Bent low, we creep back to our seats. As he re-enters, we talk of horses, dogs, and airplanes.

"I would never forgive myself for disappointing such hosts," says the English major with a small smile around the corners of his mouth. We thank him seriously and ceremoniously.

Next morning, a short, bushy-bearded reservist calls for the prisoner, who turns around often to wave at us.

Five days later Meyer brings curious news from Ghent. An Englishman has overpowered his guard and escaped in a German uniform. From the toilet of a moving express train. His guard was found there, locked in.

"Was it a major?" asks Mousetooth excitedly.

"Are you clairvoyant?" asks Meyer. "It sure was, an Air Force major."

"So, he used the W.C. after all," shouts Mousetooth.

Meyer looks around with surprise. We all laugh until our jaws ache.

Sometimes we fly alone, sometimes with the entire *staffel*, but we fly every day. Almost every day brings a fight. On March 28 I am under way with Gussmann. A patrol toward Albert. It is afternoon, and the sun already stands in the west. Its glaring light bites at the eyes. From time to time, the light must be screened off with the thumb so that the horizon may be searched for the enemy. Otherwise you'll be surprised. The late Guynemer has taught his lessons to the entire front. Suddenly, an Englishman is above us anyway. He comes down on Gussmann, who avoids him by diving. A hundred meters below I see them maneuvering around. I watch for a spot where I can take the Englishman without hitting Gussmann.

I lift my head for a moment and see a second Englishman making for me. He is barely 150 meters off. At eighty meters he opens fire. It is impossible to avoid him, so I go straight toward him. Tack . . . tack . . . tack bellows mine at him, tack . . . tack . . . tack bellows his back at me.

We are still twenty meters apart, and it looks as though we will ram each other in another second. Then, a small movement, and he barely skims over me. His propwash shakes me, and the smell of castor oil flows past me.

I make a tight turn. "Now begins the dogfight," I think. But he has also turned, and again we come at each other, firing like two tournament knights with lances at rest. This time I fly over him.

Another bank. Again, he is straight across from me, and once more we go for each other. The thin, white trails of the tracers hang in the air like curtains. He skims over me with barely a hand's width to spare . . . "8224" it says on his fuselage in black numerals.

The fourth time. I can feel my hands getting damp. That fellow over there is a man who is fighting the fight of his life. Him or me . . . one of us has to go . . . there is no other way. For the fifth time! The nerves are taut to the bursting point, but the brain works coldly and clearly. This time the decision must fall. I line him up in my sights and go for him. I am resolved not to give an inch.

A flash of memory! I saw a dogfight at Lens. Two machines went for each other and collided head on. The fuselages went down in a ball of metal, fused together, and the wings continued on alone for quite a piece before they fluttered to the ground.

We come at each other like mad boars. If he keeps his nerve, we will both be lost!

Then, he turns off to avoid me. At this moment he is caught by my burst. His aircraft rears, turns on its back, and disappears in a gigantic crater. A fountain of earth, smoke. . . . Twice I circle around the impact area. Field gray shapes are standing below, waving at me, shouting.

I fly home, soaked through and through, and my nerves are still vibrating. At the same time, there is a dull, boring pain in my ears.

I have never thought about the opponents I have brought down. He who fights must not look at the wounds he makes. But this time I want to know who the other guy was. Toward evening, at dusk, I drive off. A field hospital is close to where I shot him down, and they will have probably brought him there.

I ask for the doctor. His white gown shines ghostly in the glaring light of the carbide lamp. The pilot had received a head shot and died instantaneously. The doctor hands me his wallet. Calling cards: Lieutenant Maasdorp, Ontario RFC 47." A picture of an old woman and a letter. "You mustn't fly so many sorties. Think of your father and me."

A medic brings me the number of the aircraft. He had

cut it out, and it is covered with a fine spray of blood flecks. I drive back to the *staffel*. One must not think about the fact that a mother will cry for every man one brings down.

During the following days, the ear pains become worse. It is as though one were chiseling and boring within my head. One April 6. I bring down another one. A Sopwith Camel taken out of the middle of an enemy gaggle. It is my twenty-fourth victory.

As I land, I am so overcome by pain I can hardly walk. Richthofen stands on the airstrip, and I stumble past him without salute toward the quarters.

We only have a hospital corpsman. The group has not yet been authorized a doctor. The corpsman is a nice, heavyset guy, but I don't have too much faith in his medical competence. He digs around my ear with his instruments so I think he wants to saw open my head. "The back of the ear is filled with pus," he finally pronounces.

The door opens, and the captain enters.

"Udet, what's the matter with you?" he asks. The corpsman explains.

The captain pats me on the shoulder: "Now be gone with you, Udet."

I protest: "Maybe it'll go away."

But he cuts me off: "You'll take off tomorrow. Out here you have to be healthy."

It is hard for me to leave my new *staffel*, to interrupt my success. He knows this, because we all more or less believe in the Rule of the Series.* Because of this he escorts me to the two-seater himself next morning. He stands on the airstrip and waves at me with his cap. His blond hair glistens in the sun.

The train arrives in Munich early in the morning. The city is still asleep, the streets are almost empty, the stores

---

* *That any break in a run of victories ended one's luck.*

closed, and only here or there the snarl of shades being drawn up. I amble along Kaufingerstrasse, past Stachus. "Home again," I think, "back home." But the feeling of home, the warm familiarity with the things about, still eludes me. A city at dawn is as remote as a person asleep.

I go into a cigarette shop and phone my father at his office. In spite of the early hour, he is already there. He holds much store in always being the first in the office.

"Ernie," he says, and I hear him take a few deep breaths, "Ernie, you are here?"

Then we arrange not to let mother know and that I will call for him at the factory shortly before lunchtime. First, I want to see a doctor.

It is our old family doctor, and he receives me with a booming hello. With many, this may be a professional touch, but with him it comes from the bottom of his big generous heart. Then he examines me and becomes serious.

"Finished with flying, young man," he says, "your eardrum is gone and the inner ear infected."

"That's impossible." In spite of all efforts I can't prevent my voice from shaking.

"Well," he pats me on the shoulder, "perhaps Uncle Otto can patch this thing together again. It would be better if we would stay on the ground, though."

The visit has depressed me. On the way to my father, I can't shake my thoughts. No more flying – that can't be so. This would be like putting black glasses on me, to let me wander around for the rest of my life. Then it's better to see for a few more years and then be blind forever. I resolve to follow the advice of the doctor only so long as I decide it is best for me as far as I am concerned.

And then I meet my father. As soon as I step into his office, he comes out from behind his desk and toward me in big strides. "Boy, my dear boy," he says and stretches both hands out to me. For a moment we stand and look at each other, and then he speaks, a bit breathlessly.

So Sergeant Barlet's Winchester, a bit of booty, had

reached him safely and he had already taken it hunting twice.

How simple it is for men in France. They know no embarrassment when they say hello or good-bye. They embrace and press bearded kisses into each other's face, regardless of where they walk or stand. I have often observed this in railroad stations. We sit across from each other, separated by the desktop. "By the way, you wrote me the other day about a Caudron you couldn't bring down. Maybe the machine was armored?"

I shake my head.

"But, yes, you wouldn't know," he continues intently. "I thought we should also armor our planes, at least the cockpit and the motor. Then the greatest danger for the pilot would be alleviated."

I disagree. For the artillery "rabbits" this may be all right, but for a fighter it would be completely out of the question. With a crate thus armored, one certainly couldn't climb above one thousand meters.

"That doesn't matter. The main business is the safety of the pilot."

"But Dad," I say a bit loftily, "what strange ideas you have about flying."

The enthusiastic zeal in his face flags. "Yes, you are probably right," he says in a tired voice, and at the same moment I feel a rueful shame come up within me. How little I understood him. The armor had been forged in his heart to protect me, and I had tossed it onto the scrap heap without even looking at it.

"At Krupp's they are supposedly trying out a new light metal that is bulletproof," I say in an attempt to pick up the lost thread, but he waves me off: "Let it lie, son. Let's call Mother to let her know I'm bringing a guest so she'll set an extra place on the dinner table."

And then we are home. Father walks into the room ahead of me. Mother is setting the table. I hear the clatter of the silver and then her voice: "Did you read the Army report? Our Ernie has shot down his twenty-fourth."

I can no longer hold back. I run into the room. She throws the silver onto the table, and we are in each other's arms. Then she takes hold of my head and holds me at arm's length: "Sick, son?"

"Oh, only a little bit in the ears."

She calms down immediately. This is singular about her: She is absolutely certain that nothing untoward is going to happen to me in this war, and she insists upon this with a certainty as though God had made her a personal promise, sealed with a handshake. Sometimes it makes me smile, sometimes I am touched by the innocent trust in her belief, but slowly her confidence crosses over to me, and I often believe myself that the bullet has not been cast for me this time.

We eat. In between she plies me with questions, and I answer with discretion. I don't speak of my fight with Maasdorp. I don't want to disquiet father, but I am also held back by an unaccountable aversion. Across sauer-braten and dumplings I cannot speak of a man who was all man with a hero's heart and who fell through my doing.

Yes, now I am home. One is immersed into this feeling like a warm bath. Everything relaxes, one sleeps late, eats much, and gets spoiled. I rarely go to town during the first days. What should I do there? My buddies are in the Army, many already dead, and I don't feel like strolling among strangers.

But I should really go see old Bergen. But I dread this visit. The old man is said to have become a depressive since he received the news of his son Otto's crash. What can I say to console him? It is easier to fight than to stand by idly to look at the wounds wrought by the war.

I have to go to the doctor every day. He is not very happy with the healing process. I let him talk now; it no longer touches me like it did the first time. One morning, just as I return from one of my visits, I meet Lo* in the Hofgarten. We had known each other from the old days as

* *An old girlfriend of Udet; he painted her name on his successive Fokker triplanes.*

youngsters know one another. We had danced together a few times and had been on picnics in company with others.

We walk along together. In her delicately patterned silk dress she looks as though she had blossomed just this morning. When one looks at her, one can hardly believe that there can be such a thing as war. But then she tells me that she is working as an auxiliary nurse in an Army hospital. In her station lies a man with a bullet in his spine who has been dying for months. Every few weeks, his relatives make a long trip to see him, take leave of him, and he continues to live on. But he must die, so all the doctors say.

She looks at me with surprise, as I interrupt her curtly: "Wouldn't you rather talk about something else?"

For a while she is offended. She pushes out her lower lip and looks like a child who just had a chocolate bar taken away from it. In front of her house we make up and make a date for an evening at the Ratskeller.

In the afternoon I go to Bergen's. The maid leads me into the living room where old Bergen sits behind a newspaper. He is all by himself. Hans and Claus are in the field, and his wife died a long time ago. He lets the paper sink and looks at me over his pince-nez. His face has become startlingly old and withered, his Van Dyke hangs like a snowy icicle.

How helpless is one before the pain of another. "I wanted to . . ." I stammer . . . "because of Otto . . ."

"Let it be, Ernst, you wanted to look up Otto once more." He gets up and shakes my hand. "Come."

He opens the door and precedes me up the stairs. We stand in Otto's room, the little mansard Otto occupied as a student.

"So," says old Bergen with a flitting wave of the hand, "you can see everything here."

Then he turns around and walks out. His footfall diminishes down the stairs. I am alone with Otto.

In the little room, everything is as it was then. On the chest and on the book shelves stand model airplanes that

Otto had built himself. They look beautiful, these models.
All the types known at that time, reproduced to the most
minute detail. But when they flew, they fell like stones.
That was ten years ago.

I step up to the children's desk with the green, ink-
spotted cover and fold up the top. They are still there, the
composition books, the diary of the Aero Club Munich,
1909. Its members were between ten and thirteen years
old. Every Wednesday there was a model building group
in our attic, every Saturday a big airplane meet by the
Stadtbach or the Isar. Otto's planes were always the most
beautiful, but mine, ugly sparrows though they were, flew
farthest. Somehow, I had the knack. And in his neat,
child's handwriting he had noted down everything in his
capacity as secretary of the club. "the aviator, *Herr* Ernst
Udet, was awarded first prize for the successful channel
crossing of his model U-11" it says there, because my type
had gotten across the Isar without accident.

Everything is so neatly placed, as though he had arranged everything before taking his final leave. There are
letters, all the letters I had written to him, packed in small
bundles and marked with the year they were written. On
top is the last, unopened. In it, there is news that I have
finally succeeded in getting him released for my *staffel*.
The letter closes: "Hurrah, Otto!"

There are the drawings. He always did the right half, I
the left. The photographs all are there, beginning with
those from earliest childhood. He has even saved the ones
from the "Meet at Niederschau." I jumped with the first
glider constructed by the Aero Club and cracked up. The
bird broke its beak and Willi Goetz, our chairman, informed the people of Niederschau that the ground mag-
netism in the area was too strong for flying. Then, group
shots from the first days of dancing school loves, then the
war, motorcyclists, the first flying suits, after the first
victory. Under each photo the date and in neat lettering
the caption in white ink. He had lived my life with me.

There is something strange about the friendship of

boys. We would have rather bitten our tongues than to admit even by a single word that we cared for each other. Only now do I see it all before me.

I close the desk and go down the stairs. Old Bergen again sits behind his paper. He gets up and shakes my hand; there is no pressure, no warmth.

"If you want some of Otto's things, Ernst," he says, "take what you like. He liked you most of all his friends."

He turns away and begins to clean his pince-nez. I have none, and a few tears run across my face. I stand in the hallway for a while before I step out into the street.

I was twenty-one then, and Otto was my best friend.

In the evening I meet Lo at the Ratskeller. I wear "civvies" because I want to forget the war for an evening. But Lo feels hurt. I don't look sufficiently heroic.

We eat tough, stringy veal and large, bluish potatoes that look as though they were anemic and had spent too much time in the water. Only the wine has ripe sweetness and gives no indication of the war.

An old lady comes by with roses. Lo glances sideways at the flowers. "Leave them be," I say in a low voice, "they're all wired anyhow."

But the old one has heard me; she puts down her basket and plants herself squarely in front of us.

"This I like fine," she shrieks in a broad Bavarian dialect and stems her arms into her hips. "Such a fine little snot sits around, all dolled up, and wants to take the bread out of the mouth of an old woman. In the trenches, that's where you belong, young man, that much I tell you."

People at the neighboring tables, their attention attracted by the old lady's clamor, are looking at us. This would be pretty embarrassing if I were a dodger but, since I'm not, it amuses me, but Lo has blushed to the roots of her hair.

"Well," I say, "so give me a couple of bundles."

The transformation is miraculous. Her ire has passed with the speed of a theater storm, and her face is suffused with sweetness and courtesy. She hastily fishes around among her bundles of roses.

"Never mind me, young man," she babbles on, "anyone can see you are still much too young to go out. I just let my temper run away with me. All you have to do is look to see," she says, turning to the people at the surrounding tables, "any child can tell that this boy just celebrated his confirmation."

I wave her off. Lo has an ominous wrinkle between her eyebrows.

"Just confirmed," she snaps.

I reach for her small, sun-tanned hand, lying on the white tablecloth.

"You know," I say, "just once, I would like to be alone with you, away from everything." It is an attack straight out of the sun. She is so surprised, I can almost read the thoughts behind the round, childlike forehead.

"We would have to drive out," I said, "somewhere in the country. Perhaps we could go to Lake Starnberg; Gustav Otto has invited me. Perhaps we could also go farther up into the mountains. We could be free and unencumbered and enjoy nature, as though we were in another world."

At first she smiles, then she purses her lips.

"But we could hardly do this. What would my parents say?"

"Please forgive me," I say, "but I have left my manners in the field."

We go. It is a humid night, and the wind rustles the treetops. We stop under a lantern, and she pats me on the arm.

"Please don't be angry."

I shrug: "Angry? No!"

But I feel something is amiss. Out in the field, everything has changed. Things that were once important are no longer of any value. Other things as important as life itself. But back here, life has stood still. I can't put it into words, but suddenly I feel homesick for my buddies.

We stop at the garden gate in front of Lo's home. She lingers, but I quickly kiss her hand quite correctly and make a fast getaway.

On the next day I go out by myself. I'm in a rotten mood. I can't get back to the front. When I brought up the subject, the doctor read me the riot act. But back here I feel lost. When I come home, my parents are already asleep.

On one evening, however, all windows are still alight. I run up the stairs as the door opens and my mother stands on the jamb, her face red and shining with happiness. She is waving a piece of paper in her hand, a telegram from the group, advising that I had been awarded the *Pour le Mérite*.

I am happy, really happy, even though it doesn't come as a complete surprise. After a certain number of victories, the *Pour le Mérite* comes – it is almost automatic. But the real joy is that which reflects from my mother. She is beside herself and has kept everyone up to wait for me, even my little sister. She has cut a medal out of paper and now hangs it around my neck with a piece of yarn.

My father shakes hands with me. "Congratulations, son," he says, nothing else. But he has opened a bottle of Stein-berger Kabinett, 1884 vintage, one of the family heirlooms. This says more than words. The wine is golden yellow and flows like oil. Its fragrance permeates the entire room. We touch glasses.

"To peace, a good peace," says father.

Next morning, in bed, I think of Lo. If I had my *Pour le Mérite*, I would make a date with her, as if nothing had happened. I jump out of bed, get dressed, and go into town.

I go to an orders jeweler on Theatinerstrasse. The salesman shrugs his shoulders: "*Pour le Mérite?* – No! Insufficient demand." Too bad. I thought I could surprise Lo. But it will be at least two weeks before the medal will reach me from my unit. Slowly I amble along the street, mechanically returning salutes to soldiers and officers passing by. There comes a naval officer; it is Wenninger, commander of a submarine. At his throat, a *Pour le Mérite* glistens in the sun.

It is the inspiration of the moment. I go toward him, saluting, and ask: "Excuse me, but do you per chance happen to have a second *Pour le Mérite?*"

He gives me a wide-eyed look, and I explain. He laughs loudly and embarrassingly long. No, he doesn't have a second one, but he gives me the address of a store in Berlin where I can order one, by telegram if I so desire. I thank him, a little chagrined, and salute formally.

Two days later, the order arrives from Berlin. It lies like a star in a red velvet case. I give Lo a call to make a date. She laughs and accepts at once. Waiting for her, I parade up and down in front of her house. Then she comes and spots the order around my neck at once. "Ernie," she shouts, and comes hopping along like a bird trying to take off. In the middle of the street, in front of everyone, she throws here arms around my neck and kisses me.

It is a bright, sunny, spring morning. Side by side, we walk slowly and loose-jointed toward the center of town. When soldiers pass, they salute especially sharply, and most turn around. Lo counts: Out of forty-three, twenty-seven have turned around. We walk along Theatinerstrasse, the main artery of Munich, from which life seems to radiate and where it returns. In front of the Residenz* stands the sentry, a short reservist with bristling beard and button nose. Suddenly, with a voice of proportions unexpected from such a small chest, he shouts:

"The Guard, fall out!"

The men come piling out. "Fall in," commands the officer. "Left shoulder arms! *Achtung!* Present arms!"

I look around. There is no one else near. Then I remember my *Pour le Mérite*. I am almost past when I return the salute. It comes off a bit small, too hasty and without dignity.

---

* *The King of Bavaria's palace.*

"What was that all about?" asks Lo, looking at me with big eyes.

"God," I say loftily, "before a *Pour le Mérite*, the Guard has to fall out."

"You're kidding!"

"No, I'm not!"

"Good, then we'll try once more."

At first I object a little, but I finally give in. After all, I'm still not all that certain myself.

This time we are well prepared and enter into this affair with good posture. "Guards, fall out," shouts the sentry. At the same moment Lo hooks into my arm and, with a gracious nod, she troops the short line at my side.

Woman's vanity is insatiable. If she had her way, we would spend the rest of the afternoon chasing the Guard in and out. But I go on strike. The Guard detail is no toy for little girls. Lo pouts.

They are days of blue silk. Never again did I experience such a spring. We meet every day, strolling through the English Garden, drinking tea or going to the theater. The war is far, far away.

CRASHES AND COCKTAILS

JOHN McGAVOCK GRIDER

Grider, whose diary is extracted below, was an American aviator serving with the Royal Flying Corps in France, 1917–18.

November 18th

Cal and I went down to Stamford to spend the day and nearly died laughing. Our stomachs are still sore.

There was a sort of straff going on that day. They had a new C.O. and he was an ex-Guards officer and had a grudge against the Huns and wanted to get on with the war. There were a lot of young English kids that had been there some time swinging the lead and he sent for them all and lined them up. He told them that there was a war on and that pilots were needed badly at the front and that they were all going solo that afternoon. They nearly fainted. Some of them had had less than two hours of air work and none of them had had more than five.

We all went out to the airdrome to see the fun. I guess there were about thirty of them in all. The squadron was equipped with D.H. Sixes which are something like our Curtiss planes except they are slower and won't spin no matter what you do to them.

The first one to take off was a bit uneasy and an

instructor had to taxi out for him. He ran all the way across the field, and it was a big one, and then pulled the stick right back into his stomach. The Six went straight up nose first and stalled and hung on its propeller. Then it did a tail slide right back into the ground.

The next one did better. He got off and zig-zagged a bit but instead of making a circuit he kept straight on. His instructor remarked that he would probably land in Scotland, because he didn't know how to turn.

Another one got off fairly well and came around for his landing. He leveled off and made a beautiful landing – a hundred feet above the ground. He pancaked beautifully and shoved his wheels up thru the lower wings. But the plane had a four-bladed prop on it and it broke off even all around. So the pupil was able to taxi on into the hangar as both wheels had come up the same distance. He was very much pleased with himself and cut off the engine and took off his goggles and stood up and started to jump down to the ground which he thought was about five feet below him. Then he looked down and saw the ground right under his seat. He certainly was shocked.

Another took off fine but he had never been taught to land and he was a bit uncertain about that operation. He had the general idea all right but he forgot to cut off his motor. He did a continuous series of dives and zooms. A couple of instructors sang a dirge for him:

The young aviator lay dying, and as 'neath the wreckage he lay
To the Ak Emmas around him assembled, these last parting words did he say:
"Take the cylinder out of my kidney, the connecting rod out of my brain,
From the small of my back take the crankshaft, and assemble the engine again!"

There were a lot more verses but I can't remember them.

We thought sure he was gone but he got out of it all right and made a fairly decent landing but not where he had expected.

The next one didn't know much about landing either. He came in too fast and didn't make the slightest attempt to level off. The result was a tremendous bounce that sent him up a hundred feet. He used his head and put his motor on and went around again. He did that eight times and finally smashed the undercarriage so that next time he couldn't bounce. Then he turned over on his back. The C.O. congratulated him and told him he would probably make a good observer.

They finally all got off and not a one of them got killed. I don't see why not tho. Only one of them got hurt and that was when one landed on top of the other one. The one in the bottom plane got a broken arm. I got quite a thrill out of that.

May 13th

The great McCudden, now Major McCudden, V.C., D.S.O., M.C., E.T.C.,* just back from the front to get decorated again, came into Murray's last night for dinner and, oh, boy, what a riot he caused. All the officers went over to his table to congratulate him and the women – well, they fought to get at him just like they do at a bargain counter back home. He's the hottest thing we have now – 54 Huns, five more than Bishop** and he's just gotten the V.C. and a bar to his D.S.O. He held a regular levee. I think there are only five airmen living that have the V.C. The first thing you have to do to get it is to get killed.

The girl with him thought she was the Queen of Sheba. She started to pretend she didn't know us. I should have reminded her where we met but I didn't. I saved her life once.

Well, I'm not jealous. I'm going to hot myself some day.

* See pp 91–159
** See pp 61–75

I'm either coming out of the war a big man or in a wooden kimono. I know I can fight, I know I can fly, and I ought to be able to shoot straight. If I can just learn to do all three things at once, they can't stop me. And Bishop is going to teach me to do that. I've got to make a name for myself, even if they have to prefix "late" to it.

May 14th

All aboard for France. Our orders have come thru and we leave next Wednesday.

A ferry pilot brought over my new machine day before yesterday and smashed it all to pieces landing. He got tangled up in the wires coming in. So I decided I'd fetch my own service machine and got Springs to fly me over to Brooklands in an Avro yesterday and I flew it back. It certainly is a beauty. I like these 180 Viper Hispanos made by Wolsey much better than the 220 Peugeots. Brooklands used to be an automobile race track but is now the depot and test park for the R.F.C. I saw some of the new experimental planes down there. One was the Snipe, which has the 200 Bentley motor and is going to take the place of the Camel at the front. Another was the Snark which has the big A.B.C. air-cooled radial. It has a wonderful performance but I understand there's some hitch about it. The Salamander and the Hippo and the Bulldog were all there too. The Hippo is a sort of two-seater Dolphin.

I gave my new plane a work-out in the air to-day. It flies hands off; I put it level just off the ground and it did 130. Then I went up high and did a spinning tail slide. Nothing broke so I have perfect confidence in it. I've been cleaning and oiling the machine guns, tuning up the motor and testing the rigging. The best part of it is that it's mine – no one else has ever flown it and no one else ever will. It's painted green and I have named it the Julep and am having one painted on the side of the fusilage. Nigger has the Gin Palace II. and Springs has the Eggnog First.

To-morrow, I've got to synchronize my gun gear, set my sights, swing my compass and then I'm ready.

May 17th

We had a bunch of Brass Hats from the War Office down at Hounslow to-day and we put on an exhibition of formation flying and stunting for them that was pretty good. Nineteen machines in close battle formation are a stirring sight. Everything went off well except Springs's landing. His wheel hit a soft spot and turned him and the other wheel gave way and he turned over on his back and his head was shoved into the mud. He was a great sight when he came walking back to the tarmac where all the generals were standing. He had on slacks and a white shirt and wasn't wearing helmet or goggles and his face and head were all covered with mud. He's got to go over to Brooklands again to-morrow after another plane. I'm going to fly him over in an Avro.

Mrs. Bishop had a lady with her and she invited us to tea with them. We explained that we were all pretty dirty, which we were, but she said to never mind that and come along as we were; so we did. We all went into the squadron office and had tea brought over from the mess. The lady with her proved to be very nice and was very much interested in Americans and America. She was the most patriotic person I've met over here because she was always talking about the King. When I told her how much all the Americans liked serving with the British, she said she was so glad and she knew the King would be delighted to hear it. That sounded a bit far fetched to me. We got on fine with her and we told her some funny stories and she nearly died laughing. We had a taxi waiting for us and offered to take her back to town with us as soon as we got dressed. She said she'd rather take a bus and get the air and it would take her right by the palace. I didn't get that either. As we went out we saw Cunningham-Reed's mother and she nearly broke a leg curtsying and I noticed Mrs. Bishop do the same thing when we left her and took the lady out to the bus. I asked Cunningham-Reed why the gymnastics and he told me it was for royalty. I asked him wherefore and he told me the lady was Princess Mary Louise. All three of us have been trying to remember whether we cracked any jokes about the King or not.

May 25th

France!

Here's where we sober up and get down to real serious work.

Here I am at the front, the victim of many emotions. We had a fine send off and come what may, nothing can ever take away from me the joy that has been mine.

We left Hounslow about eleven and our take-off was a scream. Billy and Babs were there over at one end, Dora and Lillian and Cecil were also present in another group. Nigger's fiancée was there with her family, and the Princess was there with Mrs. Bishop. We nearly broke our necks running from one group to another and pretending we didn't know anybody else. Then the staff arrived from the American Headquarters. We hadn't expected them – Col. Morrow, Col. Mitchell, Jeff Dwyer and a couple of others. We tried to get in the ground but couldn't find a hole.

The Princess was very cordial. She said she told the King about us and that he was very pleased to hear that American pilots were so enthusiastic about serving with the R.F.C. and that he hoped some day he would have the opportunity to decorate one of us. Mrs. Bishop made us promise to stick to the major and not let a Hun get on his tail.

That was one morning when I would rather not have been so conspicuous. Our style was badly cramped. Col. Morrow was very nice and spoke of the time I had come to him to enlist and only had one letter of recommendation. But that was from the ex-secretary of war so he wrote the other one for me himself.

Dora was much interested in our silk skull caps that we wear under our fur helmets. She wanted to know whose stocking mine was made from.

All nineteen machines were arranged in position for taking off in formation and the engines warmed up. The major's machine was out front in the center and the three flights arranged in a V on each side and in back of him. We'd practised getting off that way and it was all right as long as no machine got directly behind another and hit the backwash.

Bishop lined us up before the crowd and some general made us a little speech. Then Bishop gave us our final instructions. He told us that Lympe would be our first stop and to be sure and take a good look at the wind sock and to land squarely into the wind. But he didn't call it a sock. He called it by the name we always call it on the field when there are no ladies or gentlemen present. He turned red and the ladies lowered their parasols and he ran and jumped in his machine and we all took off together. I got in Spring's backwash and nearly cracked up getting off.

Cal didn't get far. He disappeared from the formation about fifteen minutes after we took off, and didn't get here until today. He had an air bubble in his water line and he had to land in a field south of London to let his motor cool off and get some more water. He got down all right and got out of the field again and decided he'd stop at Croydon and get his radiator drained. He made a bad landing at Croydon and crashed. So he went back to London for another night and got a new machine from Brooklands the next day.

We stopped at Lympe near Folkestone for lunch and Brown cracked up there. We took off after lunch and Canning cracked up on the beach when his motor conked. We landed at Marquis near Boulogne, for tea. We had a beautiful trip across the channel. It was as clear as a bell and we crossed at eight thousand feet. My motor was missing a little and I kept picking out destroyers and trawlers below to land beside in case it gave out. MacDonald crashed at Marquis when he landed short in the rough and turned over and Cunningham-Reed washed out his plane by pancaking.

On the way across, Springs motioned for me to come up close to him. I flew up to his wing tip and he took out his flask and drank my health. I didn't have a thing with me but a bottle of champagne and that was in my tool box and I couldn't get to it.

We arrived at our airdrome about six.

June 2nd

There are six machines in a flight. Nigger leads and MacGregor and Cal are on his right, behind and a little above. Springs and I are on the left and Thompson is in the center in the space between Cal and me. We fly in the form of a triangle with the back corners high. MacGregor is deputy flight commander and takes command in case anything happens to Nigger. We fly pretty close together and have a set of signals. If Nigger is going to turn sharp, he drops his wing on that side. If he is going to dive steep, he holds up his arm. If he wants us to come up close or wants to call our attention to something he shakes both wings. If it's a Hun, he shakes his wings and points and fires his guns. If he means "yes" he bobs his nose up and down and if he means "no" he shakes his wings. If we see a Hun and he doesn't, we fire our guns and fly up in front and point. We fly at three-quarters throttle so we can always pull up. If he has trouble and wants us to go on, he fires a red light from his Very pistol. If he wants us to follow him out of a fight, he fires a white light. If he wants to signal the other flights, he fires a green light.

MacGregor has been out before. He was out on Pups for six months when they were service machines. He came over with the Australian infantry. Thompson has been out before too. He was out last fall on Camels but crashed too many of them.

We've been doing rather well. We have a score board in

the mess and there's a big red 6 staring me in the face now. We don't count any unless they go down in flames or break up in the air or someone sees them crash. The wing commander, Col. Cunningham, is over here all the time and is tickled to death because all this is voluntary for we aren't supposed to get into action the first two weeks. I'm going to get a Hun this week if I pull a wing off in the attempt.

June 6th

I went up and had a private battle of my own. I saw a Hun two-seater away the hell and gone over Roulers. I chased him a bit but couldn't catch him. Then about three Archie batteries opened up on me! The whole sky turned black. A barrage grew up in front of me like a bed of mushrooms and I swung around just in time to avoid it. Scared? Of course, I was scared. There were heavy clouds below me and I didn't know where the lines were. My compass was spinning around so fast that I couldn't tell anything from it. Then I forgot whether the sun set in the east or the west and had to stop and figure it out. Every time Archie would get close to me, my heart would skip a beat. It has an awful sound when it's close, like a giant clapping his hands and it has a sort of metallic click. So I put my nose down and ran for it. First Archie would be 'way behind me and then he'd get 'way in front and I'd zoom and he'd be a mile away. I crossed the lines down below Wipers where I didn't know the country and for a few minutes I was lost. I got out my maps and found a town on the map that I located on the ground and then I came on back by Bergues.

June 10th

What a nightmare this war is! I'm beginning to understand the term "Anti-Christ." Both the Allies and the Germans pray to the same God for strength in their slaughter! What a joke it must seem to Him to see us puny insignificant mortals proclaiming that we are fighting for Him and that He is helping us. Think of praying to the God of Peace for help in War! The heavens must shake with divine mirth.

I can't kick. It's the best war I know anything about. It's been worth a lot to me so far. Sooner or later I'll join the company of the elect but I want to get a Hun first. I want to get one sure one – a flamer or a loose-winged flop. I know how hard it is, but unless I get one, the government will simply be out all it cost to train me. If I get one, it'll be an even break. If I get two, I'll be a credit instead of a debit on the books.

June 30th

We got into a dogfight this morning with the new brand of Fokkers* and they certainly were good. They had big red stripes on the fusilage diagonally so they must be Richthofen's old circus. There were five of us and we ran into five Fokkers at fifteen thousand feet. We both started climbing, of course. And they outclimbed us. We climbed up to twenty thousand five hundred and couldn't get any higher. We were practically stalled and these Fokkers went right over our heads and got between us and the lines. They didn't want to dogfight but tried to pick off our rear men. Inglis and Cal were getting a pretty good thrill when we turned back and caught one Hun napping. He half rolled slowly and we got on his tail. Gosh, it's unpleasant fighting at that altitude. The slightest movement exhausts you, your engine has no pep and splutters; it's hard to keep a decent formation, and you lose five hundred feet on a turn. The other Huns came in from above and it didn't take us long to fight down to twelve thousand. We put up the best fight of our lives but these Huns were just too good for us. Cal got a shot in his radiator and went down and Webster had his tail plane shot to bits and his elevator

* *The Fokker DVII, max speed 124 mph, armed with 2 Spandau 7.92mm machine guns.*

control shot away. He managed to land with his stabilizer wheel but cracked up. I don't know what would have happened if some Dolphins from 84 hadn't come up and the Huns beat it. I think we got one that went down in a spin while Cal was shooting at it but we couldn't see it crash.

I got to circling with one Hun, just he and I, and it didn't take me long to find out that I wasn't going to climb above this one. He began to gain on me and then he did something I've never heard of before. He'd be circling with me and he'd pull around and point his nose at me and open fire and just hang there on his prop and follow me around with his tracer. All I could do was to keep on turning the best I could. If I'd straightened out he'd have had me cold as he already had his sights on me. If I had tried to hang on my prop that way, I'd have gone right into a spin. But this fellow just hung right there and sprayed me with lead like he had a hose. They have speeded up guns too. All I could do was to watch his tracer and kick my rudder from one side to the other to throw his aim off. This war isn't what it used to be. Nigger has noted the improvement in the Huns and is awful thoughtful.

We went to see Springs this afternoon and he seems to be doing all right. He's got lips like a nigger minstrel's and a mouthful of thread and a couple of black eyes. We took him a couple of bottles of champagne but he didn't need it as they serve it to him there. Things have been sort of quiet at the front lately in this sector and there were only three of them in there. One is a brigadier general who had been wounded seven times before this last shot in his leg. He and Springs were full of champagne and have a bar rigged up in a tent outside. The third is a Chink from a labor battalion who has been parted from his appendix forcibly.

There are about eighteen nurses there and it is the custom for all the nurses from the Duchess down to walk by and ask each patient how he feels each morning. The general says if they just had short skirts on and would whistle he'd applaud and join the chorus. Spring's face is going to be all right because they sewed it up from the inside.

Mac made a date to call on a pretty little nurse. That boy is a fast worker. I'll bet he gets sick in a few days.

July 20th

Mannock* is dead, the greatest pilot of the war. But his death was worthy of him. Inglis had been doing a lot of fighting but had never gotten a Hun. But he tried hard and Mannock told him that he would take him out alone and get him a Hun. So just the two of them went out late in the afternoon. Mannock picked up a two-seater over Estaires and went down after him. Mannock has a special method of attacking a two-seater. He takes them from the front at an angle and then goes under them if he misses his first burst. It is very hard to do but is unquestionably the best method. Instead of going under and getting him for himself, he held his fire and turned the Hun and held him for Inglis. Inglis got him and they started back but they were down low. Mannock got hit by machine gun fire from the ground just like Richthofen and dove right on into the ground. Inglis went back and flew right down to the ground and saw the wreck and is sure he's dead.

August 11th

Again I've got that feeling, gee, it's great to be alive! The last three days have been particularly strenuous and eventful. Ordinarily I wouldn't be able to sleep at all, but I'm so tired that I slept like a baby last night. And I'm getting so bored at being shot at that I don't bother to dodge any more. I sat up in the middle of Archie bursts

* *Edward "Mick" Mannock, born 1887, killed in action on 26 July, not 20 July as in the diary. The highest scoring English fighter ace of WWI, with 61 aerial victories (and perhaps as high as 73, since he frequently shared "kills" or failed to claim them).*

yesterday for five minutes, yawned and refused to turn until they knocked me about a hundred feet. I used to be scared to death of Archie and gunfire fire from the ground. Now it almost fails to excite even my curiosity.

Day before yesterday we had four dogfights. In the morning we attacked five Huns. I paired off with a Fokker on my level and we maneuvered for a couple of minutes trying to get on each other's tail. I finally got inside of him, put one hundred rounds into him and he went down out of control. Another one was after me by that time and we had quite a scrap but he made the fatal blunder of reversing his bank and I got on his tail and pumped about two hundred rounds into him. I couldn't see what happened to him as another one was coming down on me from above. This one should have gotten me but he didn't. He had every advantage and one of my guns jammed. I was down on the carpet by that time and had to come back low for five miles with this Hun picking at me while I was trying to clear the stoppage and do a little serious dodging.

Yesterday we did ground straffing down south. That's my idea of a rotten way to pass the time. Orders came thru after dinner and all night I felt just like I did that night before the operation. I shivered and sweated all night. I took off with four little twenty-pound bombs strung under my fusilage; then we flew over about four miles across the lines at three thousand feet. Nigger gave the signal when he saw what we were after which was Hun transport and we split up and went down on the carpet. All the machine guns on the ground opened up and sprayed us with tracer and a few field guns took a crack at us but we got thru somehow and dropped our messages with pretty good effect and shot up everything we could see on the ground. I saw what looked like a battery and emptied my guns into it and then chased home zigzagging furiously. As soon as we got back, they told us to get ready to go out and do it again. So over we went and this time I saw a road packed with gun limbers. I dropped my bombs on them and then started raking the road with my guns. My bombs hit right on the side of the road and everything scattered. Two planes were shot up pretty badly and A flight lost a man. Don't know what happened to him.

Then we did a high patrol with A flight. They got after a two-seater and there were some Fokkers up above them that didn't see us on account of the clouds. We went down after them and three of them pulled up to fight us. Inglis and I took them on and the rest went on down. I got into a regular duel with one of them and we fought down from eight thousand to about fifteen hundred. He did a half roll and I did a stall turn above him and dropped right onto his tail. I'd have gotten him if the other one hadn't come on down after me. Then it was my turn to half roll and I was careful to do a good one and not lose any altitude. He half rolled with me a couple of times but the dogfight was working down and he decided to postpone the engagement and dove for home.

Zellers and Dietz and Paskill have been killed.

August 20th

The British seem to be going after the control of the air. So far neither side has ever had the control of the air. First one side and then the other has had the supremacy of the air depending on superiority of planes and pilots but neither side has ever been able to do its air work unmolested or keep the other side from doing theirs. Both sides have accomplished certain things and had to fight constantly to do it. But the British seem to be planning to drive the Huns out of the air by carrying the aerial warfare back to their airdromes. I understand that the Huns have a decided supremacy over the French and Americans. I'd like to get down on the American Front with a British squadron and get some cold meat. I'm tired of having to go so far over. Makes the odds too high against you.

If I was running the war the first thing I would do would be to get control of the air no matter what it cost. That's what's saved England all these centuries – control of the seas. And her fleet is big enough to keep control without fighting. The Air Force would do the same thing.

August 21st

More rumors of more battles. We were in the Folkestone in Boulogne and Henry told us that there is going to be a big push shortly. Push? What's a push to us? That's for the Poor Bloody Infantry to worry over. We push twice a day, seven days in the week. We go over the top between each meal. Oh, yes, the flying corps is the safe place for little Willy – that is as long as he doesn't have to go near the front!

Nigger and I flew up for tea with Springs. He was not too good. He and Bim have had tombstones made for themselves. They are hollow and if they go down on the Hun side, they are to be filled with high explosive and dropped over, if they are killed on this side, they are to be filled with cognac so it will leak on them.

Mac is back with a new version of the widow of Malta.

Hilary Rex has been killed. He was in a fight with a Fokker and his machine was disabled and he had to land. He landed all right and got out of his plane. The Hun dove on him and shot him as he was standing by his plane.

Armstrong is in the hospital with an explosive bullet in his back.

August 27th

We've lost a lot of good men. It's only a question of time until we all get it. I'm all shot to pieces. I only hope I can stick it. I don't want to quit. My nerves are all gone and I can't stop. I've lived beyond my time already.

It's not the fear of death that's done it. I'm still not afraid to die. It's this eternal flinching from it that's doing it and has made a coward out of me. Few men live to know what real fear is. It's something that grows on you, day by day, that eats into your constitution and undermines your sanity. I have never been serious about anything in my life and now I know that I'll never be otherwise again. But my seriousness will be a burlesque for no one will recognize it. Here I am, twenty-four years old, I look forty and I feel ninety. I've lost all interest in life beyond the next patrol. No one Hun will ever get me and I'll never fall into a trap, but sooner or later I'll be forced to fight against odds that are too long or perhaps a stray shot from the ground will be lucky and I will have gone in vain. Or my motor will cut out when we are trench straffing or a wing will pull off in a dive. Oh, for a parachute! The Huns are using them now. I haven't a chance, I know, and it's this eternal waiting around that's killing me. I've even lost my taste for licker. It doesn't seem to do me any good now. I guess I'm stale. Last week I actually got frightened in the air and lost my head. Then I found ten Huns and took them all on and I got one of them down out of control. I got my nerve back by that time and came back home and slept like a baby for the first time in two months. What a blessing sleep is! I know now why men go out and take such long chances and pull off such wild stunts. No discipline in the world could make them do what they do of their own accord. I know now what a brave man is. I know now how men laugh at death and welcome it. I know now why Ball went over and sat above a Hun airdrome and dared them to come up and fight with him. It takes a brave man to even experience real fear. A coward couldn't last long enough at the job to get to that stage. What price salvation now?

No date

The worst thing about this war is that it takes the best. If it lasts long enough the world will be populated by cowards and weaklings and their children. And the whole thing is so useless, so unnecessary, so terrible! Even those that live thru it will never be fit for anything else. Look at what the Civil War did for the South. It wasn't the defeat that wrecked us. It was the loss of half our manhood and the demoralization of the other half. After the war the survivors scattered to the four corners of the earth; they roamed the West; they fought the battles of foreign nations; they became freebooters, politicians, prospectors, gamblers, and those who got over it, good citizens. My great-uncle was a captain in the Confederate Army and served thruout the war. He became a banker, a merchant, a farmer and a good citizen, but he was always a little different from other men and now I know where the difference lay. At the age of seventy he hadn't gotten over those four years of misery and spiritual damnation. My father used to explain to me that he wasn't himself. But he was himself, that was just the trouble with him. The rest were just out of step. My father used to always warn me about licker by telling me that uncle learned to drink in the army and it finally killed him. I always used to think myself that as long as it took forty years to do it, he shouldn't speak disrespectfully of uncle's little weakness. And as the old gentleman picked up stomach trouble from bad food in the campaign of '62, I always had a hunch that perhaps the licker had an unfair advantage of him.

The devastation of the country is too horrible to describe. It looks from the air as if the gods had made a gigantic steam roller, forty miles wide and run it from the coast to Switzerland, leaving its spike holes behind as it went.

I'm sick. At night when the colonel calls up to give us our orders, my ears are afire until I hear what we are to do the next morning. Then I can't sleep for thinking about it all night. And while I'm waiting around all day for the afternoon patrol, I think I am going crazy. I keep watching the clock and figuring how long I have to live. Then I go out to test out my engine and guns and walk around and have a drink and try to write a little and try not to think. And I move my arms and legs around and think that perhaps to-morrow I won't be able to. Sometimes I think I am getting the same disease that Springs has when I get sick at my stomach. He always flies with a bottle of milk of magnesia in one pocket and a flask of gin in the other. If one doesn't help him he tries the other. It gives me a dizzy feeling every time I hear of the men that are gone. And they have gone so fast I can't keep track of them; every time two pilots meet it is only to swap news of who's killed. When a person takes sick, lingers in bed a few days, dies and is buried on the third day, it all seems regular and they pass on into the great beyond in an orderly manner and you accept their departure as an accomplished fact. But when you lunch with a man, talk to him, see him go out and get in his plane in the prime of his youth and the next day someone tells you that he is dead – it just doesn't sink in and you can't believe it. And the oftener it happens the harder it is to believe. I've lost over a hundred friends, so they tell me – I've seen only seven or eight killed – but to me they aren't dead yet. They are just around the corner, I think, and I'm still expecting to run into them any time. I dream about them at night when I do sleep a little and sometimes I dream that someone is killed who really isn't. Then I don't know who is and who isn't. I saw a man in Boulogne the other day that I had dreamed I saw killed and I thought I was seeing a ghost. I can't realize that any of them are gone. Surely human life is not a candle to be snuffed out. The English have all turned spiritualistic since the war. I used to think that was sort of far fetched but now it's hard for me to believe that a man ever becomes even a ghost. I have a sort of a feeling that he stays just, as he is and simply jumps behind a cloud or steps thru a mirror. Springs keeps talking about Purgatory and Hades and the Elysian Fields. Well, we sure are close to something.

When I go out to get in my plane my feet are like lead – I am just barely able to drag them after me. But as soon as I take off I am all right again. That is, I feel all right, tho I know I am too reckless. Last week I actually tried to ram a Hun. I was in a tight place and it was the only thing I could do. He didn't have the nerve to stand the gaff and turned and I got him. I poured both guns into him with fiendish glee and stuck to him tho three of them were on my tail. I laughed at them.

I saw Springs the other day in Boulogne. He said his girl at home sent him a pair of these Ninette and Rintintin luck charms. Since then he's lost five men, been shot down twice himself, lost all his money at blackjack and only gotten one Hun. He says he judges from that that she is unfaithful to him. So he has discarded them and says he is looking for a new charm and that the best one is a garter taken from the left leg of a virgin in the dark of the moon. I know they are lucky but I'd be afraid to risk one. Something might happen to her and then you'd be killed sure. A stocking to tie over my nose and a Columbian half dollar and that last sixpence and a piece of my first crash seem to take care of me all right, tho I am not superstitious.

The diary ends here due to the author's death in combat.

PRISONER OF WAR

JAMES NORMAN HALL

*During World War I "Jimmie" Hall served in both the
French Lafayette Escadrille (which was composed of
American volunteers for the Tricolour) and the 94th
pursuit squadron of the US Army Air Service. He also
found time to write up his aerial exploits for* Atlantic
Monthly. *On May 7th 1918, after scoring six victories,
Hall crash-landed behind German lines when the fabric
on the wing of his Nieuport tore off during a dive. He
escaped with a broken ankle, and saw out the remainder
of the war in a POW camp. A letter of Hall's written
from* Offiziers Kriegsgefangenen Lager, Karlsruhe,
Baden, Deutschland, *is reprinted below.*

July 27 1918

I've been wondering about the ultimate fate of my poor
old "High Adventure"* story, whether it was published
without those long promised concluding chapters which I
really should have sent on had I not had the misfortune to
be taken prisoner. I hope the book has been published,
incomplete as it is. Not that I am particularly proud of it as
a piece of literature!

* *A memoir based on Hall's* Atlantic Monthly *articles.*

I told you briefly, on my card, how I happened to be taken prisoner. We were a patrol of three and attacked a German formation at some distance behind their lines. I was diving vertically on an Albatross when my upper right plane gave way under the strain. Fortunately, the structure of the wing did not break. It was only the fabric covering it, which ripped off in great strips. I immediately turned toward our lines and should have reached them, I believe, even in my crippled condition; but by that time I was very low and under a heavy fire from the ground. A German anti-aircraft battery made a direct hit on my motor. It was a terrific smash and almost knocked the motor out of the frame. My machine went down in a spin and I had another of those moments of intense fear common to the experience of aviators. Well, by Jove! I hardly know how I managed it, but I kept from crashing nose down. I struck the ground at an angle of about 30 degrees, the motor, which was just hanging on, spilled out, and I went skidding along, with the fuselage of the machine, the landing chassis having been snapped off as though the braces were so many toothpicks. One of my ankles was broken and the other one sprained, and my poor old nose received and withstood a severe contact with my wind-shield. I've been in hospital ever since until a week ago, when I was sent to this temporary camp to await assignment to a permanent one. I now hobble about fairly well with the help of a stick, although I am to be a lame duck for several months to come, I believe.

Needless to say, the lot of a prisoner of war is not a happy one. The hardest part of it is, of course, the loss of personal liberty. Oh! I shall know how to appreciate that when I have it again. But we are well treated here. Our quarters are comfortable and pleasant, and the food as good as we have any right to expect. My own experience as a prisoner of war and that of all the Frenchmen and Englishmen here with whom I have talked, leads me to believe that some of those tales of escaped or exchanged prisoners must have been highly imaginative. Not that we

are enjoying all the comforts of home. On the contrary, a
fifteen-cent lunch at a Child's restaurant would seem a
feast to me, and a piece of milk chocolate – are there such
luxuries as chocolate in the world? But for prisoners, I for
one, up to this point, have no complaint to make with
respect to our treatment. We have a splendid little library
here which British and French officers who have preceded
us have collected. I didn't realize, until I saw it, how book-
hungry I was. Now I'm cramming history, biography,
essays, novels. I know that I'm not reading with any
judgment but I'll soon settle down to a more profitable
enjoyment of my leisure. Yesterday and to-day I've been
reading "The Spoils of Poynton," by Henry James. It is
absurd to try cramming these. I've been longing for this
opportunity to read Henry James, knowing that he was
Joseph Conrad's master. "The Spoils of Poynton" has
given me a foretaste of the pleasure I'm to have. A prisoner
of war has his compensations. Here I've come out of the
turmoil of a life of the most intense nervous excitement, a
life lived day to day with no thought of to-morrow, into
this other life of unlimited bookish leisure.

We are like monks in a convent. We're almost entirely out
of touch with the outside world. We hear rumors of what is
taking place at the front, and now and then get a budget of
stale news from newly arrived prisoners. But for all this we
are so completely out of it all that it seems as though the
war must have come to an end. Until now this cloistered
life has been very pleasant. I've had time to think and to
make plans for a future which, comparatively speaking,
seems assured. One has periods of restlessness, of course.
When these come I console myself as best I may. Even for
prisoners of war there are possibilities for quite interesting
adventure, adventure in companionship. Thrown into
such intimate relationships as we are here, and under
these peculiar circumstances, we make rather surprising
discoveries about ourselves and about each other. There
are obvious superficial effects which I can trace back to

causes quite easily. But there are others which have me guessing. By Jove! this is an interesting place! Conrad would find material here which would set him to work at once. I can imagine how he would revel in it.

Well, I'm getting to be a very wise man. I'm deeply learned in many kinds, or, better, phases, of human psychology and I'm increasing my fund of knowledge every day. Therefore, I've decided that, when the war is over, I'll be no more a wanderer. I'll settle down in Boston for nine months out of the year and create deathless literature. And for vacations, I've already planned the first one, which is to be a three months' jaunt by aeroplane up and down the United States east and west, north and south. You will see the possibilities of adventure in a trip of this sort. By limiting myself somewhat as to itinerary I can do the thing. I've found just the man here to share the journey with, an American in the British Air Force. He is enthusiastic about the plan. If only I can keep him from getting married for a year or so after getting home!

I had a very interesting experience, immediately after being taken prisoner on May 7th. I was taken by some German aviators to their aerodrome and had lunch with them before I was sent on to the hospital. Some of them spoke English and some of them French, so that there was no difficulty in conversing. I was suffering a good deal from my twisted ankles and had to be guarded in my remarks because of the danger of disclosing military information; but they were a fine lot of fellows. They respected my reticence, and did all they could to make me comfortable. It was with pilots from this squadron that we had been fighting only an hour or so before. One of their number had been killed in the combat by one of the boys who was flying with me. I sat beside the fellow whom I was attacking when my wing broke. I was right "on his tail," as we airmen say, when the accident occurred, and had just opened fire. Talking over the combat with him in their pleasant quarters, I was heartily glad that my affair ended as it did. I asked them to tell me frankly if they did not feel rather bitterly toward me as one of an enemy patrol which had shot down a comrade of theirs. They seemed to be surprised that I had any suspicions on this score. We had "a fair fight in an open field." Why should there be any bitterness about the result. One of them said to me, "Hauptmann, you'll find that we Germans are enemies of a country in war, but never of the individual." My experience thus far leads me to believe that this is true. There have been a few exceptions, but they were uneducated common soldiers. Bitterness toward America there certainly is everywhere, and an intense hatred of President Wilson quite equal in degree and kind to the hatred in America of the emperor . . .

NORMAN HALL

A REGULAR DOG-FIGHT AND THE STRAFING OF A DRACHEN

EDDIE V. RICKENBACKER

Captain Eddie Rickenbacker was the "ace of aces" of the US Army Air Service in World War I, shooting down 26 German aircraft over the Western Front in an operational career that spanned a mere eight months. Throughout he flew with the "Hat-in-the-Ring" 94th Aero squadron USAAS, eventually becoming its commanding officer. With the conclusion of the war, he formed the Rickenbacker Motor Company, which carried as its marque the old "Hat-in-the-Ring" insignia of the 94th Aero Squadron. Later Rickenbacker ran Eastern Air Lines. He died at the age of 82 in 1973.

On the afternoon of October 10th [1918] the 94th Squadron received orders to destroy two very bothersome enemy balloons, one of which was located at Dun-sur-Meuse, the other at Aincreville. The time for this attack was fixed for us at 3.50 P.M. sharp. A formation of defending planes from 147 Squadron was directed to cover our left wing while a similar formation from the 27th was given the same position on our right. I was placed in command of the expedition and was to arrange all minor details.

Selecting Lieutenants Coolidge and Chambers to act as the balloon executioners, I sent orders to all the pilots who were to accompany our secret raid to assemble their formation at 3,000 feet above Montfaucon at 3.40 o'clock precisely. Then with Coolidge and Chambers ahead of us, the united force would proceed first to the Dun balloon, where we would protect the two Strafers against Hun aeroplanes while they went in to attack their objective. Then, after destroying the first, if circumstances permitted, we should proceed on to Aincreville, destroy that balloon and beat a retreat straight for home. If Coolidge and Chambers encountered any hostile aircraft they were instructed to avoid fighting, but retire immediately to the protection of our formation.

A clear afternoon made it certain that the Boche machines would be thick about us. According to our Secret Intelligence Reports the enemy had here concentrated the heaviest air force against the Americans that had ever been gathered together since the war began. Both the Richthofen Circus and the Loezer Circus were now opposed to us and we had almost daily seen the well-known red noses of the one and the yellow-bellied fusilages of the other. Also we had distinguished the Checker-Board design of the No. 3 Jagstaffel and the new scout machines which the Huns had but lately sent to the front – the Sieman-Schuckard, which was driven by a four-bladed propeller and which had a much faster climb than had the Spad. Further reports which came to us stated that the new Fokkers now arriving at the front had four instead of two guns mounted forward, two as of yore fastened along the engine top and two others attached to the top wing. Personally I have never seen one of these "Roman Candle" affairs which so startled several pilots who reported having fights with them. They may have been in use along our front, of course, but I have never met one nor seen a pilot who was certain that he had met one. It was said that when all four guns began firing their tracer bullets at an enemy machine, the exhibition resembled the setting off of Fourth of July

Roman Candles, so continuous a stream of tracer bullets issued from the nozzles of the four machine-guns.

This heavy consolidation of enemy aircraft along our front was necessary to the Germans for two reasons. The retreating Hun infantry must hold the Meuse front until they had time to withdraw their troops from Belgium and the north or the latter would be cut off; secondly, the allied bombing squadrons which were now terrifying the Rhine towns were all located along this front and must be prevented from destroying those Prussian cities so dear to the heart of the Hun. General Trenchard of the British Independent Air Force proved he was right when he demonstrated that his bombing of enemy cities would necessarily withdraw from the battle front much of the enemy's air strength to defend those helpless cities against such attacks.

So it is not necessarily to be believed that Germany was actually in such fright over the appearance of the American airmen that she straightway sent all her best aviators to the Verdun region to oppose us. She really had quite other objects in view. But such a move nevertheless resulted in filling the skies opposite us with the best fighting airmen in the German service. It promised to be a busy month for us.

Fourteen of my Spads then left the ground on October 10th at 3.30 in the afternoon, with eight of 147's machines and seven of those from 27 Squadron taking their places on the right and left of us as arranged. I pushed my Spad No. 1 up several thousand feet above the flotilla to watch their progress over the lines from a superior altitude. The enormous formation below me resembled a huge crawling beetle, Coolidge and Chambers flying in exact position ahead of them to form the stingers. Thus arranged we proceeded swiftly northwest in the direction of Dun-sur-Meuse.

We arrived over the lines to be welcomed by an outlandish exhibition of Archie's fury, but despite the large target we made no damage was received and none of our

Spads turned back. Reaching a quieter region inside German territory I looked about me. There indeed was our Dun balloon floating tranquilly in the sunshine. It was 3.40 by my watch. We had ten minutes to maneuver for position and reach our objective. I looked down at my convoy and found that 147's Formation at the left had separated themselves somewhat widely from the others. Then studying the distant horizon I detected a number of specks in the sky, which soon resolved themselves into a group of eleven Fokkers flying in beautiful formation and evidently just risen from their aerodrome at Stenay, a dozen miles beyond Dun. They were approaching from the west and must reach the detached formation of 147's pilots before the rest of my flight could reach them, unless they immediately closed up. I dived down to dip them a signal.

On my way down I glanced around me and saw approaching us from Metz in quite the opposite direction another formation of eight Fokkers. Certainly the Huns had wonderful methods of information which enabled them to bring to a threatened point this speedy relief. While I debated an instant as to which danger was the most pressing I looked below and discovered that the enemy balloon men were already engaged in pulling down their observation balloon, which was the object of our attack back of Dun-sur-Meuse. So they suspected the purpose of our little expedition! It lacked yet a minute or two of the time set for our dash at the balloon and as I viewed the situation it would not be wise for Coolidge and Chambers to take their departure from our formation until we had disposed of the advancing Fokkers from the west. Accordingly I kept my altitude and set my machine towards the rear of the Stenay Fokkers, which I immediately observed wore the red noses of the von Richthofen Circus. They were heading in at the 147 Formation which was still separated almost a mile away from our other Spads. Lieutenant Wilbur White of New York was leading No. 147's pilots. He would have to bear the brunt of the Fokker attack.

Evidently the Fokker leader scorned to take notice of me, as his scouts passed under me and plunged ahead towards White's formation. I let them pass, dipped over sharply and with accumulated speed bore down upon the tail of the last man in the Fokker formation. It was an easy shot and I could not have missed. I was agreeably surprised, however, to see that my first shots had set fire to the Hun's fuel tank and that the machine was doomed. I was almost equally gratified the next second to see the German pilot level off his blazing machine and with a sudden leap overboard into space let the Fokker slide safely away without him. Attached to his back and sides was a rope which immediately pulled a dainty parachute from the bottom of his seat. The umbrella opened within a fifty foot drop and settled him gradually to earth within his own lines.

I was sorry I had no time to watch his spectacular descent. I truly wished him all the luck in the world. It is not a pleasure to see a burning aeroplane descending to earth bearing with it a human being who is being tortured to death. Not unmixed with my relief in witnessing his safe jump was the wonder as to why the Huns had all these humane contrivances and why our own country could not at least copy them to save American pilots from being burned to a crisp!

I turned from this extraordinary spectacle in midair to witness another which in all my life at the front I have never seen equaled in horror and awfulness. The picture of it has haunted my dreams during many nights since.

Upon seeing that my man was hit I had immediately turned up to retain my superiority in height over the other Huns. Now as I came about and saw the German pilot leap overboard with his parachute I saw that a general fight was on between the remaining ten Fokkers and the eight Spads of 147 Squadron. The Fokker leader had taken on the rear Spad in White's Formation when White turned and saw him coming. Like a flash White zoomed up into a half turn, executed a renversement and came back at the Hun leader to protect his pilot from a certain death. White was one of the finest pilots and best air fighters in our group. He had won seven victories in combat. His pilots loved him and considered him a great leader, which he most assuredly was. White's maneuver occupied but an instant. He came out of his swoop and made a direct plunge for the enemy machine, which was just getting in line on the rear Spad's tail. Without firing a shot the heroic White rammed the Fokker head on while the two machines were approaching each other at the rate of 230 miles per hour!

It was a horrible yet thrilling sight. The two machines actually telescoped each other, so violent was the impact. Wings went through wings and at first glance both the Fokker and Spad seemed to disintegrate. Fragments filled the air for a moment, then the two broken fusilages, bound together by the terrific collision fell swiftly down and landed in one heap on the bank of the Meuse!

For sheer nerve and bravery I believe this heroic feat was never surpassed. No national honor too great could compensate the family of Lieutenant White for this sacrifice for his comrade pilot and his unparalleled example of heroism to his Squadron. For the most pitiable feature of Lieutenant White's self-sacrifice was the fact that this was his last flight over the lines before he was to leave for the United States on a visit to his wife and two small children. Not many pilots enter the service with loved ones so close to them!

This extraordinary disaster ended the day's fighting for the Hun airmen. No doubt they valued their own leader as much as we did Lieutenant White, or perhaps they got a severe attack of "wind-up" at witnessing the new method of American attack. At any rate they withdrew and we immediately turned our attention to the fight which was now in progress between the Spads of 27 Squadron at our right and the Hun formation from Metz. It looked like a famous dog-fight.

As I came about and headed for the mixup I glanced below me at Dun and was amazed to see one of our Spads piquing upon the nested balloon through a hurricane of flaming projectiles. A "flaming onion" had pierced his wings and they were now ablaze. To add to his predicament, a Hun machine was behind his tail, firing as he dived. I diverted my course and started down to his rescue, but it was too late. The fire in his wings was fanned by the wind and made such progress that he was compelled to land in German territory, not far from the site of the balloon. In the meantime other things were happening so rapidly that I had little opportunity to look about me. For even as I started down to help this balloon strafer I saw another Spad passing me with two Fokkers on his tail, filling his fusilage with tracer bullets as the procession went by. A first glance had identified the occupant of the Spad as my old protégé – the famous Jimmy Meissner! For the third time since we had been flying together Providence had sent me along just in the nick of time to get Jimmy out of trouble. Twice before on the old Nieuports Jimmy had torn off his wings in too sudden a flip and his unscrupulous antagonists had been about to murder him as he wobbled along, when I happened by. Now, after a four months' interlude Jimmy comes sailing by again, smiling and good-natured as ever, with two ugly brutes on his tail trying their best to execute him.

I quickly tacked onto the procession, settling my sights into the rear machine and letting go a long burst as I came within range. The Hun fell off and dropped down out of control, the other Fokker immediately pulling away and diving steeply for home and safety.

Two other Fokkers fell in that dog-fight, neither of which I happened to see. Both Coolidge and Chambers, though they had been cheated of their balloon, brought down a Fokker apiece, which victories were later confirmed. The Spad which had dropped down into German hands after being set afire by the flaming onions belonged to Lieutenant Brotherton, like White and Meissner, a member of the 147th Squadron. Four more victories were thus added to 94's score by this afternoon's work. We did not get the balloons but we had done the best we could. I was never in favor of attacking observation balloons in full daylight and this day's experience – the aroused suspicions of the observers, the pulling down of the balloon as strong aeroplane assistance at the same time arrived, and the fate of Lieutenant Brotherton, who tried unsuccessfully to pass through the defensive barrage – is a fair illustration, I believe, of the difficulties attending such daylight strafings. Just at dawn or just at dusk is the ideal time for surprising the Drachen.

Our captured Hanover machine, it will be recalled, had been brought back to our aerodrome and by now was in good condition to fly. We left the Hun Maltese Cross and all their markings exactly as we found them and after telephoning about to the various American aerodromes in our vicinity that they must not practise target shooting at a certain Hanover aeroplane that they might encounter while wandering over our part of the country, we took the machine up to see how it flew. The Hanover was a staunch heavy craft and had a speed of about one hundred miles an hour when two men (a pilot and an observer) were carried. She handled well and was able to slow down to a very comfortable speed at landing. Many of us took her up for a short flip and landed again without accident.

Then it became a popular custom to let some pilot get aloft in her and as he began to clear the ground half a dozen of us in Spads would rise after him and practise piquing down as if in an attack. The Hanover pilot would twist and turn and endeavor to do his best to outmaneuver the encircling Spads. Of course, the lighter fighting machines always had the best of these mock battles, but the experience was good for all of us, both in estimating the extent of the maneuverability of the enemy two-seaters and in the testing of our relative speeds and climbings.

While engaged in one of these mock combats over our field one afternoon we came down to find Captain Cooper, the official Movie Picture expert, standing below watching us. He had his camera with him and had been attempting to grind out some movie films while we were flying overhead. He spent the night with us and after some planning of the scenario we decided to take him up in the rear seat of a Liberty aeroplane and let him catch with his camera a real movie of an aeroplane combat in mid-air. All the details carefully arranged, we gathered next morning on the field, put him in the rear seat of the Liberty and helped him strap in his camera so that the pressure of the wind would not carry it overboard. Jimmy Meissner was to be his pilot. Jimmy climbed in the front seat, warmed up his motor and when everything was ready and we other "actors" were sitting in our seats waiting for him to get away, Jimmy gave the signal, opened up his motor and began to taxi over the grass. Several hundred feet down the field he turned back, facing the wind, which was blowing from the west. Here he prepared for his real take-off. His machine rushed along with ever quickening speed until the tail lifted, the wheels next skimmed the ground and the Liberty rose gradually into the air. Just as they approached the road which skirts the west side of the aerodrome, the Liberty's engine stopped. A line of wires ran along the roadside some fifteen feet above ground. Jimmy saw them and attempted to zoom over them – but in vain. The Liberty crashed full in the middle of the highway, bounded up a dozen feet and after a half somersault, stuck her nose in the ground the other side of the road and came to a rest.

We hurried over, expecting to find the occupants badly injured, as the Liberty herself appeared to be a total wreck. But out stepped Jimmy and Captain Cooper, neither of them the worse for their experience. And to complete our surprise, the camera, although covered with the debris of the machine, was quite unhurt!

That ended our little movie show for this day. We had no other two-seater machine on hand. But we were delighted to find that Captain Cooper, in spite of his narrow escape, was quite determined to go through with the show.

So we went to the Supply Station for another machine and again put the Captain up for the night while awaiting its coming.

Next day, October 19th, I was directed to appear before General Patrick at Souilly to receive the American decoration, the Distinguished Service Cross, with four oak leaves. These oak leaves represent the number of citations in Army Orders that the wearer of a decoration has received.

The usual formalities, which I have already described, attended the ceremony. Over twenty pilots of the American Air Service were presented with the D.S.C. by General Patrick, after which the military band played the National Anthem while we all stood at attention.

I could not help thinking of the absent pilots whose names were being read out but who did not answer, and for whom decorations were waiting for deeds of heroism that had ended with their death. There was White, for whom the whole Group mourned. What a puny recognition was a simple ribbon for heroism such as his! There was Luke – the most intrepid air-fighter that ever sat in an aeroplane. What possible honor could be given him by his country that would accord him the distinction he deserved!

One thing was certain. The reputation of these great American airmen would live as long as the comrades who knew them survived. Perhaps none of us would ever live to see our homeland again. I glanced down the line of honor men who were standing immobile in their tracks, listening to the last notes of "The Star Spangled Banner"! Who will be the next to go, I wondered, knowing only too well that with every fresh honor that was conferred came a corresponding degree of responsibility and obligation to continue to serve comrade and country so long as life endured.

Observation balloons, or "Drachen" as the Boches call them, provide a most valuable method of espionage upon the movements of an enemy and at the same time are a most tempting bait to pilots of the opposing fighting squadrons.

They are huge in size, forming an elongated sausage some two hundred feet in length and perhaps fifty feet in diameter. They hang swinging in the sky at a low elevation – some two thousand feet or under, and are prevented from making any rapid effort to escape from airplane attack by reason of the long cable which attaches them to their mother truck on the highway below.

These trucks which attend the balloons are of the ordinary size – a three-ton motor truck which steers and travels quite like any big lorry one meets on the streets. On the truck bed is fastened a winch which lets out the cable to any desired length. In case of an attack by shell fire the truck simply runs up the road a short distance without drawing down the balloon. When it is observed that the enemy gunners have again calculated its range another move is made, perhaps back to a point near its former position.

Large as is its bulk and as favourable and steady a target as it must present to the enemy gunners three miles away, it is seldom indeed that a hit from bursting shrapnel is recorded.

These balloons are placed along the lines some two miles back of the front-line trenches. From his elevated perch two thousand feet above ground, the observer can study the ground and pick up every detail over a radius of ten miles on every side. Clamped over his ears are telephone receivers. With his telescope to his eye he observes and talks to the officers on the truck below him. They in turn inform him of any special object about which information is desired. If our battery is firing upon a certain enemy position, the observer watches for the bursts and corrects the faults in aim. If a certain roadway is being dug up by our artillery, the observer notifies the battery when sufficient damage has been done to render that road impassable.

Observation balloons are thus a constant menace to

contemplated movements of forces and considered as a factor of warfare they are of immense importance. Every fifteen or twenty miles along the front both sides station their balloons, and when one is shot down by an enemy airplane another immediately runs up to take its place.

Shelling by artillery fire being so ineffective it naturally occurs to every airplane pilot that such a huge and un-wieldy target must be easy to destroy from the air. Their cost is many times greater than the value of an airplane. They cannot fight back with any hope of success. All that seems to be required is a sudden dash by a fighting airplane, a few shots with incendiary bullets – and the big gas bag bursts into flames. What could be more simple?

I had been victorious over five or six enemy airplanes at this time and had never received a wound in return. This balloon business puzzled me and I was determined to solve the mystery.

I lay awake many nights pondering over the stories I had heard about attacking these Drachen, planning just how I should dive in and let them have a quick burst, sheer off and climb away from their machine-gun fire, hang about for another dive and continue these tactics until a sure hit could be scored.

I would talk this plan over with several of my pilots and after working out all the details we would try it on. Perhaps we could make 94 Squadron famous for its destruction of enemy balloons. There must be some way to do it, provided I picked out the right men for the job and gave them a thorough training.

After discussing the matter with Major Atkinson, our commanding officer, who readily gave me his approval, I sought out Reed Chambers, Jimmy Meissner, Thorn Taylor, and Lieutenant Loomis. These four with myself would make an ideal team to investigate this situation.

First we obtained photographs of five German balloons in their lairs, from a French Observation Squadron. Then we studied the map and ascertained the precise position each occupied: the nature of the land, the relative position of the mountains and rivers, the trees and villages in the vicinity of each, and all the details of their environment.

One by one we visited these balloons, studying from above the nature of the roadway upon which their mother trucks must operate, the height of the trees along this roadway and where the anti-aircraft defenses had been posted around each Drachen. These latter were the only perils we had to fear. We knew the reputation of these defenses, and they were not to be ignored. Since they alone were responsible for the defense of the balloons, we presumed that they were unusually numerous and accurate. They would undoubtedly put up such a heavy barrage of gunfire around the suspended Drachen that an airplane must actually pass through a steady hailstorm of bullets both in coming in and in going out.

Major Willy Coppens*, the Belgian ace, had made the greatest success of this balloon strafing. He had shot down over a score of German Drachens and had never received a wound. I knew he armed his airplane with flaming rockets which penetrated the envelope of the gas bag and burned there until it was ignited. This method had its advantages and its disadvantages. But another trick that was devised by Coppens met with my full approval.

This was to make the attack early in the morning or late in the evening, when visibility was poor and the approach of the buzzing engine could not be definitely located. Furthermore, he made his attack from a low level, flying so close to the ground that he could not be readily picked up from above. As he approached the vicinity of his balloon he zoomed up and began his attack. If the balloon was being hauled down he met it halfway. All depended upon the timing of his attack and the accuracy of his aim.

On June 25, 1918, my alarm clock buzzed me awake at 2:30 o'clock sharp. As I was the instigator of this little

* *Willy Coppens de Houthulst, born 1892, died 1986. Flew a bright blue Hanriot HDI biplane for most of his 37 victories. Invalided 14 October 1918 after being hit by an incendiary bullet in the leg.*

expedition, I leaped out of bed and leaned out of my window to get a glimpse of the sky. It promised to be a fine day!

Rousing out the other four of my party, I telephoned to the hangars and ordered out the machines. The guns had been thoroughly serviced during the night and special incendiary bullets had been placed in the magazines. Everything was ready for our first attack and we sat down to a hurried breakfast, full of excitement and fervor.

The whole squadron got up and accompanied us to the hangars. We were soon in our flying suits and strapped in our seats. The engines began humming and then I felt my elation suddenly begin to dissipate. My engine was stubborn and would not keep up its steady revolutions. Upon investigation, I found one magneto unserviceable, leaving me with but one upon which I could rely! I debated within myself for a few seconds as to whether I should risk dropping into Germany with a dud engine or risk the condolences of the present crowd which had gathered to see us off.

The former won in spite of my best judgment. Rather than endure the sarcasm of the onlookers and the disappointment of my team, I prayed for one more visitation of my Goddess of Luck and gave the signal to start.

At 4:30 o'clock we left the ground and headed straight into Germany. I had decided to fly eight or ten miles behind the lines and then turn and come back at the balloon line from an unexpected quarter, trusting to the discipline of the German army to have its balloons ascending just as we reached them. Each pilot in my party had his own balloon marked out. Each was to follow the same tactics. We separated as soon as we left the field, each man taking up his own course.

Passing high over Nancy I proceeded northward and soon saw the irregular lines of the trenches below me. It was a mild morning and very little activity was discernible on either side. Not a gun was flashing in the twilight which covered the ground and as far as my eye could reach nothing was stirring. It was the precise time of day when weary fighters would prefer to catch their last wink of sleep. I hoped they would be equally deaf to the sounds of my humming Nieuport.

Cutting off my engine at fifteen thousand feet over the lines. I prayed once more that when the time came to switch on again my one magneto would prove faithful. It alone stood between me and certain capture. I could not go roaring along over the heads of the whole German army and expect to conceal my presence. By gliding quietly with silent engine as I passed deeper and deeper within their territory I could gradually lose my altitude and then turn and gain the balloon line with comparatively little noise.

"Keep your Spunk Up – Magneto, Boy!" I sang to my engine as I began the fateful glide. I had a mental vision of the precise spot behind the enemy balloon where I should turn on my switch and there discover – liberty or death! I would gladly have given my kingdom that moment for just one more little magneto!

At that moment I was passing swiftly over the little village of Goin. It was exactly five o'clock. The black outlines of the Bois de Face lay to my left, nestled along the two arms of the Moselle. I might possibly reach those woods with a long glide if my engine failed me at the critical moment. I could crash in the treetops, hide in the forest until dark and possibly make my way back through the lines with a little luck. Cheery thoughts I had as I watched the menacing German territory slipping away beneath my wings!

And then I saw my balloon! The faithful fellows had not disappointed me at any rate! Conscientious and reliable men these Germans were! Up and ready for the day's work at the exact hour I had planned for them! I flattened out my glide a trifle more, so as to pass their post with the minimum noise of singing wires. A mile or two beyond them I began a wide circle with my nose well down. It was a question of seconds now and all would be over. I wondered how Chambers and Meissner and the others were getting on. Probably at this very instant they were throbbing with joy over the scene of a flaming bag of gas!

Finding the earth rapidly nearing me, I banked sharply to the left and looked ahead. There was my target floating blandly and unsuspiciously in the first rays of the sun. The men below were undoubtedly drinking their coffee and drawing up orders for the day's work that would never be executed. I headed directly for the swinging target and set my sights dead on its center. There facing me with rare arrogance in the middle of the balloon was a huge Maltese Cross – the emblem of the Boche aviation. I shifted my rudder a bit and pointed my sights exactly at the center of the cross. Then I deliberately pressed both triggers with my right hand, while with my left I snapped on the switch.

There must be some compartment in one's brain for equalizing the conflicting emotions that crowd simultaneously upon one at such moments as this. I realized instantly that I was saved myself, for the engine picked up with a whole-souled roar the very first instant after I made the contact. With this happy realization came the simultaneous impression that my whole morning's work and anguish were wasted.

I saw three or four streaks of flame flash ahead of me and enter the huge bulk of the balloon ahead. Then the flames abruptly ceased.

Flashing bullets were cutting a living circle all around me too, I noticed. Notwithstanding the subtlety of my stalking approach, the balloon's defenders had discovered my presence and were all waiting for me. My guns had both jammed. This, too, I realized at the same instant. I had had my chance, had shot my bolt, was in the very midst of a fiery furnace that beggars description but thanks to a benignant Providence, was behind a lusty engine that would carry me home.

Amid all these conflicting impressions which surged through me during that brief instant, I distinctly remember that I had failed in my mission! With the largest target in the world before my guns, with all the risks already run and conquered, I had failed in my mission simply because of a stupid jamming of my guns.

I had swerved to the right of the suspended gas bag and grazed the distended sides of the enemy Drachen. I might almost have extended my hand and cut a hole in its sleek envelope, as I swept by. The wind had been from the east, so I knew that the balloon would stretch away from its supporting cable and leave it to the right. More than one balloon strafer has rushed below his balloon and crashed headlong into the slim wire cable which anchors it to the ground.

I had planned every detail with rare success. The only thing I had failed in was the over-all result. Either the Boche had some material covering their Drachens that extinguished my flaming bullets, or else the gas which was contained within them was not as highly inflammable as I had been led to believe. Some three or four bullets had entered the sides of the balloon – of this I was certain. Why had they failed to set fire to it?

Later on I was to discover that flaming bullets very frequently puncture observation balloons without producing the expected blaze. The very rapidity of their flight leaves no time for the ignition of the gas. Often in the early dawn the accumulated dews and moisture in the air serve to dampen the balloon's envelope and hundreds of incendiary bullets penetrate the envelope without doing more damage than can be repaired with a few strips of adhesive plaster.

As I flew through the fiery curtain of German bullets and set my nose for home I developed a distinct admiration for the Belgian Willy Coppens de Houthulst. And since he had proved that balloon strafing had in fact a possibility of success, I was determined to investigate this business until I too had solved its mysteries.

Then I began to laugh to myself at an occurrence that until then I had had not time to consider. As I began firing at the sausage, the German observer who had been standing in his basket under the balloon with his eyes glued to his binoculars, had evidently been taken entirely by surprise. The first intimation he had of my approach was the bullets which preceded me. At the instant he dropped his glasses he dived headlong over the side of his basket with his parachute. He did not even pause to look around to see what danger threatened him.

Evidently the mother truck began winding up the cable at the same time, for as the observer jumped for his life the balloon began to descend upon him. I caught the merest glimpse of his face as I swept past him, and there was a mingled look of terror and surprise upon his features that almost compensated me for my disappointment.

On my way homeward I flew directly toward a French observation balloon that swung on the end of its cable in my path. Without considering the consequences of my act, I sheered in and passed quite close to the Frenchman who was staring at me from his suspended basket.

Suddenly the Froggy leaped headlong from his perch and clutching his parachute rigging with his two hands began a rapid descent to earth. And not until then did I realize that coming directly at him, head on from Germany as I did, he had no way of reading my cocards which were painted underneath my wings. He had decided that I was a Boche and did not care to take any chances at a jump with a blazing gas bag about his ears.

Fortunately for me, the French gunners below could read my insignias from the ground and they suffered me to pass, without taking any revenge for the trick I had played upon their comrade.

Arriving at the aerodrome at 5:45, I found that I was the last of my little party of balloon strafers to land. The other four were standing together, looking rather sheepishly in my direction as I walked toward them.

"Well, what luck?" I inquired as I came up to them. Nobody spoke. "I thought I saw a big blaze over in your direction, Jimmy!" I went on, addressing myself to Lieutenant Meissner. "Did you get him?"

"No!" replied Jimmy disgustedly. "The balloon was

not up in the air at all. I didn't get a sight of it. I didn't even see where they had hidden it."

"Did you get yours, Reed?" I asked, turning to Chambers.

"Hell, no!" retorted Lieutenant Chambers emphatically. "I shot the thing full of holes, but she wouldn't drop."

The other two pilots had much the same stories. One had failed to find his balloon and the other had made an attack but it had brought no results. All had been subjected to a defensive fire that had quite reversed their opinions of the Archibald family.

"I suppose you burned yours all right, Rick?" said Reed Chambers rather enviously as we walked up to the mess together. "What do you think of us fellows anyway?"

"I think, Reed," replied I, "that we are the rottenest lot of balloonatical fakers that ever got up at two-thirty in the morning. But I am happy to discover," I added, thinking of my one operative magneto, "that none of us had to land in Germany."

ACTION

PAUL RICHEY

With the British declaration of war against Nazi Germany on September 3 1939, Paul Richey was dispatched to France with the RAF's No. 1 (Fighter) Squadron as part of the "British Expeditionary Force Air Component". Fortunately for No 1 Squadron they had recently converted from the hopelessly out-dated Hawker Fury biplanes to the Hurricane Mark 1 (which had a top speed of 328 mph at 20,000 feet, and was armed with 8 Browning .303 inch machine guns). After some ten months of "Sitzkrieg", the Germans invaded the Low Countries on May 10 1940, with France the next stop. Here is Richey's record of his actions on May 11 1940.

We were up again at two forty-five AM, refreshed by a sound sleep. We had to be on the airfield half an hour before dawn, but grabbed a biscuit and a cup of tea in the Mess first.

The Bull decided that our concrete pilots' hut was too obvious a target. We guessed the German bomber had been aiming at it the previous evening, and considering he was flying at 18,000 feet his bombing had been damned accurate. Accordingly the Bull chose a spot some 250 yards away on the fringe of the trees, and we spent the first few hours of daylight rigging up a tent into which we moved the telephone to Wing, a couple of desks and our flying-kit. There was a shallow trench and dug-out nearby that looked as though they might be useful. They were . . .

We climbed into our cockpits at eight as there was a hell of a lot of bombing going on. We sat ready and strapped in, gazing into the sky to the east, with an aircraftsman sitting beside each plugged-in starter-battery. The scheme was to get the aircraft off the ground and out of harm's way if there was a raid, and perhaps to knock down a few bombers – although this was not our primary job. In this particular case "B" Flight were ordered to get off first and chase the Huns, with "A" Flight to follow and circle the airfield, or engage if there was a chance.

My aircraftsman suddenly stood up and peered at the sky behind me. I had my helmet on and couldn't hear much, but I could pick up a lot of crumps going off. I twisted round as far as my straps would let me and looked up. Yes, there was something up there all right! Shells from a nearby British ack-ack battery were bursting all over the place. A "B" Flight engine burst into life at the other end of the line. I waved to the aircraftsman and in a moment my prop was whirling in front of me and the machine vibrating. As I waited for "B" Flight to get off I watched engine after engine start up. In a minute the first "B" Flight aircraft roared off across our noses, followed in quick succession by the other five. I looked up right as the aircraftsman waggled my aileron and pointed. Yes! There were the buggers, turning away east at a good 15,000 feet.

Soon I too was off. No time to lose, no time to join up even, and I started climbing flat-out beside two "B" Flight aircraft – one of them with Billy's "P" on its side – after the raiders. They must have seen us take off, and we thought later we had probably foiled a heavy attack on the airfield, for they were now climbing at full throttle dead into the sun: good tactics. They were Heinkels – about twelve – in very open formation, probably because they were flat-out. We were catching them slowly, but it became apparent that if we ever made it we would probably be over Berlin. One of the "B" Flight Hurricanes rolled over and dived away for home, in what must have been disappointed disgust. Billy kept on. It was obvious there wasn't much hope now, so I looked around for something, maybe, within reach.

I found it – about five miles away to the right and below me. I couldn't see what it was, but it stood out clearly against the top of the haze, and as I turned sharply towards it, it gave the clue to its nationality by turning from its westerly course and diving steeply east, evidently having seen me too. I nearly lost it in the haze, but soon got nearer and saw it was a Dornier 215. Having made quite sure, I attacked from astern. The fellow was moving bloody fast and it was all I could do in my slow old wooden-blader to get within range. Long before I did so the Hun rear gunner betrayed his feelings by loosing off wildly, the tracers flashing past me all over the place. I fired a short preliminary burst at long range, partly to put him off and partly to steady my aim, and having closed and got my sights on, I opened fire.

The German started turning, first one way, then the other. The rear gunner stopped firing. Realizing that once he was on the deck any shooting would be difficult, I fired longish bursts following each other as rapidly as possible. Soon he was right down on the trees, slowing but still travelling fast. Each time I fired I saw whitish smoke pump from one engine or the other – doubtless glycol – but the determined bloody man kept right on flying. I ran out of ammunition, but must have hit his oil system as my windscreen was splattered with black oil.

I pulled off and watched him from above. Still no fire from the rear gun, but something glowing like a Vérey light floated up towards me; I thought at the time it was a defiant shot from the Hun's Vérey pistol, his gun being jammed, but decided later it was probably a French tracer-shell from the ground. Anyway, as soon as he saw I'd stopped attacking, he turned half-right and flew straight due east. I did a roll over the top of him to wish him luck and left, as he showed no signs of coming down now and I didn't know where I was. If his engines lasted long enough without glycol and oil he probably made it all right, and I rather hope he did. Either my shooting was bloody poor or he was loaded with armour, or both. But I felt he'd got the best of me, so I metaphorically raised my hat to him and departed.

I circled uneasily for a few minutes trying to pick up my bearings. The country was thickly wooded and green. Luxembourg? Belgium? Somewhere round there, I thought. As usual my luck held. I came to an airfield with Potez 63s parked round the edge and honeycombed with bomb-craters varying in diameter from six feet to sixty. I was in the right country, but short of fuel, so I landed. In trying to dodge one of the smaller bomb holes, which were invisible at a distance, I swerved violently and dug my port wing in, bending the tip.

I taxied over, wondering what the hell I was going to do about dear old "G", my aeroplane. The airfield was Mézières. I dug out the French squadron CO, who got an engineer to look my Hurricane over. The engineer said it definitely could not fly, as engineers will. The ailerons still worked, though, and I thought it would fly with full right aileron. The CO left the decision to me but emphasized that he wouldn't fly it. He thought it would misbehave coming in to land. As he was a pilot of some twenty-five years' experience I decided to follow his advice.

The French CO was a tall, hard-looking man, bursting with efficiency and quite undisturbed by the numerous delayed-action bombs scattered about the airfield. "Oh, those!" he said contemptuously, "they've been going off all night. One gets used to anything in time . . ."

His squadron was engaged in bombing and reconnaissance, operating with the French light mechanized units which had advanced into Luxembourg and southern Belgium. They had not suffered many losses yet. "But," he added despondently, "if *only* we had more fighters . . ."

He very decently put an aircraft at my disposal to fly me back to Berry, and having taken my maps and parachute out, I said *au revoir* to poor old "G" with her gay red spinner. It was to be goodbye, but I still feel sentimental about her. Three days later Sammy took a lorry and a party of riggers to Mézières to patch her up and bring her home. He was only there five minutes when there was a whine and a roar from the sky, whereupon he was compelled to recline in a ditch for two and a half hours while the airfield was wholeheartedly strafed by low-flying Dorniers. Sammy said he could actually see the pilots and gunners as they flew up and down a matter of yards away bombing and machine-gunning. They did their stuff beautifully, setting fire to all fifteen Potez's and an assortment of other aircraft and leaving the place a write-off. Sammy's lorry was shot up. But worst news of all to me, poor old "G" was sieved with bullets. I can only hope she burned before the Huns laid their rude hands on her.

During the trip back I spent most of the time fiddling about with the machine-gun in the rear cockpit. The aeroplane was a Mureau – a very ancient open parasol monoplane with a Hispano engine; it looked like a First War effort. The pilot kept glancing round anxiously to see what I was playing at, while I was hoping no German fighters would appear, at any rate until I'd got the gun working. A fat lot of use it would have been anyway.

Back with the Squadron, I didn't claim the Dornier, but entered it as a "possible" in my log book. Wing had kicked up a fuss about our taking off to chase up bombing-raids, and AHQ at Reims pointed our curtly that since we were there primarily to provide cover for our bombers on their missions, how the blazes could we rush off all over the sky every time we saw an enemy bomber? We were *not* –, repeat *not* – to take off without orders. If a bombing-raid came over we were to lie down and lump it. All very fine for them deep down in their champagne-cellar shelters. But we supposed they were right; they sometimes were. However, we learnt with relish that three jumbo bombs

had dropped just outside their Reims château, wiping out
some transport and frightening the pants off them. "What
did they expect, setting-up their HQ in a perfect target?"
said Prosser tartly.

That same afternoon we were ordered to patrol AHQ at
Reims! We were up an hour and a half but saw nothing. I
believe the chaps at Headquarters felt a little more confident seeing us droning about over the city. Reims had
been bombed, but I couldn't see any damage. I hoped to
God the Germans wouldn't knock the cathedral down
again; the restorers had only just finished making good the
World War I damage.

Back at the airfield, "A" Flight dashed off to Ponta-
vert for tea. I had eaten nothing that day and had been
up since three, so I wasn't sorry. We swallowed the hot
tea and bread-and-jam, then rushed back to the airfield
as a message came through from Wing that a big
formation of bombers was heading for Reims – forty-
five, they said!

As I doubled across to my new aircraft I met Squadron
Leader White, the Roman Catholic padre to the local
Battle squadrons. I had met him on our previous visit
to Berry in April and thought him a damn good chap. He
asked me if I wanted absolution, puffing along beside me.
I confessed briefly. He asked if there were any other
Catholics who might want absolution. I said "Only old
Killy in that Hurricane over there – he hasn't been active
for ten years, but you can try!" We laughed and I waved
him goodbye. But confess Killy did – sitting in his cockpit
with the padre standing on the wing beside him. He was a
good man, that padre. I never saw him again.

Five minutes later we were off. "Patrol Panther" (A H
Q Reims) "Angels 10" came over the R/T. Up we climbed
– Johnny leading, Hilly No 2 on his right, myself No 3 on
the left, and Killy and Soper 4 and 5 respectively, doing
the cross-over behind. After fifteen minutes over Reims
we were called up: "Two enemy aircraft going west from
Sedan – two Dorniers going west – angels 5." We closed in

and shot off north, rubbing our hands at the thought of only two Dorniers to five Hurricanes at 5,000 feet.

Approaching Sedan Johnny called: "There they are! There they are! Straight ahead!" I couldn't see them at first, but suddenly I did, and my heart raced. As we came nearer I counted them – thirty Dorniers in two squadrons of fifteen more or less in line abreast, covered by fifteen 110s* in groups of twos and threes wheeling and zig-zagging slowly above, ahead, beside and behind the bombers. They were going west across our noses from right to left.

Johnny rocked his wings for us to close in tighter and pressed straight on, climbing a little to 7,000 feet, then turning left and diving at the Huns from astern. "Now keep in – keep in – and keep a bloody good look-out!" he said steadily. I was swivel-eyed as we approached, to make sure we were not being attacked by something unseen, for the Huns continued straight on although we were closing on them. They must have seen us long before, but it was not until the last moment that the 110s wheeled, some to the right and some to the left, going into aircraft-line-astern in twos and threes.

We went in fast in a tight bunch, each picking a 110 and manoeuvring to get on his tail. I selected the rear one of two in line-astern who were turning tightly to the left. He broke away from his No 1 when he had done a half-circle and steepened his turn, but I easily turned inside him, holding my fire until I was within fifty yards and then firing a shortish burst at three-quarters deflection. To my surprise a mass of bits flew off him – pieces of engine-cowling and lumps of his glass-house (hood) – and as I passed just over the top of him, still in a left-hand turn, I watched with a kind of fascinated horror as he went into a spin, smoke pouring out of him. I remember saying "My God, how ghastly!" as his tail suddenly swivelled sideways and tore off, while flames streamed over the fuselage. Then, I saw a little white parachute open beside it. Good!

* *Messerschmitt 110, two seater fighter, later withdrawn from daylight service because of its lack of manoeuvrability.*

Scarcely half a minute had passed, yet as I looked quickly around me I saw four more 110s go down – one with its tail off, a second in a spin, a third vertically in flames, and a fourth going up at forty-five degrees in a left-hand stall-turn with a little Hurricane on its tail firing into its side, from which burst a series of flashes and long shooting red flames. I shall never forget it.

All the 110s at my level were hotly engaged, so I searched above. "Yes – those buggers up there will be a nuisance soon!" Three cunning chaps were out of the fight, climbing like mad in line-astern to get above us to pounce. I had plenty of ammunition left, so I climbed after them with the boost-override pulled. They were in a slight right-hand turn, and as I climbed I looked around. There were three others over on the right coming towards me, but they were below. I reached the rear 110 of the three above me. He caught fire after a couple of bursts and went down in flames. Then I dived at the trinity coming up from the right and fired a quick burst at the leader head-on.

I turned, but they were still there; so were the other two from above. In a moment I was in the centre of what seemed a stack of 110s, although there were in fact only five. I knew I hadn't the speed or height in my wooden-blader to dive away and beat it, so I decided to stay and make the best of it. Although I was more manoeuvrable at this height than the Huns, I found it impossible to get an astern shot in because every time I almost got one lined up, tracers came whipping past from another on my tail. All I could do was keep twisting and turning, and when a 110 got behind me make as tight a turn as possible, almost spinning, with full engine, and fly straight at him, firing a quick burst, then push the stick forward and dive under his nose. I would then pull up in a steep climbing turn to meet the next gentleman.

Obviously they couldn't all attack at once without colliding, but several times I was at the apex of a cone formed by the cannon and machine-gun fire of three of them. Their tactics consisted mostly of diving, climbing and taking full deflection shots at me. Their shooting seemed wild. This manoeuvre was easily dealt with by turning towards them and popping over their heads, forcing them to steepen their climb until they stalled and had to fall away. But I was not enjoying this marathon. Far from it. My mouth was getting drier and drier, and I was feeling more and more desperate and exhausted. Would they run out of ammunition? Would they push off? Would help come? I knew I couldn't hold out much longer.

After what seemed an age (actually it turned out to be fifteen minutes, which is an exceptionally long time for a dog-fight) I was flying down head-on at a 110 who was climbing up to me. We both fired – and I thought I had left it too late and we would collide. I pushed the stick forward violently. There was a stunning explosion right in front of me. For an instant my mind went blank. My aircraft seemed to be falling, limp on the controls. Then as black smoke poured out of the nose and enveloped the hood, and a hot blast and a flicker of reflected flame crept into the dark cockpit, I said "Come on – out you go!" pulled the pin out of my harness, wrenched open the hood and hauled myself head-first out to the right.

The wind pressed me tightly against the side of the aircraft, my legs still inside. I caught hold of the trailing edge of the wing and heaved myself out. As I fell free and somersaulted I felt as if a giant had me on the end of a length of wire, whirling me round and round through the air. I fumbled for and pulled the rip-cord and was pulled the right way up with a violent jerk that winded me. My head was pressed forward by the parachute back-pad that had slipped up behind, and I couldn't look up to see if the parachute was O K. I had no sensation of movement – just a slight breeze as I swung gently to and for. For all I knew the thing might be on fire or not properly open.

I heard the whirr of Hun engines and saw three of the 110s circle me. I looked at the ground and saw a shower of flaming sparks as something exploded in an orchard far below: my late aeroplane.

The Hun engines faded and died. I rolled the rip cord round its D-ring and put it in my pocket as a souvenir. I was still bloody frightened, as I was smack over a wood and thought I'd probably break my legs if I landed in it; and I confess without shame that I reeled off several prayers, both of thanks and supplication, as I dangled in the air. I was soon low enough to see my drift. It was towards a village, and it looked as though I might clear the trees only to hit a roof. But no – it was to be the wood all right. I was very low now, swinging gently. I saw two French motor-cycle troops running along the road, first one way, then the other. I waved to them. The trees rushed up at me. Now for it! I relaxed completely, shutting my eyes calmly. There was a swish of branches and a bump as I did a back-somersault on the ground. I had fallen between the trees.

I jumped up as the two French soldiers came crashing through the trees, one with a revolver in his hand and the other carrying a rifle. "*Haut les mains!*" they shouted, pointing their weapons at me. I raised my arms as they advanced cautiously. I was wearing white overalls over my uniform, and still had my helmet and oxygen-mask on. I spoke through the mask with difficulty. They refused to believe I was English, but I eventually managed to persuade them to look for the RAF wings under my overalls. Having done this, they put down their weapons and embraced me warmly.

I tore off my helmet and threw it on the ground, shouting, "*Ces salauds de Boches!*" which relieved my feelings slightly. We gathered up my parachute and moved on to the village. I rode in the side-car of their motorcycle combination. The entire population of Rumigny had witnessed the fight and had seen six Huns come down nearby; they later found four more, making a total of ten. They had watched me fighting the remaining five and said it had lasted at least fifteen minutes, perhaps more.

When I got back to the Squadron I found that Johnny claimed to have shot down one definitely, and perhaps two, Hilly two, Killy two and Soper two. With my two that made exactly the number found – ten – leaving the number I had fought as five (total fifteen as counted before the fight). The villagers on the ground had seen two enemy tails come off – presumably one was mine; the other was Killy's. The police presented me with one of the fins – with the black-and-white swastika pierced by two bullets, it made a respectable match for the two First War fins we had with the Black Cross emblems on them.

Donald Hills, our equipment officer, came over to collect me in the Renault, but as it was late we decided to stay the night. We ate and drank well. The French were enthusiastic over our victory, and I was encouraged to hear that the thirty Dorniers had turned and beetled off when we tackled their fighter escort. The French had taken prisoner the pilot of the first 110 to crash, which had been mine, and we rang up during dinner to find out if we could see him. He had a bullet in the thigh and was in hospital. When we got through, he had just been taken away by French Air Intelligence, but an officer who had spoken to him gave us some details; he was twenty-three, a fanatical Austrian Nazi from Vienna and said he was furious to be knocked out of the war so soon. He must have been a liar too, for he claimed to have shot me down. As I went down a good fifteen minutes later (after his departure) I thought his claim a trifle extravagant.*

There was only one bed available, so Donald and I had to share it. We'd wined and dined too well to care. Before dinner I had tramped a good seven miles across country looking for one of the Huns, led by a tough little *Chasseur*, so I was extremely tired.

We woke up in the grey dawn to the reverberations of very heavy bombing. Liart and Hirson, two neighbouring towns with railway junctions, were being flattened out

---

* *In retrospect I think that either this pilot was suffering from "dog-fight confusion" or he was mis-interpreted by the French.* [P.R.]

with a big civilian death-roll. As one of the Frenchmen had said to me at dinner, "*Il est fort, ce Bosche!*"

We got back to the Squadron at tea-time on May 12th, displaying my fin in triumph. Killy told me he had seen me stuck with the Huns but could only say "Poor bastard!" to himself and buzz off, as he had no ammunition left, and neither had anyone else. It was my own stupid fault for getting stuck anyway.

The airfield had been bombed twice during my absence. "B" Flight had been at it again – Leslie Clisby got two Dornier 17s at Avaux, where he had landed on a French airfield and been shot up by the ground defences doing so. Prosser and Boy each got a 110 in the fight.

Richey returned to England wounded on June 14th, 1940, and was awarded the Distinguished Flying Cross. On regaining his medical flying category, he served with No 609 (Fighter) squadron, 74 (Fighter) Squadron, and commanded No 165 (Fighter) Wing and then No 189 (Fighter) Wing in the Far East. After being invalided with tropical diseases, Richey served as a staff officer with SHAEF (Supreme Headquarters Allied Expeditionary Force) and ended the war as a wing commander operations with 2nd Tactical Air Force. During the Korean War he was recalled to regular service.

BATTLE OF BRITAIN DIARY

D.H. WISSLER

After the fall of France, Hitler turned his attention to Britain, determining upon invasion of the island in the autumn of 1940. First, however, there was the small matter of sweeping the fighters of the Royal Air Force from the skies. Herman Goering, head of the Luftwaffe, believed that it would take his fighters, now operating from their new bases in occupied Europe, just four days to eradicate the RAF from the south of England. As it turned out, it took the Luftwaffe one month – 12 August to 15 September 1940 - to lose the "Battle of Britain". Although the numerical advantage lay with the Luftwaffe (which initially put up some 980 fighters against the RAF's 700), the range of the principal German fighter, the Messerschmitt Bf109, when used as an escort to bombers, was limited to the south-east corner of England, and then for a relatively short period only, something in the region of ten minutes. Or, put another way, RAF fighters could fly for longer over the main area of the battle. They also had the advantage of a ground system of radar which detected the enemy and a fighter control which directed them to the target, removing the need for patrol. This said, the Luftwaffe came close to winning the Battle in September, when it destroyed 185 British aircraft for the loss of 225 German (including bombers) in the first week, and the RAF began to run precariously low on men and machines. The RAF might have triumphed anyway, but Hitler made sure that they did. In a fit of of pique following the RAF's bombing raid on Berlin of 25 August, he ordered the Luftwaffe's bombers to switch their aim from Britain's airfields to its cities, particularly London. On 7 September the Luftwaffe sent nearly 400 bombers and more than 600 fighters in two waves to attack the East End of London. The damage was considerable; but it did nothing to lessen the effectiveness of Fighter Command. Nor did the ensuing raids on Britain's cities. On 17 September, Hitler suspended his plans for the invasion of Britain. Total losses of aircraft incurred during the Battle stood at 922 British, 1,767 German. The Third Reich had lost its first battle. A Hurricane pilot with 17 Squadron, Wissler fought throughout the Battle of Britain.

Diary 15 August 1940 [Martlesham Heath]

I did not get up until 8 this morning and then went down to flight. I did a convoy patrol this morning, acting as section leader. Then in the afternoon there was a flap and took off. Joined Red section and went hunting. The aerodrome was bombed, several 1000lb bombs being dropped not doing too much damage. We didn't even get a chance to fire although F/1 Harper was shot down, but managed to jump, though wounded. In the evening we watched a raid over Harwich being machine-gunned and shelled. He[Heinkels] dropped one large bomb!

Monday, 19 August

I was recalled from leave today . . . The squadron is moving to TANGMERE. I flew "X", which was due for an inspection, to Debden. "V", my own plane not ready, so I spent the night in a comfortable bed for a change . . .

Tuesday, 20 August

I took off from Debden at about 10.15 and flew to Tangmere. I navigated my way ok but being on the coast this wasn't very hard. Tangmere is in a shocking state. The buildings being in an awful shambles, several 1000lb bombs having fallen. We were put to 30 mins at 1, and did nothing for the rest of the day. The dispersal hut is most cozy and puts ours at Debden to shame.

Wednesday, 21 August

We did some flap flying patrols today . . . but the Flight commander only saw one E/A [enemy aircraft] and then only for a second when it was between some clouds. The other section in our flight shot down a Ju88 as did yellow section in "A" flight. After it was quite dusk we were sent up on patrol but having got to 7000 ft over the aerodrome we were recalled.

Friday, 23 August

I did not fly at all today, in fact it was very quiet. We were released at 1 p.m. and went up [to London] on train. I went home.

Saturday, 24 August

There was an air raid warning in Blackheath and thought I should miss my train. However, we caught it and arrived back ok. In the afternoon we went up on a flap and saw dozens of E/A going out to sea, however did not fire although the CO and P/O Stevens got an He111. We had one very short patrol after this, but nothing was seen.

Sunday, 25 August

This was our hard day being at 15 mins and readiness the day long. At about half past seven we had a hell of a scrap over Portland in which 100 a/c were engaged. F/L Bayne made an attack below and astern quarter. The ME110 whipped up in a slow turn and I gave him a long burst while he was in a stalled condition, it fell over and went down. I then went on my own and made an He111 break formation. I gave it another burst and it went down towards the sea. F/L Bayne shot down but ok. F/L Williams lost wing. Shot off.

Saturday, 31 August

We did four patrols today ending up with one in which we intercepted about 30 Do[rnier]17s and 20–30 Me 109s. I got on an Me 109s tail, after an ineffectual attack on the bombers, and got in several long bursts at about 300 yards, however nothing was observed in the way of damage. Another got on my tail and I had to break away. I succeeded in throwing him off in a steep turn but not before he had put a explosive bullet through my wing. Sgt Stewart was shot down, but was safe. I lost another tail wheel today.

Tuesday, 3 September

We did two patrols, in the first intercepted about 100 E/A (Do.215 and Me 110). F/Lt Bayne and I got on an Me 110's tail and firing together sent it down in flames. We then attacked a Do 215, [?] Leary finishing the attack and the bomber crashed in a field just North of the River Crouch. I collected a bullet in the radiator and got covered with glycol, force landing at Castle Camps. Collected a Hurricane off 111 Sqd., flew back to Debden . . . We did one more patrol over the Thames. Then in the night I was aerodrome Control Pilot.

Saturday, 7 September

I did two types again today, the one in the morning was uneventful, the second at 5.30, on which we used V.H.F. for the first time, we saw four huge enemy formations but as we were only 6 we did not engage. We had one short scrap with Me 109's, but I only had one short burst – with no effect. These raids created a lot of damage in London. The provisional casualty list say 400 dead, 15,000 seriously injured: what complete swine these Jerries are.

Sunday, 8 September

Did not fly today and got afternoon off. Went on 4 days leave. Air raids have messed up London quite a bit.

Sunday, 15 September

I flew once today but missed the Big Blitz owing to my a/c being unservicable. Nothing was claimed by anyone because there were so many Jerries, over 200 in all. I am at 15 mins readiness tonight, and will be second off, if we have to fly. The RAF claimed 167 e/a destroyed, boy oh boy what a total. We had the station dance band in the mess tonight, and it turned into quite a party. Czernin is now DFC.

Tuesday, 17 September

We did a couple of patrols today but neither came to anything. I feel very depressed tonight. I don't know why, just a passing mood. Alf Bayne's engine cut taking off, and he had a glorious pile up, completely wrecking the Hurricane but only getting an odd bruise himself.

Wednesday, 18 September

We did four patrols today of over an hour each. On the first we saw lots of Huns way above us we could not engage, and anyway they were fighters. Nothing happened on any of the other patrols although there appear to have been lots of e/a about. We tried most unsuccessfully to play a game of snooker in the evening but the lights kept going out: switched out by the Control room when a Hun is about, how they flap here!!

Friday, 20 September

I went to the Sergeants' Mess this evening for a party and got to know a sweet little W.A.A.F. named Margaret Cameron and we had quite a kissing session after the party was over.

Tuesday, 24 September

I had just one (patrol) and one blitz only (8.30). We were attacked by ME 109s and having made our attack on an Me 109 I was making a second . . . when I realized I should let it all go. I levelled off. Suddenly there was a blinding flash on my port wing and I felt a hell of a blow on my left arm, and the blood running down. I went into a hell of a dive and came back to Debden. A cannon shell had hit my wing and a bit of it had hit me just above the elbow and behind. The shell had blown away most of my port flap. So I tried to land without flaps and I could not stop and crashed into a pile of stones just off the field, hitting my face and cutting it in two places. I was taken to Saffron Walden General Hospital, they operated but had to leave small pieces in . . .

Thursday, 26 September

Hospital.

Sunday, 29 September

Did nothing during the day but there was the usual band in the mess and when they packed up I completed the party at the Sergeants' Mess. Met Edith Heap and fell in love with her at sight. I rather cut Margaret Cameron and I am not as popular as I was!!!

Monday, 7 October

Returned to Debden, had grand party, and met Edith Heap, my God it seems to be the real thing this time. She is so sweet and seems to like me as much as I like her.

PO Wissler was reported missing in November 1940.

FINEST HOUR

JOHN BEARD

Pilot Officer John Beard was 23 at the time of the Battle of Britain. He flew a Hawker Hurricane Mk I, the mainstay RAF fighter during the Battle of Britain.

I was supposed to be away on a day's leave but dropped back to the aerodrome to see if there was a letter from my wife. When I found out that *all* the squadrons had gone off into action, I decided to stand by, because obviously something big was happening. While I was climbing into my flying kit, our Hurricanes came slipping back out of the sky to refuel, reload ammunition, and take off again. The returning pilots were full of talk about flocks of enemy bombers and fighters which were trying to break through along the Thames Estuary. You couldn't miss hitting them, they said. Off to the east I could hear the steady roll of anti-aircraft fire. It was a brilliant afternoon with a flawless blue sky. I was crazy to be off.

An instant later an aircraftsman rushed up with orders for me to make up a flight with some of the machines then reloading. My own Hurricane was a nice old kite, though it had a habit of flying left wing low at the slightest provocation. But since it had already accounted for fourteen German aircraft before I inherited it, I thought it had some luck, and I was glad when I squeezed myself into the same old seat again and grabbed the "stick".

We took off in two flights [six fighters], and as we started to gain height over the station we were told over the R. T. [radio-telephone] to keep circling for a while until we were made up to a stronger force. That didn't take long, and soon there was a complete squadron including a couple of Spitfires which had wandered in from somewhere.

Then came the big thrilling moment: ACTION ORDERS. Distantly I heard the hum of the generator in my R. T. earphones and then the voice of the ground controller crackling through with the call signs. Then the order "Fifty plus bombers, one hundred plus fighters over Canterbury at 15,000 heading northeast. Your vector [steering course to intercept] nine zero degrees. Over!"

We were flying in four V formations of three. I was flying No. 3 in Red flight, which was the squadron leader's and thus the leading flight. On we went, wing tips to left and right slowly rising and falling, the roar of our twelve Marlins drowning all other sound. We crossed over London, which, at 20,000 feet, seemed just a haze of smoke from its countless chimneys, with nothing visible except the faint glint of the barrage balloons and the wriggly silver line of the Thames.

I had too much to do watching the instruments and keeping formation to do much thinking. But once I caught a reflected glimpse of myself in the windscreen – a goggled, bloated, fat thing with the tube of my oxygen supply protruding gruesomely sideways from the mask which hid my mouth. Suddenly I was back at school again, on a hot afternoon when the Headmaster was taking the Sixth and droning on and on about the later Roman Emperors. The boy on my right was showing me surreptitiously some illustrations which he had pinched out of his father's medical books during the last holidays. I looked like one of those pictures.

It was an amazingly vivid memory, as if school was only

yesterday. And half my mind was thinking what wouldn't I then have given to be sitting in a Hurricane belting along at 350 miles an hour and out for a kill. *Me* defending London! I grinned at my old self at the thought.

Minutes went by Green fields and roads were now beneath us. I scanned the sky and the horizon for the first glimpse of the Germans. A new vector came through on the R. T. and we swung round with the sun behind us. Swift on the heels of this I heard Yellow flight leader call through the earphones. I looked quickly toward Yellow's position, and there they were!

It was really a terrific sight and quite beautiful. First they seemed just a cloud of light as the sun caught the many glistening chromium parts of their engines, their windshields, and the spin of their airscrew discs. Then, as our squadron hurtled nearer, the details stood out. I could see the bright-yellow noses of Messerschmitt fighters sandwiching the bombers, and could even pick out some of the types. The sky seemed full of them, packed in layers thousands of feet deep. They came on steadily, wavering up and down along the horizon. "Oh, golly," I thought, "golly, golly . . ."

And then any tension I had felt on the way suddenly left me. I was elated but very calm. I leaned over and switched on my reflector sight, flicked the catch on the gun button from "Safe" to "Fire", and lowered my seat till the circle and dot on the reflector sight shone darkly red in front of my eyes.

The squadron leader's voice came through the earphones, giving tactical orders. We swung round in a great circle to attack on their beam – into the thick of them. Then, on the order, down we went. I took my hand from the throttle lever so as to get both hands on the stick, and my thumb played neatly across the gun button. You have to steady a fighter just as you have to steady a rifle before you fire it.

My Merlin screamed as I went down in a steeply banked dive on to the tail of a forward line of Heinkels. I knew the air was full of aircraft flinging themselves about in all directions, but, hunched and snuggled down behind my sight I was conscious only of the Heinkel I had picked out. As the angle of my dive increased, the enemy machine loomed larger in the sight field, heaved toward the red dot, and then he was there!

I had an instant's flash of amazement at the Heinkel proceeding so regularly on its way with a fighter on its tail. "Why doesn't the fool *move?*" I thought, and actually caught myself flexing my muscles into the action *I* would have taken had I been he.

When he was square across the sight I pressed the button. There was a smooth trembling of my Hurricane as the eight-gun squirt shot out. I gave him a two-second burst and then another. Cordite fumes blew back into the cockpit making an acrid mixture with the smell of hot oil and the aircompressors.

I saw my first burst go in and, just as I was on top of him and turning away, I noticed a red glow inside the bomber. I turned tightly into position again and now saw several short tongues of flame lick out along the fuselage. Then he went down in a spin, blanketed with smoke and with pieces flying off.

I left him plummeting down and, horsing back on my stick, climbed up again for more. The sky was clearing, but ahead toward London I saw a small, tight formation of bombers completely encircled by a ring of Messerschmitts. They were still heading north. As I raced forward, three flights of Spitfires came zooming up from beneath them in a sort of Prince-of-Wales's-feathers manoeuvre. They burst through upward and outward, their guns going all the time. They must have each got one, for an instant later I saw the most extraordinary sight of eight German bombers and fighters diving earthward together in flames.

I turned away again and streaked after some distant specks ahead. Diving down, I noticed that the running progress of the battle had brought me over London again.

I could see the network of streets with the green space of Kensington Gardens, and I had an instant's glimpse of the Round Pond, where I sailed boats when I was a child. In that moment, and as I was rapidly overhauling the Germans ahead, a Dornier 17 sped right across my line of flight, closely pursued by a Hurricane. And behind the Hurricane came two Messerschmitts. He was too intent to have seen them and they had not seen me! They were coming slightly toward me. It was perfect. A kick at the rudder and I swung in toward them, thumbed the gun button, and let them have it. The first burst was placed just the right distance ahead of the leading Messerschmitt. He ran slap into it and he simply came to pieces in the air. His companion, with one of the speediest and most brilliant "get-outs" I have ever seen, went right away in a half Immelmann turn. I missed him completely. He must almost have been hit by the pieces of the leader but he got away. I hand it to him.

At that moment some instinct made me glance up at my rearview mirror and spot two Messerschmitts closing in on my tail. Instantly I hauled back on the stick and streaked upward. And just in time. For as I flicked into the climb, I saw the tracer streaks pass beneath me. As I turned I had a quick look round the "office" [cockpit]. My fuel reserve was running out and I had only about a second's supply of ammunition left. I was certainly in no condition to take on two Messerschmitts. But they seemed no more eager than I was. Perhaps they were in the same position, for they turned away for home. I put my nose down and did likewise.

Only on the way back did I realize how hot I was. I had forgotten to adjust the ventilator apparatus in all the stress of the fighting, and hadn't noticed the thermometer. With the sun on the windows all the time, the inside of the "office" was like an oven. Inside my flying suit I was in a bath of perspiration, and sweat was cascading down my face. I was dead tired and my neck ached from constantly turning my head on the lookout when going in and out of dogfights. Over east the sky was flecked with A. A. puffs, but I did not bother to investigate. Down I went, home.

At the station there was only time for a few minutes' stretch, a hurried report to the Intelligence Officer, and a brief comparing of notes with the other pilots. So far my squadron seemed to be intact, in spite of a terrific two hours in which we had accounted for at least thirty enemy aircraft.

But there was more to come. It was now about four p.m. and I gulped down some tea while the ground crew checked my Hurricane. Then, with about three flights collected, we took off again. We seemed to be rather longer this time circling and gaining height above the station before the orders came through on the R.T. It was to patrol an area along the Thames Estuary at 20,000 feet. But we never got there.

We had no sooner got above the docks than we ran into the first lot of enemy bombers. They were coming up in line about 5,000 feet below us. The line stretched on and on across the horizon. Above, on our level, were assorted groups of enemy fighters. Some were already in action, with our fellows spinning and twirling among them. Again I got that tightening feeling at the throat, for it really was a sight to make you gasp.

But we all knew what to do. We went for the bombers. Kicking her over, I went down after the first of them, a Heinkel 111. He turned away as I approached, chiefly because some of our fellows had already broken into the line and had scattered it. Before I got up he had been joined by two more. They were forming a V and heading south across the river.

I went after them. Closing in on the tail of the left one, I ran into a stream of crossfire from all three. How it missed me I don't know. For a second the whole air in front was thick with tracer trails. It seemed to be coming straight at me, only to curl away by the windows and go lazily past. I felt one slight bank, however, and glancing quickly, saw a small hole at the end of my starboard wing. Then, as the

Heinkel drifted across my sights, I pressed the button – once – twice . . . Nothing happened.

I panicked for a moment till I looked down and saw that I had forgotten to turn the safety-catch knob to the "Fire" position. I flicked it over at once and in that instant saw that three bombers, to hasten their getaway, had jettisoned all their bombs. They seemed to peel off in a steady stream. We were over the southern outskirts of London now and I remember hoping that most of them would miss the little houses and plunge into fields.

But dropping the bombs did not help my Heinkel. I let him have a long burst at close range, which got him right in the "office". I saw him turn slowly over and go down, and followed to give him another squirt. Just then there was a terrific crash in front of me. Something flew past my window, and the whole aircraft shook as the engine raced itself to pieces. I had been hit by A.A. fire aimed at the bombers, my airscrew had been blown off, and I was going down in a spin.

The next few seconds were a bit wild and confused. I remember switching off and flinging back the sliding roof almost in one gesture. Then I tried to vault out through the roof. But I had forgotten to release my safety belt. As I fumbled at the pin the falling aircraft gave a twist which shot me through the open cover. Before I was free, the air stream hit me like a solid blow and knocked me sideways. I felt my arm hit something, and then I was falling over and over with fields and streets and sky gyrating madly past my eyes.

I grabbed at the rip cord on my chute. Missed it. Grabbed again. Missed it. That was no fun. Then I remember saying to myself, "This won't do. Take it easy, take it slowly." I tried again and found the rip cord grip and pulled. There was a terrific wrench at my thighs and then I was floating still and peacefully with my "brolly" canopy billowing above my head.

The rest was lovely. I sat at my ease just floating gradually down, breathing deep, and looking around. I was drifting across London again at about 2,000 feet.

TALLY HO!

ROGER HALL

A transferred army officer, Hall gained his RAF wings in August 1940, being almost immediately posted to 152 Squadron in Fighter Command's 10th Group (which covered South West England). The Battle of Britain was at its height.

Beneath us, as we reached thirty-thousand feet and levelled out, there was a flat carpet of cloud, pure white in the bright sunlight. Above us, apart from a few delicate and remote wisps of cirrus, the sky was an intense blue, the sort of blue you find on an artist's palette. Behind us and slightly to our starboard the sun was still high in the sky and was dazzling to look into. To the east the stratus cloud was beginning to disperse and we could see across the North Sea to the Dutch Islands. Visibility was limited only by the curvature of the Earth.

The entire firmament, the vault of the heavens, was revealed to us. It stretched from Lille and St. Omer in the rolling plains of the Pas-de-Calais to the south, eastwards down the sandy coastline of Northern France, past Dunkirk to the Belgian frontier, beyond that to the Dutch Islands and past them to the faint line of the German coast, and up as far north as the Norfolk coast of our own country. Such was a panorama that confronted us as we levelled out five miles above the earth and higher than the highest mountain.

"Hallo Mandrake," Maida Leader called. "Maida Squadron now at angels three-zero – Bandits in sight – Tally Ho." "Well done, Maida Leader – Good luck – Good luck – over to you," Mandrake replied.

Yes, there they were all right. Very many bandits, too. The sky was full of black dots, which, from where we were at the moment, might have been anything; but we knew only too well what they were. They were coming from the south; squadron upon squadron, fleet upon fleet, an aerial Armada the size of which I don't suppose Jules Verne or even Wells had envisaged. The main body of them was below us by quite ten thousand feet, but above them as escort, winged the protective fighter screen proudly trailing their long white plumes of vapour.

Our position was somewhere over Surrey at the moment, and as we approached the enemy formations which were still some miles away, we saw our own fighters – the eleven group squadrons and some from twelve group in the Midlands – coming up from the north. There seemed to be quite a number of us. They too were black dots, climbing in groups of twelve or thirty-six in wing formation. Most of them were Hurricanes.

The enemy appeared to be disposed in three distinct and separate groups each comprising a hundred or more bombers. Above each group were about fifty fighters – M.E. 109's, and M.E. 110's. The bombers were Heinkels, Dorniers and Junkers 88's.

"Line astern formation – Maida squadron," ordered Maida Leader. We took up our battle formations at once, with "A" Flight in the order of Red, Yellow and White. There were two machines behind me and three in front. "Come up into line abreast 'B' Flight" came the next order from Red one. When we had completed this change the squadron was disposed in two lines of six machines flying abreast and at a distance of about fifty yards between each Flight.

We were ready to attack. We were now in the battle area and three-quarters of an hour had elapsed since we had taken off.

The two bomber formations furthest from us were already being attacked by a considerable number of our fighters. Spitfires and Hurricanes appeared to be in equal numbers at the time. Some of the German machines were already falling out of their hitherto ordered ranks and floundering towards the earth. There was a little ack-ack fire coming from up somewhere on the ground although its paucity seemed pathetic and its effect was little more than that of a defiant gesture.

We approached the westernmost bomber formation from the front port quarter, but we were some ten thousand feet higher than they were and we hadn't started to dive yet. Immediately above the bombers were some twin-engined fighters, M.E. 110's. Maida Leader let the formation get a little in front of us then he gave the order "Going down now Maida aircraft," turning his machine upside-down as he gave it. The whole of "A" Flight, one after the other, peeled off after him, upside-down at first and then into a vertical dive.

When they had gone "B" Flight followed suit. Ferdie and I turned over with a hard leftward pressure to the stick to bring the starboard wing up to right angles to the horizon, and some application to the port or bottom rudder pedal to keep the nose from rising. Keeping the controls like this, the starboard wing fell over until it was parallel to the horizon again, but upside-down. Pulling the stick back from this position the nose of my machine fell towards the ground and followed White one in front, now going vertically down on to the bombers almost directly below us. Our speed started to build up immediately. It went from three hundred miles per hour to four and more. White one in front, his tail wheel some distance below me but visible through the upper part of my windscreen, was turning his machine in the vertical plane from one side to the other by the use of his ailerons. Red Section had reached the formation and had formed into a loosened echelon to starboard as they attacked. They were coming straight down on top of the bombers, having gone slap through the protective M.E. 110 fighter screen, ignoring them completely.

Now it was our turn. With one eye on our own machines I slipped out slightly to the right of Ferdie and placed the red dot of my sight firmly in front and in line with the starboard engine of a Dornier vertically below me and about three hundred yards off. I felt apprehensive lest I should collide with our own machines in the mêlée that was to ensue. I seemed to see one move ahead what the positions of our machines would be, and where I should be in relation to them if I wasn't careful. I pressed my trigger and through my inch thick windscreen I saw the tracers spiralling away hitting free air in front of the bomber's engine. I was allowing too much deflection. I must correct. I pushed the stick further forward. My machine was past the vertical and I was feeling the effect of the negative gravity trying to throw me out of the machine, forcing my body up into the perspex hood of the cockpit. My Sutton harness was biting into my shoulders and blood was forcing its way to my head, turning everything red. My tracers were hitting the bomber's engine and bits of metal were beginning to fly off it. I was getting too close to it, much too close. I knew I must pull away but I seemed hypnotised and went still closer, fascinated by what was happening. I was oblivious to everything else. I pulled away just in time to miss hitting the Dornier's starboard wing-tip. I turned my machine to the right on ailerons and heaved back on the stick, inflicting a terrific amount of gravity on to the machine. I was pressed down into the cockpit again and a black veil came over my eyes and I could see nothing.

I eased the stick a little to regain my vision and to look for Ferdie. I saw a machine, a single Spitfire, climbing up after a dive about five hundred yards in front of me and flew after it for all I was worth. I was going faster than it was and I soon caught up with it – in fact I overshot it. It was Ferdie all right. I could see the "C" Charlie alongside our squadron letters on his fuselage. I pulled out to one side and back again hurling my machine at the air without any finesse, just to absorb some speed so that Ferdie could catch up with me. "C" Charlie went past me and I thrust my throttle forward lest I should lose him. I got in behind him again and called him up to tell him so. He said: "Keep an eye out behind and don't stop weaving." I acknowledged his message and started to fall back a bit to get some room. Ferdie had turned out to the flank of the enemy formation and had taken a wide sweeping orbit to port, climbing fast as he did so. I threw my aircraft first on to its port wing-tip to pull it round, then fully over to the other tip for another steep turn, and round again and again, blacking out on each turn. We were vulnerable on the climb, intensely so, for we were so slow.

I saw them coming quite suddenly on a left turn; red tracers coming towards us from the centre of a large black twin-engined M.E. 110 which wasn't quite far enough in the sun from us to be totally obscured, though I had to squint to identify it. I shouted to Ferdie but he had already seen the tracers flash past him and had discontinued his port climbing turn and had started to turn over on his back and to dive. I followed, doing the same thing, but the M.E. 110 must have done so too for the tracers were still following us. We dived for about a thousand feet, I should think, and I kept wondering why my machine had not been hit.

Ferdie started to ease his dive a bit. I watched him turn his machine on to its side and stay there for a second, then its nose came up, still on its side, and the whole aircraft seemed to come round in a barrel-roll as if clinging to the inside of some revolving drum. I tried to imitate this manoeuvre but I didn't know how to, so I just thrust open the throttle and aimed my machine in Ferdie's direction and eventually caught him up.

The M.E. 110 had gone off somewhere. I got up to

Ferdie and slid once more under the doubtful protection of his tail and told him that I was there. I continued to weave like a pilot inspired, but my inspiration was the result of sheer terror and nothing more.

All the time we were moving towards the bombers; but we moved indirectly by turns, and that was the only way we could move with any degree of immunity now. Four Spitfires flashed past in front of us, they weren't ours, though, for I noticed the markings. There was a lot of talking going on on the ether and we seemed to be on the same frequency as a lot of other squadrons. "Hallo Firefly Yellow Section – 110 behind you" – "Hallo Cushing Control – Knockout Red leader returning to base to refuel." "Close up Knockout 'N' for Nellie and watch for those 109's on your left" – "All right Landsdown Squadron – control answering – your message received – many more bandits coming from the east – over" – "Talker White two where the bloody hell are you?" – "Going down now Sheldrake Squadron – loosen up a bit" – "You clumsy clot – Hurricane 'Y' Yoke – what the flaming hades do you think you are doing?" – "I don't know Blue one but there are some bastards up there on the left – nine o'clock above" – Even the Germans came in intermittently: "Achtung, Achtung – drei Spitfeuer unter, unter Achtung, Spitfeuer, Spitfeuer." "Tally Ho – Tally Ho – Homer Red leader attacking now." "Get off the bastard air Homer leader" – "Yes I can see Rimmer leader – Red two answering – Glycol leak I think – he's getting out – yes he's baled out he's o.k."

And so it went on incessantly, disjointed bits of conversation coming from different units all revealing some private little episode in the great battle of which each story was a small part of the integral whole.

Two 109's were coming up behind the four Spitfires and instinctively I found myself thrusting forward my two-way radio switch to the transmitting position and calling out "Look out those four Spitfires – 109's behind you – look out." I felt that my message could hardly be of less importance than some that I had heard, but no heed was taken of it. The two 109's had now settled themselves on the tail of the rear Spitfire and were pumping cannon shells into it. We were some way off but Ferdie too saw them and changed direction to starboard, opening up his throttle as we closed. The fourth Spitfire, or "tail-end Charlie", had broken away, black smoke pouring from its engine, and the third in line came under fire now from the same 109. We approached the two 109's from above their starboard rear quarter and, taking a long deflection shot from what must have been still out of range, Ferdie opened fire on the leader. The 109 didn't see us for he still continued to fire at number three until it too started to trail Glycol from its radiator and turned over on its back breaking away from the remaining two. "Look out Black one – look out Black Section Apple Squadron – 109's– 109's came the belated warning, possibly from number three as he went down. At last number one turned steeply to port, with the two 109's still hanging on to their tails now firing at number two. They were presenting a relatively stationary target in us now for we were directly behind them. Ferdie's bullets were hitting the second 109 now and pieces of its tail unit were coming away and floating past underneath us. The 109 jinked to the starboard. The leading Spitfire followed by its number two had now turned full circle in a very tight turn and as yet it didn't seem that either of them had been hit. The 109 leader was vainly trying to keep into the same turn but couldn't hold it tight enough so I think his bullets were skidding past the starboard of the Spitfires. The rear 109's tail unit disintegrated under Ferdie's fire and a large chunk of it slithered across the top surface of my starboard wing, denting the panels but making no noise. I put my hand up to my face for a second.

The fuselage of the 109 fell away below us and we came into the leader. I hadn't fired at it yet but now I slipped out to port of Ferdie as the leader turned right steeply and over on to its back to show its duck-egg blue belly to us. I came up almost to line abreast of Ferdie on his port side and fired at the under surface of the German machine, turning upside-down with it. The earth was now above my perspex hood and I was trying to keep my sights on the 109 in this attitude, pushing my stick forward to do so. Pieces of refuse rose up from the floor of my machine and the engine spluttered and coughed as the carburettor became temporarily starved of fuel. My propeller idled helplessly for a second and my harness straps bit into my shoulders again. Flames leapt from the engine of the 109 but at the same time there was a loud bang from somewhere behind me and I heard "Look out Roger" as a large hole appeared near my starboard wing-tip throwing up the matt green metal into a ragged rent to show the naked aluminium beneath.

I broke from the 109 and turned steeply to starboard throwing the stick over to the right and then pulling it back into me and blacking out at once. Easing out I saw three 110's go past my tail in "V" formation but they made no attempt to follow me round. "Hallo Roger – Are you O.K.?" I heard Ferdie calling. "I think so – where are you?" I called back.

"I'm on your tail – keep turning" came Ferdie's reply. Thank God, I thought. Ferdie and I seemed to be alone in the sky. It was often like this. At one moment the air seemed to be full of aircraft and the next there was nothing except you. Ferdie came up in "V" on my port side telling me at the same time that he thought we had better try to find the rest of the squadron.

The battle had gone to the north. We at this moment were somewhere over the western part of Kent, and a little less than a quarter of an hour had elapsed since we had delivered our first attack on the bombers. Ferdie set course to the north where we could see in the distance the main body of aircraft. London with its barrage balloons floating unconcernedly, like a flock of grazing sheep, ten thousand feet above it, was now feeling the full impact of the enemy bombers. Those that had got through – and the majority of them had – were letting their bombs go. I recalled for an instant Mr Baldwin's prophecy, not a sanguine one, made to the House of Commons some five years before when he said that the bomber will always get through.

Now it was doing just that. I wondered if it need have done. As we approached South London the ground beneath us became obscured by smoke from the bomb explosions which appeared suddenly from the most unlikely sort of places – an open field, a house, a row of houses, a factory, railway sidings, all sorts of things. Suddenly there would be a flash, then a cloud of reddish dust obscuring whatever was there before and then drifting away horizontally to reveal once more what was left of the target.

I saw a whole stick of bombs in a straight line advancing like a creeping barrage such as you would see on the films in pictures like "Journey's End" or "All quiet on the Western Front", but this time they were not over the muddy desolation of No-Man's Land but over Croydon, Surbiton and Earl's Court. I wondered what the people were like who were fighting the Battle of Britain just as surely as we were doing but in a less spectacular fashion. I thought of the air raid wardens shepherding their flocks to the air raid trenches without a thought of their own safety; the Auxiliary Firemen and the regular fire brigades who were clambering about the newly settled rubble strewn with white-hot and flaming girders and charred wood shiny black with heat, to pull out the victims buried beneath; the nurses, both the professional ones and the V.A.D.'s in their scarlet cloaks and immaculate white caps and cuffs, who were also clambering about the shambles to administer first aid to the wounded and give morphine to the badly hurt; the St John's Ambulance brigade who always were on the spot somehow no matter where or under what circumstances an accident or emergency occurred, helping, encouraging and uplifting the victims without thought for themselves; the Red Cross and all the civilian volunteers who, when an emergency arises, always go to assist. Not least I thought of the priests and clergy who would also be there, not only to administer the final rites to the dying but to provide an inspiration to those who had lost faith or through shock seemed temporarily lost. The clergy were there all right and showed that their job was not just a once-a-week affair at the Church, but that religion was as much a part of everyday living as was eating and sleeping.

I felt humble when I thought of what was going on down there on the ground. We weren't the only people fighting the Battle of Britain. There were the ordinary people, besides these I've mentioned, all going about their jobs quietly yet heroically and without any fuss or complaint. They had no mention in the press or news bulletins, their jobs were routine and hum-drum and they got no medals.

We were now in the battle area once again and the fighting had increased its tempo. The British fighters were becoming more audacious, had abandoned any restraint that they might have had at the outset, and were allowing the bombers no respite at all. If they weren't able to prevent them from reaching their target they were trying desperately to prevent them from getting back to their bases in Northern France. The air was full of machines, the fighters, British and German, performing the most fantastic and incredibly beautiful evolutions. Dark oily brown streams of smoke and fire hung vertically in the sky from each floundering aircraft, friend or foe, as it plunged to its own funeral pyre miles below on the English countryside. The sky, high up aloft, was an integrated medley of white tracery, delicately woven and interwoven by the fighters as they searched for their opponents. White puffs of ack-ack fire hung limply in mid-air and parachute canopies drifted slowly towards the ground.

It was an English summer's evening. It was about a quarter to six. We had been in the air now for about an hour and a quarter and our fuel would not last much longer. We had failed to join up with the rest of the flight, but this was understandable and almost inevitable under the circumstances. I don't suppose the others were in any formation other than sections now.

Beneath us at about sixteen thousand feet, while we were at twenty-three, there were four Dorniers by themselves still going north and I presumed, for that reason, they hadn't yet dropped their bombs. Ferdie had seen them and was making for them. Three Hurricanes in line astern had seen the same target, had overtaken them, turned, and were delivering a head-on attack in a slightly echeloned formation. It was an inspiring sight, but the Dorniers appeared unshaken as the Hurricanes flew towards them firing all the time. Then the one on the port flank turned sharply to the left, jettisoning its bomb load as it went. The leading Hurricane got on to its tail and I saw a sheet of flame spring out from somewhere near its centre section and billow back over the top surface of its wing, increasing in size until it had enveloped the entire machine except the extreme tips of its two wings. I didn't look at it any more.

We were now approaching the remaining three Dorniers and we came up directly behind them in line astern. "Get out to port Roger" cried Ferdie "and take the left one." I slid outside Ferdie and settled my sight on the Dornier's starboard engine nacelle. We were not within range yet but not far off. The Dorniers saw us coming all right and their rear-gunners were opening fire on us, tracer bullets coming perilously close to our machines. I jinked out to port in a lightning steep turn and then came back to my original position and fired immediately at the gunner and not the engine. The tracers stopped coming from that Dornier. I changed my aim to the port engine and fired again, one longish burst and my "De-Wilde" ammunition ran up the trailing edge of the Dornier's port wing in little dancing sparks of fire until they reached the engine. The engine exploded and the machine lurched violently for a second as if a ton weight had landed on the wing and then fallen off again for, as soon as the port wing had dropped it picked up again and the bomber still kept formation despite the damage to its engine. The engine was now totally obscured by thick black smoke which was being swept back on to my windscreen. I was too close to the bomber now to do anything but break off my attack and pull away. I didn't see what had happened to the Dornier that Ferdie had attacked and what's more I could no longer see Ferdie.

I broke off in a steep climbing turn to port scanning the sky for a single Spitfire – "C" Charlie. There were lots of lone Spitfires, there were lots of lone Hurricanes and there were lots of lone bombers but it was impossible now and I thought improvident to attempt to find Ferdie in all this mêlée. I began to get concerned about my petrol reserves as we had been in the air almost an hour and a half now and it was a long way back to base.

I pressed my petrol indicator buttons and one tank was completely empty, the other registering twenty-two gallons. I began to make some hasty calculations concerning speed, time and distance and decided that if I set course for base now and travelled fairly slowly I could make it. I could put down at another airfield of course and get refuelled, but it might be bad policy, especially for a new pilot.

I called up Ferdie, thinking, not very hopefully, that he might hear me, and told him what I was doing. Surprisingly he came back on the air at once in reply and said that he was also returning to base and asked me if I thought I had got enough fuel. He said that he thought it ought to be enough and added as an after-thought that I should make certain that my wheels and flaps were working satisfactorily before coming too low, for they could be damaged. I thanked him for his advice and listened out. I was by myself now and still in the battle area and I was weaving madly for I realised how vulnerable I was. I was easy meat to German fighters, just their cup of tea, particularly if there should be more than one of them, for the Germans always seemed to fancy themselves when the odds were in their favour, particularly numerical odds. It was past six o'clock now and the sun was getting lower in the west, the direction I was travelling in. If I were going to be attacked from the sun, then it would be a head on attack. I felt fairly secure from behind, provided I kept doing steep turns.

I could see a single Spitfire in front of me and a little lower. It must be Ferdie, I thought at once, and chased after it to catch it up. It would be nice to go back to base together. When I got closer to it I noticed a white stream of Glycol coming away from the underneath. There wasn't very much but it was enough to tell me that the machine had been hit in the radiator. It seemed to be going down on a straight course in a shallow dive. I got to within about three hundred yards of it and called up Ferdie to ask his position, feeling that he would be sure to tell me if he had been hit in the radiator, although he might not have wanted me to know in the first instance. I got no reply and for a second I became convinced that he had been attacked since I had last spoken to him. I opened up my throttle, although I ought to have been conserving my fuel. From the direct rear all Spitfires look exactly the same and I had to get up close to read the lettering. I came up on its port side and at a distance of about twenty yards. It wasn't Ferdie. I felt relief. It didn't belong to Maida Squadron at all. It was "G" for George and belonged to some totally different squadron. I made a mental note of the lettering for "Brains's" benefit. I closed in a bit to see what it was all about. The Glycol leak wasn't severe. I couldn't think what to make of it at all. Perhaps the pilot wasn't aware of the leak. Perhaps he had baled out already and the machine, as they have been known to, was carrying on alone, like the "Marie Celeste". Perhaps it was my imagination, an hallucination after the excitement and strain of the past hour. I came in very close to it as though I were in squadron formation and it no longer presented a mystery to me. The pilot was there, his head resting motionless against the side of the perspex hood. Where it was resting, and behind where it was resting, the perspex was coloured crimson. Now and then as the aircraft encountered a disturbance and bumped a little, the pilot's head moved forward and back again. The hood was slightly open at the front which gave me the impression that he had made an instinctive last minute bid to get out before he had died. The wind had blown into the cockpit and had blown the blood which must have gushed from his head, back along the entire length of the cockpit like scarlet rain. I became suddenly and painfully aware that I·was being foolhardy to stay so close as this for a sudden reflex from the pilot, dead though he was, a sudden thrust of the rudder bar or a movement from the stick could hurl the aircraft at me. I swung out and left it. I didn't look back any more. Before I left it, it had started to dive more steeply, and the Glycol flowed more freely as the nose dipped and the speed increased.

I thanked God for many things as I flew back away from the din and noise of the battle through the cool and the peace of the evening across the New Forest and above Netley to base. I landed my machine at six-thirty, stepped out and went to the hut.

Brains was very much in evidence and busy collecting reports from different people. Most of the pilots had landed and Ferdie, I was glad to see, was among them. I gave my report to Brains and Ferdie checked it. I was granted two damaged aircraft and Ferdie got one confirmed and two damaged. There were still three of our pilots unaccounted for. P/O Watty was not down and Red two and Blue two were overdue. We were allowed up to the mess in parties of six at a time, for we were still on readiness until nine o'clock. Ferdie and I went together and discussed the events of the last hour or so. We had some supper and then went down to dispersal again to relieve the others. It was unlikely, I was told, that we should be scrambled again in any strength for it was getting late now and the Germans would hardly be likely to mount another large offensive as late as this.

Brains was still down in the hut and was spending most of his time at the telephone answering calls from Group Intelligence and making enquiries from other stations as to the possible fate of our own missing pilots. Eventually news came through that Watty was safe but had been shot down near Southampton on his way back to base. He had been attacked by two M.E. 109's in this area and his machine had been hit in the Glycol tank but he had managed to force-land. He was taken to the hospital there because the Medical Officer had found a rip in his tunic which, upon further investigation, had revealed that he had got some shrapnel of some sort into his arm. We heard later that Red two and Blue two had both been shot down and both of them had been killed. Blue two had gone down in flames in front of a M.E. 110 and Red two had pressed his attack too closely to a Heinkel 111 and had gone into it. Both of these were sergeant pilots.

The squadron, according to Brains's assessment, had accounted for eight confirmed aircraft, three probables and seven damaged. There was no further flying that day and we were released at nine o'clock. We went up to the mess as usual and after some drinks we got into our cars and left the camp. We were to rendezvous at The Sunray.

We got to The Sunray after five minutes or so. It wasn't far from the aerodrome and was tucked away at the end of a lane leading from the main Weymouth-Wareham road.

The Sunray was blacked out and it was pitch dark outside when we switched off our lights. We groped our way to the door which Chumley seemed able to find in some instinctive manner. He opened the front door calling to me "Switch your radar on Roger" and pulled aside a blanket which had been rigged up to act as a further precaution to prevent the light from escaping as the main door was opened. We got inside to find the others already drinking. Cocky seemed to be in the chair as Chumley and I came in and he called out "Lost again White Section – biggies coming up for both of you."

The Sunray was an old pub and full of atmosphere. The

ceilings were low and oak beams ran the entire length of them. In between the beams, the ceiling itself was made of wood of the same colour. It seemed dark at first but there was a liberal amount of lamps, not on the ceiling itself but on the walls, and these gave a soft light that was distinctly cosy. There were tables of heavy oak around which were chairs made out of barrels, highly polished and each containing soft plushy cushions. Around the walls ran an almost continuous cushion-covered bench, and the windows, from what I could see of them, for they were heavily curtained, were made of bottle-glass and were only translucent. The serving bar in the middle of the room was round and from it hung a varied assortment of brilliantly polished copper and brass ornaments. There were roses in copper vases standing on some of the tables and a bowl or two on the bar itself. There were sandwiches beneath glass cases and sausage-rolls as well. The visible atmosphere in the room was cloudy with tobacco smoke which seemed to reach its optimum height a foot or so from the ceiling where it appeared to flatten out and drift in horizontal layers until someone passed through it and then it appeared to follow whoever did so for a moment. There was wireless somewhere in the room, for I could hear music coming from near where I was standing.

I was by the bar with the others and I had finished my third pint of bitter and was talking to Cocky. The night was quite early yet and Bottle was standing up at the bar with Dimmy, Chumley and Pete; they were all laughing at the top of their voices and a bit further along was Ferdie listening to what might, I think, have been a rather long-drawn-out story from one of the sergeant pilots, while two others seemed impatiently trying to get him to the point. Ferdie seemed to be quite amused at the process. There were two of our Polish pilots here too, both non-commissioned and their names were so difficult to pronounce that we simply called them "Zig" and "Zag". They didn't seem to take any offence at this abbreviation. They were excellent pilots, both of them.

The wireless now started to play the theme of Tchaikovsky's "Swan Lake" ballet and when I'd got my sixth pint I mentally detached myself from the rest for a moment.

"Wotcher Roger, mine's a pint of black and tan – have one yourself." I was jolted back to reality by this, accompanied by a hearty slap on the back from Ferdie, who had wormed his way across to me.

I had my seventh pint with Ferdie and we both edged up closer to the bar where the main body of the squadron seemed to have congregated. It was Cocky who, high spirited and irrepressible as ever, said "Come on boys, we've had this – next stop The Crown." We picked up our caps and made for the door. "Mind the light," someone shouted as the protective blanket was thrust aside for a moment. The air outside was cold and it hit me like a cold shower for a brief second while I gathered my wits. Chumley piled into the passenger seat. I was feeling perhaps a little too self-confident after the drinks but I felt sure I would make it somehow.

We got on to the main road again and Chumley directed us to The Crown in Weymouth. The road was fairly free of traffic and I gave the little car full rein for a while. It was dark and just in front of me there seemed to be an even darker but obscure sort of shape which I found difficulty in identifying for a moment. "For Christ's sake, man," Chumley shouted. Cocky's large Humber had pulled up on the verge and its occupants were busy relieving themselves by the roadside, but one of them was standing in front of the rear light and obscuring it. We were travelling at not much less than seventy-five m.p.h. when Chumley shouted at me and the Humber was only about thirty yards from us when I recognised it. My slow-wittedness only now became evident but I felt quite confident and in complete control of my faculties as I faced the emergency. I pulled the wheel over to the right, not abruptly but absolutely surely and with a calculated pressure to allow me only inches, inches enough to guide the left mud-guard past the Humber's off rear bumper. At the time I was in full control and thinking how fine and assured were my reactions, how much finer they were now than they ever were when I had had no drink. The sense of complete infallibility and the consequent denial of any risk had overtaken me and the feeling, if anything, became accentuated when the little car had passed Cocky's large Humber, which it did by the barest fraction of an inch, to the accompanying shout of "Look out, 109's behind" from those who were standing by the verge and otherwise engaged. "No road sense, those boys," Chumley remarked.

The Crown was quite a different sort of place from The Sunray. From the outside it was distinctly unpretentious in appearance, just a flat-sided building flanking the back street down by the harbour. It had four windows, two top and bottom and a door in the middle. We went in, and as I had rather expected, it was an ordinary working-man's pub. There were no furnishings to speak of, the floor was just plain wooden boards and the few tables were round with marble tops and the conventional china ash-trays advertising some type of lager or whisky. The bar occupied the whole one side of the room and the barman greeted us warmly as we arrived. Chumley ordered two pints of bitter. Apparently the squadron were well-known and held in high esteem.

The others arrived soon after we got there and the drinks were on me this time. There was a dart-board in the corner of the room and, not surprisingly, we threw badly. What did it matter how we played I thought, as long as we let off some steam.

When we left The Crown at closing time I was drunk, but we didn't return to the aerodrome. Bottle had some friends in Bournemouth and it was to Bournemouth that he'd decided to go. I was too drunk to drive and so was Chumley, who had left The Crown before closing time and taken up his position in the passenger seat of my car where he was now fast asleep. Dimmy and I lifted him out, still asleep, into the back of Cocky's Humber. Dimmy, who, so he claimed, was more sober than I, said he would drive my car. I made no protest. I relapsed into the passenger seat and fell asleep as the car gathered speed towards Bournemouth. I woke up as soon as the car came to a standstill, feeling a lot more sober. It was about half-past eleven when we went through the door of this quite large private house. Bottle's and Cocky's car had already arrived and the occupants had apparently gone inside. The door opened and a girl greeted us. "I'm Pam, come on in the others are here," she said. Everyone was seated in or on some sort of chair or stool and all had a glass of some sort in their hand. There were two other girls there besides Pam.

I was beginning to feel rather tired about this time and I would have been glad to get back to camp, especially as I had to be on dawn readiness again. The atmosphere here didn't seem conducive to any sort of rowdery like The Crown or The Compass and the girls didn't somehow seem to fit into the picture. They weren't on the same wave-length. It was about two-thirty in the morning when we finally left.

We arrived back at the mess just after four o'clock, having stopped at an all-night café for eggs and bacon and coffee. I had to be on readiness at five-thirty and it seemed hardly worth-while going to bed, so I decided to go straight down to dispersal, to find I was the only one there. I had just an hour and a half's sleep before I was due to take-off on dawn patrol.

Hall was withdrawn from active service in September 1942, shortly afterwards suffering a mental breakdown. He made a full recovery.

SHALL I LIVE FOR A GHOST?

RICHARD HILLARY

*A Spitfire pilot with No. 603 Squadron, Hillary was
shot down on September 3 1940.*

I was falling. Falling slowly through a dark pit. I was dead.
My body, headless, circled in front of me. I saw it with my
mind, my mind that was the redness in front of the eye, the
dull scream in the ear, the grinning of the mouth, the skin
crawling on the skull. It was death and resurrection.
Terror, moving with me, touched my cheek with hers
and I felt the flesh wince. Faster, faster. . . . I was hot now,
hot, again one with my body, on fire and screaming
soundlessly. Dear God, no! No! Not that, not again.
The sickly smell of death was in my nostrils and a confused roar of sound. Then all was quiet. I was back.

Someone was holding my arms.

"Quiet now. There's a good boy. You're going to be all
right. You've been very ill and you mustn't talk."

I tried to reach up my hand but could not.

"Is that you, nurse? What have they done to me?"

"Well, they've put something on your face and hands to
stop them hurting and you won't be able to see for a little
while. But you mustn't talk: you're not strong enough
yet."

Gradually I realized what had happened. My face and

hands had been scrubbed and then sprayed with tannic acid. The acid had formed into a hard black cement. My eyes alone had received different treatment: they were coated with a thick layer of gentian violet. My arms were propped up in front of me, the fingers extended like witches' claws, and my body was hung loosely on straps just clear of the bed.

I can recollect no moments of acute agony in the four days which I spent in that hospital; only a great sea of pain in which I floated almost with comfort. Every three hours I was injected with morphia, so while imagining myself quite coherent, I was for the most part in a semi-stupor. The memory of it has remained a confused blur.

Two days without eating, and then periodic doses of liquid food taken through a tube. An appalling thirst, and hundreds of bottles of ginger beer. Being blind, and not really feeling strong enough to care. Imagining myself back in my plane, unable to get out, and waking to find myself shouting and bathed in sweat. My parents coming down to see me and their wonderful self-control.

They arrived in the late afternoon of my second day in bed, having with admirable restraint done nothing the first day. On the morning of the crash my mother had been on her way to the Red Cross, when she felt a premonition that she must go home. She told the taxi-driver to turn about and arrived at the flat to hear the telephone ringing. It was our Squadron Adjutant, trying to reach my father. Embarrassed by finding himself talking to my mother, he started in on a glamorized history of my exploits in the air and was bewildered by my mother cutting him short to ask where I was. He managed somehow after about five minutes of incoherent stuttering to get over his news.

They arrived in the afternoon and were met by Matron. Outside my ward a twittery nurse explained that they must not expect to find me looking quite normal, and they were ushered in. The room was in darkness; I just a dim shape in one corner. Then the blinds were shot up, all the lights switched on, and there I was. As my mother remarked later, the performance lacked only the rolling of drums and a spotlight. For the sake of decorum my face had been covered with white gauze, with a slit in the middle through which protruded my lips.

We spoke little, my only coherent remark being that I had no wish to go on living if I were to look like Alice. Alice was a large country girl who had once been our maid. As a child she had been burned and disfigured by a Primus stove. I was not aware that she had made any impression on me, but now I was unable to get her out of my mind. It was not so much her looks as her smell I had continually in my nostrils and which I couldn't disassociate from the disfigurement.

They sat quietly and listened to me rambling for an hour. Then it was time for my dressings and they took their leave.

The smell of ether. Matron once doing my dressing with three orderlies holding my arms; a nurse weeping quietly at the head of the bed, and no remembered sign of a doctor. A visit from the lifeboat crew that had picked me up, and a terrible longing to make sense when talking to them. Their inarticulate sympathy and assurance of quick recovery. Their discovery that an ancestor of mine had founded the lifeboats, and my pompous and unsolicited promise of a subscription. The expectation of an American ambulance to drive me up to the Masonic Hospital (for Margate was used only as a clearing station). Believing that I was already in it and on my way, and waking to the disappointment that I had not been moved. A dream that I was fighting to open my eyes and could not: waking in a sweat to realize it was a dream and then finding it to be true. A sensation of time slowing down, of words and actions, all in slow motion. Sweat, pain, smells, cheering messages from the Squadron, and an overriding apathy.

Finally I was moved. The ambulance appeared with a cargo of two somewhat nervous A.T.S. women who were to drive me to London, and, with my nurse in attendance, and wrapped in an old grandmother's shawl, I was carried aboard and we were off. For the first few miles I felt quite well, dictated letters to my nurse, drank bottle after bottle of ginger beer, and gossiped with the drivers. They described the countryside for me, told me they were new to the job, expressed satisfaction at having me for a consignment, asked me if I felt fine. Yes, I said, I felt fine; asked my nurse if the drivers were pretty, heard her answer yes, heard them simpering, and we were all very matey. But after about half an hour my arms began to throb from the rhythmical jolting of the road. I stopped dictating, drank no more ginger beer, and didn't care whether they were pretty or not. Then they lost their way. Wasn't it awful and shouldn't they stop and ask? No, they certainly shouldn't: they could call out the names of the streets and I would tell them where to go. By the time we arrived at Ravenscourt Park I was pretty much all-in. I was carried into the hospital and once again felt the warm September sun burning my face. I was put in a private ward and had the impression of a hundred excited ants buzzing around me. My nurse said good-bye and started to sob. For no earthly reason I found myself in tears. It had been a lousy hospital, I had never seen the nurse anyway, and I was now in very good hands; but I suppose I was in a fairly exhausted state. So there we all were, snivelling about the place and getting nowhere. Then the charge nurse came up and took my arm and asked me what my name was.

"Dick," I said.

"Ah," she said brightly. "We must call you Richard the Lion Heart."

I made an attempt at a polite laugh but all that came out was a dismal groan and I fainted away. The house surgeon took the opportunity to give me an anaesthetic and removed all the tannic acid from my left hand.

At this time tannic acid was the recognized treatment for burns. The theory was that in forming a hard cement it protected the skin from the air, and encouraged it to heal up underneath. As the tannic started to crack, it was to be chipped off gradually with a scalpel, but after a few months of experience, it was discovered that nearly all pilots with third-degree burns so treated developed secondary infection and septicaemia. This caused its use to be discontinued and gave us the dubious satisfaction of knowing that we were suffering in the cause of science. Both my hands were suppurating, and the fingers were already contracting under the tannic and curling down into the palms. The risk of shock was considered too great for them to do both hands. I must have been under the anaesthetic for about fifteen minutes and in that time I saw Peter Pease killed.

He was after another machine, a tall figure leaning slightly forward with a smile at the corner of his mouth. Suddenly from nowhere a Messerschmitt was on his tail about 150 yards away. For two seconds nothing happened. I had a terrible feeling of futility. Then at the top of my voice I shouted, "Peter, for God's sake look out behind!"

I saw the Messerschmitt open up and a burst of fire hit Peter's machine. His expression did not change, and for a moment his machine hung motionless. Then it turned slowly on its back and dived to the ground. I came-to, screaming his name, with two nurses and the doctor holding me down on the bed.

"All right now. Take it easy, you're not dead yet. That must have been a very bad dream."

I said nothing. There wasn't anything to say. Two days later I had a letter from Colin. My nurse read it to me. It was very short, hoping that I was getting better and telling me that Peter was dead.

Slowly I came back to life. My morphia injections were less frequent and my mind began to clear. Though I began to feel and think again coherently I still could not see. Two V.A.D.s fainted while helping with my dressings, the first during the day and the other at night. The second time I could not sleep and was calling out for someone to stop the beetles running down my face, when I heard my nurse say fiercely, "Get outside quick: don't make a fool of yourself here!" and the sound or footsteps moving towards the door. I remember cursing the unfortunate girl and telling her to put her head between her knees. I was told later that for my first three weeks I did little but curse and blaspheme, but I remember nothing of it. The nurses were wonderfully patient and never complained. Then one day I found that I could see. My nurse was bending over me doing my dressings, and she seemed to me very beautiful. She was. I watched her for a long time, grateful that my first glimpse of the world should be of anything so perfect. Finally I said:

"Sue, you never told me that your eyes were so blue."

For a moment she stared at me. Then, "Oh, Dick, how wonderful," she said. "I told you it wouldn't be long"; and she dashed out to bring in all the nurses on the block.

I felt absurdly elated and studied their faces eagerly, gradually connecting them with the voices that I knew.

"This is Anne," said Sue. "She is your special V.A.D. and helps me with all your dressings. She was the only one of us you'd allow near you for about a week. You said you liked her voice." Before me stood an attractive fair-haired girl of about twenty-three. She smiled and her teeth were as enchanting as her voice. I began to feel that hospital had its compensations. The nurses called me Dick and I knew them all by their Christian names. Quite how irregular this was I did not discover until I moved to another hospital where I was considerably less ill and not so outrageously spoiled. At first my dressings had to be changed every two hours in the day-time. As this took over an hour to do, it meant that Sue and Anne had practically no time off. But they seemed not to care. It was largely due to them that both my hands were not amputated.

Sue, who had been nursing since seventeen, had been allocated as my special nurse because of her previous experience of burns, and because, as Matron said, "She's our best girl and very human." Anne had been married to a naval officer killed in the *Courageous*, and had taken up nursing after his death.

At this time there was a very definite prejudice among the regular nurses against V.A.D.s. They were regarded as painted society girls, attracted to nursing by the prospect of sitting on the officers' beds and holding their hands. The V.A.D.s were rapidly disabused of this idea, and, if they were lucky, were finally graduated from washing bedpans to polishing bed-tables. I never heard that any of them grumbled, and they gradually won a reluctant recognition. This prejudice was considerably less noticeable in the Masonic than in most hospitals: Sue, certainly, looked on Anne as a companionable and very useful lieutenant to whom she could safely entrust my dressings and general upkeep in her absence. I think I was a little in love with both of them.

The Masonic is perhaps the best hospital in England, though at the time I was unaware how lucky I was. When war broke out the Masons handed over a part of it to the services; but owing to its vulnerable position very few action casualties were kept there long. Pilots were pretty quickly moved out to the main Air Force Hospital, which I was not in the least eager to visit. Thanks to the kind-hearted duplicity of my house surgeon, I never had to; for every time they rang up and asked for me he would say that I was too ill to be moved. The Masonic's great charm lay in that it in no way resembled a hospital; if anything it was like the inside of a ship. The nursing staff were very carefully chosen, and during the regular blitzing of the district, which took place every night, they were magnificent.

The Germans were presumably attempting to hit Hammersmith Bridge, but their efforts were somewhat erratic and we were treated night after night to an orchestra of the scream and crump of falling bombs. They always seemed to choose a moment when my eyes were being irrigated, when my poor nurse was poised above me with a glass undine in her hand. At night we were moved into the corridor, away from the outside wall, but such was the snoring of my fellow sufferers that I persuaded Bertha to allow me back in my own room after Matron had made her rounds.

Bertha was my night nurse. I never discovered her real name, but to me she was Bertha from the instant that I saw her. She was large and gaunt with an Eton crop and a heart of gold. She was engaged to a merchant seaman who was on his way to Australia. She made it quite clear that she had no intention of letting me get round her as I did the day staff, and ended by spoiling me even more. At night when I couldn't sleep we would hold long and heated arguments on the subject of sex. She expressed horror at my ideas on love and on her preference for a cup of tea. I gave her a present of four pounds of it when I was discharged. One night the Germans were particularly persistent, and I had the unpleasant sensation of hearing a stick of bombs gradually approaching the hospital, the first some way off, the next closer, and the third shaking the building. Bertha threw herself across my bed; but the fourth bomb never fell. She got up quickly, looking embarrassed, and arranged her cap.

"Nice fool I'd look if you got hit in your own room when you're supposed to be out in the corridor," she said, and stumped out of the room.

An R.A.S.C. officer who had been admitted to the hospital with the painful but unromantic complaint of piles protested at the amount of favouritism shown to me merely because I was in the R.A.F. A patriotic captain who was in the same ward turned on him and said: "At least he was shot down defending his country and didn't come in here with a pimple on his bottom. The Government will buy him a new Spitfire, but I'm damned if it will buy you a new arse."

One day my doctor came in and said that I could get up. Soon after I was able to totter about the passages and could be given a proper bath. I was still unable to use my hands and everything had to be done for me. One evening during a blitz, my nurse, having led me along to the lavatory, placed a prodigiously long cigarette-holder in my mouth and lighted the cigarette in the end of it. Then she went off to get some coffee. I was puffing away contentedly when the lighted cigarette fell into my pyjama trousers and started smouldering. There was little danger that I would go up in flames, but I thought it advisable to draw attention to the fact that all was not well. I therefore shouted "Oi!" Nobody heard me. "Help!" I shouted somewhat louder. Still nothing happened, so I delivered myself of my imitation of Tarzan's elephant call or which I was quite proud. It happened that in the ward opposite there was an old gentleman who had been operated on for a hernia. The combination of the scream of falling bombs and my animal cries could mean only one thing. Someone had been seriously injured, and he made haste to dive over the side of the bed. In doing so he caused himself considerable discomfort: convinced of the ruin of his operation and the imminence of his death, he added his cries to mine. His fears finally calmed, he could see nothing humorous in the matter and insisted on being moved to another ward. From then on I was literally never left alone for a minute.

For the first few weeks, only my parents were allowed to visit me and they came every day. My mother would sit and read to me by the hour. Quite how much she suffered I could only guess, for she gave no sign. One remark of hers I shall never forget. She said: "You should be glad this has to happen to you. Too many people told you how attractive you were and you believed them. You were well on the way to becoming something of a cad. Now you'll find out who your real friends are." I did.

When I was allowed to see people, one of my first visitors was Michael Cary (who had been at Trinity with me and had a First in Greats). He was then private secretary to the Chief of Air Staff. He was allowed to stay only a short time before being shoo'd away by my nurses, but I think it may have been time enough to shake him. A short while afterwards he joined the Navy as an A.B. I hope it was not as a result of seeing me, for he had too good a brain to waste polishing brass. Colin came down whenever he had leave from Hornchurch and brought me news of the Squadron.

Ken MacDonald, Don's brother who had been with "A" Flight at Dyce, had been killed. He had been seen about to bale out of his blazing machine at 1000 feet; but as he was over a thickly populated area he had climbed in again and crashed the machine in the Thames.

Pip Cardell had been killed. Returning from a chase over the Channel with Dexter, one of the new members of the Squadron, he appeared to be in trouble just before reaching the English coast. He jumped; but his parachute failed to open and he came down in the sea. Dexter flew low and saw him move. He was still alive, so Dexter flew right along the shore and out to sea, waggling his wings to draw attention and calling up the base on the R.T. No boat put out from the shore, and Dexter made a crash landing on the beach, drawing up ten yards from a nest of buried mines. But when they got up to Pip he was dead.

Howes had been killed, even as he had said. His Squadron had been moved from Hornchurch to a quieter area, a few days after I was shot down. But he had been transferred to our Squadron, still deeply worried because as yet he had failed to bring anything down. The inevitable happened; and from his second flight with us he failed to return.

Rusty was missing, but a clairvoyant had written to Uncle George swearing that he was neither dead nor captured. Rusty, he said (whom he had never seen), had crashed in France, badly burned, and was being looked after by a French peasant.

As a counter to this depressing news Colin told me that Brian, Raspberry, and Sheep all had the D.F.C., and Brian was shortly to get a bar to his. The Squadron's confirmed score was nearing the hundred mark. We had also had the pleasure of dealing with the Italians. They had come over before breakfast, and together with 41

Squadron we were looking for them. Suddenly Uncle George called out:

"Wops ahead."

"Where are they?" asked 41 Squadron.

"Shan't tell you," came back the answer. "We're only outnumbered three to one."

Colin told me that it was the most unsporting thing he had ever had to do, rather like shooting sitting birds, as he so typically put it. We got down eight of them without loss to ourselves and much to the annoyance of 41 Squadron.

Then one day I had an unexpected visitor. Matron opened the door and said "Someone to see you," and Denise walked in. I knew at once who she was. It was unnecessary for her to speak. Her slight figure was in mourning and she wore no make-up. She was the most beautiful person I have ever seen.

Much has been written on Beauty. Poets have excelled themselves in similes for a woman's eyes, mouth, hair; novelists have devoted pages to a geometrically accurate description of their heroines' features. I can write no such description of Denise. I did not see her like that. For me she had an inner beauty, a serenity which no listing of features can convey. She had a perfection of carriage and a grace of movement that were strikingly reminiscent of Peter Pease, and when she spoke it might have been Peter speaking.

"I hope you'll excuse me coming to see you like this," she said; "but I was going to be married to Peter. He often spoke of you and wanted so much to see you. So I hope you won't mind me coming instead."

There was so much I wanted to say, so many things for us to talk over, but the room seemed of a sudden unbearably full of hurrying jolly nurses who would not go away. The bustle and excitement did little to put her at her ease, and her shyness was painful to me. Time came for her to leave, and I had said nothing I wanted to say. As soon as she was gone I dictated a note, begging her to come again and to give me a little warning. She did. From then until I was able to get out, her visits did more to help my recovery than all the expert nursing and medical attention. For she was the very spirit of courage. It was useless for me to say to her any of the usual words of comfort for the loss of a fiancé, and I did not try. She and Peter were two halves of the same person. They even wrote alike. I could only pray that time would cure that awful numbness and bring her back to the fullness of life. Not that she was broken. She seemed somehow to have gathered his strength, to feel him always near her, and was determined to go on to the end in the cause for which he had given his life, hoping that she too might be allowed to die, but feeling guilty at the selfishness of the thought.

She believed passionately in freedom, in freedom from fear and oppression and tyranny, not only for herself but for the whole world.

"For the whole world." Did I believe that? I still wasn't sure. There was a time – only the other day – when it hadn't mattered to me if it was true or not that a man could want freedom for others than himself. She made me feel that this might be no mere catch-phrase of politicians, since it was something to which the two finest people I had ever known had willingly dedicated themselves. I was impressed. I saw there a spirit far purer than mine. But was it for me? I didn't know. I just didn't know.

I lay in that hospital and watched summer turn to winter. Through my window I watched the leaves of my solitary tree gradually turn brown, and then, shaken by an ever-freshening wind, fall one by one. I watched the sun change from a great ball of fire to a watery glimmer, watched the rain beating on the glass and the small broken clouds drifting a few hundred feet above, and in that time I had ample opportunity for thinking.

I thought of the men I had known, of the men who were living and the men who were dead; and I came to this conclusion. It was to the Carburys and the Berrys of this war that Britain must look, to the tough practical men who had come up the hard way, who were not fighting this war for any philosophical principles or economic ideals; who, unlike the average Oxford undergraduate, were not flying for aesthetic reasons, but because of an instinctive knowledge that this was the job for which they were most suited. These were the men who had blasted and would continue to blast the Luftwaffe out of the sky while their more intellectual comrades would, alas, in the main be killed. They might answer, if asked why they fought, "To smash Hitler!" But instinctively, inarticulately, they too were fighting for the things that Peter had died to preserve.

Was there perhaps a new race of Englishmen arising out of this war, a race of men bred by the war, a harmonious synthesis of the governing class and the great rest of England; that synthesis of disparate backgrounds and upbringings to be seen at its most obvious best in R.A.F. Squadrons? While they were now possessed of no other thought than to win the war, yet having won it, would they this time refuse to step aside and remain indifferent to the peace-time fate of the country, once again leave government to the old governing class? I thought it possible. Indeed, the process might be said to have already begun. They now had as their representative Churchill, a man of initiative, determination, and no Party. But they would not always have him; and what then? Would they see to it that there arose from their fusion representatives, not of the old gang, deciding at Lady Cufuffle's that Henry should have the Foreign Office and George the Ministry of Food, nor figureheads for an angry but ineffectual Labour Party, but true representatives of the new England that should emerge from this struggle? And if they did, what then? Could they unite on a policy of humanity and sense to arrive at the settlement of problems which six thousand years of civilization had failed to solve? And even though they should fail, was there an obligation for the more thinking of them to try, to contribute at whatever personal cost "their little drop," however small, to the betterment of mankind? Was there that obligation, was that the goal towards which all those should strive who were left, strengthened and confirmed by those who had died? Or was it still possible for men to lead the egocentric life, to work out their own salvation without concern for the rest; could they simply look to themselves – or, more important, could I? I still thought so.

The day came when I was allowed out of the hospital for a few hours. Sue got me dressed, and with a pair of dark glasses, cotton-wool under my eyes, and my right arm in a sling, I looked fairly presentable. I walked out through the swing-doors and took a deep breath.

London in the morning was still the best place in the world. The smell of wet streets, of sawdust in the butchers' shops, of tar melted on the blocks, was exhilarating. Peter had been right: I loved the capital. The wind on the heath might call for a time, but the facile glitter of the city was the stronger. Self-esteem, I suppose, is one cause; for in the city, work of man, one is somebody, feet on the pavement, suit on the body, anybody's equal and nobody's fool; but in the country, work of God, one is nothing, less than the earth, the birds, and the trees; one is discordant – a blot.

I walked slowly through Ravenscourt Park and looked into many faces. Life was good, but if I hoped to find some reflection of my feeling I was disappointed. One or two looked at me with pity, and for a moment I was angry; but when I gazed again at their faces, closed in as on some dread secret, their owners hurrying along, unseeing, unfeeling, eager to get to their jobs, unaware of the life within them, I was sorry for them. I felt a desire to stop and shake them and say: "You fools, it's you who should be pitied and not I; for this day I am alive while you are dead."

And yet there were some who pleased me, some in whom all youth had not died. I passed one girl, and gazing into her face became aware of her as a woman: her lips were soft, her breasts firm, her legs long and graceful. It was many a month since any woman had stirred me, and I was pleased. I smiled at her and she smiled at me. I did not speak to her for fear of breaking the spell, but walked back to lunch on air. After this I was allowed out every day, and usually managed to stay out until nine o'clock, when I drove back through the blitz and the black-out.

NIGHT FIGHTER

RODERICK CHISHOLM

In 1940 Roderick Chisholm began operations as a night fighter pilot with the RAF's 604 Squadron.

One day at the end of October 1940 the first Beaufighter arrived at Middle Wallop. On the ground it was an ominous and rather unwieldy looking aircraft, with its outsize undercarriage and propellers and small wings, but in the air it looked just right.

There is never a new machine introduced but some people whisper that it is dangerous to fly, that its speed is disappointing and that it is, in general, a wash-out. Of such criticisms the Beaufighter had more than its fair share. The reports, however, from those few of the Squadron who first flew it were favourable. It obviously had a good take-off and it was said to be manoeuvrable and fast, doing well over 300 miles per hour at about 15,000 feet. It had tankage for five hours' patrolling, an improved type of radar, and four cannon. Most important of all, it had a cockpit out of which the pilot could see well. First impressions were favourable; but having just become accustomed to the Blenheim, I could not help feeling a bit depressed because I knew I would have to start again from scratch.

Results and operational experience were urgently

needed, and the first Beaufighter was pressed into operations immediately, the only pilots to whom it was entrusted being Mike Anderson and John Cunningham.*

Ignorant of the theoretical side of night interception and inexperienced on the practical side, I was then sceptical about its prospects. I did not believe it possible with Blenheims, quite apart from their inadequate speed and radar, and so I doubted whether Beaufighters would be any more successful. This was a doubt based only on a "hunch" of the most reactionary sort. I had already chased many aircraft and sometimes I had been told that I should be fairly near them, but I had not yet seen another aircraft in flight at night and I could not imagine a technique for interception and attack. My discouragement grew, and sometimes a fleeting and irrational doubt appeared, the fruit perhaps of a primitive instinct: seeing is believing and I was not seeing. And later it always seemed somehow incredible when, after a drawn-out and exacting chase wholly dependent on electric sight, a silhouette suddenly took shape, looming up like a lamp-post in a fog.

The news less than a month after the arrival of the first Beaufighter that John had destroyed a Junkers 88 was electrifying. For me it meant that the bombers we were sent to chase were really there and that the cover of the dark was not absolute. Had further confirmation been needed, it was supplied by Mike, who destroyed a Heinkel 111 a few nights later. There seemed something unreal about these combats. To leave a comfortable Hampshire airfield and to come upon an intruder over one's own country in the dark, to shoot at it and watch it go down like a catherine wheel and explode on hitting the ground, to break the spell and feel that the cover of darkness was no longer complete – these were strange and exciting adventures. While John with typical resourcefulness had enabled his observer, Phillipson, to get the contact by investigating a searchlight concentration, Mike had been

* *Group Captain Cunningham, D.S.O., O.B.E., D.F.C.*

guided all the way by a ground controller who, with radar, kept track both of the enemy and the Beaufighter, remotely manœuvring the latter to a position from which its own radar could see the enemy and from where Cannon, his observer, could take over. Thus radar had played a key part in both successes, and it was stimulating for some of us to think that the latter interception took place entirely in the dark and under close ground control. Perhaps there was hope yet for the less resourceful; perhaps all of us might see some action before long – such was one line of reasoning.

But contacts alone were useless. Their size and their movement had to be interpreted by the observer and a running commentary maintained to the pilot to give him a picture of what he could not see and had to imagine, and every now and again a quick instruction had to be inserted like "slow down", "faster", "climb a little", "down a bit" or "steady, hold it there". This and the flying of the aircraft made the teamwork which would bring the Beaufighter to a position from which the pilot could see with his own eyes; then it was all up to him, and the four 20-millimetre cannon he controlled. It sounded straightforward; yet I, for one, was still dubious. I doubted my ability to achieve the high standard of flying which seemed vital to this sort of blind-man's bluff, this groping for the enemy. To fly in the dark and at the same time to search for the visual contact by a systematic concentration on the sky seemed a very far-off feat to one who had only just begun to realise that concentration on instruments need not, in some conditions, be incessant. It was plain that we all needed much training and practice; how we were to get it was less obvious.

Radar control from the ground had been on trial in our sector for some months, and many of us had had experience of it in practices, taking the part alternately of the bomber and the fighter. These early experiments were not encouraging, but they had about them an air of scientific investigation that made them interesting for us, although we knew little about the gear used, which then was "top secret" and was referred to simply as G.C.I. There was an academic ring about the instructions given by the scientist designers (who were then the controllers) to the pilot who, miles high above the sleeping land, was charging about blindfold and trusting. It seemed that the thanks proffered over the radio at the end of a practice or a patrol were appropriate to the completion of a valuable but inconclusive laboratory experiment. But inconclusive though it consistently was so far as I was concerned, G.C.I. was now no longer experimental. We had proof that G.C.I. could direct a radar fighter near enough to an enemy bomber for a contact, and we knew that the Beaufighter had the speed to overhaul it.

The problems facing the higher command must at this time have been exceedingly grave. The enemy were flying over us at night with all but immunity from interception, and our cities were being systematically destroyed. To deal with the night bomber there were plans in profusion; more anti-aircraft guns, more searchlights, more radar fighters, more cat's-eye fighters and more special devices; but with successes so few and experience so slender, there can have been no certainty that priorities were being rightly allocated, and there must have been much relief that there was now a clear indication. A new radar fighter had succeeded in one sector with both ground control and searchlights, and informed circles were probably now optimistic. The pioneering efforts of Mike and John and their observers, and their rewards, were probably as far reaching in their effect on policy as they were laudable in their execution.

We, the aircrew, were happily unconscious of the bigger issues, and our only anxieties outside our own flying task were such seemingly vital domesticities as the establishing of the right to late breakfast, the night-flier's extra egg, or petrol for leave. The activities of the Squadron were really all that mattered in the war, and they were all engrossing. Nevertheless, we could see the proportions of the task in our own sector and it was enormous. It was, in fact, only a small part of that confronting Fighter Command.

Controllers, radar operators and pilots had to be trained in the use of new equipment and in new techniques. When John scored the first success there were but three pilots fit to fly the Beaufighter at night and the same number of competent operators. Method had to be worked out between pilots and their observers and pilots and ground controllers. Each separate operation had to be practised, and then dress rehearsals were needed. Yet the urgency of operations virtually ruled out practice at night because all available aircraft were required for the programme. We all needed practice, but when could we get it? Which comes first, training or operations, the chicken or the egg? This perpetual quandary, which must always beset the high commands in modern war, was very acute just then.

We were up against poor serviceability of new equipment, and ignorance. The Beaufighters had their teething troubles which, though mostly minor, could become serious in night flying. The radar was new and delicate; it broke down frequently; and the mechanics who knew much about it were few. Our radar officers never spared themselves, working, it seemed, day and night, and often flying on operations as well as in tests and practices. The observers had had only the scantiest training, a number of them having been airgunners who had been given a short conversion course. As soon as a pilot was considered fit, he and his observer became operational as a crew. Thereafter they had to practise on the Germans. I shall remember it always by a not unusual incident during a daylight test flight in a Blenheim. I flew some distance behind another aircraft and I told my observer to turn on the radar. There was an "O.K.", a silence and suddenly, a little later, an excited cry "I can see it!", and then, after a few moments of suspense, "It's gone!", and further silence. And that was more than usually occurred, since on most occasions there was nothing to be seen on the radar tubes at all.

By the end of 1940 we had been completely re-equipped, and sufficient pilots, six in all, had been scraped together to allow the operational programme to proceed exclusively with Beaufighters. The Blenheim had disappeared from night fighting so far as we were concerned, and those like myself who had not had the opportunity of flying a Beaufighter at night became non-operational. With impatience we waited for an opportunity for Beaufighter night solos, the essential prelude to becoming operational again; we were short of aircraft and at this season the weather was often bad, and so it was that Mike, John, Georgie, Spekie, Alastair and Jackson were on operations every night for about a month.

After weeks of depressing inactivity, I was given a chance. With low, broken cloud and a forecast of deterioration, the weather was not ideal, but I was no longer a novice and, needing time only for one or two take-offs, circuits and landings, I was let go. What followed was not all my fault, nor can it be attributed wholly to the weather, for soon after I had taken off the control went off the air and all calls were ignored, with the result that I and the three others also airborne assumed the radio, either ground or air, to have failed. There was dangerous confusion. In that weather the decision to land while we knew we were near base was inevitable. It was every man for himself and, with the cloud at about 1,000 feet, we came in and landed as we could. I broke cloud, saw the aerodrome lights and, making an ill-judged and hurried approach, came straight in. I was too high and, to make matters worse, I held off too early and opened up a little to reduce the bump. The aircraft touched down and ran on with all the momentum of ten tons moving at eighty miles per hour. I braked hard, but we were on wet grass – there were no runways then and the flare-path, laid out into the wind, was sometimes too short to cover faults – and the boundary lights of the Andover-Salisbury road seemed to be approaching alarmingly. A moment later I was in the road and at rest at last. Suddenly everything was still. I got out and walked away from what had been a perfectly good Beaufighter, feeling rather an ass.

A few nights later I tried again and, all going well, we were reinstated on the operational programme, so that one of the original six crews could then have one night off in six.

With experience my confidence grew. I felt I was becoming accustomed to the Beaufighter and its idiosyncrasies. It was then unstable fore and aft, and so was not ideal for night flying. It always seemed – and this was in the imagination of an anxious mind – that the darker the night the worse was the effect of this instability. If there were sufficient external guides, lights in good visibility, a skyline or moonlit ground, it was easy enough to fly steadily, as in daylight; but if those aids were absent, the night dark and visibility poor, the instruments were the only guides, and instrument flying in the early Beaufighter called for unceasing and most exacting concentration. There were times when the loss or gain of a few hundred feet in the gentle undulation of its normal trajectory could not be afforded, and at such times there had to be no relaxing.

In bad weather a return to base and landing became something of an ordeal. Effective blind approach and airfield lighting systems were yet to come, and at the end of 1940 we had to find our own way as best we could, depending on homing bearings and on recognition of the dim flare-path lights when we were near the airfield.

Condensation and frost, which formed on both sides of the one-and-a-half-inch-thick windscreen as one came down into warmer air, were further impediments and, since the windscreen was close to one's face, there was nothing to do but peer ahead through the small windows on either side of it.

The Beaufighter tended to tighten up in turns, and this, accentuating the ever-present difficulty of making accurate turns on instruments, resulted – at least in my experience – in unwitting gains or losses in height in all but gentle turns. Being usually frightened and so cautious, I made a practice of very gentle turns at low altitude, imagining the consequences of losing too much height, and knowing only too well the embarrassment of blundering back into cloud again by gaining it. The airfield might come into view too late, and going obliquely across the flare-path, unable to make the steep turn that might have got me in, I would have to go on in a wide sweep into the outer darkness again and away from those feeble but homely lights, hoping that when I saw them again I would be better aligned for landing. I would see some lights, but from low altitude their pattern was not plain. Suddenly they became the flare-path, not exactly where I had expected it but off to one side; still I might be able to "make" it. Perhaps in the act of putting the wheels down hurriedly I would let the machine gain some height. The airfield lights seemed to go out. My immediate instinct was to push the nose down, to lose height and to regain contact with the ground and the guidance of the lights quickly, but my caution made me lose height gingerly; it might yet be all right when, out of cloud, I saw the lights again, or it might not, and then the whole anxious process might have to be repeated.

Finding base and getting down to Mother Earth could be both long and anxious. It seemed that there were no rules to learn, and sometimes when I landed I found myself in a cold sweat, knowing that I had been lucky and wondering what would happen next time.

The acme of unpleasantness was reached one night when the enemy made a serious mistake about the weather and lost five aircraft, probably through icing: a loss which the Press attributed incorrectly but perhaps intentionally to our fighters. The blitz was on Southampton and we were making a maximum effort. The weather was awful. As a new experience for me, there was an icy, electric haze in which I was still floundering at 22,000 feet, unable to reach the clear air. There was a constant bluish discharge from one side of the windscreen to the other and on the airscrew blades, and a ghostly light in the cockpit which made it impossible to see anything outside.

Dependent only on the blind-flying instruments and their dazzling, sickly green needles, I began to feel, as I grew tired, that my power over the machine was becoming uncertain and that I might suddenly find myself unable to control it. My senses denoted turns; yet the needles showed straight flight. I tried to turn left and, depending on my senses (other than my vision), operated the stick and rudder to produce a left turn; but the instruments insisted that I was not turning, and a vicious pull on the controls to produce a turn which the needles would admit caused such sensations that I dared not continue it. But a turn to the right could be made, I found, according to the needles and the pressure on my seat, and so I turned right handed, the long way round. Chasing the enemy was a hopeless proposition. In these conditions it was all I could do to keep myself poised, somewhat unsurely, with my machine more or less under control. My only chance of destroying an enemy in that sort of weather (and, I then thought, in any sort of weather for that matter) was haphazard collision.

As I was feeling my way back to base, a load of incendiaries was dropped just behind me. I was at a few hundred feet only and the glare from them, as they burnt, was reflected in and diffused by the haze in which I was flying in a way that was distracting and, until I guessed its source, alarming. There was a good deal of tight-rope walking that night.

As I have said, we had few opportunities for training at night because all serviceable aircraft were usually required for operations, but on one memorable occasion absence of enemy activity coincided with good local weather and we were able to carry out some interception practice. Grouping about in the dark at close on three hundred miles an hour called for steady flying and a cold-blooded nervelessness that I had not got. I had always had vague doubts about it: now I would see what it was like.

Using navigation lights, we took off in pairs, one behind the other, and set off. When all was ready the crew in front extinguished lights and the crew behind tried to approach on radar to within visual range. Instead of the daylight swoop to attack, there had to be a steady and deliberate stalk to close range, then a search, the pilot looking where his observer told him for a small patch that was darker than its surroundings; and finally a stealthy closing up to point-blank range. This much I knew; but how to put theory into practice was another matter, and the machine behind – when it was mine – wandered and weaved about, trying to close in and just maintaining radar contact, sheering off or shooting underneath as the target suddenly loomed up as it were out of a fog, converging frighteningly. After this, my first practice, I was despondent; I felt out of my depth.

At that time, I think, most of us were ignorant as well as inexperienced. We had yet to understand the full significance of the illumination of the background and the size of the silhouette to appreciate that, against bright starlight, a Beaufighter could be seen from a thousand feet below, while against the ground it remained invisible down to about 300 feet. We had not yet learnt that the correct technique was to search (exploiting the fact that our sight is more acute on the periphery than at the centre of the eye) with speeds synchronised so as to avoid blundering on when the invisible opponent, though left behind, would still appear as radar "blips", seeming (until the observers too had acquired experience) to be drawing away ahead. We did not yet possess the encouraging knowledge that most aircraft, except our Beaufighters, had tell-tale exhausts, and that surprise could always be on the side of the radar fighter against a bomber without radar. There was much we had to discover and develop for ourselves, for it was new ground we were breaking.

That winter (1940) there was a short spell of brilliantly clear and very cold nights, and the enemy took full advantage of them, keeping up his raids, it seemed to us, all night long. We did all we could, flying long patrols on several consecutive nights, but it was of no avail. Six crews reported about seventy radar contacts, but all were lost inconclusively. In our contribution of thirteen hours' patrolling during those three nights, my observer and I got and lost our first contact on an enemy aircraft.

It seemed to me that our efforts had reached a crisis, and while I had the small satisfaction of knowing that I was not alone in being unsuccessful, I was concerned about my own part in it. I was tired, having had no adequate leave for what seemed many months – the crew shortage allowed us only to snatch a day or two here and there – and I had sore eyes, caused by prolonged exposure to draught (it came up through the crack between the escape hatch and the fuselage side; it curled up over your head and caught you straight in the eyes) and my confidence had recently been badly shaken by some unnerving returns and land-ings of the sort I have already tried to describe. I was beginning to think that I would not be able to pull it off the next time and that I would fall off the tight-rope; and in that low state of mind I was relieved to be sent away for a fortnight's course on beam flying and blind approach.

This gave me a welcome change from night flying, and incidentally allowed my eyes to recover. I learnt a way of approaching, unseeing, to land at an airfield by using a beam transmitted from that airfield as a guide. It would be possible, in any weather, to approach from a distance with deliberation, and the certainty that, on breaking cloud, one would be correctly placed to land straight ahead. Thus the tempo of the operation would be slowed down and it would become more manageable.

The operation (hitherto hit-and-miss so far as I was concerned) of finding and landing at an airfield in bad weather could now be done by following rules, and then safe arrivals, which had been accidental and so destructive of confidence, would now, if achieved by following the rules, have just the opposite effect. I returned from the course with new confidence and feeling well and re-freshed.

*   *   *

On the night of March 13th, 1941, the unexpected happened. I destroyed two enemy aircraft. This was luck unbounded, and these were experiences which I knew could never be equalled. For the rest of that night it was impossible to sleep; there was nothing else I could talk about for days after; there was nothing else I could think about for weeks after.

With these victories – and even one of them would have sufficed – a great deal had suddenly become worth while, and this was success such as I had never dreamt of; it was sweet and very intoxicating. I saw my name in the papers, and the Squadron, so long in obscurity, coming into the limelight; for these were its sixth and seventh confirmed successes. It became suddenly 'a famous night-fighter squadron''. The public was let into the secret; it was equipped with Beaufighters and there were veiled allusions to a secret weapon. There was a lot of glamour and excitement attached to being a night-fighter pilot; we felt a good deal beyond ourselves.

On that night there was an almost full moon and the weather was very fine. We had been flying for more than an hour when we were put on to a bomber that was going back empty. We were overtaking fairly well, and by the time we passed over Bournemouth were about a mile behind. We closed in a bit more and Ripley, my observer, got a close radar contact over to the left. I turned a little to the left, and I could hardly believe my eyes, for there was another aircraft about a hundred yards away and on the same level. It was black and its fish-like fuselage glistened dully in the moonlight; it was unmistakably a Heinkel.

Converging rapidly, I turned to come behind and dropped below with an automatism that surprised me; my machine seemed to be on rails, so easily did it slide into position. I was afraid I would be seen in that light – and the Beaufighter would have been a sitter – but interceptions were not expected then, and the enemy gunners were not keeping a good look-out. I was able to creep up unmolested until I was within a hundred yards and forty-five degrees below. The machine looked enormous; the wings seemed to blot out the sky above me; now, a squat silhouette, it had lost its recognisable form. I saw the four rows of exhausts, each with six stubs, and now and again one of them would belch out a bigger flame than usual.

The moment had come to shoot; it was now or never. Holding my breath I eased the stick back a little and the Heinkel came down the windscreen and into the sight. It went too far and I found myself aiming above. Stick forward a bit and the sight came on it again. How ham-fisted this was! I pressed the firing-button. There was a terrific shaking and banging, and to my surprise I saw flashes appearing, as it seemed, miraculously on the shape in front of me. Pieces broke away and came back at me. I kept on firing, and it turned away to the right slowly, apparently helplessly and obviously badly damaged. My ammunition finished I drew away farther to the right. I had overshot, and I could see the Heinkel over my left shoulder still flying all right. Nothing happened, perhaps nothing was going to happen, and suddenly I thought that it was going to get away. I had had a chance, a sitter, and I had not hit it hard enough. It seemed that I had succeeded in the almost impossible feat of firing two hundred 20-millimetre shells at this aircraft at point-blank range without destroying it. It had been like the crazy kitchen side-show at a fair, impossible not to hit something; but here, so I began to think, I had hit nothing vital.

And then I saw a lick of flame coming from the starboard engine. It grew rapidly, and enveloped the whole engine and soon most of the wing. The machine turned east and started to go down slowly; it looked by now like a ball of flame. We followed it down from 11,000 feet until, minutes later, it hit the sea, where it continued to burn.

It was said that the crew baled out, but none was picked up. I did not think of them any more than they probably had thought of the people they had been bombing. This kind of warfare, though in some ways cold-blooded murder, was as impersonal as it was mechanical. This was a big-game hunt, and thought was focused on personal achievement. In the aftermath it was satisfactory to know that the enemy bomber force had been reduced by one, but immediately it was the elation of personal success with neither regrets nor outraged scruples that monopolised my thoughts.

We had one or two more chases which came to nothing and, having been on patrol for three and a half hours, we went back to land. The aircraft was refuelled and rearmed, and within thirty minutes we were again at "readiness". It was about midnight, and although activity usually stopped by midnight, there were on that night still a few enemy bombers going back from the Midlands. We were ordered off.

A chase started soon after take-off; it went on, and I began to despair, for I knew that these bombers without their loads would be going back quickly. After nearly fifteen minutes I was told to turn back north and come home. We were then at about 10,000 feet over the sea, and there was a lane of reflected moonlight on the water stretching south to a small bank of cloud. As I started to turn left towards the north I saw far below a sight which I could hardly believe – the navigation lights of an aircraft flying south. I called up and asked if there were any friendly aircraft about, and the answer came "No", so I made to follow the lights I had seen. Enemy aircraft had been seen before now flying home brazenly with all lights on; this perhaps was another of them.

I watched the lights intently and started to lose height, trying not to overshoot them. Then they went out and I followed blindly. The thin layer of cloud I had seen to the south intervened, and I reckoned that if the aircraft was skimming along the top, I would have a good chance of seeing it – it was tempting, day or night, to skim along just above the cloud – but I saw nothing. We were now at 5,000 feet and we went down to 4,000, where we were below cloud. As we came out into clear air, Ripley got a contact ahead and close. I started to search and soon, in that light, I saw an aircraft about 2,000 feet away and dead ahead.

I closed in quickly and, recognising it as a Heinkel, dropped below and crept up to sure firing range. Coming up I opened fire from about a hundred and fifty yards. There were flashes on the fuselage and the starboard engine, which lost a cowling and started to emit smoke and sparks. I drew away to await developments, thinking that it would be forced down at once, but instead it started to climb, making for the cloud layer not far above. Hurriedly I opened fire again, but the rear gunner, recovered by now, opened fire and red streaks came past which made me wince and break away to the left.

I followed, climbing well above so that I might see it against the cloud below. Soon I saw that about a mile ahead there was clear air, the cloud ending abruptly. This Heinkel was hard hit and its chances of getting back were, I reckoned, nil; and then I saw ahead – how far I could not judge, but it was perhaps not more than a few miles – a vivid explosion on the sea. We went to the spot and circled, but there was nothing to be seen. I called up to report the combat and find my position, and I was surprised that we were only a few miles south of the Isle of Wight.

We went home to bed, tired after five hours very active flying and blissfully contented. After this successful but wakeful night, I discovered that I had become, according to the more exaggerated Press accounts, a minor "ace".

These were brilliant times for us. Successes, once they had started, came fast, and the lessons learnt from each by aircrews and controllers brought more successes. Although the nation's fortunes of war were as low as they had ever been, our particular war was then being loudly acclaimed as a victory of a sort, and that was all that mattered to most of us.

The enemy was sending picked crews ahead of his raids to find the targets and start fires as guides to the bombing force which was following. Late one evening we intercepted one of these pathfinders. There was that groping pursuit, then the sight of twinkling exhausts and the stealthy unseen approach to a position below and close enough for there to be no mistakes. I came up and opened fire, and it was all over very quickly. It was not surprising that the two survivors of the crew did not know what had hit them, for the aircraft exploded, seeming to burst open after the first few rounds, and we were left alone, with the sky to ourselves, the only visible reminder of that aircraft being the oil which smothered our windscreen and forced us to return to base. Well I remember the quiet "Well done" from the station commander, who was waiting on the tarmac. Later that night I destroyed a second Heinkel and two nights later a third. It was characteristic of this sort of warfare that these two nights' flying alternated with attendances at the Sadler's Wells ballet, which was performing at a nearby camp.

I had passed a milestone in my flying by the completion of one hundred hours at night; I had become fairly experienced. This seemed a long way from the timid flying at the training school.

With such successes came a heady self-confidence and the conviction that interception was not only the best counter-measure to the night bomber, being within the powers of even average crews, but that it should seldom fail. From being incredulous and sceptical I quickly became over-confident, forgetting that moonlight or near twilight (and even navigation lights) and the unawareness of the enemy had allowed me to score. Then my confidence would disappear with a succession of failures, reminders that the real dark multiplied difficulties incredibly, and doubts about the adequacy of my own flying assailed me. It was testing to be close to an opponent, unseen though known to be within visual range, sometimes flying through his slipstream with a sickening bump, and to persevere, waiting for the hail of bullets from an alert gunner (which, in fact, seldom came), with the suspicion growing all the time that the radar was at fault – for this early type could lie most perfectly. Did I fly steadily enough when things were not going well? How did my flying compare with that of others? Their accounts were usually most reticent, and I wondered whether most were more stable or simply less impressionable than I.

With these failures came the suspicion that the enemy, now expecting interception though probably unaware of the approach of individual fighters, was taking routine evasive action: a small turn off course then back being enough to keep the pursuer always at a distance, noticing the turns after they had started and swinging about always on the outside of them.

A dark night when Plymouth was being blitzed for the fourth time in succession was typical of the many occasions when all this was brought disconcertingly home to me. We were sent after an enemy aircraft which was leaving the target and, getting an early contact, we overhauled it steadily. Hopes began to rise and then, as we reached a position from which I might have seen it (but only after a search and knowing which section of the sky to scan), some relative movement started. The enemy slid off quickly to one side, and we had to turn hard to keep the contact. Soon we were weaving about doing hard turns first one way and then the other as if we were on the end of a whip. We lost distance and our oscillations diminished until we were able to settle down to an approach again. Each time we closed in the same thing happened, and finally we were called off and sent after another bomber which was approaching the target. Again all went well until we were a few hundred yards away. We had climbed to 19,000 feet, and I believed that in the glare of the burning city I would not fail to see this aircraft; it should be flying steadily here for its bombing run. But there ensued the same depressing sequence of turns one way and then the other, sometimes becoming hard turns so as to keep the enemy ahead in our radar's field of vision, with never a moment to steady up and endeavour to construe what was happening. And having seen in the inferno far below the flashes of bomb bursts, bombs perhaps dropped by our opponent, we had again to give up. That night the streets of Plymouth stood out, clear dark furrows in the flames. We went home considerably chastened.

Comparing notes the next day with John, I learnt that he and Jimmie★ (his air gunner since 1936 and now his radar operator) had chased one aircraft almost to Cherbourg before they had had to give up, and then I felt less dejected.

By May 1941 the Squadron score, which had been mounting steadily, was in the thirties; we led others by a comfortable margin. The system for doing what a year before was almost unheard of was no longer experimental but firmly established. There was no knowing how far the technique would develop before the war ended. It seemed that night was slowly being turned into day. How long, I wondered, would it take for defence to overcome the disadvantage of the dark. How long would it be worth bombing at night? How long would it take us to develop radar to a pitch that would allow us to repulse bombers at night as we had by day? These were interesting speculations.

My luck deserted me. One thing after another went wrong, and sometimes I seemed fated to choose a wrong course when decisions had to be made quickly and there was one right course that might earn the much-needed success. I had a glimpse of an enemy aircraft over Bristol, silhouetted against the glow of fires on the cloud a thousand or so feet below. Perhaps prompt action, a steep dive, would have let me keep it in sight until my observer could pick out the radar contact, but I hesitated and it passed out of sight, screened by one of the engines, and did not reappear. Some nights later my guns jammed when I was behind a Heinkel, close and unseen – this would have been a certainty – and having fired a round or two I could

★ *Squadron Leader C.F. Rawnsley, D.S.O., D.F.C., D.F.M.*

do nothing but try to avoid the return fire and save our own skins. On a night in May a deplorable error was saved from having tragic results by what then seemed a miracle.

We were sent down to the coast west of Portland to look for low-flying enemy aircraft which had been reported. It was late and we had already been on patrol for an hour and a half. There was little chance of success, but I hoped and expected that my luck would change; there was a moon and the weather was good. Approaching the coast, I reduced height. It was a beautiful night, and flying south it was easy to see, as we crossed it, the irregular line of demarcation between complete and incomplete blackness which was the coastline. "Vector one eight zero for ten miles and then patrol east and west." The controller had little else to say, and I guessed rightly that not much was known about those low-flying aircraft. It was a wild-goose chase and my confidence evaporated; I was pleased to be soon told to return to base.

Near the coast the radio voice warned me of the presence of another aircraft, saying ominously: "You are being followed by another aircraft. Orbit once." Without any further clue as to the identity of my shadower, I construed that it was the needle in the haystack which, in my optimism, I almost expected to find. I turned the switch that cut off all contact with the outside world so as to have uninterrupted conversation with my observer. We started to search and soon got a contact. After a few changes of course, we were going west and were closing in comfortably. Then I saw a small indistinct shape, barely a silhouette, about 2,000 feet away; for there was a half moon.

We had found to our cost that the enemy were, by then, keeping a good look-out in moonlight; they had been able to get away several times, diving as the fighter closed in or opening fire unexpectedly early. I wanted no mistake this time, and with my eyes glued to this almost shapeless patch of darkness I came in fast, all set to fire as soon as I was satisfied that it was what I expected it to be, hostile.

The shape became more distinct; it had all the squatness of the Heinkels I had seen before; there was no doubt in my mind: it was a Heinkel. My approach was not seen, and I was able to close well in before opening fire. I gave a burst and I saw hits on the starboard wing. With another there was a big flash on the port engine; the port wheel came down. It was still flying, but probably, damaged as it was, it would not get home. We had only to follow, reload the guns and finish it off, if it had not already fallen into the sea. The experimental graticule pattern in the gunsight which I was using had done nothing to improve my shooting; it had perhaps made it worse.

I was overtaking all the time, and I overshot, pulling away to the right. The damaged machine turned left towards the sea and across the moon. As the moon caught it I saw something that I would not accept; that tail was familiar. Was it familiar? A thought came to my mind, and I smothered it. It was not possible; it was unthinkable. There was no question that this was not an enemy aircraft; I had been told it was hostile. But had I? One had to make up one's mind in moonlight quickly and from a long way off; otherwise the chance would be lost. And once one's mind was made up there was no drawing back; the rear gunner might shoot first, and his aim would be deliberate. Perhaps it was not a Heinkel; it might be a Junkers 88; I had never seen one of them at night. But there was the shape of that tail, and back came the awful doubt.

All this flashed through my mind, and then I called up, as was the normal procedure, to report that I had had a combat. The answer to my excited message was calm and there were no congratulations. The voice said: "That was probably a friendly aircraft. Follow it and report its position. How badly damaged is it?" I felt as if I had taken an ice-cold plunge. The bottom fell out of my world. I knew now why the tail of that aircraft had looked familiar. The two men inside it were on my side and I had probably killed them; probably they were from my

Squadron. John Cunningham and Edward Crew were flying; it might be either of them.

"Why the hell didn't you tell me that it was a 'friendly' which was following me?"

"We could not get in touch with you." Of course they could not get in touch with me when it was too late. Why could they not have warned me at once, when they told me I was being followed? What I had done scarcely bore contemplation.

We followed the crippled aircraft, with one wheel hanging grotesquely down, for four or five minutes as it turned slowly from south to east and then towards north. And then, against a darker part of the sky, I lost sight of it. That this aircraft was still flying did not mean that the pilot was still alive; damaged aircraft can fly on with no one in control for some time. But there was a little hope. Then on the radio I heard:

"One engine is still working. They hope to make their base." That meant that the pilot was still alive.

"Follow close and report your position if you can."

"I have lost sight of him and I do not know my position."

"The crew is going to bale out. Is it over the sea or land?"

"I do not know."

I was instructed to return to base; there was nothing I could do now. The sight, some minutes later, of a fire on the ground suggested that the machine had crashed on land, and that the crew, had it been possible to bale out, was safe. I reported what I had seen and went home, my mind a seething, unhappy turmoil. I had done a terrible thing. Was it possible, I wondered, that the crew was safe and sound? It would have been a miracle if neither member had been touched.

It seemed to take an age to fly the eighty miles to base. I landed, taxied in, got out and stumbled towards the "readiness" room. I pushed the door open and went in, blinking and dazzled by the lights. Someone – I forget who it was – was lying on a bed; he was the only chap left there. He said sleepily: "Hullo." I said: "I've shot down a Beau," and he said: "God! I'm sorry. Bloody bad luck." That, I felt, was decent of him. I would not have been surprised had he said something like "I never want to speak to you again." A stupid idea, but that is how I felt.

I telephoned to Operations and was told what I had realised, that it had been a machine from a squadron in a neighbouring sector. There was no news of the crew, but from the radio conversation it seemed that both members were untouched. A little later I heard that the pilot was safe, and after a further agonising wait came like news about the observer. A load was lifted from me. No longer did I brand myself a fratricide. A mistake had been made; the results were not fatal and that was all that mattered to me just then.

At the enquiry on the next day I met the crew of the machine which I had destroyed, the men whom I had, not so long before, done my best to kill, and I found that I knew the pilot fairly well, having been on a course with him only a few weeks before. Together at this meeting, the strangeness of which we both appreciated, we had an interesting post-mortem on the affair. He asserted that a tip I had given him while we were on that course had let him make good his exit by parachute. We had learnt that of the two escape hatches the pilot's was often difficult to open (there was an automatic release which was not dependable), and it had been made a standard drill that if a crew had to bale out the observer would come forward to help to open the pilot's hatch before going out by his own. In this case it was only by their joint efforts that the pilot's hatch was opened. Despite the poor marksmanship, largely attributable to the experimental gunsight graticule – for the range was very close – the damage done, they said, was heavy. Both engines were hit and one stopped at once; both petrol tanks were holed; the hydraulics were wrecked and, as I had seen, a wheel came down; a few shells had whistled over the pilot's head and gone out just above the windscreen. As often as not an aircraft well hit by cannon shells would blow up. I thought that it was more than luck that had saved that Beaufighter crew.

Some weeks after this baleful episode my luck turned and we intercepted in quick succession two Heinkels heading for the Midlands. In the ensuing combats one was only damaged, but the second blew up after a short burst, like a match being struck, and spun down leaving only a plume of smoke.

DOGSBODY

JAMES "JOHNNIE" JOHNSON

James "Johnnie" Johnson joined the Royal Air Force Volunteer Reserve in 1939 as a sergeant pilot. He served throughout the war in Fighter Command, first with 616 (South Yorkshire) Squadron, and later with, among others, 610 (County of Chester), 144 Canadian Spitfire Wing and 125 Wing. By the time of victory in Europe, "Johnnie" Johnson had been promoted to Group Captain and secured the ranking position as Allied top-scoring pilot with 38 victories. Johnson retired the service in 1966 as an Air-Vice-Marshall. He died in 2001.

Here Johnson recounts the Spitfire days of high summer 1941 whilst serving with the legendary Douglas Bader (call sign: "Dogsbody") in 616 Squadron, then operating out of Tangmere in Sussex.

High summer at Tangmere. I shall never forget those stirring days, when it seemed that the sky was always blue and the rays of the fierce sun hid the glinting Messerschmitts; or when there was a high layer of thin cirrus cloud (although this filtered the sun and lessened the glare, it was dangerous to climb through it, for your grey-green Spitfire stood out against the white-backcloth); when the grass was burnt to a light brown colour and discoloured with dark oil-stains where we parked our Spitfires, and when the waters of the Channel looked utterly serene and inviting as we raced out of France at ground-level, hot and sweating in that tiny green-house of a cockpit.

High summer, and the air is heavy with the scent of white clover as we lounge in our deck-chairs watching a small tractor cut down the long clover and grass on our airfield. In some places it is almost a foot high, but it is not dangerous and we know that if we are skilful enough to stall our Spitfires just when the tips of the grasses caress the wheels then we shall pull off a perfect landing.

It is Sunday, and although it is not yet time for lunch we have already escorted some Stirlings to bomb an inland target. For some obscure reason the Luftwaffe seem to oppose our week-end penetrations with more than their usual ferocity, and now we are waiting for the second call which will surely come on this perfect day.

For once our chatter is not confined to Messerschmitts and guns and tactics. Yesterday afternoon Nip and I borrowed the Padre's car, a small family saloon, and drove to Brighton for dinner. Before the return journey we collected two pilots from 145 Squadron, and in the small hours, wedged together, began the journey back to Tangmere. Nip was driving, the rest of us asleep, and along the front at Hove he had a vague recollection of some confusion and shouting and a half-hearted barrier stretched across part of the road. He pressed on and thought little of the incident, but soon after the engine ran unevenly and became very hot. Somehow we coaxed the car home. Next morning a close inspection revealed a sinister hole just below the rear window. Shocked, we traced the path of the bullet, for it turned out that a sentry at Hove had challenged us and, not receiving a suitable reply, had opened fire. The bullet had passed between the two pilots on the back seat, had continued between Nip and me at shoulder height, drilled a neat hole through the dashboard, grazed the cylinder head and ploughed out through the radiator. Small wonder that the little car had barely struggled back to Tangmere! The Padre is more concerned with our lucky escape than the damage to his car, but Billy Burton is incensed that his pilots should have to run a gauntlet of fire at Hove. He is busy penning a letter to the military, but we keep out of his way, for we think that he is opening his attack from a very insecure base.

There is a fine haze and the soft bulk of the South Downs is barely discernible. We can just see the spire of Chichester cathedral, but above the haze the visibility is excellent and you can see Lille from fifty miles.

Lille! It lies seventy miles inland from Le Touquet and marks the absolute limit of our daylight penetrations over France. We often escort bombers to Lille, for it is a vital communications centre and contains important heavy industries. Not unnaturally the Luftwaffe are very sensitive about it. Their ground-control organization has time to assess our intentions and bring up fighter reinforcements, and the run-up to the target is always strongly contested. We can be sure of a stiff fight when Lille is the target for the bombers.

The ops. phone rings and the airman who answers it calls out to the C.O.; Billy Burton listens and replaces the receiver.

"That was the wing commander. Take-off at 1325 with 610 and 145. We shall be target-support wing to the bombers. It's Lille again."

Suddenly the dispersal hut is full of chatter and activity. We shall be the last Spitfires in the target area, for our job is to see that the beehive leaves the area without interference. The sun will be almost directly overhead, and the Messerschmitts will be there, lurking and waiting in its strong glare. We shall fight today.

Highly coloured ribbons are pinned across the large map on the wall to represent the tracks of the beehive and the six supporting fighter wings, so that the map looks like one of those bold diagrams of London's Underground system. The two flight sergeants talk with their respective flight commanders about the serviceability of our Spitfires, and our names and the letters of our aircraft are chalked up on a blackboard which shows three sections of finger-fours.

It is fascinating to watch the reactions of the various pilots. They fall into two broad categories; those who are going out to shoot and those who secretly and desperately know they will be shot at, the hunters and the hunted. The majority of the pilots, once they have seen their names on the board, walk out to their Spitfires for a pre-flight check and for a word or two with their ground crews. They tie on their Mae Wests, check their maps, study the weather forecast and have a last-minute chat with their leaders or wingmen. These are the hunters.

The hunted, that very small minority (although every squadron usually possessed at least one), turned to their escape kits and made quite sure that they were wearing the tunic with the silk maps sewn into a secret hiding-place; that they had at least one oilskin-covered packet of French francs, and two if possible; that they had a compass and a revolver and sometimes specially made clothes to assist their activities once they were shot down. When they went through these agonized preparations they reminded me of aged country-women meticulously checking their shopping-lists before catching the bus for the market town.

A car pulls up outside and our leader stumps into the dispersal hut, breezy and full of confidence. "They'll be about today, Billy. We'll run into them over the target, if not before. Our job is to see the Stirlings get clear and cover any stragglers. Stick together. Who's flying in my section?"

"Smith, Cocky and Johnnie, sir," answers Billy Burton.

"Good," Bader grins at us. "Hang on and get back into the abreast formation when I straighten out. O.K.?"

"O.K. sir," we chorus together.

The wing commander makes phone calls to Stan Turner and Ken Holden. Brief orders followed by a time check. Ten minutes before we start engines, and we slip unobtrusively to our Spitfires, busy with our own private thoughts. I think of other Sunday afternoons not so very long ago when I was at school and walked the gentle slopes of Charnwood Forest clad in a stiff black suit. Our housemaster's greatest ambition was to catch us seniors red-handed smoking an illicit cigarette. And I think of my own father's deep-rooted objections to any form of strenuous activity on the Sabbath during the holidays at Melton Mowbray.

My ground crew have been with the squadron since it was formed and have seen its changing fortunes and many pilots come and go. They know that for me these last few moments on the ground are full of tension, and as they strap me in the cockpit they maintain an even pressure of chatter. Vaguely I hear that the engine is perfect, the guns oiled and checked and the faulty radio set changed and tested since the last flight. The usual cockpit smell, that strange mixture of dope, fine mineral oil, and high-grade fuel, assails the nostrils and is somehow vaguely comforting. I tighten my helmet strap, swing the rudder with my feet on the pedals, watch the movement of the ailerons when I waggle the stick and look at the instruments without seeing them, for my mind is racing on to Lille and the 109s.

Ken starts his engine on the other side of the field and the twelve Spitfires from 610 trundle awkwardly over the grass. Bader's propeller begins to turn, I nod to the ground crew and the engine coughs once or twice and I catch her with a flick of the throttle and she booms into a powerful bass until I cut her back to a fast tick-over. We taxi out to the take-off position, always swinging our high noses so that we can see the aircraft ahead. The solid rubber tail-wheels bump and jolt on the unyielding ground and we bounce up and down with our own backbones acting as shock absorbers.

We line our twelve Spitfires diagonally across one corner of the meadow. We wait until Ken's squadron is more than half-way across the airfield and then Bader nods his head and we open out throttles together and the

deep-throated roar of the engines thunders through the
leather helmets and slams against our ear-drums. Airborne, and the usual automatic drill. We take up a tight
formation and I drop my seat a couple of notches and trim
the Spitfire so that it flies with the least pressure from
hands and feet.

One slow, easy turn on to the course which sends us
climbing parallel to the coast. Ken drops his squadron
neatly into position about half a mile away and Stan flanks
us on the other side. Woodhall calls from the ops. room to
his wing leader to check radio contact:

"Dogsbody?"

"O.K., O.K."

And that's all.

We slant into the clean sky. No movement in the cockpit
except the slight trembling of the stick as though it is alive
and not merely the focal point of a superb mechanical
machine. Gone are the ugly tremors of apprehension
which plagued us just before the take-off. Although we
are sealed in our tiny cockpits and separated from each
other, the static from our radios pours through the earphones of our tightly fitting helmets and fills our ears with
reassuring crackles. When the leader speaks, his voice is
warm and vital, and we know full well that once in the air
like this we are bound together by a deeper intimacy than
we can ever feel on the ground. Invisible threads of trust
and comradeship hold us together and the mantle of
Bader's leadership will sustain and protect us throughout
the fight ahead. The Tangmere Wing is together.

We climb across Beachy Head, and over Pevensey Bay
we swing to the starboard to cross the Channel and head
towards the French coast. Some pilot has accidentally
knocked on his radio transmitter and croons quietly to
himself. He sounds happy and must be a Canadian, for he
sings of "The Chandler's Wife" and the "North Atlantic
Squadron". He realizes his error and we hear the sudden
click of his transmitter, and again the only sound is the
muted song of the engine.

Now Bader rocks his wings and we level out from the climb and slide out of our tight formation. We take up our finger-four positions with ourselves at 25,000 feet and Ken and Stan stacked up behind us. It is time to switch the gun button from "safe" to "fire" and to turn on the reflector sight, for we might want them both in a hurry.

"O.K. Ken?" from Bader.

"O.K., Dogsbody."

"Stan?" from Bader again.

"You bet."

The yellow sands of the coast are now plainly visible, and behind is a barren waste of sandhills and scrub. Well hidden in these sandhills are the highly trained gunners who serve the 88 mm. batteries. We breast the flak over Le Touquet. The black, evil flowers foul the sky and more than the usual amount of ironmongery is hurled up at us. Here and there are red marker bursts intended to reveal our position to the Messerschmitts. We twist and pirouette to climb above the bed of flak, and from his relatively safe position, high above, Stan sees our plight and utters a rude comment in the high-pitched voice he reserves for such occasions. The tension eases.

On across the Pas de Calais and over the battlefields of a half-forgotten war against the same foe. From the Tangmere ops. room Woodhall breaks the silence:

"Dogsbody, from Beetle. The beehive is on time and is engaged."

"O.K."

"Fifty-plus about twenty miles ahead of you," from Woodhall.

"Understood," replies Bader.

"Thirty-plus climbing up from the south and another bunch behind them. Keep a sharp look-out," advises the group captain.

"O.K. Woodie. That's enough," answers the wing leader, and we twist our necks to search the boundless horizons.

"Look's like a pincer movement to me," comments

some wag. I suspect it is Roy Marple's voice, and again the tension slackens as we grin behind our oxygen masks. Woodhall speaks into his microphone with his last item of information.

"Dogsbody. The rear support wing is just leaving the English coast." (This means we can count on some help should we have to fight our way out.) "Course for Dover – 310 degrees." (This was a last-minute reminder of the course to steer for home.) Woodhall fades out, for he has done his utmost to paint a broad picture of the air situation. Now it is up to our leader.

"Dogsbody from blue one. Beehive at twelve o'clock below. About seven miles."

"O.K. I see them," and the wing leader eases his force to starboard and a better up-sun position.

The high-flying Messerschmitts have seen our wing and stab at Stan's top-cover squadron with savage attacks from either flank.

"Break port, Ken." (From a pilot of 610).

"Keep turning."

"Tell me when to stop turning."

"Keep turning. There's four behind!"

"Get in, red section."

"We're stuck into some 109s behind you, Douglas." (This quietly from Stan.)

"O.K. Stan."

"Baling out."

"Try and make it, Mac. Not far to the coast." (This urgently from a squadron commander.)

"No use. Temperatures off the clock. She'll burn any time. Look after my dog."

"Keep turning, yellow section."

So far the fight has remained well above us. We catch fleeting glimpses of high vapour trails and ducking, twisting fighters. Two-thirds of the wing are behind us holding off the 109s and we force on to the target area to carry out our assigned task. We can never reform into a wing again, and the pilots of 145 and 610 will make their way home in twos and fours. We head towards the distant beehive, well aware that there is now no covering force of Spitfires above us.

The Stirlings have dropped their heavy load of bombs and begin their return journey. We curve slowly over the outskirts of Lille to make sure the beehive is not harried from the rear. I look down at a pall of debris and black smoke rising from the target five miles below, and absurdly my memory flashes back to contrast the scene with those other schoolboy Sunday afternoons.

"Dogsbody from Smith. 109s above. Six o'clock. About twenty-five or thirty."

"Well done. Watch 'em and tell me when to break."

I can see them. High in the sun, and their presence only betrayed by the reflected sparkle from highly polished wind-screens and cockpit covers.

"They're coming down, Dogsbody. Break left." And round to port we go, with Smith sliding below Bader and Cocky and me above so that we cover each other in this steep turn. We curve round and catch a glimpse of four baffled 109s climbing back to join their companions, for they can't stay with us in a turn. The keen eyes of Smith saved us from a nasty smack that time.

"Keep turning, Dogsbody. More coming down," from Cocky.

"O.K. We might get a squirt this time," rejoins Bader. What a man, I think, what a man!

The turn tightens and in my extreme position on the starboard side I'm driving my Spitfire through a greater radius of curve than the others and falling behind. I kick on hard bottom rudder and skid inwards, down and behind the leader. More 109s hurtle down from above and a section of four angle in from the starboard flank. I look round for other Spitfires but there are none in sight. The four of us are alone over Lille.

"Keep turning. Keep turning." (From Bader.) "They can't stay with us." And we keep turning, hot and frightened and a long way from home. We can't keep turning all bloody day, I think bitterly.

Cocky has not re-formed after one of our violent breaks. I take his place next to Bader and the three of us watch the Messerschmitts, time their dives and call the break into their attacks. The odds are heavily against us.

We turn across the sun and I am on the inside. The blinding light seems only two feet above Bader's cockpit and if I drop further below or he gains a little more height, I shall lose him. Already his Spitfire has lost its colour and is only a sharp, black silhouette, and now it has disappeared completely, swallowed up by the sun's fierce light. I come out of the turn and am stunned to find myself alone in the Lille sky.

The Messerschmitts come in close for the kill. At this range their camouflage looks dirty and oil-stained, and one brute has a startling black-and-white spinner. In a hot sweat of fear I keep turning and turning, and the fear is mingled with an abject humiliation that these bastards should single me out and chop me at their leisure. The radio is silent, or probably I don't hear it in the stress of trying to stay alive. I can't turn all day. Le Touquet is seventy hostile miles away; far better to fight back and take one with me.

Four Messerschmitts roar down from six o'clock. I see them in time and curve the shuddering, protesting Spitfire to meet them, for she is on the brink of a high-speed stall. They are so certain of my destruction that they are flying badly and I fasten on to tail-end Charlie and give him a long burst of fire. He is at the maximum range, and although my shooting has no apparent effect some of my despair and fear on this fateful afternoon seems to evaporate at the faint sound of the chattering machine guns. But perhaps my attack has its just reward, for Smith's voice comes loud and clear over the radio.

"One Spit behind, Dogsbody. A thousand yards. Looks like he's in trouble."

Then I see them. Two aircraft with the lovely curving wings that can only belong to Spitfires. I take a long breath and in a deliberately calm voice:

"It's me Dogsbody – Johnnie."

"O.K. Johnnie. We'll orbit here for you. Drop in on my starboard. We'll get a couple of these—"

There is no longer any question of not getting home now that I am with Bader again. He will bring us safely back to Tangmere and I know he is enjoying this, for he sounds full of confidence over the radio. A dozen Messerschmitts still shadow our small formation. They are well up-sun and waiting to strike. Smith and I fly with our necks twisted right round, like the resting mallard ducks one sees in the London parks, and all our concentration focussed on the glinting shoal of 109s.

"Two coming down from five o'clock, Dogsbody. Break right," from me. And this time mine is the smallest turn so that I am the first to meet the attack. A 109 is very close and climbing away to port. Here is a chance. Time for a quick shot and no danger of losing the other two Spitfires if I don't get involved in a long tail chase. I line up my Spitfire behind the 109, clench the spade-grip handle of the stick with both hands and send short bursts into his belly at less than a hundred yards. The 109 bursts apart and the explosion looks exactly the same as a near burst of heavy flak, a vicious flower with a poisonous glowing centre and black swirling edges.

I re-form and the Messerschmitts come in again, and this time Bader calls the break. It is well judged and the wing leader fastens on to the last 109 and I cover his Spitfire as it appears to stand on its tail with wisps of smoke plummeting from the gun ports. The enemy aircraft starts to pour white smoke from its belly and thick black smoke from the engine. They merge together and look like a long, dirty banner against the faded blue of some high cirrus cloud.

"Bloody good shooting, sir."

"We'll get some more."

Woodhall – it seems an eternity since we last heard him – calls up to say that the rear support wing is over Abbeville. Unbelievably the Messerschmitts which have tailed us so long vanish and we are alone in the high spaces.

We pick up the English coast near Dover and turn to port for Sussex and Tangmere. We circle our airfield and land without any fuss or aerobatics, for we never know until we are on the ground whether or not a stray bullet has partially severed a control cable.

Woodhall meets us and listens to his wing leader's account of the fight. Bader has a tremendous ability to remember all the details and gives a graphic résumé of the show. The group captain listens carefully and says that he knew we were having a hard time because of the numerous plots of enemy formations on his operations table and our continuous radio chatter. So he had asked 11 Group to get the rear support wing over France earlier than planned, to lend a hand. Perhaps the shadowing Messerschmitts which sheered off so suddenly had seen the approach of this Spitfire wing.

Bader phones Ken and Stan while the solemn Gibbs pleads with us to sit down and write out our combat reports.

"Please do it now. It will only take two minutes."

"Not likely Gibbs. We want some tea and a shower and . . ."

"You write them and we'll sign them," suggests a pilot.

Cocky walks in. He came back on the deck after losing us over Lille and landed at Hawkinge short of petrol.

"Dinner and a bottle at Bosham tonight, Johnnie?"

"Right," I answer at once.

"Count me in, too," says Nip.

The group captain is trying to make himself heard above the din.

"You chaps must watch your language. It's frightful. And the Waafs seem to be getting quite used to it. They don't bat an eyelid any more. But I'm sure you don't know how bad it sounds. I had it logged this afternoon." And he waves a piece of paper in his hand.

Someone begins to read out from the record. We roar

with laughter, slap each other on the back and collapse weakly into chairs, but this reaction is not all due to the slip of paper. Woodhall watches us and walks to the door hoping that we don't see the grin which is creasing his leathery countenance.

We clamber into our meagre transports, one small van per flight, and drive to Shopwhyke. We sit on the lawn and drink tea served by Waafs. These young girls wear overalls of flowered print and look far more attractive and feminine than in their usual masculine garb of collar and tie. One of our officers is a well-known concert pianist and he plays a movement from a Beethoven concerto, and the lovely melody fills the stately house and overflows into the garden. The sweat from the combats of but an hour ago is barely dry on our young bodies.

THE FLYING TIGERS

CLAIRE L. CHENNAULT

The legendary Flying Tigers squadron – more properly the American Volunteer Group of the Chinese Nationalist Airforce – was the brainchild of Claire Chennault, a former USAAF pilot who had become the air adviser to the Chinese government of Chiang Kai Chek. Chennault's appointment in 1937 had virtually coincided with the Japanese invasion of China, to which the CNAF had only been able to put up a token resistance. Eventually, though, Chennault persuaded the Chinese government to bolster its airforce by buying 100 Curtiss Tomahawk fighters (P-40s) from the US, while he himself – with President Roosevelt's permission – recruited volunteer pilots for it from the US airforces. By spring 1941, 109 pilots from the US Marine Corps, the US Navy, the USAAF and civilian flying clubs had joined the American Volunteer Group (AVG).

Training lasted until December 1941, in which month the AVG flew its first missions against the Japanese. By now the USA itself was at war with Japan, but the Tigers retained their volunteer status until the summer of 1942, when they were reorganized as the 23rd Fighter Group of the USAAF. In the seven months of its existence as a fighting unit, the AVG and its shark-mouthed P-40s shot down 297

> *Japanese aircraft over the skies of China and Burma*
> *for the loss of 80 planes.*
>
> *Below is Colonel Claire L. Chennault's personal*
> *account of the first AVG sorties against the Japanese,*
> *flown in December 1941.*

My worst fears in thirty years of flying and nearly a decade of combat came during the first weeks after the attack on Pearl Harbor over the possibility of getting caught on the ground by a Japanese air assault on the A.V.G. at Toungoo. This fear had been gnawing at me ever since mid-October when the volunteer group began to take shape as a combat unit and I ordered the first aerial reconnaissance over the Japanese-built airfields in Thailand. I knew the Japanese were well informed on the condition of my group. I also knew they would have scant regard for the neutrality of Burma if they considered the A.V.G. a real menace to their activities in China. After Pearl Harbor I considered a Japanese attack on Toungoo a certainty. My only thought was to meet it with my planes in the air. During my long fight against the Japanese I constantly strove to put myself in the place of the enemy air commanders and diagnose their probable tactics. Generally my experience proved I allotted them too much credit.

Nearly half the A.V.G. men at Toungoo were Navy men and many of them had served at Pearl Harbor. I too had my own memories of Hawaii in the days when the 19th Fighter Squadron, which I commanded, was based on Ford Island as part of the air defenses of Pearl Harbor. In 1925 we experienced one of the Japanese attack scares that periodically swept the islands. It proved to be a baseless rumor. However, for three weeks I had the 19th Fighter Squadron warming up their planes in the dark of early morning. We took off before the first streaks of dawn to rendezvous over. Oahu at 10,000 feet where it was already day. We patrolled the approaches to Pearl Harbor until long after sunrise hit the ground. There were no orders from my superiors to stand this alert, and our squadron took a lot of ribbing for the performance. I knew, as does every Regular Army officer, that the first responsibility of a unit commander – whether he heads an infantry platoon or an air force – is to take measures to ensure his own unit against tactical surprise by the enemy. The transition from peace to war comes hard for civilians, but for professional soldiers there is no excuse. If I had been caught with my planes on the ground, as were the Air Corps commanders in the Philippines and in Hawaii, I could never again have looked my fellow officers squarely in the eye.

The lightness with which this cardinal military sin was excused by the American high command when committed by Regular Army officers has always seemed to me one of the more shocking aspects of the war. Americans have been prone to excuse the failings of their military leaders partly because of the glow of final victory and partly because they still lack all the facts from which to form an honest and accurate appraisal – facts that have been carefully withheld from the public under the guise of censorship allegedly necessary to military security. It is high time the American people made it their business to find out more about why the men they paid for twenty years to provide for the national defense were so pitifully unprepared for the catastrophe that nearly engulfed us all. The penalty for the failure to do so will be a new and even more disastrous Pearl Harbor.

The Japanese attack on Hawaii confronted me with an abrupt change in plans. Although my fighter squadrons at Toungoo were ready for action, other phases of the project were in a more precarious state. Except for the P-40 tires sent by General MacArthur and Admiral Hart from the Philippines, we had no spares so vitally needed to keep the planes repaired after combat. Hudson bombers for the Second American Volunteer Group were parked on Lockheed's airport at Burbank, California. They were immediately taken over by the Air Corps, and we heard no more of them until they arrived in China for the Chinese Air Force in the late summer of 1942. A sizeable group of bomber crews already at sea on their way to Burma were diverted to Australia and inducted into the U.S. Army. First shipment of replacement fighter pilots met the same fate.

Events of December 7 and 8 made it clear that the fighter group was the only salvage from all the elaborate plans that had been so painstakingly woven in Washington. Had I known then that for over a year this fighter group would be the only effective Allied air force to oppose the Japanese on the Asiatic mainland I probably would not have entered the combat with such high hopes.

It was immediately evident that both ends of the Burma Road would have to be defended from heavy air assaults since the wrecking of Rangoon, the port of entry, and Kunming, the main division point in China, by air attack would offer a relatively cheap and effective means of tightening the Japanese fingers on China's throat without draining the far-flung enemy offensives in the southern Pacific. Rangoon was the only funnel through which supplies could still come to China. Kunming was the vital valve in China that controlled distribution of supplies to the Chinese armies in the field.

From the beginning there was dissension among the new Allies. The Generalissimo offered the British six divisions of his best troops and all of his heavy motorized artillery for the defense of Burma. The British spurned the offer, and Chiang's troops sat idle in Yunnan until March 1942 when the fall of Rangoon finally convinced the British they needed help. The British however showed no such reluctance over the American Volunteer Group of the Chinese Air Force. They pressed hard for transfer of the entire group to Rangoon to operate under R.A.F. command.

I opposed this transfer just as stubbornly as the British refused the help of Chinese ground troops. Early in the fall I conferred with Group Captain Manning over the aerial defense of Rangoon. He then had no warning net and only a single runway at Mingaladon, ten miles from Rangoon, on which to base his fighters. I suggested he build some dispersal fields to the west of Rangoon and fill in the gap between the new fields and the Thailand border with a network of air spotters' posts linked by special telephone and radio. With those facilities our fighters would have been able to meet the enemy over Rangoon with plenty of warning and altitude and be securely protected on the ground at fields beyond the Japs' range. I had learned early in this long game against the Japanese that it is suicide to fight air battles without adequate warning of the enemy's attacks and a main base out of his range. Manning, however, regarded his single runway within Japanese range as adequate and placed a reliance on his combination of radar and long-distance phone that was never borne out by experience. Manning had also committed the R.A.F. under his command to combat tactics that I regarded as suicidal. By serving under his command, I would have lost my own authority over the group and forced my pilots to accept his stupid orders. All during the period we were negotiating for transfer of all or a part of the A.V.G. to Rangoon, Manning refused to allow me to enter his fighter-control room or become familiar with any of the facilities that we were supposed to use jointly in the air defense of Rangoon.

We finally worked out an agreement, satisfactory to both the Generalissimo and the British, whereby one squadron of the A.V.G. would assist the R.A.F. in the defense of Rangoon with the other two squadrons to be stationed at Kunming, the China end of the Burma Road, where we had adequate warning net and dispersal fields. The Rangoon squadron remained under my direct command subject-only to operational control by the senior R.A.F. officer in Burma. In this way the American pilots remained free to use their own tactics while coming under strategic direction of the R.A.F. Manning agreed to provide housing, transportation, food, and communications for the American squadron at Rangoon. This he failed to do.

The day after Pearl Harbor (December 9 by our calendar) we had half a dozen false alerts. With each new clang of the brass warning bell, Tom Trumble, my secretary, grabbed his rifle and tin hat and dashed for the slit trenches while I slung on my binoculars and trotted to the control tower. On December 10 Thailand "surrendered" to the Japanese, and enemy troops, ships, and planes poured into Bangkok to establish a base for the assault on Burma and Malaya. I sent Erik Shilling on a photo-reconnaissance mission over Bangkok in a special stripped-down P-40 equipped with an R.A.F. aerial camera. This improvised photo plane was about 18 miles per hour faster and could climb 3,000 feet higher than the average P-40, but it was completely outclassed by the speedy Japanese high-altitude photo planes that continued to do their work unmolested over Asia until the first Lockheed Lightnings (P-38) arrived in China in the summer of 1943. Escorted by Ed Rector of Marshal, North Carolina, and Bert Christman of Fort Collins, Colorado, in regular P-40s, Shilling photographed the docks and airfields of Bangkok from 26,000 feet.

When I saw his pictures, I exploded. Docks along the Menam River were jammed with enemy transports disgorging troops and supplies. Don Maung airdrome outside the city was packed with Japanese aircraft, parked wing tip to wing tip and awaiting dispersal to the chain of advanced bases closer to the Burma border. A dozen bombers could have wrecked the Japanese air offensive in twenty minutes.

This was but one of the many times during the war when a kingdom was lost for want of a few planes.

The Third A.V.G. Squadron commanded by Arvid Olson, of Hollywood, California, moved to Mingaladon airdrome on December 12 to join the R.A.F. in the defense of Rangoon. At Toungoo we encouraged every possible movement rumor about the rest of the group to confuse the Burmese spies while we tied up our loose ends preparatory to establishing a new base at Kunming. There were still twenty-five pilots not sufficiently trained to be turned loose in combat and a dozen P-40s under repair at Toungoo, but when the radio crackled from Kunming that the Japanese were bombing the city on December 18, it was apparent that the time to move had come.

The group was so organized that everything essential to immediate combat operations could be airborne. Permanent base personnel and supplies left Toungoo by truck convoy up the Burma Road. Three C.N.A.C. transports swooped down on Toungoo on the afternoon of the eighteenth and whisked me, my combat staff, and the oxygen, ammunition, and spare parts we needed for fighting to Kunming before dawn the next day.

The First and Second Squadrons flew from Toungoo to Kunming on the afternoon of the eighteenth with a refueling stop at Lashio. At Toungoo the First Squadron circled on patrol covering the Second Squadron's take-off, and at Kunming the roles were reversed as the Second stayed in the air until the First Squadron had landed, refueled, and was ready for combat again at Kunming.

By dawn on the nineteenth we had thirty-four P-40s ready to fight at Kunming with a fighter-control headquarters hooked into the Yunnan warning net and the Chinese code rooms that were monitoring Japanese operational radio frequencies and decoding enemy messages. For the first time since mid-October I breathed easier.

It was this kind of lightning mobility that was necessary to realize the full potential of airpower. To achieve it meant that I would always have to operate on a skeletonized basis with airmen doubling in ground duties and a few key men doing the work of an entire staff. It meant that I could never afford the excess staff personnel required by more orthodox military organizations.

It was this ability to shift my combat operations six hundred and fifty miles in an afternoon and a thousand miles in twenty-four hours that kept the Japanese off balance for four bloody years and prevented them from landing a counterpunch with their numerically superior strength that might easily have put my always meager forces out of business.

We had little strain on our patience for the first pay-off on these tactics. December 19 passed quietly with three P-40 reconnaissance patrols over southern Yunnan but no sign of life from the enemy. At 9:45 A.M. on the twentieth my special phone from the Chinese code room rang. It was Colonel Wong Shu Ming, commander of the Chinese Fifth Air Force and Chinese chief of staff for the A.V.G. His message said, "Ten Japanese bombers crossed the Yunnan border at Laokay heading northwest."

From then on the battle unfolded over Yunnan as it had done a hundred times before in my head. Reports filtered in from the Yunnan net as the enemy bombers penetrated deeper into China.

"Heavy engine noise at station X-10."

"Unknowns overhead at station P-8."

"Noise of many above clouds at station C-23."

Position reports recorded on our fighter-control board added up to a course designed to bring the enemy bombers to about fifty miles east of Kunming, from which point they would probably begin the circling and feinting tactics designed to confuse the warning net before their final dash to the target.

I ordered the Second Squadron to make the interception. Jack Newkirk, of Scarsdale, New York, led one four-plane element in search of the bombers while Jim Howard, of St. Louis, son of former medical missionaries in China, led another four-plane formation on defensive patrol above Kunming. Sixteen planes of the First Squadron commanded by Robert Sandell, of San Antonio, Texas, were held in reserve in the stand-by area west of Kunming, ready to join the fray at the decisive moment.

I fired a red flare sending the Second and First Squadrons into the air and drove with my executive officer, Harvey Greenlaw, and interpreter, Colonel Hsu, to the great timbered clay pyramid looming above the grassy mounds of a Chinese graveyard on a gentle slope overlooking the field. This was our combat-operations shelter with a duplicate set of radio and phone communications. Inside the dark, dank interior we studied the plotting board by the light of matches held by Greenlaw while Hsu took phone reports from the Chinese net. Outside, the winter air of the Kunming plateau was crisp and clear. Scattered puffball clouds floated lazily above the city at 10,000 feet. Weather reports to the south indicated a solid overcast brushing the mountain peaks.

This was the decisive moment I had been awaiting for more than four years – American pilots in American fighter planes aided by a Chinese ground warning net about to tackle a formation of the Imperial Japanese Air Force, which was then sweeping the Pacific skies victorious everywhere. I felt that the fate of China was riding in the P-40 cockpits through the wintery sky over Yunnan. I yearned heartily to be ten years younger and crouched in a cockpit instead of a dugout, tasting the stale rubber of an oxygen mask and peering ahead into limitless space through the cherry-red rings of a gunsight.

Suddenly voices broke through the crackling radio static.

"There they are."

"No, no, they can't be Japs."

"Look at those red balls."

"Let's get 'em."

Then maddening silence. I ordered Sandell's reserve squadron to dive to Iliang about thirty miles southeast of Kunming along the Japs' line of probable approach. There was nothing more on the radio. The Chinese net reported the bombers had reversed course and were heading back toward Indo-China. Sounds of gunfire were heard, and the heavy fall of Japanese bombs in the mountains near Iliang was reported. There was nothing to do but return to the field and wait.

Chinese were already streaming back to the city from their refuge among the grave mounds, incredulous that no bombs had fallen. Howard's patrol over Kunming came down. They had seen nothing. Newkirk's flight returned, sheepish and chagrined over a bad case of buck fever on their first contact with the enemy. They had sighted the Jap formation of ten gray twin-engined bombers about thirty miles southeast of Kunming, but for a few incredulous seconds could hardly believe the bombers were really Japs. The bombers jettisoned their bombs, put their noses down for speed, and wheeled back toward Indo-China. By the time Newkirk's flight recovered and opened fire, the bombers had too big a lead – too big that is for everybody except Ed Rector. The last the other pilots saw of Rector he was still chasing the Japs at full throttle.

Finally Sandell's squadron came straggling in. From the whistling of the wind in their open gun barrels and the slow rolls as they buzzed the field, we knew they had been in a fight. They had sighted the Jap formation in full retreat over Iliang about thirty miles southeast of Kunming, scuttling along on top of a solid overcast with Rector still in pursuit.

As the P-40s dived to attack, everybody went a little crazy with excitement. All the lessons of Toungoo were forgotten. There was no teamwork – only a wild mêlée in which all pilots agreed that only sheer luck kept P-40s from shooting each other. Pilots tried wild 90-degree deflection shots and other crazy tactics in the 130-mile running fight that followed. Fritz Wolf of Shawano, Wisconsin, shot down two bombers and then cursed his armorer because his guns jammed.

When he landed and inspected the guns, he found they were merely empty. When the P-40s broke off three Jap bombers had gone down in flames and the remainder were smoking in varying degrees. Ed Rector was the only A.V.G. casualty. His long chase left him short of gas, forcing him to crash-land his P-40 in a rice paddy east of Kumming with minor injuries.

Back at the field most of the pilots were too excited to speak coherently.

"Well, boys," I told the excited pilots, "it was a good job but not good enough. Next time get them all."

I herded them into the operations shack for an hour before I let them eat lunch. We went over the fight in minute detail pointing out their mistakes and advising them on how to get all the bombers next time. Not until the spring of 1945 did I learn how close Sandell's flight had come to getting all the Japs in that first fight of the A.V.G.

Lewis Bishop of De Kalb Junction, New York, an A.V.G. pilot shot down five months after the Iliang battle and taken prisoner in Indo-China, met the Japanese pilot who led the raid. The Jap said his crew had been the sole survivors of the mission. Nine of the ten bombers had failed to return.

Bishop was a prisoner of the enemy for three years. He finally escaped by jumping from a moving train in North China while being transferred from Shanghai to Manchuria. He reached me in Kunming early in 1945 to write the final footnote to the A.V.G.'s first fight.

Japanese airmen never again tried to bomb Kunming while the A.V.G. defended it. For many months afterward they sniffed about the edges of the Yunnan warning net and dropped a few bombs near the border but never ventured near Kunming. Our border patrols shot down a half dozen of these half-hearted raiders, and by the spring of 1942 we were on the offensive carrying the war deep into Indo-China with dive-bombing and strafing missions. The Japs waited until sixteen months after their first defeat to launch another mission against Kunming in the spring of 1943, when they knew I was in Washington attending the Trident Conferences of the British-American Combined Chiefs of Staff. Then they brought thirty fighters to protect their bombers.

Although the A.V.G. was blooded over China, it was the air battles over Rangoon that stamped the hallmark on its fame as the Flying Tigers. The cold statistics for the ten weeks the A.V.G. served at Rangoon show its strength varied between twenty and five serviceable P-40s. This tiny force met a total of a thousand-odd Japanese aircraft over southern Burma and Thailand. In 31 encounters they destroyed 217 enemy planes and probably destroyed 43. Our losses in combat were four pilots killed in the air, one killed while strafing, and one taken prisoner. Sixteen P-40s were destroyed. During the same period the R.A.F., fighting side by side with the A.V.G., destroyed 74 enemy planes, probably destroyed 33, with a loss of 22 Buffaloes and Hurricanes.

Winston Churchill, then prime minister of the United Kingdom, added his eloquence to these statistics, cabling the Governor of Burma, "The victories of these Americans over the rice paddies of Burma are comparable in character if not in scope with those won by the R.A.F. over the hop fields of Kent in the Battle of Britain."

Air Vice Marshal D. F. Stevenson, who replaced Manning in January 1942, noted that while the ratio of British to German planes in the Battle of Britain had been 1 to 4, the ratio of Anglo-American fighters to Japanese planes over Rangoon was 1 to from 4 to 14.

The Japanese began their aerial assault on Rangoon with a strength of 150 fighters and bombers based on a few fields in southern Thailand. In Burma, the Allies could muster only 16 P-40s of the A.V.G., 20 Buffaloes of the R.A.F., some ancient British Lysanders of the India Air Force, and a few Tiger Moth training planes. As I anticipated, the radar-phone combination of the R.A.F. warning system failed to provide adequate warning. Many times the only warning my pilots received was a hurried phone call, "Bombers overhead," or the noise and dust of the R.A.F. Buffaloes scrambling for an alert. Numerous A.V.G. interceptions were made only after the enemy finished bombing and was leaving the target due to the inadequate warning. When the R.A.F. indicated that its only attempts to bolster the warning system consisted of providing advanced ground troops with heliographs to flash warning messages, I fought vigorously to withdraw the A.V.G. from what I considered an unnecessarily exposed position. Only the heavy pressure of the Anglo-American Combined Chiefs of Staff and the Generalissimo prevented me from doing so.

Shortly before the Rangoon battles began, the A.V.G. suffered its final blow from William D. Pawley. The contract between Pawley and the Chinese government provided that I could call on Pawley's Central Aircraft Manufacturing Company for technical personnel, tools, and materials for repairing damaged P-40s of the A.V.G. At a conference with General Chow, chief of the Chinese Aeronautical Commission, in September it was agreed that all A.V.G. repair work west of the Salween River would be handled by CAMCO's Loi-Wing plant, located in Yunnan just across the Burma border, while the Chinese Air Force repair shop in Kunming would do all servicing east of the Salween.

As damaged planes began to pile up during training at Toungoo, I made repeated requests to Pawley for men and materials from his Loi-Wing plant to repair them. A few CAMCO men were sent to Toungoo but it was decided to do only emergency work there and to ship badly damaged planes over the Burma railroad to Lashio and thence by truck to the Loi-Wing factory. A number of P-40s were shipped to Loi-Wing, but after they arrived, little work was done on them.

CAMCO was engaged in the assembly of Curtiss-Wright Model 21 fighters and some trainers, which Pawley had already sold to the Chinese government. Pawley had that repairing A.V.G. planes interfered with his assembly program. I argued that repair of proven combat planes for experienced pilots rated higher priority than the assembly of trainers and experimental fighters. We also disagreed over the need for an A.V.G. squadron to be stationed at Loi-Wing for the protection of his factory. At that time the possibility of enemy air action against Loi-Wing was too remote to be considered seriously.

In mid-December Pawley issued an order to his American employees at Loi-Wing, forbidding them to touch an A.V.G. plane, and followed this with a radio to me that, as of January 1, CAMCO would do no more repair work on A.V.G. P-40s. I replied that Pawley's inability to do this work was regretted, but we would manage without him.

Loss of the CAMCO repair base was a serious blow to the group since we were already fighting over Rangoon. I took the matter to the Generalissimo in Chungking. He ordered the Chinese manager of CAMCO, Colonel Chen, to continue repairing A.V.G. planes. Chen did an excellent job for us until the plant was burned and abandoned in the face of the Japanese advance into Yunnan. The Chinese government acquired Pawley's interest in CAMCO, and he flew off to India where he had already begun construction of another aircraft plant.

I have always suspected that Pawley, like the Japanese, thoroughly believed the British and American intelligence reports that the A.V.G. would not last three weeks in combat. At any rate on the occasions when he had a chance to provide the A.V.G. with badly needed assistance, Pawley exhibited what I considered a remarkable lack of co-operation. It was only after the A.V.G.'s combat record had made the organization world famous that Pawley made strenuous efforts to have himself identified with it, even to the extent of attempting to secure an honorary membership of the Flying Tigers Incorporated, the only authentic postwar organization of former A.V.G. men, by offering a ten-thousand-dollar contribution to the corporation's funds. His offer was flatly rejected by the membership, who apparently felt that a few repaired P-40s during the dark days of 1941–42 would have been more valuable to them than a postwar check. After a succession of wartime manufacturing ventures, Pawley embarked on a diplomatic career as ambassador to Peru and Brazil. No doubt he found the Medal for Merit awarded him for "organizing the Flying Tigers" useful in his new work.

Two days before Christmas the Japanese shot their first aerial bolt against Rangoon with 54 bombers escorted by

20 fighters. The low fighter-bomber ratio indicated that the Japanese were confident and expected little trouble from the Allied air defense. There was no warning at Mingaladon. The Third Squadron was casually ordered to clear the field. While still climbing they were informed by R.A.F. fighter control, "Enemy approaching from the east."

The Japanese had finished bombing and were on their way home before the A.V.G. sighted the formation. Jap fighters were diving on the city, strafing the crowds of civilians who jammed the streets to watch the raid. One bomber formation hit Mingaladon Field, and the other laid their eggs along the docks. In the brief fight that followed, the Americans shot down six Japanese planes and lost two of their own pilots – Neil Martin of Texarkana, Arkansas, riddled by a quartet of Jap fighters, and Henry Gilbert of Bremerton, Washington, blown up by the top-turret fire of the bomber formations. The R.A.F. failed to make contact.

This raid put the torch of panic to Rangoon. Those who were rich enough to do so fled for their lives to India. Native Burmese rioted, looted, and began potting stray Britons. All the native cooks and servants fled from Mingaladon, leaving the A.V.G. without a mess. For two days they lived mainly on stale bread and canned beer, of which there seemed to be an ample stock.

On a cloudless Christmas day with the temperature at 115 degrees in the sun the Japanese came back to finish off Rangoon. They figured 60 bombers and 30 fighters would be ample for the job. This time 12 P-40s were waiting at altitude and sailed into the Japanese formations as they droned toward the city. "Like rowboats attacking the Spanish Armada," one observer on the ground described the attack. The R.A.F. put 16 Buffaloes into the fray later.

"It was like shooting ducks," Squadron Leader Olson radioed me at Kunming. "We got 15 bombers and 9 fighters. Could put entire Jap force out of commission with whole group here."

A.V.G. losses were 2 planes. Both pilots bailed out safely. The R.A.F. got 7 Jap planes and lost 9 Buffaloes and 6 pilots.

William Pawley happened to be in Rangoon that memorable Christmas and apparently suffered a slight change of heart in his attitude toward the A.V.G. He loaded a truck full of food and drink in Rangoon and drove it to Mingaladon to present the Third Squadron with Christmas dinner. Under the shade of banyan trees around the airport rim, with the smoke of burning Japanese wrecks still rising from the jungles beyond, the Third Squadron squatted to a dinner of ham and chicken liberally lubricated by beer and Scotch. The rest of the group, eight hundred miles to the north on the frosty Kunming plateau, dined on Yunnan duck and rice wine.

After the Christmas battle, the Third Squadron had only 11 serviceable P-40s left. Olson radioed for help, and I sent the Second Squadron, led by Newkirk, to relieve him. By the first week in January the transfer was completed, and the pattern of the Japanese effort against Rangoon became apparent.

While they gathered strength for another mass daylight assault, the Japanese sent night bombers to harass Rangoon, slipping in singly all night long to gain maximum nuisance value. A.V.G. efforts to halt them were unsuccessful, but the R.A.F. bagged several. Meanwhile the A.V.G. took the offensive, prowling the enemy fields in Thailand to smash their planes on the ground. Newkirk and "Tex" Hill led many of these early strafing attacks on the Jap airfields.

While the A.V.G. P-40s fought to keep the port of Rangoon open, our ground crews were working like beavers on the docks loading truck convoys with lend-lease equipment for shipment up the Burma Road to China. It was during this period, with the hot breath of the Japanese blowing on our necks, that the Burma Road first delivered twenty thousand tons a month to China. These supplies, trucked out of Burma before the fall of Rangoon, enabled the A.V.G. to continue operations in China long after every land line of communication with that unhappy land had been severed by the enemy. Every type of A.V.G. nonflying personnel, including our chaplain, Paul Frillman, of Maywood, Illinois, sweated like coolies on the Rangoon docks during those hectic weeks.

By the last week in January the Japanese were ready for another knockout attempt on Rangoon. From January 23 to 28 six major attacks of up to one hundred planes each rolled over the Burmese port. It was a tribute to the Anglo-American fighter pilots that the Japanese formations had switched to a three-to-one ratio of fighters protecting small bomber formations.

On January 23 and 24 the Japanese tried to floor the A.V.G. with a series of one-two punches. They led with a fighter sweep designed to get the Allied fighters into the air and use up their fuel. Then a second wave was scheduled to deliver the knockout punch while the A.V.G. and R.A.F. were on the ground refueling. It was a good plan but it didn't work. A.V.G. ground crews were too fast on refueling and rearming the P-40s and had them ready to fight again before the second wave of Japs appeared. By January 28 the Japs were sending over only large fighter formations, and the score for this offensive stood at 50 Jap planes destroyed against a loss of 2 A.V.G. pilots and 10 R.A.F. pilots killed.

Newkirk radioed Kunming, "The more hardships, work, and fighting the men have to do the higher our morale goes. Squadron spirit really strong now."

However strong the Second Squadron's spirit, they were down to ten P-40s, so I sent Bob Sandell and his First Squadron to take up the burden at Rangoon. The Japanese ground offensive into Burma had begun to roll during the last weeks in January, and it was evident that the British had neither the men, equipment, nor leadership to stop it.

Before I left the United States in the summer of 1941 I asked a few friends in Louisiana to watch the newspapers and send me any clippings about the A.V.G. Now I was being swamped with clippings from stateside newspapers, and my men were astonished to find themselves world famous as the Flying Tigers. The insignia we made famous was by no means original with the A.V.G. Our pilots copied the shark-tooth design on their P-40s' noses from a colored illustration in the *India Illustrated Weekly* depicting an R.A.F. squadron in the Libyan desert with shark-nosed P-40s. Even before that the German Air Force painted shark's teeth on some of its Messerschmitt 210 fighters. With the pointed nose of a liquid-cooled engine it was an apt and fearsome design. How the term Flying Tigers was derived from the shark-nosed P-40s I never will know. At any rate we were somewhat surprised to find ourselves billed under that name. It was not until just before the A.V.G. was disbanded that we had any kind of group insignia. At the request of China Defense Supplies in Washington, Roy Williams of the Walt Disney organization in Hollywood designed our insignia consisting of a winged tiger flying through a large V for victory.

Although the Flying Tiger victories made ready front-page copy for an Allied world rocked by a series of shattering defeats, I noticed too much tendency to attribute our success to sheer derring-do or some mystical quality and not enough on the solid facts on which our triumphs were really based.

Whatever its later shortcomings, the Curtiss-Wright P-40 was an excellent fighter for the battles over Rangoon, all of which were fought below 20,000 feet. At those altitudes the P-40 was better than a Hurricane and at its best against the Japanese Army Nates and Navy Model Zeros. The two .50-caliber machine guns gave the P-40 a heavy, fast-firing gun that neither the British nor Japs could match. Pilot armor saved many a P-40 pilot's life, and the heavy rugged construction, though a disadvantage in maneuverability, was certainly an advantage in field maintenance and putting damaged planes back into battle. P-40s could be repaired after damage that would have made a Japanese plane a total loss.

The ground crews were a vital factor that most news-paper correspondents on the spot overlooked. It was the speed with which the ground crews repaired, refueled, and rearmed the P-40s that kept the A.V.G. from being floored by the Japanese one-two punches. The ground crews displayed ingenuity and energy in repairing battle-damaged P-40s that I have seldom seen equaled and never excelled. Their performance at Rangoon was in many ways symbolic, for in all the long years of the war to come, it was American maintenance that was one of the keystones in our eventual arch of triumph. Until the very end of the Rangoon holocaust our ground crews managed to keep a minimum of 10 P-40s ready to fight every day. In contrast the R.A.F. commander, Air Vice Marshal Ste-venson, complained of his maintenance men who allowed a squadron of 30 Hurricanes arriving in January to slump to 11 planes fit for combat by mid-February and only 6 by March. I had never favored liquid-cooled engines for combat planes but the Allison engines in our P-40s cer-tainly did more than the manufacturer claimed for them.

Our leadership at Rangoon was also superior. All of the squadron leaders who saw action there – Olson; Sandell and Newkirk before they were killed; "Tex" Hill of Hunt, Texas; and Bob Neale, of Seattle, Washington, were leaders of the highest quality. It was no accident that Hill and Olson became full colonels and commanded Army Air Forces fighter groups in combat or that the A.A.F. offered a lieutenant colonelcy to Bob Neale, who entered the A.V.G. as a Navy ensign.

Above all it was the kind of teamwork that is so typically American, wherein there is plenty of scope for individual brilliance but everybody contributes toward a common goal. You can see it on an autumn Saturday afternoon in a top-notch football team. It will take the same kind of well-co-ordinated teamwork to operate a guided-missile or push-button group in the next war or to pull us through the perils of peace.

In January my annual attack of chronic bronchitis laid

me low in Kunming, and a projected trip to Rangoon had to be canceled. I alternated between brief spells in my airfield office and longer sieges in my sickbed at the University of Kunming where the A.V.G. was quartered. A radio was installed near my bed, so I could listen to the radio chatter of my pilots during their fights over Rangoon. It was over this radio that I heard of the Japanese attack on Toungoo, February 4. They struck at 6 A.M. There was no warning. All personnel were asleep. The operations building and a hangar were destroyed by direct hits; three P-40s still under repair were wrecked; and half a dozen R.A.F. Blenheims burned. That might all too easily have been the fate of the entire A.V.G. eight weeks earlier.

After the fall of Singapore in mid-February, the Japanese transferred the crack air units that blasted the R.A.F. out of the Malayan air to Thailand to join the assault on Rangoon. These reinforcements boosted enemy plane strength available to attack Rangoon to four hundred planes. Before the month's end, they were hammering at the city with two hundred planes a day.

It was during this period that a handful of battered P-40s flown by Bob Neale's First Squadron pilots wrote the final lurid chapter in the A.V.G. history of Rangoon. Neale had become First Squadron leader after the death of Bob Sandell, who died flight-testing a repaired P-40 over Mingaladon. Since the fall of Rangoon was already looming, Neale no longer retained damaged planes at Mingaladon but had them flown or shipped north by rail. About this time I also ordered Neale to cease all strafing and bomber-escort missions due to the worn condition of the P-40 engines, which were long overdue for overhaul. The fact that shark-nosed planes were observed flying north and were no longer seen over Thailand airdromes or accompanying R.A.F. bombers gave rise to rumors that the A.V.G. had left Rangoon. Neale radioed me for orders regarding the actual evacuation. I replied, "Expend equipment. Conserve personnel utmost. Retire with last bottle oxygen."

Neale took me literally. With 9 P-40s he waited for the final Japanese daylight assaults with their crack units from Singapore. R.A.F. strength had dwindled too. All the Buffaloes had been lost in combat or accidents. Thirty Hurricane reinforcements had shrunk to a dozen serviceable planes. New reinforcements of 18 Hurricanes and Spitfires being ferried from Calcutta to Rangoon cracked up in the Chin Hills with a loss of 11 pilots. When the Japanese began their final aerial assault on February 26, there were only 15 Allied fighters to meet the attack by 166 enemy planes. They fought off three raids on the twenty-fifth with the A.V.G. bagging 24 Jap planes. The next day was even worse, with 200 enemy planes over Rangoon. The A.V.G., now reduced to 6 P40s, bagged 18 Jap fighters to bring their two-day total to 43 enemy aircraft without loss to themselves.

In those two days of almost constant air fighting Neale's detachment turned in one of the epic fighter performances of all time. With the best of equipment it would have been a brilliant victory, but under the conditions Neale and his eight pilots fought, it was an incredible feat. The report of Fritz Wolf, who left Rangoon just before the final battles began, describes those conditions well.

Planes at Rangoon are almost unflyable. Tires are chewed up and baked hard. They blow out continually. We are short on them, and battery plates are thin. When we recharge them, they wear out within a day. There is no Prestone oil coolant in Rangoon. British destroyed the battery-charging and oxygen-storage depots without any advance warning to us so we could stock up. We are completely out of auxiliary gear shifts and they are wearing out in the planes every day.

Fresh food of any kind is completely lacking. We are living out of cans. Water is hard to get. Most of the city water supply has been cut off.

Dust on the field fouls up the P-40 engines considerably. It clogs carburetion so much that it is dangerous to increase manifold pressure when the engine quits cold. Entire carburetion systems are cleaned on the ground, but they are as bad as ever after a single day's operations. This tendency of engines to quit makes it hard to dogfight or strafe. Of the eight planes that took off for an air raid two days ago, only five got off the ground.

Conditions in Rangoon are getting dangerous. Authorities have released criminals, lunatics, and lepers to fend for themselves. Natives have broken into unguarded liquor stocks and are in a dangerous state. There are continual knifings and killings. Three British were killed near the docks a few nights ago. Stores are all closed. At least twenty-five blocks of the city are burning furiously. All fire trucks were sent up the Prome Road to Mandalay several weeks ago.

Our only contact with British intelligence was a visit from one officer about ten days ago. There seems to be little co-operation between the R.A.F. and British Army and less between the R.A.F. and us. It seems certain that the Japanese have crossed the Sittang River (only eighty miles from Rangoon), but we have had no word on it.

On the night of February 27 the R.A.F. removed the radar set from Rangoon without previous notice to the A.V.G. For Neale that was the last straw. The next morning he sent four of his remaining six P-40s to cover the route of the last A.V.G. truck convoy to leave Rangoon. He and his wingman, R. T. Smith, later an A.A.F. fighter group commander, stayed to make a final search for an A.V.G. pilot who had bailed out over the jungle some days before. Neale ripped out his own radio and enlarged the baggage compartment to hold a stretcher case if the pilot turned up injured. Neale and Smith sweated out February 28 waiting for news of the lost pilot, Edward

Liebolt. The next day the Japanese cut the Prome Road, last land line of retreat from Rangoon. Neale and Smith jammed two cases of whisky into Neale's baggage compartment and took off for Magwe, two hundred miles to the north. Two days later the Japanese Army entered Rangoon.

The battle of southern Burma was over.

TO KILL A MAN

GUNTHER BLOEMERTZ

*Bloemertz was one of the famed "Abbeville Boys",
flying Me 109s out of Abbeville in Northern France
during the German Occupation.*

What was it father said long ago – "You want to be an
airman? Now think, my boy. Downstairs there's a family
like ours: father, mother and child, saying grace before
supper – and you want to go and drop a bomb into all this
peacefulness!"

"No," I replied, "no, father, I want to be a fighter pilot,
one of the ones who shoots bombers down."

Then I was stretching both hands out of the window of
the railway carriage, with mother quietly crying and father
saying in a low voice, "Come back safely, my . . ." The
first flight over the fields and the wide forest, above the
red tiled roofs of the town . . . the heavy suitcases when I
arrived at the front. Oh – they *were* heavy! I had put them
down and entered the dusty, dry barracks. That was in
Abbeville . . . Abbeville – the front.

The spare man in the plain linen flying-suit standing
before me was the Kommandeur of the Abbeville Boys. A
bright yellow life jacket hung loosely across his shoulder
and chest, and a black, white and red ribbon stood out
from under his collar.

"How old?"

"Nineteen, Herr Major."

His lower lip came forward and he stared at me for a moment. "Have you any request to make?"

It sounded like an execution. But I did actually have a request – to get near two of my friends. Werner and Ulrich were a reminder of home . . .

The sun-warmed air was shimmering above the long concrete runways and wide stretches of grass. I had to walk on for quite half an hour with my heavy cases to the other side of the airfield. Close above the horizon, far beyond the shimmering layer, something sparkled for a second. A dozen fine streaks lay mutely across the sky: twelve fighters were either flying away from me or would be over my head in a few seconds. The streaks grew larger. Soon cockpits, wings and armament could be made out – the aircraft were already flying so low over the grass that in the hot eddying air they seemed to fuse with the ground, and still I could hear no engine noise. I saw the heads behind the goggles, the blunt noses of the motors hurtling towards me. A thin singing hum grew momentarily louder, then they were roaring over my head in lightning and thunder – and away.

I turned my head. The twelve trails with their dots in front were once again high in the sky. So those were they: the Tommies called them the "Abbeville Boys", and feared and respected them.

"Line-shooters!" I said to myself.

The line-shooters returned. Banking steeply, they circled the airfield and then swept in to land, whistling and bellowing, sharp explosions punctuating the flat accompaniment of idly-turning propellers. For a fraction of a second they displayed their flat, silver-blue bellies, drew down ever more closely towards their shadows on the grass, and alighted carefully with legs spread wide. Perhaps that's my squadron, I thought, perhaps Werner and Ulrich are with them. Or had they already been killed? I hauled my suitcases on a bit further, spurred by the joyful anticipation of seeing two old friends again.

At that very moment, from the squadron dispersal area, a "bird" rose in a leisurely, awkward fashion into the air. Its engine roaring, it vibrated slowly along towards me, splaying out its thin stork-like legs as though about to land again any moment. In fact the "Storch" landed scarcely thirty paces away on the greensward. The pilot jumped out, clowning in dumb show.

"Hallo, old boy! What a sight for my poor old eyes. You, too, taking your bones to market?"

Ulrich was standing before me: Ulrich, the dark-eyed, spare-framed reservist with the long, almost black hair – Ulrich, my pal of recruit days, who had worn his service nightshirt with such lazy distinction and had climbed every night into the topmost bunk of the row.

"Ulrich, old fellow, how did you know I was here?" I mumbled.

"Slow as ever in the uptake! How did I know you were here? Caught sight of you during the approach, recognised your old moon face quite plainly. Hawk's eyes, old boy – hawk's eyes! Cigarette?"

Ulrich's lapels smelt as they always had done of *Soir de Paris*.

"Incidentally, you look a regular porter," he went on unkindly. "There wasn't a car handy at the squadron but a Storch is just as good. Simple, isn't it? Coming?"

We went laughing to the aircraft. Ulrich's walk was as it used to be, leaning forward so you expected him to fall on his nose any moment. Around his mouth and at the corners of the eyes there had appeared finely drawn wrinkles.

"Yes, the Abbeville Boys have had a good deal of scrapping," he grinned. "And this evening we're going to drown it all."

"Where's Werner?" I asked, hesitating.

"Baled out an hour ago over St Orner. Got a bit above himself. The little Spitfires gave him a bellyful. Poor chap rang up just now. He's flying back with a replacement in the morning. Chuck your cigarette away!"

We climbed in to the cockpit of the Storch, and the shortest air journey of my career began. A few seconds later we climbed out between two dispersal hangars.

"The one in front is the Kapitän," Ulrich muttered under his breath. The Kapitän might well have been a cadet, for his fresh, brown face made him look just like an eighteen-year-old. The pilots were lying back in their easy chairs between the aircraft and waiting for the next sortie. The Kapitän led me round from one to the other, and Ulrich drew me finally to a chair next to his own.

The pair to my right were called Vogel and Meyer II, a strange couple who seemed only to exist for each other.

"The best of the whole squadron," whispered Ulrich, indicating them with his eyes.

The pilots' attention was jerked to the loudspeaker. Ulrich listened tautly with his lips pressed together. Only a hum could be heard at first – the current as it was switched on – and then came the announcement.

"*Achtung! achtung! Enemy aircraft forming up in strength over London, probably four-engined bombers.*"

Ulrich swallowed a curse. "Off we go again."

Drawing nervously at his cigarette he turned abruptly away, making for his machine. The other pilots were already clambering into their cockpits.

"*Immediate readiness!*" came through the loudspeaker, and the latecomers sprang into their aircraft. I stood on the wing beside Ulrich, who was crouched in the narrow cockpit, fastening his harness.

"Do your stuff!"

Laughing, he punched me in the chest.

"Can do," he nodded, and then, softly and nervously, "can do–can do. . . ."

His fists were clenched and I could see he had become suddenly serious. His eyes, lost in an unearthly distance, reflected something strange and rare, not fear – but perhaps a certain figure with a scythe coming towards him across the wide field. Since I had got to know Ulrich it was this curious expression in the eyes which had led me to the fancy that he might be a visitor from another planet wishing to study affairs on earth, moving among human beings to experience their habits, joys and sorrows, so he, too, could love, fight and die like any of them.

"*Achtung! Achtung! Squadron take off at once! Enemy formation airborne over Thames Estuary. Course Flushing.*"

The two-thousand-h.p. engines sprang into deafening life, their slip-stream forcing me backwards, as if eighty thousand horses were thundering all around. Forty small, compact single-seaters roared across the airfield, rose laboriously from the ground and drove with gathering speed towards the enemy.

That very day one of the pilots in our squadron had won his twenty-fifth victory in the air. In the evening a crowd of fellows came into our mess to celebrate in the company of their successful comrade. The Kommandeur with his staff, the Kapitäns of the neighbouring units and the pilots of our own squadron were all there. The men of the morning had changed very much in appearance, for instead of oily flying-suits they were wearing smart white or dark-blue uniforms, white shirts and – in accordance with a special squadron custom – loosely fitting white socks. Even in the Palace of Versailles you would not have found greater correctness in social conduct than here; but in spite of this, the conversation was pretty easy.

The Welfare Officer of our squadron was there too, a reserve major who always wore uniforms of English cut. Known as "Papi", he could easily have been the father of any one of us. He got now to telling a story about the evening a strange guest had been entertained in a small château not far from St Omer: a legendary Englishman who had already lost both his legs and who had now been shot down in combat. The brave Englishman had landed safely, but his artificial limbs had been smashed. So there was the captured enemy airman, the renowned Wing-Commander Bader from the other side, sitting in the middle of a group of German pilots – the Fighter General himself had invited him to an evening party.

The two of them, both experts at their craft, had sat in deep armchairs by the fireplace, their gaze fixed on the crackling embers. The atmosphere was rather oppressive, everyone appreciating the feelings of their guest, the airmen's immobile expressions flung into relief by the light of the flaming logs. No one spoke a word. Every now and again they sipped their drinks quietly and with reserve, never forgetting the little formalities which went with it. Germans are incapable of behaving in any other way – they honoured their guest as the man who had forgotten both his legs were missing to go out and fight for his country.

The strangeness of the occasion and reflections about their shot-down opponent led every man's thoughts the same way, suddenly to anathematise the war and that fate which throws a man into one particular society at his birth, and makes it his duty to conform to it. Why hadn't each of them been born in England? That would have given England one more pilot. Why was the Englishman sitting by the fireplace not a German? He might perhaps have been a kommodore of our own. Hadn't we often enough in peacetime sat down at table with those whom today it seemed our highest duty to kill? It was suddenly impossible to understand how men of the same sort, with the same feelings, desires, and needs could come to mangle one another to death.

The Englishman might well have been thinking somewhat similar thoughts, but he too had found himself unable to solve this problem and so perhaps had let it rest. At that, as he looked up, they raised their glasses to him. And subsequently there slowly developed between him and the German General an intimate discussion about fights experienced in common, told after the usual manner of fighter pilots – the sort of conversation only good friends can have.

That same evening the guest had asked if his reserve

legs could be sent across from England, and a few hours afterwards a British radio operator was holding the message in his hands – the Germans had offered an escort at a pre-arranged time, at a specified point where the legs could be dropped by parachute. But over there they didn't seem to trust "the Jerries" very much, for next day the Germans received a message to the effect that the legs had been dropped at a different time and in another area.

Our close attention had rewarded the Major for his narrative. I had quite recently heard more about the remarkable R.A.F. officer who continuously encouraged his companions in the prisoner-of-war camps to escape. He had finally got away himself, and it was even suggested our General had given him encouragement in doing so: at any rate the former had sworn heartily when he heard the British party had been recaptured.

As the last words of the narrator died away a disconcerted silence settled over the company. Few of my fellow pilots had known that memorable fireside circle at the Château of St Omer: the others were no longer living. It was not surprising we were silent.

The Kommandeur rose to his feet.

"*Kameraden!* The Abbeville boys come, do their duty and go. They follow the example of their fallen friends with all that they have in them. These friends have bequeathed to us their knightly spirit. May every one of us carry this spirit in him, and hand it on even when the enemy wins a victory. To the health of all true knights!"

Subdued strains of jazz could be heard from the next room, I thought to myself – in every age there'll always be knights.

Late that evening, with glasses of brandy in our hands, Ulrich and I received orders to take off at first light from a small airfield north of Abbeville. This field lay at the edge of the Forest of Crécy, and was one of those which the English had used during the First World War. From it we were to intercept two Spitfires which used to fly over from

Biggin Hill each morning at the same time and patrol along the coast. A reconnaisance at daylight from the English point of view was a small risk, comparable to that which defence against such early risers presented to us. But the Tommies didn't believe we ever sat ready in our aircraft at this hour, and we counted on this. For this reason both we and the English used to let a learner go out on these operations, a "guinea-pig" so to speak, this being the quickest way of giving him his baptism of fire.

And now I was the guinea-pig. It was striking six when I put my right leg out of bed. In an hour's time someone would be shooting at me and I would perhaps be training my guns for the first time on a human being.

I took things as they came, as millions had done before me, trying to banish all such thoughts from my mind. I looked at my "new" aircraft: perhaps I should soon be lying in the ground in company with it. But really it was so old one could almost attribute to it a consciousness and experience of its own; some people even maintained it could fly without a pilot and shoot down an enemy aircraft of its own accord. I put on my dressing-gown.

That moment there came the order: "*Tommies close off the mouth of the Somme. Take off at once!*"

The Englishmen would certainly not have spent last night drinking brandy! I ran to my machine. Ulrich, too, with puffy eyes and in pyjamas was hurrying to his aircraft. As the engine revved up someone threw a life-jacket round me and someone else fastened my parachute harness and belt.

Full throttle! As I left the ground and swept low over the tree tops of the Forest of Crécy beside Ulrich, I put on my helmet and goggles with my left hand, adjusted the R/T pads around my neck, retracted the under-carriage, raised the flaps, set the trimmer and made the innumerable small manual adjustments which were required.

We were already over the sea, with a visibility of barely a thousand metres. Then, through the grey, damp morning mist, the two Spitfires were all at once rushing towards us.

To wrench the stick round, sight, turn, aim and fire was a matter of seconds in which body and brain acted with automatic precision – a mechanical reaction for which I had prepared myself for two years, against a target which I now hit quite without conscious volition or regard to the consequences. The enemy crumpled under my fire. Victory! A transport of happiness and pride possessed me, from which it took me a moment to recover. Finally I turned my aircraft and looked round with anxious eyes for Ulrich. Far astern, guns were sparkling in the clear sky over the mainland: the adversaries pursuing one another in a series of steep, tight turns. Before I could help, a small white mushroom unfolded, and slowly sank towards the earth. Ulrich's aircraft spun into a wood, and the Tommy flew on his way.

I circled low over my friend, whose pyjamas were flapping in the breeze. Ulrich waved to me, seemingly unhurt. He had scarcely landed in a small meadow when from all directions gallant infantrymen with rifles at the ready came hurrying to take him prisoner. They had obviously mistaken him for the defeated enemy and me for the victorious German. For the first time since the fight I actually began to laugh – Ulrich, the "captured Tommy" was standing down there in his pyjamas with his hands above his head!

I had too much to attend to in my machine to watch this spectacle for long, but I saw them taking Ulrich away, and I had already flown a good part of the journey home when I looked round again. To my horror I saw another aircraft on my quarter, apparently almost within touching distance. Just as well it wasn't a Tommy. The unknown pilot put his hand to his helmet, and I returned his salute. The other was smiling all over his face.

"Good morning, old man," came through my earphones. I looked again, more closely.

"Werner, hallo Werner!"

I had to look ahead again, but now I understood. Werner had baled out yesterday near St Omer and was now flying a new machine back to Abbeville. I looked across at him again – he was staring before him and spoke without turning his head.

"Are you landing at Abbeville?"

"Can't very well. Look at this!" I lifted the skirt of my dressing-gown to the window of the cockpit. It was a little while before Werner understood.

"Good show," he laughed. I didn't know whether he meant my dressing-gown, Ulrich's pyjamas or this strange reunion. And when, a few minutes later, I dropped away over Crécy and we waved to each other again it was as though a few days only had passed, instead of five long years, since we had last seen one another.

That welcome night brought to an end what had been a difficult day. I lay awake and thought of the daylight hours just passed. They had been commonplace for many, decisive for some. Today, as for many years past, death and mourning, victory and ecstasy had been arbitrarily apportioned among us. Friend and foe alike had been under the same illusion as they said their prayers, of supplication or gratitude, hurriedly, humbly or proudly, each one wishing only to love the good and to hate evil. And we too belonged to that company.

From time to time we openly recognised the meaninglessness of this existence. More often we simply sensed it. But, at moments like these, what could our disgust alone do against the links of this fateful chain made up of our own bodies and souls, dragging us all along? Good motives there were – here as well as "over there" – our own country, our own wives and children at home must be protected as stoutly as those on the other side. We young men were incapable of comprehending the meaning of it all. Fate plunged onwards down its ordained path, and however we might try to protect ourselves it struck us exactly as it pleased. I couldn't block its way; and you – you who had wanted to kill me early in the morning – you couldn't do so either. Tommy, if you still live, are you perhaps drinking at this moment in some bar in the West End? Or perhaps you're in some quiet corner, grieving over one of your own friends or squadron mates who died in the early morning; perhaps you're writing at this moment to his parents or his fiancée, who, still cheerful, have as yet no idea what has happened? Tommy, I know you would do that, just as I should.

How joyfully I grasped my comrades' hands! I jumped beaming from the cockpit, while a soul went up from the still warm body of a man I had killed. How proud I had still been in the time before the bell tolled for him whom I had shot.

The day passed in jollity, dancing and girls' laughter. I wanted to forget the morning, to wipe the vision of blood and shining roundels from before my eyes. Now the silent night lay over all. I was very tired, but I couldn't sleep. Agonising thoughts still passed through my head. Did every soldier experience this feeling when he had killed a man for the first time?

I listened to Ulrich's quiet breathing. Perhaps he would laugh if I asked him about it.

"You could have saved yourself the last burst!" he had said smilingly, not ironically or frivolously, and certainly not sadly. I could see it still, the Tommy in his Spitfire hovering in the air close in front of me. I have no idea whether I have hit him. But I fire – for whole seconds in my excitement. Then we go into turns, the tightest possible turns. It seems any moment I must go into a spin. The rough sea spray is scarcely a hundred metres below me, and we are far out from the shore. I am still lying not quite right astern of the enemy, and the correct deflection for hitting him has not yet been reached. Nerves are stretched to the uttermost. My quarry hauls his machine all of a sudden right round in front of me, so that heavy vapour-trails appear in the sky. I react instantaneously and take a chance between crashing the aircraft and getting the final ounce out of it. Heaving the stick towards me with both hands, for the fraction of a second I achieved the correct firing-angle. My index-finger shifts by a milli-metre on the triggers of my guns, and the burst flashes into the enemy's fuselage.

He plunges almost vertically, but regains control just above the surface with desperate strength, and climbs steeply – mortally hit. I see him struggling to get out – he wants to jump, He's like a hunted quarry during any such chase and I feel with him – pray feverishly for him.

There she goes! The damaged aircraft's climbing ver-tically in front of me in its last convulsion, the great roundels on the wings standing out bright and hostile – filling me only with horror. In the seconds which decide a man's life my finger again crooks automatically one milli-metre – and the burst streaks redly out! – I shudder. It shouldn't have happened, it wasn't necessary. But I can't bring those deadly jewels back; it's done now.

"Jump! man, jump!" I shouted aloud in despair. In-stead I see him bathed in the red of his own blood; his body strains half over the side to hang there, mutilated. Then the waves close over him. . . .

Perhaps it was only the trembling of my finger that brought death to that man? I didn't know. But again it came to me – how fate goes its own way and strikes us down as it pleases. I couldn't stop it, and nor could you – whoever you may have been.

I turned over on my pillow and reached for the reading-lamp and the cigarettes. For a long while I gazed medita-tively at the pictures of my parents. Perhaps tomorrow they would be weeping for me.

"Still awake?" Ulrich asked softly, although he knew well I wasn't sleeping. He too was staring at the ceiling. "What are you thinking about?"

"What am I thinking about. . . ." I repeated, rather at a loss. It was a difficult question; as a soldier I had had to forget how to talk from the heart. But it was easier to talk lying there gazing upwards – you can speak so much more easily and naturally to the ceiling.

"What am I thinking about, Ulrich? The Tommy of

this morning," I confessed. "It simply wasn't necessary. Why didn't the man jump before he did?"

"You must forget it," Ulrich replied. "One gets used to anything, including shooting people down . . . but even so, war's a pretty bloody business." We were silent. "But, you know," he began again after a pause, "it's a great deal bloodier for someone like me who does it all without any real conviction."

Nothing more was said. I don't know how long we lay there with our eyes open, and the light was still burning when the dawn woke us.

THE STRAITS OF MESSINA

JOHANNES STEINHOFF

*A veteran of the Battles of Britain and Stalingrad,
Steinhoff assumed command of* Jagdgeschwader 77
*(77th Fighter Group) in 1943, shortly before its with-
drawal from Tunisia in the face of Allied victory there.
The evacuation was carried out in dramatic fashion, with
Group pilots carrying mechanics in the fuselage of their
Messerschmitt 109s over the sea to Sicily. The* Jagd-
geschawder 77 *found little peace in Sicily, however, for
on 10 July 1943 the Allied invasion of Sicily began. Here
is an extract from Steinhoff's diary of 12 July, 77's last
day on the island. It was a turning point of the war for
Steinhoff, the moment at which he understood that the
Luftwaffe had "been assigned a task which was incapable
of execution". It was also the selfsame day that Goering
issued his infamous order to the fighter pilots of the
Second Air Force demanding "an immediate improvement in fighting spirit". This blithely ignored the real
reason for Luftwaffe fighter arm's lack of success – which
is that German aircraft were generally unable to match
the speed and armament of Allied planes.*

The remorseless jangling of the telephone dragged me
from my sleep. The noise was unpleasantly loud and in a
daze I felt for the receiver in the darkness.

"Teleprint from Air Corps, sir. We made contact at midnight but we've lost it again now. Shall I read it out?"

"Wait a moment. I'll have to turn the light on."

I looked for the switch in the dark, but when at last I found it, I turned it in vain. There was no current. Eventually I managed to find some matches with which to light the candle stump on the plate beside my camp-bed. My movements were slow, for I was unspeakably tired. As I lay down again in my sweat-soaked pyjamas and picked up the receiver my limbs felt heavy as lead.

"Will you read it out, please."

In expressionless tones the teleprinter operator, a lead-ing aircraftsman, began to read: " 'To the Second Air Force. Together with the fighter pilots in France, Norway and Russia, I can only regard you with contempt. I want an immediate improvement in fighting spirit. If this im-provement is not forthcoming, flying personnel from the commander down must expect to be remanded to the ranks and transferred to the eastern front to serve on the ground. Göring, Reichsmarschall' . . . Are you still there, sir?"

"Yes, thank you. Will you bring it over to the ops room."

As I replaced the receiver, the airman gave the three short rings prescribed by regulations. Then the room was deathly still. The candle's flickering flame cast grotesque, dancing shadows on the walls. All at once I could hear my own breathing. I held my breath and remained quite motionless. Everywhere in this small house people were wrapped in soothing sleep, wholly unaware of this fresh insult. As yet the air-craftsman on the teleprinter and I were the only people here to know of the strictures passed by the most senior officer in the Luftwaffe. I tried to imagine what the man on the other end of the line looked like, for I must have seen him often enough. Perhaps he had been a schoolmaster in civilian life; he might even be old enough to be my father. All at once I was conscious of a strange bond between this invisible airman and myself.

But the mood passed quickly, thrust aside by the realization of the sheer brutality of the unbelievable message I had just heard. What ought I to do about the signal? Ought I to read it out in front of a muster parade? But if I were to appear before them and talk about "fighting spirit" they would look at me in mute reproach. Their expressions would tell me that my duty as a C.O. was to spare them such phrases.

So this was what had come of our general's efforts to save us from court martial. Fighting spirit indeed! In an hour's time another day would begin and with it yet another feat of improvisation such as had been demanded of us every single day since our return to Sicily. With what we could scrape together of the remnants of the group, we would fly along the north coast and over Etna's crater towards the Straits of Messina where we would fling ourselves at the Flying Fortresses in a series of unco-ordinated attacks. Our numbers were so few that we would do little damage, and even that little depended upon our breaking through to the bombers.

Afterwards we would land in Gerbini if the airfield was still usable, or else at Catania. We would refuel our aircraft by hand-pump, rearm and top up with oil. We would leap into slit trenches and shelters and wait for the bomb carpets to unroll over us. And then we would crawl out again, haul the wrecked aircraft to one side, repair any minor damage and, provided we still had enough machines to make up a modest formation, take off on the next patrol. This was what all these men had had to go on doing day after day. And now I was expected to talk to them about fighting spirit!

I doubted whether we would be able to hold out in Trapani for the remainder of the day. The bombers appeared without warning since they came in too low to be picked up by our direction finders. Flying in close formation, they had been showering down bombs on the airfield until it resembled a lunar landscape. The advanced landing ground near Corleone would therefore have to be our last refuge. Up to now, however, it had been nothing more than a long field covered with yellow wheat stubbled and marked out with whitewashed stone slabs.

We would be like hunted animals seeking cover. And without either telephone or supplies we would be cutting ourselves off from the outside world. Nor was there another airfield left in western Sicily.

I must have fallen asleep, for again the telephone jerked me out of a brief spell of blissful unconsciousness. "Four o'clock, sir."

The first light of day was filtering through the Venetian blinds as I got up to open the shutters. I still felt utterly exhausted; indeed, I seemed to be in a permanent state of fatigue. I had but one desire and that was to sleep.

In the next room Tubby was opening the shutters, putting the chairs in place and rattling the breakfast crockery. It had become a little cooler. In the wan light before dawn, the sickle-shaped bay, the terraces, gardens and white houses were lightly shrouded in mist through which black pines thrust upwards and smoke from chimneys rose perpendicularly into the sky.

Bachmann and Straden, who were sitting at the table when I entered the day room, answered my "good morning" in low, morose voices. None of us felt any desire to converse. What we really wanted to do, as we drank Tubby's strong hot coffee, was to cradle our heads in our arms on the table and sleep.

Kegel came in, sat down and pushed the teleprint over to me without speaking. The white strips of printed text had been pasted neatly on to the pale pink paper of the official form. The first words to spring to the eye, appearing as they did well below the main portion of the long signal, were "Göring, Reichsmarschall".

". . . regard you with contempt . . ." I had no wish to read to the end. It was not my habit to shirk what was unpleasant but this repelled me. It seemed to be directed at myself alone; I was the man responsible for this group and I, personally, was the object of his contempt.

I handed the signal across the table. Straden took it and he and Bachmann began to read. Then, slowly and carefully, he put the paper down on the table, rose, took his cap from its hook and left the room without a word. Bachmann looked after him uncertainly, then at me and Kegel, eased his chair back and followed Straden. On his way out he said quietly: "I'm driving to the ops room, sir."

The telephone rang. "It's the general, sir."

The general's voice came from a long way away and was overlaid with crackles and hisses. So as to hear him better I held my breath and motioned to Kegel and Tubby to keep quiet.

"We're near Taormina," the general said. "We're surrounded – d'you understand me? Comiso is no longer usable."

"Yes, sir."

"I wanted to call you last night before that signal went out but I couldn't get through to you . . ."

"Yes, sir."

"Listen, you're not to take it seriously. I did what I could. I've been urging him to abandon the whole business, but then he sent this signal to Air Corps."

He did not continue and I remained silent. Finally he asked: "Can you still hear me?"

"Yes, sir."

"Collect all the aircraft in western Sicily and go to Gerbini. The airfield is usable. By now your 3 Wing will be on its way from Sardinia and they will also land at Gerbini. Your job is to protect the Straits of Messina. Can you tell me how many aircraft will be arriving?"

"Between fifteen and twenty belonging to 2 Wing and Group H.Q. No. 1 hasn't reported yet."

"Have you any questions?"

I had indeed, lots of them, but in terms of German military tradition most were not of the kind a major can ask a general.

"Yes, sir. What's the situation? How far have the Allies got?"

"The pressure on our ground troops has increased enormously and we shall be concentrating our defence in the eastern portion of the island. It's possible that you'll have to move soon. The enemy is pressing on towards the centre of the island."

"But where is the group to move to, sir?"

"I don't know yet," was his somewhat irritable reply. "For the time being no German soldier may leave Sicily. But you should get all your vehicles ready for a move. There'll be no transport aircraft – Air Corps haven't a Ju left. And once again: don't take that teleprint too seriously. D'you promise me that?"

What could I say over a telephone line that might go dead at any time? We had already discussed this question once before for several hours and had found no solution, so it was quite pointless to say anything further now. I therefore replied:

"Yes, sir."

I felt almost ashamed of my attitude when speaking to the general. It seemed to me that I had been an accessory to an act of treachery of which our pilots were the victims. At the same time I realized how diabolical was the dilemma in which the general found himself. I had thrown in the sponge, simply answering "Yes, sir". In this answer lay that trust in one's superior – a whole attitude towards life – which had been instilled into us, into our fathers and into their fathers before them. For us soldiers it had hitherto been the only right attitude, indeed the only conceivable one. The obedience practised for centuries by the German soldier had always presupposed an unshakeable trust that the orders he received would be sensible orders and that the high command would search their hearts very carefully before sacrificing whole formations. And the many who were sacrificed died in the certainty that this was so. Increasingly of late I had found this reflected in the mute expressions of my pilots though for some time there had been a distinct note of interrogation. It still holds good, doesn't it, sir? they seemed to be asking me. It surely must have some sense if the high command demands it of us, surely it must!

But supposing that something had gone wrong with part of this old military equation? Who were the "high command" anyway? Supposing that after 1933 a new factor had entered this hierarchy of obedience, a factor which had suddenly allowed the high command to do what it liked, even something senseless?

Questions, questions! A man would need leisure to reflect on them. He would have to have caught up with his sleep. He would need time, would need someone else to discuss them with. In our business such matters were not discussed. Yet it might have been better if they had been, for in that way our doubts could perhaps have been dispelled.

For the past few minutes I had been standing beside the telephone table with the receiver in my hand. Kegel and Tubby were looking at me thunderstruck. From the earpiece came a quacking voice: "Are you still speaking? Have you finished? I'm disconnecting you."

These were no thoughts for the C.O. of a group at the start of a day's operations. I grabbed my belt and pistol from the back of the chair where they usually hung and buckled the belt round my waist. For a soldier there is something extremely salutary in this gesture: he is taking a grip on himself, discarding all unnecessary thoughts, focusing his mind on immediate things, on essentials.

How I detested those flights to Gerbini! Whenever I stood on that barren expanse under the blazing sun, a landscape pockmarked with bomb craters and covered with wrecked aircraft, the scene always brought home to me the hopelessness of our battle for the island.

"Tubby, let the ops room know that I'm on my way to fetch Captain Straden and Mr. Bachmann. We're flying to Gerbini."

Kegel got into the Kübelwagen with me and we drove between gardens along a narrow, deserted lane which debouched into the main road through a constricted alleyway. Spread out below us in the morning mist, the western tip of the island with the airfield and the white houses of Trapani presented a magnificent spectacle. It was the brief hour before sunrise when a semblance of freshness could be felt coming off the sea, before the scorching heat descended on the countryside from the eternally clear southern sky. Over on the horizon, above Marsala, a row of dark blue smudges floated above the mist – flak bursts. The idyll was deceptive and the war went on. It was five o'clock in the morning and the day was going to go on for ever.

As we drove up to the operations room I gave Kegel the necessary instructions regarding the preparations for the move.

"All ground personnel," I told him, "other than those needed for the final servicing of the aircraft, should be dispatched to Messina. Check our loading lists and make arrangements to destroy the equipment we can't take with us."

When we arrived, Kegel and I jumped out of the Kübelwagen and climbed the few steps into the hut. Straden was already walking towards me.

"The general wants to speak to you," he said.

He was continuing to avoid my eyes. I had the impression that the Reichsmarschall's insults were still sticking in his throat. But it was a case of swallow or choke.

While I perched on the folding chair and waited to be connected, my eyes travelled over the plain.

The direction finders near Marsala had reported the approach of heavy bombers. There would, however, be no point in sending up our few available aircraft against them since our intention was to leave for Gerbini in a few minutes' time. The attack might be directed against our airfield, but equally the target could be Palermo harbour. The Allies' intention was to cut off our supplies so as to lighten their task on the island. To achieve that end they would have to attack the Straits of Messina as well as Palermo harbour. Probably they would attack both at once

– they certainly possessed sufficient equipment to do so.

The firing of warning shots by the flak was followed by the immediate cessation of all activity on the airfield below. In front of the hut a number of airmen were gesticulating and pointing towards Chinisia. And then I, too, saw a long stream of bombers approaching from the west. Suddenly the white strip of runway, which usually gleamed in the sun, was veiled in an enormous cloud of dust. The bomb carpet must have been very wide for the whole length of the airfield was obscured. Only then did we hear the rumble of explosions. As I shouted into the handset, vainly trying to get my connection, the first black clouds of petrol smoke from burning aircraft began to rise up out of the gloom.

The sight of Chinisia's blasted airfield reminded me of my visit to the Italian fighter wing stationed there, and at the same time I realized that I had almost completely forgotten about the existence of the Italian fighter arm. During the gruesome finale on this island it was a case of every man for himself. The heavy attacks had begun before we had had time to establish signals communications with each other or to co-ordinate our tactics – steps we would have taken as a matter of course had conditions been anything like normal. This meant that each air force had begun fighting its own war. And, in circumstances where relations between the Italian and German high commands were far from good, not only were the arrangements for controlling the units of the two nations entirely separate but the orders they received were also different, so that any co-ordination in the operation field was out of the question. Indeed, that had been the main defect of the joint command ever since the start of the Mediterranean campaign: the two controlling organizations had been so much concerned with prestige that each had taken all possible steps to prevent its own units being placed under the other's command. Thus, although the battle was a common one, the assignments and orders were invariably different.

A bomb carpet is a terrible weapon when used against an airfield and is extremely demoralizing for the airfield personnel, even though they may have a measure of protection while squatting in bunkers or slit trenches. Particularly effective were the smaller bombs which the enemy released by the thousand. The made only shallow craters and the fragments, projected outwards at high velocity and close to the ground, shredded the outer skins of our aircraft as though they were made of paper.

How would the Italian fighter wing be feeling now, unaccustomed as they were to such attacks and knowing that their superiors had moved them to Sicily only with reluctance? A few day previously I had gone to make my number with the commander of the Italian group. On landing I had noted the surprisingly good condition of the airfield. Having taxied up the long runway, I was directed to a pen surrounded by a protective rampart of white tuff. Macchi fighters, still in the desert camouflage of the North African campaign, occupied the neighbouring pens.

In front of the flying-control building I was approached by an officer who introduced himself as Major Visconti, the commander of the fighter unit. He said that his C.O. had his operations room and his quarters on Mount Erice, if I should wish to visit him there.

The man walking beside me had a virile and extremely likeable face. His small white cap with its short peak was pulled down well over his forehead almost as far as his bushy, prominent eyebrows. Beneath the aquiline nose was a black, curling moustache. There was no hint of timidity as he looked at me with his expressive, surprisingly blue eyes. His name was familiar, for I had heard much about him. He had been known to the veterans of my group since the days in North Africa and they spoke of him as a gallant and outstanding fighter pilot.

He began talking about their wretched communications, his main command channel being a field telephone which, however, seldom enabled him to communicate with his C.O. Moreover, he had no contact with the German direction finders near Marsala and when he saw the German fighters take off to attack, having been alerted in good time, he could only look on enviously, for he had learnt that without guidance from the ground any success was a matter of chance. Nobody, he told me, warned him of the approach of the enemy and in the air he received no orders whatsoever.

I could sympathize with his position. If we ourselves felt misunderstood by our high command, what must he feel? Wondering how I could help him, I felt something like pride when I compared his own hopeless situation with ours. At least we had the technical means to wage a successful battle – indeed we still had them! And it was a poor sort of C.O. who sat back, high up on a mountainside, watching part of his group lying idle on a first-rate airfield until such time as it should be knocked out by an accurate massed bombing attack! As I shook Visconti's hand and turned towards my aircraft, I resolved to call on his C.O. as soon as our daily operations allowed.

The present attack on Chinisia airfield reminded me of the resolution and the prediction I had made then. I was surprised that the Allies had not attacked this admirable airfield before. Had they, perhaps, ceased to take the Italians seriously? Had they ever taken them seriously?

It was a line of thought I did not wish to pursue, for it somehow seemed uncomradely towards Visconti with whom I felt a bond. At all events I intended to seek out his peculiar C.O. up on Mount Erice.

Then the preparations for take-off, the take-off itself and the task of leading my small formation into the air claimed the whole of my attention. Again and again the demands of the moment prevented us from reflecting and this was just as well. For one way or the other, anyone who gave himself over to brooding was lost: either he would be killed through lack of concentration and resolution at the crucial moment of the battle or else, faltering even before he had made contact with the enemy, he would turn back, not once but again and again, until finally he would have to be posted away, his days as a fighter pilot at an end.

We circuited Gerbini airfield, searching for the landing strip which had been marked out for us with small, barely identifiable flags. At last, having formed a picture of the layout, I decided to land. In the fields much of the yellow stubble had been burnt. The plain, a notably fertile one, was patterned hideously with bomb craters and the black scars of fires. Descending towards them I felt an almost overpowering reluctance to land. As the machine came to a standstill opposite the hut, the propeller continued to give a few fitful jerks accompanied by loud bangs. It was much too hot for the engines when one had to taxi at walking pace. I had had some trouble in finding my dispersal pen and the mechanics had guided me half-way round the airfield before I arrived at the hut and the place reserved for me. In the chaos of bomb craters and skeletons of aircraft among the burnt olive trees it was difficult to keep one's bearings, much more so than it had seemed when coming in to land.

Straden, Bachmann and Zahn had parked their 109s close by. Even at this hour of the morning they were already exhausted and they dragged their feet as they walked towards the hut. Outside it was a bench made of a few stone slabs and a balk of timber, and on this they sat down without further ado.

I walked past them in silence and went into the hut where I began trying to make contact with the Fighter Leader, Air Corps or indeed any other higher formation. Eventually Sergeant Korn came in – how on earth had he got here? – and announced that no purpose would be served by contacting any of the head-quarters since orders had already arrived for us to "refuel, take off and fly cover over the Straits of Messina".

Armed with this cut-and-dried information I joined the men on the bench who, with legs outstretched, were dozing in the scanty shade. Resting my head against the hot wall, I, too closed my eyes. From all sides came the familiar noises of an advanced landing ground: the click of the fuel hand-pumps, the shouts of the mechanics, the rising howl of an engine being run up on test, I heard it all and as I listened I consciously registered the passing of every minute.

In this place we were utterly exposed. It had only to occur to the enemy to come here; he need only pass this way by chance, and it would be the end of us. Nervously we awaited the completion of refuelling, well aware that we would be lucky if we managed to get into the air unscathed.

When the dull rumbling crumps of a distant bombing raid assailed our ears we leapt instantly into the slit trenches. As though at the touch of a spectral hand all signs of life disappeared from the surface of the field. The flak to the south began firing heavily and then fell silent again. This time the attack was being directed against another part of the huge plain, not against us. It was only when the distant drone of aircraft engines had diminished in volume to the level which persisted, almost without intermission, throughout each day, that we emerged suspiciously and very cautiously from our trenches. An Me 109 was taxiing across the airfield in a cloud of dust and someone in the group operations room reported that Colonel Larsen had just landed.

He threaded his way between the bomb craters and parked his machine close to the hut. As Larsen was climbing out, my chief mechanic, Schwarz, told me that my engine needed a change of plugs. This meant that the aircraft would be out of action for an hour.

"Straden, get through to No. 1 and tell them that Godert is to lead the group. Will you take over H.Q. Flight, please."

"Right, sir."

While I was still greeting Larsen engines began springing to life round the edge of the airfield and the remnants of the group started to move. A few minutes later they were in the air, their task the protection of the Straits of

Messina. Larsen removed his life-jacket and handed it to
the mechanic who was to refuel his machine. As we walked
slowly towards the hut I caught myself scanning our
surroundings, instinctively registering the location of
the nearest slit trench. I steered him towards a spot where
some empty ammunition boxes had been piled up to form
a kind of seat beside a deep trench. Probably some of the
airmen had had a game of skat here the previous evening.

"I'm sorry about that signal. You may be certain that we
did everything we could to stop it."

Reluctantly I looked my old friend straight in the eye.
His present appointment being what it was, even he was
probably not wholly immune to the prevailing doubletalk.

"Franzl," I said, "I'm utterly sick of hearing that.
You're all apologizing to us – you yourself, the general,
Air Corps – now I'm only waiting for the field marshal!
Perhaps you'll start complimenting us again if you find
that it makes us fight better and go more cheerfully to our
doom. First you send us that shameful signal and a bit
later you're slapping us jovially on the back saying: 'Don't
take it so seriously, ha ha ha,' or else 'Chins up! It'll soon
be forgotten.' At the same time you know as well as I do
that every teleprinted section, every H.Q. between us and
the Reichsmarschall has taken note of our disgrace without your being able to explain to them the whole thing is
not to be taken too seriously. I can't help it, Franzl, but the
whole performance strikes me as utterly vile. It's just
slaughtering our reputation as soldiers."

He returned my gaze and answered calmly: "Of course
you're right – the thing's impossible and we're all in the
same boat. I agree that as an example of leadership it
couldn't be worse. But what are we to do? The Luftwaffe
is in an atrocious situation. The Reichsmarschall has been
under fire ever since the Fortresses began penetrating east
of Berlin. The Führer blames him for the failure of the air
arm and he gets out of it by saying over and over again,
'It's not me, it's the fighter pilots!' I've found out for
myself that it's no longer possible to converse rationally

with the Reichsmarschall in the way officers ought to converse. Believe me, I often have grave doubts . . ."

He broke off without divulging the nature of those doubts. I had them, too, but these were things that could not be said by people in our situation. For to do so would have precipitated a conflict of conscience unendurable to a fighting soldier. So we both remained silent for a while, each of us perfectly aware of what the other was thinking. At last I said:

"I haven't announced the contents of the signal although all the pilots know about it, of course. I've pigeon-holed it."

"No one's going to ask about that . . ."

"How much longer d'you give us in Sicily?"

Larsen lit a cigarette, expelling the smoke with a hiss.

"The spearhead of the British Eighth Army is now about twenty-five miles south of here," he said. "The American Seventh has advanced from Gela presumably with the intention of linking up with the British here on the plain of Catania. What that signifies for you in western Sicily and for the defence of the island as a whole is pretty obvious."

"You mean evacuation – an orderly withdrawal if possible?"

"What else?" replied Larsen. His voice was expressionless but his look spoke volumes as he continued: "And who has greater experience of that than you?"

"What do you think this withdrawal is going to be like? In Tunisia the order arrived much too late. But in our service, paradoxically enough, it's not called an order but permission, as though the high command kept nursing a secret hope that there might be some intrepid individuals who would prefer to fight to the last gasp in a series of Thermopylaes rather than take advantage of their magnanimous offer. But here there's nothing left to salvage. This time I've made up my mind to get every single man over to the mainland, even if it means burning or blowing up most of the equipment. We're slowly reaching a stage when everyone is going to be needed. In any case, the really skilled, responsible ground crews will become fewer and fewer if these bomb carpets continue to drop on us."

"You may be right there," he said thoughtfully. "Aircraft and other equipment can be replaced; experienced mechanics can't. If you can get your people across the Straits of Messina safe and sound, we'll be able to re-equip the group. Did you know that we are now turning out a thousand fighters a month and can possibly go even higher? Admittedly our losses are also very heavy. We're losing hundreds at the training stage alone."

At that moment two fighters flew unsteadily across the airfield, and then the group, their operation concluded, came in to land, the pilots following each other down in rapid succession. Immediately all was again dust and din and apparent chaos.

"Captain Straden has baled out quite close by," called Sergeant Korn through the window of the hut; he had to shout as loud as he could to make himself heard above the noise. "We need a Storch!"

He settled down to some brief but concentrated telephoning and shortly after was able to announce: "No. 2 are sending their Storch, sir. They know where he baled out."

Bachmann then reported and told me about the battle. Apparently they had climbed on a westerly course so as to be up-sun when they pounced on the Fortresses. But they had still been climbing over grid square "Martha" when they had seen Boeings beneath them heading north. Instantly Godert had commenced the attack, which had proceeded almost in text-book fashion. At the same moment, however, a squadron of Spitfires had dived on them and split them up. Keeping close formation, Straden and H.Q. Flight had pressed on and, under intense fire, had managed to get within range of the rear section of bombers. Suddenly his machine had started climbing away and he reported that he had been hit and wounded. He had then turned round and gone into a steep glide in the direction of Gerbini. Almost immediately, however, he had jettisoned his hood, half-rolled and baled out. Bachmann had seen his parachute open.

The Storch, with Straden on board, landed a few yards from the hut. Carefully the stretcher was lowered out of the aircraft and the M.O. attached to No. 1 Wing of the 53rd Fighter at once began slitting the wounded man's blood-drenched trouser leg as far as the hip.

"Another one come to grief," I said to Larsen as we walked up and down close by. "No. 1 say they have lost three. The group keeps on losing more and more pilots. It's going to be the finish here, Franzl."

He seemed to be working out a picture in his mind of the operation on which we were engaged. As the Inspector, South, he had, of course, little influence on tactical decisions in this theatre, but his words nevertheless carried some weight in the councils of the men round the General of Fighters. Maybe this first-hand impression would facilitate the decision to break off the unequal struggle on the island.

I had seen dead and dying men. In four years of war, four years of almost uninterrupted operations, an eternity, I had seen them crash and bleed and burn: some mere boys; fledgelings who had been instantly struck down by what is called fate; others, older men, veterans whose experience exceeded that of all the rest yet whose hour had suddenly struck. Admittedly Straden was "only" wounded but I was not going to see him for a long time, perhaps never again, and so the scene of the pilots standing round the Storch while the doctor attended to Straden became indelibly branded on my mind.

This was now one of the last bases on the island. The sun shone pitilessly down on the yellow plain about which groups of men like ourselves were hectically engaged in putting the few available aircraft into the air against the enemy, a process that inevitably resulted in fewer aircraft still. While the mechanics, with speed born of practice, refuelled the aircraft and rattled ammunition belts over the engine cowlings, the pilots, wilting and expressionless, stood or squatted beneath the dusty olive trees. Barely a word was exchanged. Every man knew that he and his companions were at the end of their tether.

There was nothing now to recall the dashing, stylish fighter pilot with his yellow scarf and his imaginatively modified uniform. Our outward appearance accurately reflected the pass to which we had come: crumpled, filthy, oil-stained trousers, ancient, greasy life-jackets, emaciated and in many cases unshaven faces. Everything was a dusty brown – earth, clothes, faces, aeroplanes. There are the hardships of victory, hardships which in Russia and North Africa we cheerfully shrugged off and which, on occasion, we had not even noticed, so elated had we been by our sense of superiority. And there are the hardships of defeat, the hardships of dirt and dishonour which feed on morale, impair the fighting spirit and only serve to engender fresh defeats. This, we had been taught, was the hour of the born military commander, the hour when he would jerk his men out of their state of depression, give them a purpose, inspire them with new élan and lead them boldly to death or glory against the foe. But to all of us here, engaged in the routine task of fighting in the heat and dirt, that concept was a highly dubious one. It was a relic of the First World War, if not the days of cavalry charges, and was utterly useless in the situation in which we now found ourselves. The war in the air is a technological war which cannot be won by a technologically inferior fighting force, however high its morale or dauntless its resolution. This was a point our field marshals had failed to grasp and it was also the reason why the Reichsmarschall could think only in terms of bravery and cowardice and why, to his mind, a fighter arm which had lost its superiority could be nothing other than cowardly.

Larsen's voice suddenly intruded on my thoughts. "We've got to move you over to the mainland while there's still a nucleus round which to rebuild the group. In North Africa it was left until much too late. Obviously a group is more than just a conglomeration of aeroplanes and equipment plus a given number of men."

"Who d'you think you're telling that to?" I answered bitterly. "Tell it to the general, although he should be perfectly well aware of it. He was still a group commander himself only two years ago."

"You mustn't be unfair to him. I'm positive he's perfectly aware of all these things. After all he belongs to the same generation as we do and his experience in action has been exactly the same as ours. But what can he do . . . ?"

I shrugged my shoulders and turned towards the wounded man again. Perhaps Larsen was right. There was no solution and we had to carry on. We had invested our military leaders and the commands that issued from them with a kind of sanctity and, while we had still been winning, we had thought that splendid. Now, in time of defeat, we had no alternative but to await their orders and carry them out, even if those orders should be wrong and even if we knew them to be wrong.

After climbing out of his aircraft Bachmann had sat down under an olive tree. His eyes never strayed from the back of the doctor who was still kneeling down attending to his patient. As he gazed fixedly at the scene, he kept restlessly stroking his chin with his sunburnt hand. His attitude, it seemed to me, was that of an old man and I found myself observing his person in minute detail: the worn-down tropical shoes with their leather toe caps and canvas uppers, the greasy, shiny dye pouch attached by its snap hook to the life-jacket, the battered, shabby gloves whose only purpose was to prevent one's hands, which were invariably damp with sweat, from slipping off the stick and the other controls.

Then the doctor rose to his feet. The wounded man's leg was now heavily bandaged and he lay with his eyes closed. He had been conscious throughout but had not uttered a word. Probably he was suffering from the effects of shock.

"His right calf has been chewed up by an explosive

bullet," the doctor said. He spoke quietly so as not to be overheard by the patient. "It's impossible to say immediately whether or not the leg can be saved. We'll have to get him to hospital at once." He paused for a moment before continuing: "On the mainland if possible. I've given him morphia and anti-tetanus injections."

"We'll have to wait until dusk before we risk a Storch," I said, "but if we alert Vibo Valentia airfield, they can arrange to send him on without delay."

"Telephone, sir!" Sergeant Korn called from the hut.

It was Temme, the commander of the Focke-Wulf fighter-bombers. His people had been holding out here for days, flying mission after mission – to negligible effect, since they could administer no more than pinpricks.

"An order has just come in from Air Corps," he said. "It reads: 'Proceed to alternative landing grounds near Trapani forthwith together with H.Q. and Nos. 1 and 2 Wings 77th Fighter Group. No. 3/77th will return to Sardinia.'"

"Thank you. I'll get moving as soon as my aircraft have been refuelled and rearmed. That's to say in a few minutes. I think the airfield near Salemi is the better of the two and I suggest you make for that one."

"Fine," replied the fighter-bomber commander evenly. "But first I'll have a go at the shipping off Gela so as to give the whole thing some point."

The airfield near Salemi was the one with the farmhouse that had so annoyed the Kittyhawks. Without doubt the enemy had taken it to be a strong point, but he could, for that matter, seek us out anywhere. The airstrip near Corleone was little more than a last resort, to be used if we had to evacuate Trapani yet continue to remain in the western portion of the island.

"We'll be taking off for the advanced landing ground near Salemi," I shouted to Korn. "I'd like to know soon how many aircraft are ready."

Some of us would leave now and the aircraft still being serviced would have to follow on later. This meant that we would be flying in groups too small to constitute viable fighting formations. On our way to the west we intended to carry out ground attacks against the beach-heads. I had not seen Abben, who led my No. 3 Wing, since our arrival in Gerbini. He had reported the wing's presence by telephone and had spoken of engagements over Etna and now he was getting ready to return to Sardinia. His preparations were going ahead with the same speed as ours, for we all wished to depart as quickly as we could from our exposed position before the enemy unloaded his next bomb carpet on us.

Larsen came up to say good-bye. "I'm going to Catania," he said. "I'll be telling the general how things stand with you. If only the Führer would give us permission to evacuate the island."

The Führer, I thought absently. Yes, of course, the Führer! But at that moment the enemy seemed more important. Would the enemy, I wondered, permit us to evacuate the island?

This time, as my aircraft left the ground to carry me back to Trapani, the sense of relief that had grown stronger with every departure from Gerbini was totally absent. It might well be the last time, for the end was very near. Even if the bombing were suddenly to cease, it would be weeks before we could mount an effective attack since we lacked everything necessary to the conduct of a fighter unit's operations – skilled personnel, spares, ammunition, even petrol – and obviously we could only take off from those advanced landing grounds to which the little that was available had been transported at the cost of tremendous effort. What we had witnessed in this theatre was, to use the words Temme had quoted, "the destruction of one air arm by another in order to ensure the unhampered action of the latter's airpower and the safe deployment of its ground forces". Without doubt the operation on which I was now embarking would show the Americans that we were not completely finished – it would cost the enemy a few lives and bring destruction to some of his equipment – but by comparison with the tons of bombs he had dropped on Sicily it would be of little significance.

There were only nine Messerschmitts behind me. The remainder would take off from Gerbini as soon as they had been serviced and would rejoin us on the advanced landing ground. We were not in any sense a large formation; indeed the few aeroplanes at our disposal would be useless against the enemy bombers and their bristling array of weapons. We might, perhaps, be able to shoot down a few fighters in a dogfight but both in quantity and in quality those aircraft were our superiors.

The sky to the west had turned a steely grey and thunderclouds had started to build up over the island's central massif. With the map spread out on my knee I applied myself to skirting the wall of cloud without losing my bearings. Near Enna, which could be readily identified by the extensive remains of the Hohenstaufen *Castello*, I turned south in order to reach the Bay of Gela. Visibility was poor and the cloud so low that I throttled back as I flew down the long valley. I knew that the Americans were moving up through this valley in their northward thrust and that if I wished to reach the coast I should have to reckon with their attentions. At first I kept well away from the road, flying close to the slopes which disappeared into the mist overhead. All at once I was surrounded by strings of tracer. They looked like fireworks as they climbed towards me, inaudible above the sound of my engine. It was a pretty display but at any moment it could prove lethal. This so bewildered me that I applied full boost and raced down the valley in a series of violent evasive man-oeuvres.

A sudden torrent of rain struck the windscreen like a blow and for a few seconds I could see nothing whatever. Then the curtain of cloud parted abruptly to reveal Gela's white beach where, not long before, I had met the Italian sentry patrol. I turned to starboard so as to avoid the beach and the inevitable anti-aircraft fire from the destroyers and landing craft. I was now a few hundred feet above the road that runs parallel to the coast, flying through a continuous hail of tracer with the others behind me well closed up as though threaded on a string. By introducing an element of surprise we could use our fire-power to maximum effect before the troops on the ground managed to jump for cover or the gunners take aim.

Lorries and tanks were lined up along the road as though on parade, and as I dived, with the "pop-pop-pop" of my cannon drowning the noise of the engine, my mouth was dry and the old bitter taste was back on my tongue. I had only a few seconds firing time left and my speed built up rapidly as I pressed home the attack. The illuminated cross-wires stood out against the dark ground, and the silhouettes of vehicles flowed rapidly across them. With violent kicks on the rudder bar, I tried to line up the illuminated ring and its cross-wires with the road and the transport. A large tank loomed up rapidly in my sights and my cannon shells smacked on to its armour-plate, rico-cheting in all directions. Soldiers leapt for the verges and melted into the ground before my eyes.

Then the "g" force was pressing me hard against my parachute as I went into a climbing right-hand turn and continued my headlong progress along the coast road. Leaning my head right back I looked over the armour-plate and through the sloping Plexiglass window down on the road which was flowing away behind me as though in a greatly speeded-up film. There were burning vehicles, cannon shells bursting on the road and jeeps bumping over the ground in a wild dash for the open country. It was an absorbing sight which gave one a deceptive sense of superiority. I banked to the left and, still looking back, saw one of our aircraft going down low – far too low! – until it struck one of the vehicles in the convoy and immediately exploded in a welter of metal and a column of flame as high as a house.

This was what we termed a "fire on impact", which could be caused either by anti-aircraft fire or by inad-

vertent contact with the ground. Such a death, spectacular
and gruesome, was seen but fleetingly, with half an eye.
One heard the droning of one's engine and, in the headphones, the staccato sounds of battle. But, as in a silent
film, the tremendous explosion seemed to make no noise at
all. So it had been when Sergeant Meyer had cut a swathe
through a wood near Novgorod; when Second Lieutenant
Behrens had rolled along like a fireball in the middle of a
convoy of Russian army lorries; when Flight Sergeant
Stumpf had lost a wing while flattening out and crashed on
the steppe among the enemy tanks.

All at once there were no more streams of tracer rising
ahead of me. The pale ribbon of road below was deserted.
The front had been left behind. I wondered who the
unlucky one had been for I didn't know who had taken
off with me apart from Bachmann and Zahn. These two
were flying close by in battle formation but the others had
left Gerbini in the order that their aircraft had been
serviced and found airworthy.

Agrigento was on our left. I made a wide detour round
the town and harbour so as to avoid stirring up the anti-
aircraft guns and began to climb. The sun was shining on
my face and the wall of cloud to the east gleamed brilliantly white. My intention, provided that we did not
encounter the enemy in the meanwhile, was to fly in a
large semicircle so that I could observe Chinisia, Trapani
and the two advanced landing grounds from above.

"Odysseus One to Erice, how are you receiving me?"

"Receiving you beautifully Odysseus One. We've just
picked up a formation of Marauders with fighter escort
approaching Trapani. Report your position and height.
Over."

"Odysseus One to Erice understood. Position Castelve-
trano, 16,000. Over."

Once again those idiotic bombers were "approaching
Trapani' so as to deliver yet another load on to the same
expanse of rubble. But fundamentally the Allies were right
in doing so for we were still attacking them even though it

was with the last remnants of our effective strength. And by now they had no illusions about our toughness.

By my reckoning we should make contact in ten minutes. What sort of a bunch, I wondered, was I leading? I twisted round and tried to make out the numbers painted on the aircraft accompanying me. There were eight in all, my entire fighting force, and I had no idea who was piloting them, apart from Bachmann and Zahn, of course. These two were flying close beside me to right and left, their machines rock-steady in the calm air. I had somehow suspected that the enemy would be reported. A sense of foreboding had told me that this battle was inevitable and that, with no reserves of strength, I was nearing the end of my tether.

The Erice controller kept reporting the latest position of the bomber formation. If there had been more of us and if we had been a little fresher, this teamwork between air and ground could have been entirely pleasurable, but as things were now it was nothing more than the prelude to an unequal struggle.

"Erice to Odysseus One, Pantechnicons now immediately north of airfield, height 10,000. You'd better get a move on!"

"Message received."

By now we could see the dirty smudges of the flak bursts and, in front of them, the bombers flying in close formation. They were coming in over the mountain from the north and at any moment would be opening their bomb doors. My altimeter was showing 13,000 feet. "You'd better get a move one!" he had told me. That I was most assuredly doing, hastening towards another clash with our old acquaintances from North Africa. Where were the fighters? As yet I had seen none. The flak's shooting was brilliant. Their shells were bursting accurately among the Marauders, forcing them to make repeated changes of course.

One of the big aircraft dipped a wing and for a few seconds accompanied the formation in a side-slip – a wholly unnatural manoeuvre. Suddenly it touched another aeroplane in the section and immediately the two machines locked together and hurtled downwards in a tangle of metal. Surprisingly, two parachutes appeared above them, floating calmly in the air.

And then I saw the fighters immediately ahead of me on the same course. They were Thunderbolts with big radial engines, ambling along well above the flak bursts.

Almost subconsciously I moved the lever into position above the button on the control column, thus setting my weapons at "fire". Provided I was certain that I was going to shoot I invariably did this well beforehad. And once again the bitter taste was in my mouth.

As soon as I engaged them with my cannon the fighters broke formation. I had taken them by surprise. The section leader half-rolled and broke away in a spectacular dive. However, I hadn't hit him yet; the black smoke emerging from his exhaust stubs simply meant that he was on full boost. As the ground came racing towards me I managed to keep in position, firing at short intervals. Where my section could be I didn't know; doubtless they were locked in battle elsewhere. We were very low now, hopping over trees and houses as we neared the coast, and then suddenly we were over the sea, only a few feet above the surface of the water. I was racing in the direction of Pantelleria with little reserve of fuel, but once again the fever of the chase had me in its grip. I was faster than he was and I continued to close.

If he had turned his head he would have looked straight along my engine cowling. I had expended all my cannon ammunition. But I didn't intend to fire my machine guns just yet, because it was very easy to miscalculate when engaging fighters. The American could in his turn force me into a dogfight. I hadn't enough fuel for that but he was not to know it. Hence he was seeking safety in escape, putting his trust in his powerful engine.

"All of a sudden, acting instinctively, and independent of any conscious decision, I pulled the throttle back and began a wide turn towards the land. I returned the firing lever to the "safe" position, screwed the knob behind the sights to the left to extinguish the illuminated cross-wires, and opened the radiator flaps. A few minutes later I saw the airfield. My mind had been so empty that I had gained height and navigated almost automatically. I had to make two circuits before I identified the narrow landing strip between the bomb craters and committed myself to a landing. Just as I was touching down, the engine began to misfire violently and then suddenly cut. I had got back on my last drops of petrol. The airfield looked dead and deserted as though it had already been abandoned by the group. All at once I knew that the end had come – irrevocably.

Jagdgeschwader 77 *was withdrawn to Italy on 13 July, thereafter playing a part in the defence of Italy, France, Rumania, the Reich and Berlin. Steinhoff survived both the war and imprisonment by the Russians.*

BAA BAA BLACK SHEEP

"PAPPY" BOYINGTON

Gregory "Pappy" Boyington had a long war, beginning with Claire Chennault's Flying Tigers (see pp 335–357) in China and finishing as a prisoner of the Japanese. In between, Boyington shot down six aircraft in China, then 22 for the US Marine Corps. Almost as famous for his insubordinate plain-speaking and drunken boisterousness as for his flying, Boyington gathered around him pilots of similar hue, hence the "Black-sheep" tag accorded to his VMF-214 Squadron. After the war, he sunk into alcoholism for a decade until rescued by Alcoholics Anonymous. In this extract from his memoir Baa Baa Black Sheep, *Boyington describes his last mission for VMF-214, undertaken on 3 January 1944.*

During one of these daily hops over Rabaul I had reached a definite climax in my flying career without too much effort. I shot down my twenty-fifth plane on December 27. And if I thought that I ever had any troubles previously, they were a drop in the bucket to what followed.

There was nothing at all spectacular in this single victory, but it so happened that this left me just one short of the record jointly held by Eddie Rickenbacker of World War I and Joe Foss of World War II. Then everybody, it seemed to me, clamored for me to break the two-way tie. The reason for all the anxiety was caused by my having only ten more days to accomplish it; 214 was very near completion of its third tour, and everyone knew I would never have another chance. My combat-pilot days would close in ten days, win, lose, or draw.

Everyone was lending a hand, it seemed, but I sort of figured there was too much help. Anyway, I showed my appreciation by putting everything I had left into my final efforts. I started flying afternoons as well as mornings, and in bad weather in addition to good weather.

One pre-dawn take-off was in absolute zero-zero conditions, and all we had for references were two large searchlights on the end of the Vella strip, one aimed vertically and the other horizontally. I wasn't questioned by the tower whether I had an instrument ticket, like I am today. My last words to my pilots before I started my take-off through the fog were: "Please listen to me, fellows, and have complete faith in your instruments. If you dare to take one look out of the cockpit after you pass the searchlights, you're dead."

As I had always been unaccustomed to help or encouragement in the past, all the extra help did nothing more than upset me. But I couldn't have slowed down or stopped if I had wanted to, simply because nobody would let me.

One fight made me desperate when I could not see to shoot with accuracy, because I wasn't able to see well enough through the oil-smeared windshield. After several fruitless attempts I pulled off to one side of the fight and tried to do something to correct it. I unbuckled my safety belt and climbed from my parachute harness, then opened the hood and stood up against the slipstream, trying my darnedest to wipe off the oil with my handkerchief. It was no use; the oil leak made it impossible for me to aim with any better accuracy than someone who had left his glasses at home.

Soon I began to believe that I was jinxed. Twice I

returned with bullet holes in my plane as my only reward. Twice I ran into a souped-up version of the Zero known as the Tojo. Though not quite as maneuverable as the original, it was considerably faster and had a greater rate of climb. Still no shoot-downs, and I was lucky the Nips didn't get me instead.

Doc Ream was really concerned over the way I was affected by the pressure, suggesting we call a halt to the whole affair. He said that there were plenty of medical reasons for calling all bets off. But I knew I couldn't stop. Whether I died in the attempt made no difference. Anyway, my last combat tour would be up in a few days, and I would be shipped back to the United States. I said: "Thanks for the out, Doc, but I guess I better go for broke, as the Hawaiians say."

Never had I felt as tired and dejected as I did when I flew into Vella one afternoon in late December. Another futile attempt was behind me. The bullet holes in my plane were a far cry from the record I was striving to bring back. I was dead tired, I had counted upon the day ending, but a pilot had crawled up on my wing after I had cut my engine, and he had something important to say.

Marion Carl was scheduled to take several flights that afternoon to Bougainville, where they were to remain overnight, taking off on the following morning for a sweep. He said: "Greg, I want to give you a chance to break the record. You take my flight because you're so close I think you are entitled to it. I've got seventeen, but I still have loads of time left, and you haven't."

Carl had been out previously in the Guadalcanal days as a captain, piling up a number of planes to his credit, and was then back for the second time, as a squadron commander. He had just been promoted to major, and it was true that many chances were coming up for him. Great person that Marion Carl is, he was trying to give a tired old pilot a last crack at the title, even though it was at his own expense.

I can never forget George Ashmun's thin, pale face when I mentioned where I was going, and he insisted that he go along as my wingman. Maybe George knew that I was going to have to take little particles of tobacco from a cigarette, placing them into the corners of my eyes to make them smart so that I'd stay awake.

Those close to me were conscious of what kind of shape I was in, and they were honestly concerned. But I was also happy to find others I hadn't thought of at the time who were concerned for my welfare as well, though in most cases I didn't discover this until after the war. And that was by mail.

Some of the letters were clever, but I especially remember one from a chap who I imagine must have been about eighteen. He wrote me that, after I was missing in action, his partner, "Grease Neck", who worked on a plane with him, had said that I was gone for good, and the first chap said: "I bet you he isn't." The outcome of the discussion was that each bet a hundred and fifty dollars, one that I would, the other that I would not, be back home six months after the war was over. The six-months business referred to the fact that if you are missing six months after the war is over you are officially declared dead. And at one time I had said, just as a morale builder to the other pilots so that they would not worry about me: "Don't worry if I'm ever missing, because I'll see you in Dago and we'll throw a party six months after the war is over."

I had said it by coincidence just before taking off on what turned out to be my last fight, but the words apparently had stuck in their minds.

But to get back to this letter from the young chap, he told me how thrilled he was about my being home, and he told me about this bet he had made with "Grease Neck", and how he had just collected that hundred and fifty, and that he was going to spend the entire amount on highballs in my honor in San Diego.

It was a great feeling to get those letters and know that the boys really wanted to see you home – bets or no bets. I also hope, because I never heard any more from this young fellow, that he didn't end up in the local bastille while celebrating in my honor.

My thoughts then are much the same now in many respects. Championships in anything must be a weird institution. So often there is but a hairline difference between the champion and the runner-up. This must go for boxing and tennis, football and baseball. In my case it was something else, the record for the number of planes shot down by a United States flyer, and I was still having quite a time trying to break it.

After getting twenty-five planes, most of them on missions two hundred miles or better into enemy air, I had gone out day after day, had had many a nice opportunity, but always fate seemed to step in and cheat me: the times there was oil on the windshield and I couldn't see any of the planes I fired into go down or flame; the times my plane was shot up. Nothing seemed to work for me. Then everybody, including the pressmen, kept crowding me and asking: "Go ahead; when are you going to beat the record?" I was practically nuts.

Then came the day when the record finally was broken, but, as so often happens with one in life, it was broken without much of a gallery. And in this case without even a return.

It was before dawn on January 3, 1944, on Bougainville. I was having baked beans for breakfast at the edge of the airstrip the Seabees had built, after the Marines had taken a small chunk of land on the beach. As I ate the beans, I glanced over at row after row of white crosses, too far away and too dark to read the names. But I didn't have to. I knew that each cross marked the final resting place of some Marine who had gone as far as he was able in this mortal world of ours.

Before taking off everything seemed to be wrong that morning. My plane wasn't ready and I had to switch to another. At the last minute the ground crew got my original plane in order and I scampered back into that.

I was to lead a fighter sweep over Rabaul, meaning two hundred miles over enemy waters and territory again.

We coasted over at about twenty thousand feet to Rabaul. A few hazy clouds and cloud banks were hanging around – not much different from a lot of other days.

The fellow flying my wing was Captain George Ashmun, New York City. He had told me before the mission: "You go ahead and shoot all you want, Gramps. All I'll do is keep them off your tail."

This boy was another who wanted me to beat that record, and was offering to stick his neck way out in the bargain.

I spotted a few planes coming up through the loosely scattered clouds and signaled to the pilots in back of me: "Go down and get to work."

George and I dove first. I poured a long burst into the first enemy plane that approached, and a fraction of a second later saw the Nip pilot catapult out and the plane itself break out into fire.

George screamed over the radio: "Gramps, you got a flamer!"

Then he and I went down lower into the fight after the rest of the enemy planes. We figured that the whole pack of our planes was going to follow us down, but the clouds must have obscured us from their view. Anyway, George and I were not paying too much attention, just figuring that the rest of the boys would be with us in a few seconds, as usually was the case.

Finding approximately ten enemy planes, George and I commenced firing. What we saw coming from above we thought were our own planes – but they were not. We were being jumped by about twenty planes.

George and I scissored in the conventional Thatch-weave way, protecting each other's blank spots, the rear ends of our fighters. In doing this I saw George shoot a burst into a plane and it turned away from us, plunging downward, all on fire. A second later I did the same to another plane. But it was then that I saw George's plane start to throw smoke, and down he went in a half glide. I sensed something was horribly wrong with him. I screamed at him: "For God's sake, George, dive!"

Our planes could dive away from practically anything the Nips had out there at the time, except perhaps a Tony. But apparently George never heard me or could do nothing about it if he had. He just kept going down in a half glide.

Time and time again I screamed at him: "For God's sake, George, dive straight down!" But he didn't even flutter an aileron in answer to me.

I climbed in behind the Nip planes that were plugging at him on the way down to the water. There were so many of them I wasn't even bothering to use my electric gun sight consciously, but continued to seesaw back and forth on my rudder pedals, trying to spray them all in general, trying to get them off George to give him a chance to bail out or dive – or do something at least.

But the same thing that was happening to him was now happening to me. I could feel the impact of the enemy fire against my armor plate, behind my back, like hail on a tin roof. I could see enemy shots progressing along my wing tips, making patterns.

George's plane burst into flames and a moment later crashed into the water. At that point there was nothing left for me to do. I had done everything I could. I decided to get the hell away from the Nips. I threw everything in the cockpit all the way forward – this means full speed ahead – and nosed my plane over to pick up extra speed until I was forced by the water to level off. I had gone practically a half mile at a speed of about four hundred knots, when all of a sudden my main gas tank went up in flames in front of my very eyes. The sensation was much the same as opening the door of a furnace and sticking one's head into the thing.

Though I was about a hundred feet off the water, I didn't have a chance of trying to gain altitude. I was fully aware that if I tried to gain altitude for a bail-out I would be fried in a few more seconds.

At first, being kind of stunned, I thought: "Well, you finally got it, didn't you, wise guy?" and then I thought: "Oh, no you didn't!" There was only one thing left to do. I reached for the rip cord with my right hand and released the safety belt with my left, putting both feet on the stick and kicking it all the way forward with all my strength. My body was given centrifugal force when I kicked the stick in this manner. My body for an instant weighed well over a ton, I imagine. If I had had a third hand I could have opened the canopy. But all I could do was to give myself this propulsion. It either jettisoned me right up through the canopy or tore the canopy off. I don't know which.

There was a jerk that snapped my head and I knew my chute had caught – what a relief. Then I felt an awful slam on my side – no time to pendulum – just boom–boom and I was in the water.

The cool water around my face sort of took the stunned sensation away from my head. Looking up, I could see a flight of four Japanese Zeros. They had started a game of tag with me in the water. And by playing tag, I mean they began taking turns strafing me.

I started diving, making soundings in the old St George Channel. At first I could dive about six feet, but this lessened to four, and gradually I lost so much of my strength that, when the Zeros made their strafing runs at me, I could just barely duck my head under the water. I think they ran out of ammunition, for after a while they left me. Or my efforts in the water became so feeble that may be they figured they had killed me.

The best thing to do, I thought, was to tread water until nightfall. I had a little package with a rubber raft in it. But I didn't want to take a chance on opening it for fear they might go back to Rabaul, rearm, and return to strafe the raft. Then I would have been a goner for certain.

I was having such a difficult time treading water, getting weaker and weaker, that I realized something else would have to be done real quickly. My Mae West wouldn't work at all, so I shed all my clothes while I was treading away; shoes, fatigues, and everything else. But after two hours of this I knew that I couldn't keep it up any longer. It would have to be the life raft or nothing. And if the life raft didn't work – if it too should prove all shot full of holes – then I decided: "It's au revoir. That's all there is to it."

I pulled the cord on the raft, the cord that released the bottle of compressed air, and the little raft popped right up and filled. I was able to climb aboard, and after getting aboard I started looking around, sort of taking inventory.

I looked at my Mae West. If the Nips came back and strafed me again, I wanted to be darned sure that it would be in working order. If I had that, I could dive around under the water while they were strafing me, and would not need the raft. I had noticed some tears in the jacket, which I fully intended to get busy and patch up, but the patching equipment that came with the raft contained patches for about twenty-five holes.

"It would be better first, though," I decided, "to count the holes in this darned jacket." I counted, and there were more than two hundred.

"I'm going to save these patches for something better than this." With that I tossed the jacket overboard to the fish. It was of no use to me.

Then for the first time – and this may seem strange – I noticed that I was wounded, not just a little bit, but a whole lot. I hadn't noticed it while in the water, but here in the raft I certainly noticed it now. Pieces of my scalp, with hair on the pieces, were hanging down in front of my face.

My left ear was almost torn off. My arms and shoulders contained holes and shrapnel. I looked at my legs. My left ankle was shattered from a twenty-millimeter-cannon shot. The calf of my left leg had, I surmised, a 7.7 bullet through it. In my groin I had been shot completely through the leg by twenty-millimeter shrapnel. Inside of my leg was a gash bigger than my fist.

"I'll get out my first-aid equipment from my jungle pack. I'd better start patching this stuff up."

I kept talking to myself like that. I had lots of time. The Pacific would wait.

Even to my watch, which was smashed, I talked also. The impact had crushed it at a quarter to eight on the early morning raid. But I said to it: "I'll have a nice long day to fix you up."

I didn't, though. Instead, I spent about two hours trying to bandage myself. It was difficult getting out these bandages, for the waves that day in the old South Pacific were about seven feet or so long. They are hard enough to ride on a comparatively calm day, and the day wasn't calm.

After I had bandaged myself as well as I could, I started looking around to see if I could tell where I was or where I was drifting. I found that my raft contained only one paddle instead of the customary two. So this one little paddle, which fitted over the hand much like an odd sort of glove, was not of much use to me.

Talking to myself, I said: "This is like being up shit creek without a paddle."

Far off to the south, as I drifted, I could see the distant shore of New Britain. Far to the north were the shores of New Ireland. Maybe in time I could have made one or the other of these islands. I don't know. But there is something odd about drifting that I may as well record. All of us have read, or have been told, the thoughts that have gone through other men under similar circumstances. But in my case it was a little tune that Moon Mullin had originated. And now it kept going through my mind, bothering me, and I couldn't forget it. It was always there, running on and on:

> On a rowboat at Rabaul,
> On a rowboat at Rabaul . . .

The waves continued singing it to me as they slapped my rubber boat. It could have been much the same, perhaps, as when riding on a train, and the rails and the wheels clicking away, pounding out some tune, over and over, and never stopping.

The waves against this little rubber boat, against the bottom of it, against the sides of it, continued pounding out:

> . . . On a rowboat at Rabaul,
> You're not behind a plow . . .

And I thought: "Oh, Moon Mullin, if only I had you here, I'd wring your doggone neck for ever composing the damn song."

Boyington was "rescued" by a Japanese submarine and spent the remainder of the war in a POW camp.

HEAVY BABIES

HEINZ KNOKE

Heinz Knoke flew over 400 operational missions for the Luftwaffe during World War II, shooting down 52 Allied aircraft before being invalided in October 1944 in a road attack by Czechoslovak partisans. Below is Knoke's diary for two of those missions, 25th February 1944 and 29th April 1944, undertaken whilst serving with No. 11 Fighter Wing in its defence of the Reich against the Flying Fortress ("heavy babies") bombers of USAAF.

25th February, 1944

The Americans and British conduct their large-scale air operations in a way which leaves us no respite. They have rained hundreds of thousands of tons of high explosive and phosphorus incendiary bombs upon our cities and industrial centres. Night after night the wail of the sirens heralds more raids. How much longer can it all continue?

Once again Division Control reports those blasted concentrations in sector Dora-Dora. It is the daily waiting for the action call, the permanent state of tension in which we live, which keeps our nerves on edge. Every mission is now followed by some more pictures going up on the wall.

Concentrations in sector Dora-Dora! This report has

now come to have a different significance for us: it is a reminder that, for the moment, we are still alive. The faces of the comrades have become grave and haggard.

Concentrations in sector Dora-Dora! Today it will be the same story again. In silence we prepare for take-off. One by one we again retire into the can. That is also part of the same routine. No laxatives are needed to assist the sinking feeling Dora-Dora creates.

Take-off at 1600 hours.

The Squadron circles the airfield until it is assembled in formation.

"Climb to 25,000 feet on course due north," calls base. "Heavy babies approaching over the sea."

At 15,000 feet over Lüneberg Heath we are joined by the Flights from our Third Squadron. It is cold. I turn on the oxygen.

20,000 feet: we maintain radio silence. Base periodically gives the latest enemy position reports, "Heavy babies now in sector Siegfried-Paula."

22,000 feet: we fly strung out in open formation. The monotonous hum of the code-sign in our earphones: Di-da-di-da-di-da-di-da . . . short-long-short-long-short-long. . . .

25,000 feet: our exhausts leave long vapour-trails behind.

30,000 feet: my supercharger runs smoothly. Revs, boost, oil and radiator temperatures, instrument check shows everything as it should be. Compass registers course three-six-zero.

"On your left . . . watch for heavy babies to your left."

There is still no sign of them. Nerves are tense. I am suddenly very wide awake. Carefully I scan the skies. Vast layers of cloud cover the distant earth below as far as the eye can see. We are now at an altitude of 33,000 feet: it should be just right for bagging a few enemy bombers or fighters.

Vapour-trails ahead. There they are!

"I see them," Specht reports with a crackle of his ringing voice.

"Victor, victor," base acknowledges.

The bomber-alley lies about 6,000 feet below us – 600 to 800 of the heavy bombers are heading eastwards. Alongside and above them range the escorting fighters.

And now I am utterly absorbed in the excitement of the chase. Specht dips his left wing-tip, and we peel off for the attack. Messerschmitt after Messerschmitt follows him down.

"After them!" The radio is a babel of sound, with everybody shouting at once.

I check my guns and adjust the sights as we dive down upon the target. Then I grasp the stick with both hands, groping for the triggers with my right thumb and forefinger. I glance behind. Thunderbolts are coming down after us.

We are faster, and before they can intercept us we reach the Fortresses. Our fighters come sweeping through the bomber formation in a frontal attack. I press the triggers, and my aircraft shudders under the recoil.

"After them!"

My cannon-shells punch holes in the wing of a Fortress. Blast! I was aiming for the control cabin.

I climb away steeply behind the formation, followed by my Flight. Then the Thunderbolts are upon us. It is a wild dog-fight. Several times I try to manœuvre into position for firing at one of their planes. Every time I am forced to break away, because there are two–four–five – or even ten Thunderbolts on my tail.

Everybody is milling around like mad, friend and foe alike. But the Yanks outnumber us by four or five to one. Then some Lightnings come to join in the *mêlée*. I get one of them in my sights. Fire!

Tracers come whizzing in a stream close past my head. I duck instinctively.

Woomf! Woomf! Good shooting!

I am forced to pull up out of it in a steep corkscrew climb, falling back on my old stand-by in such emergencies. For the moment I have a breathing space. I check the instruments and controls. All seems well. Wenneckers draws alongside and points down at four Lightnings on our left.

"After them!"

Our left wing-tips dip, and we peel off. We hurtle down towards the Lightnings as they glisten in the sun. I open fire. Too fast: I overshoot the Lightning. I wonder what to do about my excessive speed.

But now a Lightning is on my tail. In a flash, I slam the stick hard over into the left corner. The wing drops. I go down in a tight spiral dive. The engine screams. I throttle back. My aircraft shudders under the terrific strain. Rivets spring from the wing-frame. My ears pop. Slowly and very cautiously I begin to straighten out. I am thrust forward and down into the seat. My vision blacks out. I feel my chin forced down on to my chest.

A Lightning passes me, going down in flames. There is a Messerschmitt on its tail.

"Got it!"

It is Wenneckers.

A few moments later he is alongside me again. I wave to him with both hands.

"Congratulations!"

"The bastard was after your hide," he replies.

It is the second time Wenneckers has shot a Yank from off my tail.

After we land I go up to Wenneckers to shake hands, congratulate him on his success, and— But Wenneckers interrupts before I am able to thank him: –

"No need for you to thank me, sir. I only wanted your wife not to be made a widow by that bastard. Besides, think what a nuisance to the Flight it would have been to have had to dispose of your remains!"

All the mechanics standing around greet this remark with roars of laughter. I dig the lanky lad in the ribs. We go together into the crew-room. Meanwhile the others have also been coming in to land. This is one day we all come back.

29th April, 1944

"Concentrations of enemy aircraft in Dora-Dora!" Here we go again! The reorganised Squadron is ready for action.

Three Bomber Divisions are launching an offensive from the Great Yarmouth area. Our formations in Holland report strong fighter escorts. My orders are to engage the escorting fighters in combat with my Squadron, draw them off and keep them occupied. Other Squadrons of Focke-Wulfs are thus to be enabled to deal with the bombers effectively without interference.

1000 hours: "Stand by, the entire Squadron!"

I have a direct ground-line from my aircraft to the control room at Division. Enemy situation reports are relayed to me all the time. They pass over Amsterdam . . . the south tip of Ijssel Bay . . . north of Deventer . . . crossing the Reich border . . . west of Rheine.

At 1100 hours the spearhead of the formation is over Rheine.

1104 hours: "Entire Squadron to take off; entire Squadron to take off!" The order booms forth from the loudspeakers across the field. Signal rockets and Vérey lights are sent up from the Flight dispersal points. Engines roar. We are off! The Flights rise from the field and circle to the left, closing in to make up a single compact Squadron formation.

I turn on the radio and contact base. "Heavy babies in sector Gustav-Quelle. Go to Hanni-eight-zero."

"Victor, victor," I acknowledge.

I continue climbing in a wide circle to the left up to the required operational altitude . . . 20,000 . . . 22,000 . . . 25,000 feet.

North and south of us other Squadrons are also climbing. They are mostly Focke-Wulfs.

"Heavy babies now in Gustav Siegfried; Hanni-eight-zero."

"Victor, victor."

I have now reached 30,000 feet. The new superchargers are marvellous.

1130 hours: off to the west and below I spot the first vapour-trails. They are Lightnings. In a few minutes they are directly below, followed by the heavy bombers. These are strung out in an immense chain as far as the eye can reach. Thunderbolts and Mustangs wheel and spiral overhead and alongside.

Then our Focke-Wulfs sweep right into them. At once I peel off and dive into the Lightnings below. They spot us and swing round towards us to meet the attack. A pack of Thunderbolts, about thirty in all, also come wheeling in towards us from the south. This is exactly what I wanted.

The way is now clear for the Focke-Wulfs. The first of the Fortresses are already in flames. Major Moritz goes in to attack with his Squadron of in-fighters (*Rammjaeger*).

Then we are in a madly milling dog-fight. Our job is done; it is a case of every man for himself. I remain on the tail of a Lightning for several minutes. It flies like the devil himself, turning, diving, and climbing almost like a rocket. I am never able to fire more than a few pot-shots.

Then a flight of Mustangs dives past. Tracers whistle close by my head. I pull back the stick with both hands, and the plane climbs steeply out of the way. My wingman, Sergeant Drühe, remains close to my tail.

Once again I have a chance to fire at a Lightning. My salvoes register at last. Smoke billows out of the right engine. I have to break away, however. Glancing back, I see that I have *eight* Thunderbolts sitting on my tail. The enemy tracers again come whistling past my head.

Evidently my opponents are old hands at the game. I turn and dive and climb and roll and loop and spin. I use the methanol emergency booster, and try to get away in my favourite "corkscrew climb". In only a few seconds the bastards are right back on my tail. They keep on firing all the time. I do not know how they just miss me, but they do.

My wingman sticks to me like glue, either behind or

alongside. I call him to "Stay right there!" whatever happens. "Victor, victor," he calmly replies.

In what I think could be a lucky break, I get a Yank in my sights. I open fire with all guns. The crate goes up in a steep climb. Then all his comrades are back again on my tail.

In spite of the freezing cold, sweat pours down my face. This kind of dog-fight is hell. One moment I am thrust down into the seat in a tight turn; the next I am upside down, hanging in the safety-harness with my head practically touching the canopy roof and the guts coming up into my mouth.

Every second seems like a lifetime.

The Focke-Wulfs have meanwhile done a good job. I have seen nearly thirty of the Fortresses go down in flames. But there are still several hundred more of the heavy bombers winging their way eastwards undaunted. Berlin is in for another hot day.

My fuel indicator needle registers zero. The red light starts to flicker its warning. Ten more minutes only, and my tank will be empty. I go down in a tight spiral dive. The Thunderbolts break away.

Just above the clouds; at an altitude of 3,000 feet, I slowly level off. I estimate that I am probably somewhere in the vicinity of Brunswick or Hildesheim.

I look at my watch. Perhaps in another forty-five minutes I shall be over the "bomber-alley" again. Perhaps then I shall be able to get a fat bomber in front of my guns. . . .

Overhead, the sky is still streaked with vapour-trails, stamped with the imprint of that infernal dog-fight. Suddenly the wingman beside me flicks his aircraft round and vanishes into the cloudbank.

So what the hell . . . ?

In a flash I glance round, and then instinctively duck my head. There is a Thunderbolt sitting right on my tail, followed by seven more. All eight open fire. Their salvoes slam into my plane. My right wing bursts into flames.

I spiral off to the left into the clouds. A shadow looms ahead: it is a Thunderbolt. I open fire. Its tail is soon in flames.

Now I can see the ground. I jettison the canopy and am ready to bale out. There is another rat-tat-tat sound of machine-guns close to my ear and more hammer-blows hit my flaming crate. That Thunderbolt is there again, not 100 feet behind me.

Blast! I shall be chewed to mincemeat in his airscrew if I try to bale out now. I huddle down and crouch low in my seat, trying to make myself as small as possible. The armour plate at my back protects me from the otherwise fatal shots. Wings and fuselage are riddled. A large hole gapes beside my right leg. The flames are licking closer now: I can feel the heat.

Crash! The instrument panel flies into splinters in front of my eyes. Something strikes me on the head. Then my engine stops: not a drop of fuel left.

Blast! There is no chance for me now.

My forward speed, of course, rapidly decreases. This causes my opponent to overshoot and pass me. For a few seconds only he is in my sights; but it is a chance to take him with me. I press both triggers. I feel myself trembling all over from the nervous tension. If I can only take him with me!

My salvo scores a perfect bull's-eye in the centre of his fuselage. He pulls up his smoking plane in a steep climb. In a moment he is in flames. The canopy opens and the body of the pilot emerges.

The ground comes up with a rush. Too late for me to bale out now. I cross some large fields. Down goes the nose and the plane settles. The flames come up reaching for my face. Earth flies into the air. There is a dull, heavy thud. The crate skids along in a cloud of dust, then digs its own grave in the soft earth. I throw up my arms to cover my face, and brace my legs against the rudder-bar. It is all over in a split second. Something crashes with stunning force on to my head.

So this must be the end! It is my last thought before losing consciousness. . . .

I have no recollection of getting clear of that burning wreck, but I suppose I must have done so. Coherent thought is beyond me: there is only that dreadful pain in my head. I remember bullets flying past my ears as the ammunition explodes. I stumble and fall, but somehow stagger to my feet again. My one idea is to get away before the final explosion. The bright flames consuming my aircraft contrast vividly against the dark smoke-pall rising into the sky behind it.

A second wreck is burning only a few hundred yards away. Dimly I realise that it must be my Yank. If only the pain would stop! My head! my head! – I hold it in both hands and sink to my knees. The world spins crazily in front of my eyes. I am overcome by recurrent nausea, until only the taste of green bile remains.

The other seven Thunderbolts keep diving at me. They are firing. It seems a long way to the edge of the field and comparative safety. I finally roll into the shallow ditch and pass out again. I am at the end of my tether. . . .

When next I recover consciousness, I become aware of a man standing motionless and staring down at me. He is as tall as a young tree – an American!

I try to sit up on the edge of the ditch. The big fellow sits down beside me. At first neither of us speak. It is all I can do to prop my elbows on my knees and hold my splitting head in my hands. Then the Yank offers me a cigarette. I thank him and refuse, at the same time offering him one of mine. He also refuses; so we both light up our own fags.

"Was that you flying the Messerschmitt?"

"Yes."

"You wounded?"

"Feels like it."

"The back of your head is bleeding."

I can feel the blood trickling down my neck.

The Yank continues: "Did you really shoot me down?"

"Yes."

"But I don't see how you could! Your kite was a mass of flames."

"Don't I know it!"

The tall American explains how he spotted me above the clouds and went down after me with his men. "It sure seemed like a bit of luck," he added.

I ask him in turn: "What was your idea in getting out in front of me when my engine died?"

"Too much forward speed. Besides, it never occurred to me that you would still be firing."

"That is where you made your mistake."

He laughs. "Guess I'm not the first you bagged, am I?"

"No; you are my twenty-sixth."

The American tells me that he has shot down seventeen Germans. In a few more days he was due to go home. He notices the ring on my finger, and asks if I am married.

"Yes; and I have two little children." I show him a picture of Lilo and Ingrid.

"Very nice," he remarks, nodding in appreciation, "very, very nice indeed."

I am glad he likes them.

He also is married. His wife over there will have to wait for him in vain now. Rather anxiously, the big fellow asks what is going to happen to him.

I explain that he will be sent to a special P.O.W. camp for American airmen. "Are you an officer?"

"Yes; a Captain."

"In that case, you will go to a camp for officers. You will be well treated. Our prisoners are just as well treated as yours."

We have a friendly chat for about half an hour. He seems like a decent fellow. There is no suggestion of hatred between us, nor any reason for it. We have too much in common. We are both pilots, and we have both just narrowly escaped death.

A squad of soldiers from a nearby searchlight battery arrives, and we are covered with raised rifles.

"Put away that damned artillery, you clods," I call over to them.

On the highway there is a truck waiting for us. Six Yanks from a Fortress are huddled in the back. They look rather gloomy. My Captain and I sit beside them. Although feeling like death myself, I try to cheer up the party with a few jokes.

On the road we collect more Yanks who were shot down. One of them is badly wounded in the leg. I see that our men lift him up carefully into the truck.

We are driven to the Brunswick airfield at Broitzum. There I say farewell to my fellow-sufferers, and we all shake hands.

"Good luck!"

"All the best!"

"*Auf Wiedersehen!*"

One hour later Barran flies over and collects me in an Aroda. The Squadron all returned without further casualties. I am the only one who was caught.

Later, in the operations-room, I collapse unconscious again. They first take me to my quarters, where I develop a raging fever. During the night I am admitted to hospital.

MISSION TO REGENSBURG

BEIRNE LAY

A view from the receiving end of Luftwaffe fighter attacks during World War II. Beirne Lay was a USAAF co-pilot flying B-17 bombers on raids over Germany.

When our group crossed the coast of Holland at our base altitude of 17,000 feet, I was well situated to watch the proceedings, being co-pilot in the lead ship of the last element of the high squadron. With all of its twenty-one B-17Fs tucked in tightly, our group was within handy supporting distance of another group, ahead of us at 18,000 feet. We were the last and lowest of the seven groups that were visible ahead on a south-east course, forming a long chain in the bright sunlight – too long, it seemed. Wide gaps separated the three combat wings.

As I sat there in the tail-end element of that many-miles-long procession, gauging the distance to the lead groups I had the lonesome foreboding that might come to the last man about to run a gantlet lined with spiked clubs. The premonition was well founded.

Near Woensdrecht, I saw the first flak blossom out in our vicinity, light and inaccurate. A few minutes later, two FW-190s appeared at one o'clock level and whizzed through the formation ahead of us in a frontal attack, nicking two B-17s in the wings and breaking away beneath us in half rolls. Smoke immediately trailed from the B-17s, but they held their stations. As the fighters passed us at a high rate of closure, the guns of our group went into action. The pungent smell of burnt powder filled our cockpit, and the B-17 trembled to the recoil of nose- and ball-turret guns. I saw pieces fly off the wing of one of the fighters before they passed from view.

Here was early action. The members of the crew sensed trouble. There was something desperate about the way those two fighters came in fast, right out of their climb without any preliminaries. For a few seconds the interphone was busy with admonitions: "Lead 'em more . . . short bursts . . . don't throw rounds away . . . there'll be more along in a minute."

Three minutes later, the gunners reported fighters climbing up from all around the clock, singly and in pairs, both FW-190s and ME-109Gs. This was only my fourth raid, but from what I could see on my side, it looked like too many fighters for sound health. A coordinated attack followed, with the head-on fighters coming in from slightly above, the nine and three o'clock attackers approaching from about level, and the rear attackers from slightly below. Every gun from every B-17 in our group and the one ahead was firing, crisscrossing our patch of sky with tracers to match the time-fuze cannon-shell puffs that squirted from the wings of the Jerry single-seaters. I would estimate that seventy-five percent of our fire was inaccurate, falling astern of the target – particularly the fire from hand-held guns. Nevertheless, both sides got hurt in this clash with two B-17s from our low squadron and one other falling out of formation on fire with crews bailing out, and several fighters heading for the deck in flames or with their pilots lingering behind under dirty yellow parachutes. Our group leader pulled us up nearer to the group ahead for mutual support.

I knew that we were already in a lively fight. What I didn't know was that the real fight, the *anschluss* of

Luftwaffe 20-mm cannon shells, hadn't really begun. A few minutes later, we absorbed the first wave of a hailstorm of individual fighter attacks that were to engulf us clear to the target. The ensuing action was so rapid and varied that I cannot give a chronological account of it. Instead, I will attempt a fragmentary report, salient details that even now give me a dry mouth and an unpleasant sensation in the stomach when I recall them. The sight was fantastic and surpassed fiction.

It was over Eupen that I looked out of my co-pilot's window after a short lull and saw two whole squadrons, twelve ME-109s and eleven FW-190s, climbing parallel to us. The first squadron had reached our level and was pulling ahead to turn into us and the second was not far behind. Several thousand feet below us were many more fighters, with their noses cocked at maximum climb. Over the interphone came reports of an equal number of enemy aircraft deploying on the other side. For the first time, I noticed an ME-110 sitting out of range on our right. He was to stay with us all the way to the target, apparently reporting our position to fresh squadrons waiting for us down the road. At the sight of all these fighters, I had the distinct feeling of being trapped – that the Hun was tipped off, or at least had guessed our destination and was waiting for us. No P-47s were visible. The life expectancy of our group suddenly seemed very short, since it had already appeared that the fighters were passing up preceding groups, with the exception of one, in order to take a cut at us.

Swinging their yellow noses around in a wide U-turn, the twelve-ship squadron of ME-109s came in from twelve to two o'clock in pairs and in fours and the main event was on.

A shining silver object sailed past over our right wing. I recognized it as a main exit door. Seconds later a dark object came hurtling through the formation, barely missing several props. It was a man, clasping his knees to his head, revolving like a diver in a triple somersault. I didn't see his chute open.

A B-17 turned gradually out of the formation to the right, maintaining altitude. In a split second, the B-17 completely disappeared in a brilliant explosion, from which the only remains were four small balls of fire, the fuel tanks, which were quickly consumed as they fell earthward.

Our airplane was endangered by hunks of debris. Emergency hatches, exit doors, prematurely opened parachutes, bodies, and assorted fragments of B-17s and Hun fighters breezed past us in the slipstream.

I watched two fighters explode not far below, disappearing in sheets of orange flame, B-17s dropping out in every stage of distress, from engines on fire to control surfaces shot away, friendly and enemy parachutes floating down and, on the green carpet far behind us, numerous funereal pyres of smoke from fallen fighters, marking our trail.

On we flew through the strewn wake of a desperate air battle, where disintegrating aircraft were commonplace and sixty chutes in the air at one time were hardly worth a second look.

I watched a B-17 turn slowly out to the right with its cockpit a mass of flames. The co-pilot crawled out of his window, held on with one hand, reached back for his chute, buckled it on, let go, and was whisked back into the horizontal stabilizer. I believe the impact killed him. His chute didn't open.

Ten minutes, twenty minutes, thirty minutes, and still no letup in the attacks. The fighters queued up like a breadline and let us have it. Each second of time had a cannon shell in it. The strain of being a clay duck in the wrong end of that aerial shooting gallery became almost intolerable as the minutes accumulated toward the first hour.

Our B-17 shook steadily with the fire of its .50s and the air inside was heavy with smoke. It was cold in the cockpit, but when I looked across at our pilot — and a good one — sweat was pouring off his forehead and over his oxygen mask. He turned the controls over to me for a while. It was a blessed relief to concentrate on holding station in formation instead of watching those everlasting fighters boring in. It was possible to forget the fighters. Then the top-turret gunner's twin muzzles would pound away a foot above my head, giving an imitation of cannon shells exploding in the cockpit, while I gave an even better imitation of a man jumping six inches out of his seat.

A B-17 ahead of us, with its right Tokyo tanks on fire, dropped back to about 200 feet above our right wing and stayed there while seven of the crew bailed out successfully. Four went out the bomb bay and executed delayed jumps, one bailed from the nose, opened his chute prematurely and nearly fouled the tail. Another went out the left-waist gun opening, delaying his chute opening for a safe interval. The tail gunner dropped out of his hatch, apparently pulling the ripcord before he was clear of the ship. His chute opened instantaneously, barely missing the tail, and jerked him so hard that both his shoes came off. He hung limply in the harness, whereas the others had immediately showed some signs of life after their chutes opened, shifting around in the harness. The B-17 then dropped back in a medium spiral, and I did not see the pilots leave. I saw it just before it passed from view, several thousand feet below us, with its right wing a solid sheet of yellow flame.

After we had been under constant attack for a solid hour, it appeared certain that our group was faced with annihilation. Seven had been shot down, the sky was still mottled with rising fighters and target time still thirty-five minutes away. I doubt if a man in the group visualized the possibility of our getting much farther without 100 percent loss. I know that I had long since mentally accepted the fact of death and that it was simply a question of the next second or the next minute. I learned first-hand that a man can resign himself to the certainty of death without becoming panicky. Our group firepower was reduced thirty-three percent, ammunition was running low. Our tail guns had to be replenished from another gun station. Gunners were becoming exhausted and nerve-tortured from the prolonged strain, and there was an awareness on everybody's part that something must have gone wrong. We had been the aiming point for what seemed like most of the Luftwaffe, and we fully expected to find the rest of it primed for us at the target.

Fighter tactics were running fairly true to form. Frontal attackers hit the low squadron and lead squadron, while rear attackers went for the high. The manner of their attacks showed that some pilots were old-timers, some amateurs, and that all knew pretty definitely where we were going and were inspired with a fanatical determination to stop us before we got there. The old-timers came in on frontal attacks with a noticeably slower rate of closure, apparently throttled back, obtaining greater accuracy than those that bolted through us wide out. They did some nice shooting at ranges of 500 or more yards, and in many cases seemed able to time their thrusts to catch the top- and ball-turret gunners engaged with rear and side attacks. Less experienced pilots were pressing attacks home to 250 yards and less to get hits, offering point-blank targets on the breakaway, firing long bursts of twenty seconds, and, in some cases, actually pulling up instead of going down and out. Several FW pilots pulled off some first-rate deflection shooting on side attacks against the high group, then raked the low group on the breakaway out of a side-slip, keeping the nose cocked up in the turn to prolong the period the formation was in their sights.

I observed what I believe was an attempt at air-to-air bombing, although I didn't see the bombs dropped. A patch of seventy-five to 100 gray-white bursts, smaller than flak bursts, appeared simultaneously at our level, off to one side.

One B-17 dropped out on fire and put its wheels down while the crew bailed. Three ME-109s circled it closely, but held their fire, apparently ensuring that no one stayed in the ship to try for home. I saw Hun fighters hold their fire even when being shot at by a B-17 from which the crew was bailing out.

Near the IP, one hour and a half after the first of at least 200 individual fighter attacks, the pressure eased off, although hostiles were nearby. We turned at the IP with fourteen B-17s left, two of which were badly crippled. They dropped out after bombing the target and headed for Switzerland. The number-four engine on one of them was afire, but the plane was not out of control. The leader of the high squadron received a cannon shell in his number-three engine just before the start of the bombing run and went in to the target with the prop feathered.

Weather over target, as on the entire trip, was ideal. Flak was negligible. The group got its bombs away promptly on the leader. As we turned and headed for the Alps, I got a grim satisfaction out of seeing a column of smoke rising straight up from the ME-109 shops, with only one burst over in the town of Regensburg.

The rest of the trip was a marked anticlimax. A few more fighters pecked at us on the way to the Alps. A town in the Brenner Pass tossed up a lone burst of futile flak. We circled the air division over Lake Garda long enough to give the cripples a chance to join the family, and we were on our way toward the Mediterranean in a gradual descent. About twenty-five fighters on the ground at Verona stayed on the ground. The prospect of ditching as we approached Bône, shortages of fuel, and the sight of other B-17s falling into the drink seemed trivial matters after the nightmare of the long trip across southern Germany. We felt the reaction of men who had not expected to see another sunset.

At dusk, with red lights showing on all of the fuel tanks in my ship, the seven B-17s of the group still in formation circled over Bertoux and landed in the dust. Our crew was unscratched. Sole damage to the airplane: a bit of ventilation around the tail from flak and 20-mm shells. We slept on the hard ground under the wings of our B-17, but the good earth felt softer than a silk pillow.

FLYING HIGH

CHUCK YEAGER

Chuck Yeager achieved world fame in 1947 when he became the first test pilot to break the sound barrier, flying the Bell X-1. In this extract he recounts an earlier exploit, flying his P-51 Mustang in a wild aerial fight over Germany in the dying days of World War II and also gives his thoughts on the tactics of dogfighting. He emerged from World War II with 11.5 "kills".

On rainy nights in the flight leader's Nissen, we'd listen to Glenn Miller records on the phonograph and toast grilled cheese sandwiches on the coke stove. If we had a good day at work, we heated a poker red hot and branded another swastika on the front door. Each swastika represented a dogfight victory, and by the end of my tour, that door displayed fifty. Four of us accounted for more than half the squadron's total number of kills. During the last week in November, I became a double ace with eleven kills by shooting down four German planes during an historic dogfight – the greatest single American victory of the air war.

Andy was leading the squadron and I was leading one of the flights of four. Our job that day was to escort Mustangs carrying a bomb and a drop tank under their wings for attacking underground fuel facilities near Poznań,

Poland. We provided top cover, flying at 35,000 feet, while the bomb-carrying Mustangs cruised below. On German radar we were mistaken for a fleet of unescorted heavy bombers, and the Luftwaffe scrambled every available fighter in East Germany and Poland. Andy and I were the first to see them coming; at fifty miles or more, they were a dark cloud moving toward us. "God almighty, there must be a hundred and fifty of them," Andy exclaimed. We couldn't believe our luck. Andy called for a turn left that put me in the lead; we punched our wing tanks and plowed right into the rear of this enormous gaggle of German fighters.

There were sixteen of us and over two hundred of them, but then more Mustangs from group caught up and joined in. Christ, there were airplanes going every which way. I shot down two very quickly; one of the airplanes blew up, but the pilot bailed out of the other. I saw him jump, but he forgot to fasten his parachute harness; it pulled off in the windstream and he spun down to earth. To this day I can still see him falling.

A dogfight runs by its own clock and I have no idea how long I was spinning and looping in the sky. I wound up 2,000 feet from the deck with four kills. Climbing back to altitude, I found myself alone in an empty sky. But for as far as I could see, from Leipzig to way up north, the ground was littered with burning wreckage. It was an awesome sight.

We found out later that we hadn't even attacked their main force: the Germans put up 750 fighters against what they thought was a huge bomber fleet. They ran into two hundred Mustangs from three different fighter groups and lost ninety-eight airplanes. We lost eleven.

I climbed to 35,000 feet and saw three small specks way off and slightly higher. I still had plenty of fuel and ammo, and I just began to turn toward those specks, when I heard a familiar voice: "Bogie down south." Only one pair of eyes could've spotted me the moment I began my turn. "Andy," I asked, "is that you?" It was. And crazy bastards that we were, we raced toward each other and began to dogfight, happy as clams. He had shot down three. Andy led us home and it turned out to be one of the funny moments of our friendship.

We encountered unusually powerful headwinds, and after a couple of hours Andy assumed we were over the Channel and began his descent. We followed him down into a thick cloud over and found ourselves directly over the anti-aircraft emplacements on the Frisian Islands. I mean we could've walked home on that flak; the sky was black with it. And there we were, only 500 feet above those big guns. Man, did we cuss poor Andy. By the time we landed his ears were purple. And we kept at it for days. Hell, I still haven't let him forget that one.

That day was a fighter pilot's dream. In the midst of a wild sky, I knew that dogfighting was what I was born to do. It's almost impossible to explain the feeling: it's as if you were one with that Mustang, an extension of that damned throttle. You flew that thing on a fine, feathered edge, knowing that the pilot who won had the better feel for his airplane and the skill to get the most out of it. You were so wired into that airplane that you flew it to the limit of its specs, where firing your guns could cause a stall. You felt that engine in your bones, felt it nibbling toward a stall, throttle wide open, getting maximum maneuvering performance. And you knew how tight to turn before the Mustang snapped out on you, a punishment if you blundered. Maximum power, lift, and maneuverability were achieved mostly by instinctive flying: you knew your horse. Concentration was total; you remained focused, ignoring fatigue or fear, not allowing static into your mind. Up there, dogfighting, you connected with yourself. That small, cramped cockpit was exactly where you belonged.

You fought wide open, full-throttle. With experience, you knew before a kill when you were going to score. Once you zeroed in, began to outmaneuver your opponent while closing in, you became a cat with a mouse. You set him up, and there was no way out: both of you knew he was finished. You were a confident hunter and your finger never shook. You picked your spot: slightly below, so you could pull up, lead him a little, and avoid being hit by metal when he disintegrated. When he blew up, it was a pleasing, beautiful sight. There was no joy in killing someone, but real satisfaction when you outflew a guy and destroyed his machine. That was the contest: human skill and machine performance. You knew when you killed a pilot in his cockpit from the way his airplane began to windmill, going straight down. Then, you followed him to the deck, flipping on the camera to record the explosion and document your kill. The excitement of those dogfights never diminished. For me, combat remains the ultimate flying experience.

Tactics? Keep the sun at your back and as much altitude advantage as possible; bounce the enemy out of the sun. Not always possible, of course, and sometimes you were the one being bounced. For every action there was a possible reaction, and with experience I learned to anticipate and outguess my opponent. I knew, for example, even while I was cutting him off that he would probably try to reverse himself, so I led him a little; if I was right, I had him. If I was wrong, I had to go back to work to get him. But, really, my biggest tactical advantage was my eyes. I spotted him from great distances, knowing he couldn't see me because he was only a dim speck. Sometimes he never did see me when I bounced him out of the sun; or when he did finally see me, it was too late.

In a sky filled with airplanes, I needed to keep my neck on a swivel to avoid getting hit, being shot down, or running into somebody. The best survival tactic always was to check your tail constantly and stay alert. Dogfighting was hard work. You needed strong arms and shoulders. Those controls weren't hydraulically operated, and at 400 mph they became extremely heavy. Without cabin pressurization, flying at high altitude wore you out. And so did pulling Gs in sharp turns and steep dives. (A two-hundred-pound pilot weighs eight hundred pounds during a 4-G turn.) After a couple of minutes of dogfighting, your back and arms felt like you had been hauling a piano upstairs. You were sweaty and breathing heavily. Sometimes you could see a German's exhaustion from the way he turned and maneuvered – another advantage if you were stronger.

Dogfighting demanded the sum total of all your strengths, and exposed any of your weaknesses. Some good pilots lacked the eyes; others became too excited and lost concentration, or lost their nerve and courage; a few panicked in tight spots and did stupid things that cost them their lives. The best pilots were also the most aggressive, and it showed.

We quickly learned basic do's and don'ts. If the enemy was above, we didn't climb to meet him because we lost too much speed. When in a jam, we never ran. That was exactly what he expected. It was important to always check your back when popping out of the clouds: you could have jumped out in front of a 109. We avoided weaving around cumulus clouds; they're like boulders and you could have been easily ambushed. And we were particularly alert while flying beneath high thin cirrus clouds. Germans could look down through them and see you, but you couldn't see up through them. Whenever possible, we carefully timed our turns in a head-on attack, to avoid being caught sideways and becoming a direct target. We also tried to avoid overshooting an enemy plane, which put you in front of his gun-sights; it was like shooting yourself down. One of the guys once asked Colonel Spicer, our group commander, what to do if caught by a large force. "Rejoice, laddie," the old man said, "that's why you're here."

Some of our guys fought that way. In the middle of a vicious dogfight, I heard one of them say: "Hey, I've got six of them cornered at two o'clock. Come on up and have some fun." But one time I also heard the most horrifying scream blast into my headphones. "Oh, God, they got me.

My head, my damned head. I'm bleeding to death." That night at the officers' club, the shrieker showed up wearing a Band-Aid, a goddamned Band-Aid, taped to the back of his neck. He had been nicked by a piece of Plexiglas. So, our squadron ran the gamut. If you wanted to stay alive, you kept an eye on the weak sisters as carefully as you watched for Germans. The worst of them would get so shaken in a dogfight that they'd shoot at anybody, friend or foe. I remember how pissed we were when the worst pilot in the outfit became the first of us to score a victory and won a bottle of cognac. He was in a flight of four that got bounced by some Germans and crawled in behind his leader, only to discover he was on the tail of a 109 hammering his leader. He closed his eyes and pulled the trigger.

There were guys who became so terrified being in the same sky with Krauts that they began to hyperventilate and blacked out; a few actually shit their pants. Some were honest about their fear and asked to be relieved from combat duty. There were others who talked big during training, but once in combat turned tail at critical moments. Of course, they were screwing the rest of us. We also had a few abort artists, guys would would fly with you until a gaggle of Germans was sighted and then radio they were turning back with engine trouble. There were still others who would fire a burst, then quickly break off; or watch somebody else hammer an airplane, then, when the German was already windmilling and going down, dive in and fire a quick burst, then try to share credit for the kill. I had a guy do that to me. Believe me, he never did it again. Worst of all were wingmen who left you naked in a tight spot. A wingman's job was to stick like glue to his leader's tail, while his leader did the shooting. He was your damned life insurance, his reliability a matter of your life or death. If he failed you, there was no second chance. You got rid of him in a hurry. Eddie Simpson was Andy's wingman until Eddie got shot down. Before they flew together, Eddie said to Andy, "Let's go to London and get drunk together. Then, I'll follow you into hell." I had five or six wingmen during my tour; some had better eyesight or more discipline than others, but since I never got shot down flying as an element or squadron leader, they were competent enough, I guess.

The special closeness between the best of us – Anderson, Bochkay, Browning, O'Brien, and myself – existed because we fought the same way. Andy especially. On the ground, he was the nicest person you'd ever know, but in the sky, those damned Germans must've thought they were up against Frankenstein or the Wolfman; Andy would hammer them into the ground, dive with them into the damned grave, if necessary, to destroy them. So would I. We finished what we started every time. That's how we were raised. We did our job. We were over there to shoot down Germans, and that's exactly what we did, to the best of our ability and training. We were a pack of untested kids who grew up in a hurry. Andy called it the college of life and death. I don't recommend going to war as a way of testing character, but by the time our tour ended we felt damned good about ourselves and what we had accomplished. Whatever the future held, we knew our skills as pilots, our ability to handle stress and danger, and our reliability in tight spots. It was the difference between thinking you're pretty good, and proving it.

MARINE CRUSADER

BRUCE MARTIN

Bruce Martin was sent out to Vietnam with US Marine Fighter Squadron VMF(AW)-232 in August 1966.

When we found out we were going, the squadron roster was frozen, although we had the better part of a year before we were committed to actual combat operations. In that period we did a great amount of air-to-ground training in the F-8D and E, and in Vietnam the vast majority of our missions were ground support, although we also flew some fighter escort missions into Laos and up North. We had problems in that the Crusader was not designed for air-to-ground work. It had a lead computing gunsight and radar for air-to-air combat, so as far as bomb delivery was concerned we used the TLAR method – "That Looks About Right." You would pick a point on the gunsight and then place your target on that, allowing for drift and windage; people who had done it for a while became extremely accurate. The F-8 was a fine platform for rockets and strafing in any case, because they were flat-trajectory weapons.

The squadron was screened before going over, and we had a very capable and experienced group of pilots when we arrived in Vietnam. The senior flight leaders, including myself, were sent over early to gain combat experience

with VMF(AW)-235, the unit we were replacing at Da
Nang. Generally the first couple of missions were quiet –
maybe a little local radar bombing, usually in the daytime.
However, my first mission was with the Commanding
Officer of VMF(AW)-235 and we went on a night hop to
Tchepone in Laos, one of the hottest places in town.
Nobody even barked at us that time, but I was very
impressed with the fact that I had even gone.

We relieved VMF(AW)-235 in November 1966, but by
January 1967 around seventeen of our pilots had been
transferred out of the squadron to various Group and
Wing staff jobs. Many of the new pilots we received were
short of F-8 experience, especially in air-to-ground delivery, and had to be trained on the job. This gave the
airplane something of a bad name for a while amongst our
customers, until the new pilots gained the necessary
experience.

Our missions were usually flown in I Corps or the
northern part of II Corps; sometimes we even got across
to the Central Highlands, around Kontum and Dak To.
The large majority of them were flown from the DMZ to
south of Chu Lai. We also went into Laos on a regular
basis and did an awful lot of work along the Ho Chi Minh
Trail. We also flew two or three missions a day up North,
hitting the area around Dong Hoi and Vinh and the lower
Route Package One areas of North Vietnam. A favorite
target was the gun emplacements around the Finger Lakes
area, just across the Ben Hai River into North Vietnam.

We flew seven days a week, day and night. When we
were on strip alert we were usually armed with eight 500-
pound Snakeye finned bombs, plus our 20mm cannon. A
second plane would often carry napalm and 5-inch Zuni
rockets. The Snakeyes wore fins that would extend in
flight and retard the bombs' descent, giving us time to get
clear of the blast from the bomb if we were releasing at low
altitude.

It was hard work operating out of Da Nang. When we
first arrived we were living in open-side tents, with no air-

conditioning. The weather could be abominable, with lots of thunderstorms, heavy rain and low ceilings. If you flew at night, it was so hot in the daytime that it was difficult to sleep. We also had problems with our ground support equipment; there were never enough serviceable bomb loaders and our ordnance people often had to manhandle the 500-pound bombs onto the plane, by inserting pipes in the nose and tail where the fuses would go and muscle them on. In comparison, the Air Force on the other side of the base had airconditioned trailers, good equipment and a nice club. When General Seth McKee, one of the Air Force commanders, came to visit his son, who was a pilot in our squadron, he saw our living conditions and said, "Boy, if my guys had to put up with these conditions they would quit!" In spite of this, the squadron morale was very good throughout the tour.

I had joined the squadron in the summer of 1964, had spent a lot of time in the Crusader and was comfortable in it. I felt pretty invulnerable as far as the missions we were flying were concerned. We were getting a lot of ground fire, but it was nothing compared to what the Navy and Air Force and our A-6s were facing up North in the Red River Valley, Hanoi and Haiphong area. Normally the worst we would see would be 37 and 57mm anti-aircraft fire. Towards the end of our tour we were getting some SAM alerts down in the Route Package One area and around Khe Sanh, but I never saw one fired and, much to my dismay, I never saw a hostile aircraft.

The day that I was shot down started with a typical in-country mission for my wingman and I. Things started to go wrong when he had to abort on takeoff roll due to smoke in the cockpit. I continued the mission with my full load of eight 500-pound Snakeyes and contacted control to see if they had a single-plane mission for me. Normal SOP called for two aircraft on a mission, but exceptions were the rule, especially if we were operating below the DMZ . . .

*   *   *

When I asked control if they had any single-plane missions for me, they replied that they had an emergency
mission up near the DMZ and gave me a briefing on the
way there.* I climbed to 15,000 feet and flew up the coast,
turning inland for the last 14 miles to the target. It was a
nice hot summer day and as we were near the end of our
tour I had borrowed the Assistant Maintenance Officer's
Nikon camera to take some shots for us both. However,
there was to be little chance to do that as the day's mission
turned out to be far from routine.

As I started to let down southeast of Dong Ha there was
an F-4 coming off the target and he had been hit. I took
some pictures of him as he went by and then saw him go
into the water. It turned out the pilot was a friend of mine,
Ray Pendagraff, and neither he nor his backseater got out.

There was nothing I could do for the F-4, so I went on
in and was told to salvo all my ordnance in one go, as there
was a lot of anti-aircraft fire in the area – 37 and 57mm and
quad 50-caliber machine guns. I received a target description and they told me to go off to the west and then come
back flying parallel to the Marines lines, from west to east.

I set up a ten-degree dive and crossed over the target at
250 feet and 450 knots, but as I released all eight bombs,
everything in the cockpit lit up and the aircraft bounced.
The fire warning light came on immediately and the utility
hydraulic system failed. As I tried to pull up the Forward
Air Controller called me and told me that my bombs were
"right on." I had planned to come around again and go in
for a strafing run, but when the cockpit lit up I lost all
interest in staying in the area.

In Vietnam we had been told that the enemy owned the
land but we owned the water, so if you were hit you should
try and make it out over the water before ejecting. When it
became obvious that the airplane was holding together, I
began to climb and head out to sea. I put out a "Mayday"

* This was 2 July 1967: two companies from 1st battallion, 9th Marines,
were ambushed by an NVA unit at Con Thien, just below the Demilitarised
Zone

call and some A-4s with the callsign "Miss Muffet" that were on their way in came alongside to escort me out of the area. The flight leader said, "You have a very thin trail of smoke around your tail section, but I can't really see any big holes or anything." So I continued to climb and asked him to tell me if it got any worse.

I got out to the water and turned south and began to think about getting the aircraft back, or at least maybe to Phu Bai where they had arresting gear on the runway. I called Red Crown, the destroyer that coordinates all the rescue efforts, on the Guard channel and as I was speaking to him I looked to my right and saw that the fellow in the A-4 was giving me a vigorous "eject" signal. I looked at my instruments and saw that the exhaust gas temperature gauge was going up and heading toward the maximum reading. I looked in my mirror and there was a big cloud of black smoke behind me. Without further ado I reached up and pulled the face curtain to initiate the ejection sequence.

I felt the sensation of the aircraft falling away from me and then a lot of twisting and girating and then a terrific impact as the parachute opened. I looked around but couldn't see the airplane. I was later told that it had exploded about ten seconds after I ejected.

Since I was about six miles off the coast I reviewed what I had been told about water landings when I had jumped as FAC with the 173rd Airborne Brigade. I also recalled an article that I had seen in the National Geographic that talked about the population of sea snakes in the Tonkin Gulf and how they could raft up a quarter of a mile wide by about ten miles long. I thought that it hadn't been a very good day so far, and I really hoped I didn't land amongst those.

A number of people had been lost over the years in water landings, when they had become entangled in their parachute or shroud lines. As the parachute filled with water it had dragged them down. I was concerned about that and as I got lower I took off my oxygen mask and dropped it to gauge my height. It seemed like I still had a way to go before I hit the water. The usual procedure is to look at the horizon and wait until your feet touch the water and then release your chute and I knew that. However, I was not comfortable with that, so when it looked like I was about ten feet from the water I released the parachute and had about the longest two or three seconds of falling that anyone could imagine, because I was a little bit higher than I thought!

My lifejacket was already inflated, although the camera that I had tucked into it had, needless to say, disappeared. Once I got into the water I swam to my life raft, which had been stored in the seatpack and had come down ahead of me, inflated it and climbed in. I felt pretty good and decided to use all of the available survival aids, so I got out the signal mirror and was starting to unpack the salt water distillation kit, when I looked up, and hovering in front of me was an Air Force HH-53B Jolly Green helicopter.

They put a swimmer in the water, a para-rescueman, and I got out of the raft and into the water as well, because the downdraft from the helicopter blades was blowing the raft away. The PJ put the horsecollar around me and they pulled me up into the helicopter.

When the PJ was back on board we headed for Da Nang and it was on the way there that I realized I had been hurt. I started to stiffen up and by the time I got back to the field I was hobbling around like a 90-year-old man. It was mostly cervical strain, later diagnosed as a compression fracture, and abrasions, but at least I didn't have any holes in me.

I asked the helicopter pilot how they had got to me so quickly and he said that they were out looking for the Phantom that had gone down and saw an F-8 going by with smoke pouring out of the ass end of it. They said "That's a customer for sure" and just turned around and followed me.

I spent a night in the base hospital and had to wear a

neck brace for about ten days, and then I went back flying again. Months later, back in the USA, I received a package in the mail. When I was shot down, I had been carrying an Air Force style plastic briefing book, with codes, procedures, radio frequencies and other information in it. Apparently the charred book had been washed ashore and found by a Marine Recon Team, who saw my name in it and thoughtfully packaged it up and sent it back to me.

NIGHT MISSION ON
THE HO CHI MINH TRAIL

MARK E. BERENT

*Mark Berent served with the 497th Tactical Fighter
Squadron of the USAAF during the Vietnam War,
flying F-4s on night missions out of Thailand.*

It's cool this evening, thank God. The night is beautiful,
moody, an easy rain falling. Thunder rumbles comfortably in the distance. Just the right texture to erase the
oppressive heat memories of a few hours ago. Strange how
the Thai monsoon heat sucks the energy from your mind
and body by day, only to restore it by the cool night rain.

I am pleased by the tranquil sights and sounds outside
the BOQ room door. Distant ramp lights, glare softened
by the rain, glisten the leaves and flowers. The straight-
down, light rain splashes gently, nicely on the walkways,
on the roads, the roofs. Inside the room I put some slow
California swing on the recorder (*You gotta go where you
wanta go . . .*) and warm some soup on the hot-plate.
Warm music, warm smell . . . I am in a different world.
(*Do what you wanta, wanta do. . . .*) I've left the door open
– I like the sound of the rain out there.

A few hours later, slightly after midnight, I am sitting in
the cockpit of my airplane. It is a jet fighter, a Phantom,

and it's a good airplane. We don't actually get into the thing – we put it on. I am attached to my craft by two hoses, three wires, lap belt, shoulder harness and two calf garters to keep my legs from flailing about in a highspeed bailout. The gear I wear – gun, G-suit, survival vest, parachute harness – is bulky, uncomfortable, and means life or death.

I start the engines, check the myriad systems – electronic, radar, engine, fire control, navigation – all systems; receive certain information from the control tower, and am ready to taxi. With hand signals we are cleared out of the revetment and down the ramp to the arming area.

I have closed the canopy to keep the rain out, and switch the heavy windscreen blower on and off to hold visibility. I can only keep its hot air on for seconds at a time while on the ground, to prevent cracking the heavy screen. The arming crew, wearing bright colours to indicate their duties, swarm under the plane: electrical continuity – checked; weapons – armed; pins – pulled. Last all-round look-see by the chief – a salute, a thumbs-up, we are cleared. God, the rapport between pilot and ground crew – their last sign, thumbs-up – they are with me. You see them quivering, straining bodies posed forward as they watch *their* airplane take off and leave them.

And we are ready, my craft and I. Throttles forward and outboard, gauges OK, afterburners ignite, nose-wheel steering, rudder effective, line speed, rotation speed – we are off, leaving behind only a ripping, tearing, gut noise as we split into the low black overcast, afterburner glow not even visible anymore.

Steadily we climb, turning a few degrees, easing stick forward some, trimming, climbing, then suddenly – on top! On top where the moonlight is so damn marvellously bright and the undercast appears a gently rolling snow-covered field. It's just so clear and good up here, I could fly forever. This is part of what flying is all about. I surge and strain against my harness, taking a few seconds to stretch and enjoy this privileged sight.

I've already set course to rendezvous with a tanker, to take on more fuel for my work tonight. We meet after a long cut-off turn, and I nestle under him as he flies his long, delicate boom toward my innards. A slight thump/bump, and I'm receiving. No words – all light signals. Can't even thank the boomer. We cruise silently together for several minutes. Suddenly he snatches it back, a clean break, and I'm cleared, off and away.

Now I turn east and very soon cross the fence far below. Those tanker guys will take you to hell, then come in and pull you right out again with their flying fuel trucks. Hairy work. They're grand guys.

Soon I make radio contact with another craft, a big one, a gunship, painted black and flying very low. Like the proverbial spectre, he wheels and turns just above the guns, the limestone outcropping, called karst, and the mountains – probing, searching with infra-red eyes for supply trucks headed south. He has many engines and more guns. His scanner gets something in his scope, and the pilot goes into a steep bank – right over the target. His guns flick and flash, scream and moan, long amber tongues lick the ground, the trail, the trucks. I am there to keep enemy guns off him and to help him kill trucks. Funny – he can see the trucks but not the guns till they're on him. I cannot see the trucks but pick the guns up as soon as the first rounds flash out of the muzzles.

Inside my cockpit all the lights are off or down to a dim glow, showing the instruments I need. The headset in my helmet tells me in a crackling, sometimes joking voice the information I must have: how high and how close the nearest karst, target elevation, altimeter setting, safe bail-out area, guns, what the other pilot sees on the trails, where he will be when I roll in.

Then, in the blackest of black, he lets out an air-burning flare to float down and illuminate the sharp rising ground. At least then I can mentally photograph the target area. Or he might throw out a big log, a flare marker, that will fall to the ground and give off a steady glow. From that point he will tell me where to strike: 50 metres east, or 100 metres south, or, if there are two logs, hit between the two.

I push the power up now, recheck the weapons settings, gun switches, gunsight setting, airspeed, altitude – roll in! Peering, straining, leaning way forward in the harness, trying so hard to pick up the area where I know the target to be – it's so dark down there.

Sometimes when I drop, pass after pass, great fire balls will roll and boil upward and a large, rather rectangular fire will let us know we've hit another supply truck. Then we will probe with firepower all around that truck to find if there are more. Often we will touch off several, their fires outlining the trail or truck park. There are no villages or hooches for miles around; the locals have been gone for years. They silently stole away the first day those big trucks started plunging down the trails from up north. But there are gun pits down there – pits, holes, reveted sites, guns in caves, guns on the karst, guns on the hills, in the jungles, big ones, little ones.

Many times garden-hose streams of cherry balls will arc and curve up, seeming to float so slowly toward me. Those from the smaller-calibre, rapid-fire quads; and then the big stuff opens up, clip after clip of 37 mm and 57 mm follow the garden hose, which is trying to pinpoint me like a search light. Good fire discipline – no one shoots except on command.

But my lights are out, and I'm moving, jinking. The master fire controller down there tries to find me by sound. His rising shells burst harmlessly around me. The heavier stuff in clips of five and seven rounds goes off way behind.

Tonight we are lucky – no "golden BB". The golden BB is that one stray shell that gets you. Not always so lucky. One night we had four down in Death Valley – that's just south of Mu Gia Pass. Only got two people out the next day, and that cost a Sandy (A-1) pilot. "And if the big guns don't get you, the black karst will," goes the song. It is black, karsty country down there.

Soon I have no more ammunition. We, the gunship and I, gravely thank each other, and I pull up to thirty or so thousand feet, turn my navigation lights back on, and start across the Lao border to my home base. In spite of an air-conditioning system working hard enough to cool a five-room house, I'm sweating. I'm tired. My neck is sore. In fact, I'm sore all over. All those roll-ins and diving pull-outs, jinking, craning your head, looking, always looking around, in the cockpit, outside, behind, left, right, up, down. But I am headed home, my aircraft is light and more responsive.

Too quickly I am in the thick, puffy thunder clouds and rain of the southwest monsoon. Wild, the psychedelic green, wiry, and twisty St Elmo's fire flows liquid and surrealistic on the canopy a few inches away. I am used to it – fascinating. It's comforting, actually, sitting snugged up in the cockpit, harness and lap belt tight, seat lowered, facing a panel of red-glowing instruments, plane buffeting slightly from the storm. Moving without conscious thought, I place the stick and rudder pedals and throttles in this or that position – not so much mechanically moving things, rather just willing the craft to do what I see should be done by what the instruments tell me.

I'm used to flying night missions now. We "night owls" do feel rather élite, I suppose. We speak of the day pilots in somewhat condescending tones. We have a black pilot who says, "Well, day pilots are OK, I guess, but I wouldn't want my daughter to *marry* one." We have all kinds: quiet guys, jokey guys (the Jewish pilot with the fierce black bristly moustache who asks, "What is a nice Jewish boy like me doing over here, killing Buddhists to make the world safe for Christianity?"), noisy guys, scared guys, whatever. But all of them do their job. I mean night after night they go out and get hammered and hosed, and yet keep right at it. And all that effort, sacrifice, blood going down the tubes. Well, these thoughts aren't going to get me home. This is not time to be thinking about anything but what I'm doing right now.

I call up some people on the ground who are sitting in darkened, black-out rooms, staring at phosphorescent screens that are their eyes to the night sky. Radar energy reflecting from me shows them where I am. I flick a switch at their command and trigger an extra burst of energy at them so they have positive identification. By radio they direct me, crisply, clearly, to a point in space and time that another man in another darkened room by a runway watches anxiously. His eyes follow a little electronic bug crawling down a radar screen between two converging lines. His voice tells me how the bug is doing, or how it should be doing. In a flat, precise voice the radar controller keeps up a constant patter – "Turn left two degrees . . . approaching glide path . . . prepare to start descent in four miles."

Inside the cockpit I move a few levers and feel the heavy landing gear thud into place and then counteract the nose rise as the flaps grind down. I try to follow his machine-like instructions quite accurately, as I am very near the ground now. More voice, more commands, then a glimmer of approach lights, and suddenly the wet runway is beneath me. I slip over the end, engines whistling a down note as I retard the throttles, and I'm on the ground at last.

If the runway is heavy with rain, I lower a hook to snatch a cable laid across the runway that connects to a friction device on each side. The deceleration throws me violently into my harness as I stop in less than 900 ft from nearly 175 m.p.h. And this is a gut-good feeling.

Then the slow taxi back, the easing of tension, the good feeling. Crew chiefs with lighted wands in their hands direct me where to park; they chock the wheels and signal me with a throat-cutting motion to shut down the engines. Six or seven people gather around the airplane as the engines coast off, and I unstrap and climb down, soaking wet with sweat.

"You OK? How did it go? See anything, get anything?" They want to know these things and they have a right to know. Then they ask, "How's the airplane?" That concern always last. We confer briefly on this or that device or instrument that needs looking after. And then I tell them what I saw, what I did. They nod, grouped around, swear softly, spit once or twice. They are tough, and it pleases them to hear results.

The crew van arrives, I enter and ride through the rain – smoking a cigarette and becoming thoughtful. It's dark in there, and I need this silent time to myself before going back to the world. We arrive and, with my equipment jangling and thumping about me, I enter the squadron locker room, where there is always easy joking among those who have just come down. Those that are suiting up are quiet, serious, going over the mission brief in their minds, for once on a night strike they cannot look at maps or notes or weapon settings.

They glance at me and ask how the weather is at The Pass. Did I see any thunderstorms over the Dog's Head? They want to ask about the guns up tonight, but know I'll say how it was without their questioning. Saw some light ZPU (automatic weapons fire) at The Pass, saw someone getting hosed at Ban Karai, nothing from across the border. Nobody down, quiet night. Now all they have to worry about is thrashing through a couple of hundred miles of lousy weather, letting down on instruments and radar into the black karst country and finding their targets. Each pilot has his own thoughts on that.

Me, I'll start warming up once the lethargy of finally being back from a mission drains from me. Funny how the mind/body combination works. You are all "hypoed" just after you land, then comes a slump, then you're back up again but not as high as you were when you first landed. By now I'm ready for some hot coffee or a drink (sometimes too many), or maybe just letter writing. A lot of what you want to do depends on how the mission went.

I debrief and prepare to leave the squadron, But before I do, I look at the next days' schedule. Is it an escort? Am I leading? Where are we going? What are we carrying? My mind unrolls pictures of mosaics and gun-camera film of the area. Already I'm mechanically preparing for the next mission.

And so it goes – for a year. And I like it. But every so often, especially during your first few months, a little wisp of thought floats up from way deep in your mind when you see the schedule. "Ah, no, not tonight," you say to yourself. "Tonight I'm sick – or could be sick. Just really not up to par, you know. Maybe, maybe I shouldn't go." There's a feeling – the premonition that tonight is the night I don't come back. But you go anyhow and pretty soon you don't think about it much anymore. You just don't give a fat damn. After a while, when you've been there and see what you see, you just want to go fight! To strike back, destroy. And then sometimes you're pensive – every sense savouring each and every sight and sound and smell. Enjoying the camaraderie, the feeling of doing something. Have to watch that camaraderie thing though – don't get too close. You might lose somebody one night and that can mess up your mind. It happens, and when it does, you get all black and karsty inside your head.

I leave the squadron and walk back through the ever-present rain that's running in little rivulets down and off my poncho. The rain glistens off trees and grass and bushes, and a ripping, tearing sound upsets the balances as another black Phantom rises to pierce the clouds.

SEA HARRIER OVER THE FALKLANDS

SHARKEY WARD

Sharkey Ward commanded 801 Naval Air Squadron during the Falklands War of 1982. The squadron flew Sea Harriers which, despite being outnumbered 3-to-1 by Argentine fighters and much slower than the enemy's Mirages and Daggers, had the superior air-to-air weapon in the AIM-91 Sidewinder. The Sea Harrier's famous VSTOL capability, which enabled it to "viff" (vector thrust in forward flight), also produced turns that the anyway lesser-trained Argentine pilots had little hope of matching. Below Lieutenant-Commander Ward relates two missions from 21 May, the day of the British landings on the Falklands.

There were two ways to approach the CAP* stations, transiting north or south of the missile zone, and on this first mission we had been given the southerly CAP station. The early morning clag had abated a little but there were still extensive layers of medium to low cloud partially covering the islands, especially to the north of Falkland Sound. We descended in battle formation past Darwin and took up the CAP station, with Alasdair sticking to Steve's wing. In the morning sun the Sound was a

---

* *CAP: Combat Air Patrol*

beautiful sight with an amazing mixture of startlingly clear blues, greens and shades of turquoise. Banks of yellowish kelp seaweed took their form from the currents and the colour of the water, in sharp contrast to the muddy browns and greens of the surrounding landscape.

It was initially a quiet mission with no trade until we had commenced our climb-out after 45 minutes at low level. As we were passing about 10,000 feet the *Antrim* controller came up on the air. "I have two slow-moving contacts over the land to the south of you. Possibly helicopters or ground-attack aircraft. Do you wish to investigate?"

As soon as the controller had said the word "south", I had rolled hard to starboard and down. Steve Thomas and Alasdair followed suit.

"Affirmative. Now in descent heading 160°. Do you still hold the contacts?"

"Affirmative. 10 miles, very low."

Steve spotted them first. It was a good sighting against the indistinct colours of the gently undulating terrain. "Got them, Sharkey! Looks like two Pucaras on the deck. About 15° right of the nose."

"Not visual. You attack first." Then, as I spoke, I saw one of the Pucaras. Steve was closing in on the aircraft from its high right, 4 o'clock. I decided to attack the same aircraft from astern as I couldn't see the second target. "Got one visual now. Same one you are going for. I'll attack from his 6."

My Numbers Two and Three opened fire in unison against the target, their cannon shells ripping up the ground beyond the Pucara. I had a little more time for tracking and closed in astern of the enemy aircraft, which was hugging the ground and weaving gently – with any more bank its wing tip would have been in the dirt. I had a lot of overtake, centered the Pucara at the end of my hotline gunsight in the HUD, and squeezed the trigger. The aircraft gave its familiar shudder as the 30-mm cannon shells left the two barrels. They were on target.

The Pucara's right engine burst into flames and then the shells impacted the left aileron, nearly sawing off the wing tip as they did so. I was very close, and pulled off my target.

Meanwhile, Steve had reversed to the left of the Pucara and was turning in for a second shot from a beam position. I had throttled back, jinked hard right and left, and prepared for a second stern shot. As the ground to the right of the enemy took the full weight of Steve and Alasdair's cannon fire, I dropped half flap. I wanted to get as low as possible behind the Pucara and dropping the flap brought my nose and gun axis down relative to the wing-line. Aiming . . . hotline on . . . firing! The left engine of the Pucara now erupted into flame and part of the rear cockpit canopy shattered. My radio altimeter readout in the HUD told me I was firing from as low as 10 and not higher than 60 feet above the ground.

I pulled off a second time, fully expecting the pilot to have ejected. Must be a very brave bloke in there because he was still trying to evade the fighters. Steve's section attacked again from the right, but it just wasn't his day – the ground erupted in pain once more. I was amazed that the Pucara was still flying as I started my third and final run. Sight on – and this time you're going down. Pieces of fuselage, wing and canopy were torn from the doomed aircraft. The fuselage caught fire. I ceased firing at the last minute and as I raised my nose off the target, the pilot ejected. The aircraft had ploughed into the soft earth in a gentle skid by the time the pilot's feet hit the ground. He only had one swing in his parachute.

Later, I was to find out that the pilot's name was Major Tomba. He managed to hoof it back to his base at Goose Green after his ejection; before the war was over the man's bravery was to prove useful to both sides.

Our division of three SHARs then resumed the climb and returned to the ship. Needless to say, we were pretty short of fuel.

Everyone was keen to hear the gory details when I got to the crewroom.

Steve and I flew the next mission as a pair. There was no trade for us under the now clear blue skies, but we could see that to the south of the Sound HMS *Ardent* had seen more than enough action for the day. She was limping northwards and smoke was definitely coming from more places than her funnel. We were to see more of her on our third and final sortie of the day.

For this final "hop" we were given the station to the west of San Carlos over the land. We descended from the north-east and set up a low-level race-track patrol in a wide shallow valley. As always, we flew in battle formation – side-by-side and about half a mile apart. When we turned at the end of the race-track pattern, we always turned towards each other in order to ensure that no enemy fighter could approach our partner's 6 o'clock undetected. I had just flown through Steve in the middle of a turn at the southerly end of the race-track when I spotted two triangular shapes approaching down the far side of the valley under the hills from the west. They were moving fast and were definitely Mirages, probably Daggers. I levelled out of the turn and pointed directly at them, increasing power to full throttle as I did so.

"Two Mirages! Head-on to me now, Steve. 1 mile."

"Passing between them now!" I was lower than the leader and higher than the Number Two as they flashed past each side of my cockpit. They were only about 50 yards apart and at about 100 feet above the deck. As I passed them I pulled hard to the right, slightly nose-high, expecting them still to try to make it through to their target by going left and resuming their track. I craned my neck over my right shoulder but they didn't appear. Instead I could see Steve chasing across the skyline towards the west. My heart suddenly leapt. They are going to stay and fight! Must have turned the other way.

They had turned the other way, but not to fight. They were running for home and hadn't seen Steve at all because their turn placed him squarely in their 6 o'clock. Steve's first missile streaked from under the Sea Harrier's wing. It curved over the tail of the Mirage leaving its characteristic white smoke trail and impacted the spine of the jet behind the cockpit. The pilot must have seen it coming because he had already jettisoned the canopy before the missile arrived; when it did, he ejected. The back half of the delta-winged fighter-bomber disappeared in a great gout of flame before the jet exploded.

I checked Steve's tail was clear but he was far too busy to think of checking my own 6 o'clock. Otherwise he would have seen the third Mirage closing fast on my tail.

Steve was concentrating on tracking the second jet in his sights and he released his second Sidewinder. The missile had a long chase after its target, which was accelerating hard in full burner towards the sanctuary of the west. At missile burn-out the Mirage started to pull up for some clouds. The lethal dot of white continued to track the fighter-bomber and as the jet entered cloud, I clearly saw the missile proximity-fuse under the wing. It was an amazing spectacle.

Adrenalin running high, I glanced round to check the sky about me. Flashing underneath me and just to my right was the beautiful green and brown camouflage of the third Dagger. I broke right and down towards the aircraft's tail, acquired the jet exhaust with the Sidewinder, and released the missile. It reached its target in very quick time and the Dagger disappeared in a ball of flame. Out of the flame ball exploded the broken pieces of the jet, some of which cartwheeled along the ground before coming to rest, no longer recognisable as parts of an aircraft.

Later I was to discover that the third Mirage Dagger had entered the fight from the north and found me in his sights. As he turned towards the west and home he had been firing his guns at me in the turn, but had missed. It was the closest shave that I was to experience.

We were euphorically excited as we found each other visually and joined up as a pair to continue our CAP duties. We had moved a few miles west during the short engagement and now steadied on east for some seconds to

regain the correct patrol position. As I was looking towards San Carlos, about 10 miles distant behind the hills,
I noticed three seagulls in the sunlight ahead. Were they
seagulls?

I called *Brilliant*. "Do you have any friendlies close to
you?"

"Wait!" It was a sharper than usual reply.

A second or two later, *Brilliant* was back on the air.
"Sorry, we've just been strafed by a Mirage. Hit in the
Ops Room. Man opposite me is hurt and I think I'm hit in
the arm. No, no friendlies close to us."

Full power again. "Steve, those aren't seagulls ahead,
they're Sky Hawks!" What had looked like white birds
were actually attack aircraft that had paused to choose a
target. As I spoke the three "seagulls" stopped orbiting,
headed towards the south and descended behind the line
of hills. And from my morning flight I knew where they
were going.

"They're going for *Ardent!*" I headed flat-out to the
south-east, passing over the settlement of Port Howard at
over 600 knots and 100 feet.

In quick time I cleared the line of hills to my left and
was suddenly over the water of the Sound. Ahead and to
the left were the Sky Hawks. To the right was the stricken
Ardent, billowing smoke like a beacon as she attempted to
make her way to San Carlos. I wasn't going to get there in
time but I knew that Red Section from *Hermes* should be
on CAP on the other side of the water. "Red Section!
Three Sky Hawks, north to south towards *Ardent!* I'm out
of range to the west!"

Red Section got the message and appeared as if by
magic from above the other bank of the Sound. I saw
the smoke of a Sidewinder and the trailing A-4 exploded.
The middle aircraft then blew up (a guns kill, so I heard
later) and the third jet delivered its bombs into *Ardent*
before seeming to clip the mast with its fuselage.

I looked around to see where my Number Two had got
to.

"Steve, where are you?" He should have been in battle formation on the beam. No reply. My heart missed several beats. There was only one answer, he must have gone down!

I called *Brilliant*. "Believe I've lost my Number Two to ground fire. Retracing my track back to the CAP position to make a visual search." I didn't feel good. My visual search resulted in nothing. But I did hear the tell-tale sound of a pilot's SARBE rescue beacon. Maybe that was Steve? "*Brilliant*, I can't locate my Number Two but have picked up a SARBE signal. Could be him or one of the Mirage pilots. Can you send a helicopter to have a look, please? I'm very short of fuel and must recover to Mother immediately."

I felt infinitely depressed as I climbed to high level. Losing Steve was a real shock to my system. At 80 miles to run, I called the ship.

"Be advised I am *very* short of fuel. I believe my Number Two has been lost over West Falkland. Commencing cruise descent."

"Roger, Leader. Copy you are short of fuel. Your Number Two is about to land on. He's been hit but he's OK. Over."

"Roger, Mother. That is good news. Out".

Invincible could be clearly seen at 60 miles. She was arrowing her way through the water towards me like a speedboat, leaving a great foaming wake. Good for JJ – doesn't want to lose a Sea Jet just for a few pounds of fuel. My spirits had suddenly soared and it felt great to be alive.

I throttled back and didn't need to touch the power again until I was approaching the decel to the hover. On landing with 200 pounds of fuel remaining, I couldn't help thinking what a remarkable little jet the Sea Harrier was. The fuel was right on the button. I had calculated 200 pounds at land-on before leaving San Carlos.

On board, I heard from Steve that he had been hit in the avionics bay by 20 mm machine-gun fire from Port Howard. He had lost his radio, couldn't communicate with me, and thought he might just as well go home. I was too pleased to see him to be angry.

"What was I supposed to think, then?"

"Oh, you were hightailing it after those Sky Hawks, Boss. You can look after yourself and as I didn't have any missiles left I thought the best thing was to get the aircraft back and get it fixed."

"Steve, that is definitely worth a beer!"

It struck me later that if Red Section from *Hermes* had been capping at low level over the sound (where any 801 CAP would have been) instead of at altitude, the Sky Hawks would have had to get through them to get at *Ardent*. The A-4s would not have tangled with the SHARs so *Ardent* would not have been hit again and mortally wounded.

INTERROGATION

JOHN NICHOL

John Nichol, a navigator in a RAF Tornado GRI from XV Squadron, was shot down on 17 January 1991 during a low-level attack into Iraq during the Gulf War. Both he and the Tornado's pilot, John Peters, survived ejection from the aircraft. The pair were then captured by Iraqi soldiers. So began a seven week ordeal of interrogation and torture.

John Nichol: They dragged me back into the room. Silence. But I sensed at least two people, watching. The chair. That's what I learned to fear: backless, tubular steel, vinyl seat. When they held you down on that . . .

My body was tensed for some more of the same, but this time there was a warm, gentle voice. "It's OK, we don't want to know any information. Don't worry." They took the blindfold off. The voice turned out to be a mild-looking, middle-aged man, somebody's uncle, a twinkle in his eyes. He offered me food and drink, beside him on the table. I refused. "Look, it's not drugged, I am eating it." He asked the Big Four: name, rank, number and date of birth. I told him, that's permitted. This was a style of interrogation I recognised; I'd been warned about it in our combat survival training.

Mr Nice was talking to me again, his warm, reasonable

tones filling the room, cosy, warming, lapping gently into my thoughts: "We don't want to know any information. Here is food, here is drink. Don't worry. Relax." He started to slip in the odd question. "What squadron are you from, by the way?"

"I cannot answer that question."

"Why can't you answer that question?"

"I cannot answer that question."

And so the tournament began. He wanted me to say something else. That's the game we were playing. I'd given him the Big Four, the only other thing I could properly say now was "I cannot answer that question." If I said anything else, I would be striking up a conversation with him, and he'd have got me. I didn't want to do that. He kept on, softly, genteelly. "Why did you come to bomb my country?"

"I cannot answer that question."

"Why can't you answer that question?"

"I cannot answer that question."

"Why have you attacked us? We haven't attacked you."

"I cannot answer that question."

This is as difficult as when somebody is beating you and asking you questions. A beating is a very untechnical way of interrogating somebody. Most interrogators will tell you it is not a particularly efficient method of interrogation, because eventually you will start talking in order to stop the pain, and you will tell them what they want to hear, you will say anything, truth or not. The wheedling, the appeals to logic and reason were more subtle, undermining.

My body was still on fire from the last beating, but he was trying to be nice to me, to draw me in, to form a relationship with me. He was going through a list of things that I could actually answer, and not give any information away at all, and I thought, "I'd love to answer this, I'd love to say something different, but I can't, I've got to keep saying 'I cannot answer that question.'" It sounded ridiculous, when you kept on repeating it.

He tried a different approach: "Your friends bombed my family at the airfield tonight. What do you think of that?"

"I cannot answer that question."

"OK . . . Fine. I see you are wearing a chemical warfare suit. Why are you wearing a chemical warfare suit? Is it because you're dropping chemical weapons on my country?"

Now I was thinking, "Oh no." I desperately wanted to deny the accusation, but I could not. If I replied "No", he'd have got me. He realised from the look on my face that he was onto something; he concentrated on that for a while. "You *are* dropping chemical weapons onto my country, aren't you?"

I blocked again.

"OK. We will talk further. I know that you cannot answer these questions, but *you* know that you *will* answer them. At some point, maybe not today, maybe not tonight . . . tomorrow, maybe, the next day . . . you *will* talk to me. I know you will talk to me, you know you will talk to me."

I was thinking, "I know that as well, mate." But again, I sat and looked stupid; I looked sad, I looked very sad, I tried to get a bit of sympathy from him, but it didn't work. He continued with his questioning.

"OK," he said, "if you're not going to talk to me, I'm going to go. Do you want me to go?"

"No, no!" I thought. "Stay!" But I could not say that. I was thinking, "I know you're Mr Nice, and you're not going to hurt me." But again I replied, "I cannot answer that question."

"What do you mean, you cannot answer that question? That's stupid. All you have to say is you want me to stay, or you don't want me to stay." Psychologically, he was trying to get to me. I was desperately trying to fight that as much as I had been trying to fight the pain when they were flogging me.

In the end he decided he was going to go. He stood

behind me chatting with someone in Arabic, discussing my case, planning the rest of the evening's entertainment. Mr Nasty came in. He was not a particularly aggressive guy, but he had the threats, he was threatening quite openly: "If you do not answer my questions, we will hand you over to other people. They will hurt you, and eventually you *will* answer them. Why don't you spare yourself the pain?"

I think to myself, "Why not spare myself the pain? I know at some point I'm going to tell him what he wants."

"We will hurt you. People will beat you. You will be taken to a darkened room, it will not be nice like this, people will not offer you food and the drink that we have."

Mr Nice had attempted to persuade me, attempted to make friends with me, attempted to get me to say something else. Now he was putting his trump cards down on the table. He said, "I don't need to ask you these questions."

Now what's coming?

"I can tell you that your name is Flt Lt Nichol."

That's no problem, I've told him that.

"I can tell you that you are a navigator."

"Shit," I thought. "How does he know that? That could be a guess though; that's not a problem."

"I can tell you that you are from XV Squadron."

Now I really was worried. He knew things about me. Where had he got them from? I had a feeling that he got them from John; he could have got them from a newspaper article, but probably not, it had probably come from John. What have they done to him to get it? The same, or worse? Worse, surely. But what? When will I get it? What will it be like? What did they do?

"I know that you are from XV Squadron; I know that you are from Bahrain; I know that you fly with your Victor tankers to bomb me."

Again this was stuff that he could be guessing, or have read about in the British press. Many people in the Forces had thought that in the run-up to the war the press revealed way too much information that would be of intelligence value to the Iraqis. It was very contentious.

Now Mr Nice said, "I know that your attack did not work; I know you did not get the bombs off, and that you ditched your bombs in my desert."

So now I knew. Now a cold feeling ran right through me. John. I thought, "What the hell has happened to him? Where is he? How is he?" I was worried about him, but even more worried about myself. Deep down, I was glad that whatever had led him to talk had not yet happened to me. The questioning began again; I gave the formulaic reply. But I knew if John had talked, it was only a question of time before I followed suit.

Mr Nice got bored again: he went away, the pattern formed now. The dry mouth and sudden salivas of fear.

Still I refused to talk. In the end they gave up. Now the pain was going to start again. Sure enough, they dragged me off to another room, blindfolding me again. I was waiting, tensed, I knew something very unpleasant was going to happen to me very soon.

They left me standing against a wall in a classic stress position, designed to weaken, to break down resistance. In this position, my forehead was flat against the wall, my feet about twenty inches away from it; I was stretched right up onto my toes, arms handcuffed behind my back. My forehead was supporting my entire bodyweight against the cold surface, a surface flat as purgatory. Every time I tried to move from that position, somebody punched me, whacked me back into it. They left me like that. I tried to move my head, somebody smacked it hard against the wall, a staggering blow. My head must be thicker than I realised, or had I passed out? I tried to move my arms, manacled behind my back now for bloody hours. The handcuffs were still of the ratchet type, tightening automatically if I tried to move. Because of the beating, they were racked up tight to the last notch again, biting into my wrists, a cold, insistent metallic cutting agony. The flesh on the wrists themselves I could feel ballooning up once more over the edges of the cuffs, a two-inch step of swollen flesh, the fingers entirely numb, fluid from the sores flowing out around the steel. My shoulder muscles seized suddenly with the tearing torture of cramp, unbearable, it must be relieved. The arches of my feet were clenched hard with the strain of being on tiptoes, slow rivers of fire burned through the muscle, sinews quivering. Every fibre was shaking now with the impossible effort of maintaining the posture; I had to move, but I knew they were standing, watching, waiting for a twitch, the whip poised, the baton raised. I moved. They beat me to the floor . . .

They dragged me up, walked me around for a little bit to disorientate me, which wasn't difficult, as I was in darkness all the time. Now somebody stood me with my back to another wall in another part of the building – only this time my head was not against the wall, I was standing slightly away from it. I could not see, but I could sense somebody to one side. Suddenly, wham! they smashed my head back hard against the wall. Two seconds later, two hours later, impossible to judge, smash! my head crashed off the wall again. Nobody was asking any questions. Crack! I was thinking, "Ask me something, ask me something, at least let me say something, or hit me so I fall unconscious . . ." Crack! This went on – it could have been thirty times, it could have been a thousand times, I have no idea. Nobody asked me anything after this, nothing at all. Now, dazed, stunned like a chicken before its throat is cut, I was worried, I had lost track of how they were going to interrogate me; this was not going by the book any more. They left me. They put me in a cell with John, for the first time, but we knew they would be listening.

He said, "I've told them something."

"Don't worry, it's no problem."

They took me back out of that room, along a corridor, and attached me to the frame of what was obviously a bare iron bedstead. At the other end of the room I could hear someone being questioned. "Zaun," he said. "My name is Zaun." I wondered who Zaun was. From his accent, he was obviously American. That meant we were not alone. He had to be a flyer like ourselves.

They pushed me down onto the bed, but the agony in my wrists and hands, still ratcheted behind my back, made me catapult straight back upright again.

"What is it?" asked the guard.

"My arms. My arms." He uncuffed me, loosened off the ratchets, and cuffed my wrists back together, but this time in front. This was absolute heaven, once the worst of the pain wore off. Utterly exhausted, I curled up on the bedsprings and fell into a dead sleep. It was daylight when I awoke. The guard undid my blindfold. I looked around. I was in what we came to call "the dormitory". Several other beds, some with mattresses, were dotted around.

"It's OK," said the guard, "I'm a friend. How are you?" Thinking this was another part of the interrogation, or some sort of trick, I shook my head.

"No," he said. "Look, I'm trying to help you . . ." He brought out some cigarettes from an inside pocket.

"Do you need to see a doctor, or anything?" he asked.

At this point, I desperately, desperately wanted to say something to this guy, whom I christened "Ahmed". Though horribly scarred, his was the first friendly face in what felt already like a long age, a potential soft patch in a particularly unpleasant experience. His was the first friendly voice. But still, at the back of my mind, was the idea that he might be a more subtle form of quizmaster. He was very good though. He brought me some cold lentil soup, and I drank a tiny amount; but despite not having touched anything for twenty-four hours, I was just not interested in food; there were other things to think about.

"Where do you come from?" he asked.

"I cannot answer that question."

The heavy brigade suddenly came in; Ahmed had my

blindfold back on just in time. They began interrogating me there and then. "Stand up!" Punch, kick. I blocked them with the usual response. They became furious. "You will be sorry, Nichol, you will be sorry." A few more blows. They left.

Once they had gone, Ahmed chained me back to the bed by one wrist and took off the blindfold again. My interrogators left me there all that day. And all that day, the air raids came in, the jets screamed overhead, the Triple-A mountings on the roof hammered away, bombs crumped and rattled nearby. During one of these raids, Ahmed was in the room. A bomb went off right next to the building we were in. He looked out of the window, and then said, casually, "Someone has just been killed down there," and he pointed. I fell asleep again in the afternoon.

Later, still chained to the bed, a heavy kick in the ribs woke me: "What's your name? Rank? Number?"

"8204846."

"Where did you come from?"

"I cannot answer that question."

"You *will* be sorry, you know that, don't you, Nichol?"

"I cannot answer that question."

"We will come back for you soon. You will be sorry."

I know I'm going to be sorry. I'm already bloody sorry.

The psychological terror, the psychological torture, is just as great as the physical torture. You are shit-scared. You desperately want him to come and get you, as soon as possible, to get it over with, so that you can break, so that you can tell him something. But you haven't suffered enough yet, they haven't done enough to you yet to tell them anything. You haven't suffered enough to let anyone down, you haven't suffered enough to let yourself down; but you *do* want it to be over, to reach an end.

In the evening they came for me. They unshackled me, put the blindfold on, hauled me upright, dragged me down the stairs, round the streets, back into the interrogation centre; the familiar journey, almost routine by now. The chair: they threw me down into it. One guy was holding my arm on one side, one on the other. I knew in my heart of hearts that this was the time, I knew that it was going to get really rough now.

I was sitting with the solid fist of my own fear in my stomach.

"What squadron are you from?"

"I cannot answer that . . ."

Bang! somebody punched me in the face. Blood came pouring out of my face onto my lap, dripping. I could feel it warm on my thighs. On my lower half, I was wearing a flying-suit, a chemical-warfare suit, long-johns underneath all that, but I could still feel the blood dripping warm onto the upper part of my legs. Someone was hitting me in the face, over and over again. Question. Then somebody standing just to one side hit me hard across the skull with a solid piece of wood. Thwack! My head rang to the blow like some kind of bell. There were brilliant aching lights flashing behind the blindfold. You really do see stars. I was in the middle of the Milky Way. Question.

"I cannot answer . . ." A kick in the stomach – how he got to my stomach I don't know, they were still holding me down on the chair. I fell over to one side in the chair, my gorge rising; they dragged me up by the hair. Question.

"I cannot . . ." Whack! Someone punched me again, someone hit me with the wood, dazzling bright lights and the sudden downward spiral into blackness. Now I was disorientated, my brain was really starting to shut down, but still I thought, "It's going to take more than this, it's going to take more than this. I'm not breaking down without good cause." Somebody dragged my boot off, tearing it away with a furious wrench. "What on earth? What are they going to do to me now?" Whack! A plastic pipe filled with something hard hit me across the shins. A biting agony across the shins, on and on, biting. Question.

And now, somebody grabs the hair at the nape of my neck, and begins stuffing tissue-paper down the back of my T-shirt. That is appalling. This is terrifying now. I am sitting in a darkened room in the middle of enemy territory, and somebody has just stuffed tissue-paper down the back of my neck. "What are they doing that for?" I know straightaway what they are doing that for, I can imagine only too well. "Shit, they are going to set me on fire!" Now I really want him to ask me another question, I *am* sorry, I want to say something, I want to tell him something, anything. But he doesn't ask me a question. He just sets fire to the paper.

I throw my head violently from side to side, to try to escape from the burning, to try to shake the tissue-paper clear of my neck. They are still whacking my shins. Quite soon, mercifully soon, somebody behind me slaps out the flames.

"What squadron are you from?"

"Fifteen."

I had had enough.

APPENDIX I:
GERMAN WAR BIRDS

ANTON H.G. FOKKER

Fokker, a Dutchman, founded the Fokker aircraft factory at Schwerin in Germany in 1913, which turned over to the making of war planes for the German military with the commencement of World War I in 1914. A year later he developed the interrupter gear which allowed a machine gun to fire through the revolving propeller blades of a fighter. In this extract from his memoirs he recalls the personalities of Germany's most legendary WWI aces, Richthofen, Boelcke and Immelmann.

The contempt of the German flyers for death was only equalled by their love of life while they still had that precious possession. So complete was their disregard for the hazard of aerial combat, I sometimes thought they were hardly aware of its terrible dangers. Yet that could not be possible, for on every day they went hunting in the skies some members of the *Jagdstaffel* failed to return. When I met them in their headquarters at the Front they jested and sported as though the angel of death were not the permanent leader of their circus, and when they came to Berlin for a fortnight's holiday, they lived as riotously as though they hadn't a care in the world. That is, with a few exceptions, among them Richthofen. He was calm, cold, ambitious; a born leader of men and Germany's greatest ace.

Richthofen, Boelcke, and Immelmann, Germany's trio of aces, I knew intimately; as intimately at least as one knows men who, having stared at death so often, have learned to wear a mask lest an occasional human weakness betray their almost hypnotic gallantry. They were as different as men of the same breed can be. One by one I saw them die as I knew they must die; for they were in a contest not with a human opponent but with Time, the cruelest foe in the world. Judging their bravery by my own, I reckoned them supreme. Knowing the accuracy of the machine gun and the airplane in the hands of a skilled pilot, calculating the remote chance of surviving any prolonged campaign in the air, I would never have had the courage to face the enemy. Every man who went aloft was marked for death, sooner or later, once his wheels left the ground.

Max Immelmann, with Boelcke, was the first German pilot to win the Pour le Mérite, the Empire's highest decoration for military bravery. This medal originated by Frederick the Great, was colloquially called "the blue Max", from its colour and Frederick's name. Its French title was due to the fact that the founder of the German Empire would only speak French. Immelmann was a serious, modest youngster, intensely interested in the technical details of flying. He was popular, and originally better known than Boelcke. He came to Berlin after his fourth or fifth victory and I took him to Schwerin for a tour of my factory. We talked little of abstract matters, but always of machine guns – he was an excellent shot – of aerial maneuvers, of the relative merits of one pursuit plane over another. He had eyes like a bird of prey, and a short, athletic body capable of standing the bombardment of nerves from which every flyer suffers when alone with his imagination. At no time did he drop a hint that he considered air fighting dangerous. As far as I might have known, he had not the slightest care in the world. He gained fifteen victories before he was killed June 18, 1916.

Almost as much mystery surrounds the manner of Immelmann's death as Guynemer's, which was never adequately explained. Immelmann's plane suddenly fell to the ground as he was flying near the German front lines. It was first given out that his Fokker fighter had failed in midair. This explanation naturally did not satisfy me, and I insisted on examining the remains of the wreck, and establishing the facts of his death. What I saw convinced me and others that the fuselage had been shot in two by shrapnel fire. The control wires were cut as by shrapnel, the severed ends bent in, not stretched as they would have been in an ordinary crash. The tail of the fuselage was found a considerable distance from the plane itself. As he was flying over the German lines there was a strong opinion in the air force that his comparatively still un-known monoplane type – which somewhat resembled a Morane-Saulnier – had been mistaken for a French plane. I was finally able to convince air headquarters sufficiently so that, while it was not stated that he had been shot down by German artillery – which would have horrified his millions of admirers – neither was the disaster blamed on the weakness of his Fokker plane. The air corps exoner-ated the Fokker plane unofficially, although as far as the public was concerned the whole episode was hushed up. Because of this investigation, however, silhouettes of all German types were sent to all artillery commanders to prevent a repetition of the Immelmann catastrophe.

Boelcke, the son of a Saxon schoolmaster, was of quite a different type, although like Immelmann intensely inter-ested in the technical details of flying and aerial combat. In a desperate effort to save him from inevitable death, the High Command restricted his flying after his sixteenth victory in 1916, and sent him to Austria, Bulgaria, and Turkey to instruct others in airmanship. But he became so wearied of the relentless adulation showered on him that he begged leave to return to the Front. Until Lieutenant Boehme, of his *staffel* collided with his plane in midair causing his wing to drop off, his victories mounted, reaching a total of forty before he died. Lieutenant Boehme, who was barely restrained from suicide in his grief, was later shot down in a dogfight.

Choosing the flying corps because an asthmatic affliction kept him from harder labour, Boelcke left the signal corps shortly before the War to enter the Halberstadt flying school. After seven weeks' training he became a pilot and the first of September, 1914, saw him flying over the Western Front as an observer. It was in June of 1915 that he obtained his first Fokker single-seater in company with Immelmann and began his career as an ace. Boelcke had charm, and a kindness of heart which extended itself even to the enemies he brought down. He spent much of his leisure motoring to hospitals to cheer up his wounded opponents, leaving some gift of cigarettes or other trifle as he departed. Richthofen, who worshipped Boelcke and learned many of his flying tricks from him, records the fact that "it is a strange thing that everybody who met Boelcke imagined that he alone was his true friend. I have met about forty men, each of whom imagined that he alone had Boelcke's affection. Men whose names were unknown to Boelcke believed that he was particularly fond of them. Boelcke had not a personal enemy." Yet no one had a better record of bravery. He died on October 28, 1916.

Richthofen, with whom I became very friendly, was an entirely different sort of flyer from the other two. Without the subconscious art which Boelcke and Immelmann possessed, he was slow to learn to fly, crashing on his first solo flight and only mastering the plane at last by sheer force of superior will. Time and again he escaped death by a miracle before he managed to conquer the unruly plane which later became his willing slave. A Prussian, son of a Junker family, Richthofen was imbued with the usual ideas of a young nobleman. He flew spectacularly in his series of all-red planes which became famous over the Western Front. Flaunting himself in the face of his enemies, he built up a reputation which perhaps somewhat daunted his opponents before the fight began.

Ultimately, Richthofen became an excellent flyer and a fine shot, having always done a lot of big game hunting. But whereas many pilots flew with a kind of innocent courage which had its special kind of magnificence, Richthofen flew with his brains, and made his ability serve him. Analyzing every problem of aerial combat, he reduced chance to the minimum. In the beginning his victories were easy. Picking out an observation plane, he dived on it from the unprotected rear, opened up with a burst and completed the job almost before the enemy pilots were aware of trouble. It was something of this machine-like perfection which accounts for his near death in 1917 after his fifty-seventh victory. Richthofen himself has described the experience:

"On a very fine day, July 6, 1917, I was scouting with my gentlemen. We had flown for quite a while between Ypres and Armentières without getting into contact with the enemy.

"Then I saw a formation on the other side and thought immediately, these fellows want to fly over . . . We had an unfavorable wind – that is, it came from the east. I watched them fly some distance behind our lines. Then I cut off their retreat. They were again my dear friends, the Big Vickers . . . The observer sits in front. . . .

"My opponent turned and accepted the fight, but at such a distance that one could hardly call it a real air fight. I had not even prepared my gun for firing, for there was lots of time before I could begin to fight. Then I saw the enemy's observer, probably from sheer excitement, open fire. I let him shoot, for, at a distance of 300 yards or more, the best marksmanship is helpless. One does not hit one's target at such a distance.

"Now he flies toward me, and I hope that I will succeed in getting behind him and opening fire.

"Suddenly, something strikes me in the head. For a

moment, my whole body is paralyzed. My arms hang down limply beside me; my legs flop loosely beyond my control. The worst was that a nerve leading to my eyes had been paralyzed and I was completely blind.

"I feel my machine tumbling down – falling. At the moment, the idea struck me. "This is how it feels when one is shot down to his death." Any moment I wait for my wings to break off. I am alone in my bus. I don't lose my senses for a moment.

"Soon I regain power over my arms and legs, so that I grip the wheel. Mechanically, I cut off the motor, but what good does that do? One can't fly without sight. I forced my eyes open – tore off my goggles – but even then I could not see the sun. I was completely blind. The seconds seemed like eternities. I noticed I was still falling.

"From time to time, my machine had caught itself, but only to slip off again. At the beginning, I had been at a height of 4,000 yards, and now I must have fallen at least 2,000 or 3,000 yards. I concentrated all my energy and said to myself, "I must see – I must – I must see."

"Whether my energy helped me in this case, I do not know. At any rate, suddenly I could discern black-and-white spots, and more and more I regained my eyesight. I looked into the sun – could stare straight into it without having the least pains. It seemed as though I was looking through thick black goggles.

"Again I caught the machine and brought it into a normal position and continued gliding down. Nothing but shell holes below me. A big block of forest came before my vision and I recognized that I was within our lines.

"If the Englishman had followed me, he could have brought me down without difficulty but, thanks to God, my comrades protected me. At the beginning, they couldn't understand my fall.

"I wanted to land immediately, for I didn't know how long I could keep up consciousness. . . .

"I noticed that my strength was leaving me and that

everything was turning black before my eyes. Now it was high time.

"I landed my machine without any particular difficulties, tore down a few telephone wires, which I didn't mind at the moment. . . . I tumbled out of the machine and could not rise again. . . .

"I had quite a good-sized hole – a wound of about ten centimeters in length. At one spot, as big as a dollar, the bare white skull bone lay exposed. My thick Richthofen skull had proved itself bullet proof."

The bad news of his fall was kept from the German public which superstitiously regarded him as a superman, beyond death. It was less than a month before he was back in the air again, but never his old self. Something had gone out of him: "Manfred was changed after he received his wounds," his mother is reported to have said. Now he knew that death could reach him as well as the others, and that is no knowledge for an airman to live with, day and night.

The Richthofen "circus," as the Allies called it, was known in Germany as the *Jagdgeschwader*, composed of four *staffels* of five planes each. Toward the end of the War, there were three of these, and their size increased to forty-eight planes. They moved back and forth along the lines from July, 1917, on, wherever the fighting was thickest. It was with *Jagdstaffel* II, Boelcke's old group to whose command Richthofen succeeded, that the greatest German ace gained his long list of victories before the formation of the "circus". The Allied planes were camouflaged in colours, but as if in direct challenge, Richthofen's circus was brighter than the sun in colour. His own plane was red from propeller to tail, and the planes of his particular *staffel* were red in kind, with little distinguishing marks, such as a blue tail, white rudder, black aileron, to set them apart from the Red Knight.

For three weeks I lived with the Richthofen *Jagdstaffel*, located at the time on the Ypres front. Ten or twelve officers were living together in a pretty little Belgian

country place. This was only a short time before Richthofen was killed, when he commanded the circus and had a
great deal of executive work to attend to as well as his daily
fighting. Secretaries raced about, and orderlies came and
went all day.

Artillery sites were only about fifteen kilometers behind
the Front lines, and so, when the circus was scheduled to
go aloft, I would start an hour or so ahead of time for the
artillery camp, and follow the air fights through their
powerful range finders. As a rule the fights would not
be more than nine or ten miles off, and two or three miles
in the sky.

Spending hours at the artillery range, I saw battle after
battle in the air. *Staffel* after *staffel* would leave its airport,
circle for height, proceed to the appointed rendezvous in
the sky, and form the "circus" before cruising along the
Front in search of Allied squadrons. Richthofen would be
flying out in front, the lowest plane in an echelon of Vs,
like a flock of immobile geese, fantastically coloured and
flashing like mirrors in the sun.

Out of the western skies would come a tinier V of Allied
planes, then another and another, until the whole line of
them closed with the "circus" and the blue sky was etched
with streaking flight. Round and round, diving, zooming,
looping, with motors roaring full out, these lethal wasps
spat flaming death through the glittering propeller's disk.
Cometlike projectiles missed each other by inches in the
whirlpool of sound and fury. Suddenly, out of nowhere,
two planes in 125-mile-an-hour flight rushed at each other
too late to loop, dive, swerve. Crash! They merged,
tangling wings, clasping each other like friends long
separated, before gravity pulled them reluctantly apart
and they began a crazy descent to bury themselves eight
feet in earth miles below. Perhaps I alone noticed them.
The taut pilots in the dogfights were taking in sensations
with express train speed – flying – fighting – automatons at
the highest pitch of skill and nerve in a frenzy of killing.

Richthofen gained the tail of an enemy. The tracer

bullets were spelling out death, when the enemy's engine stopped, the plane went into a quick spin, and only levelled out for a landing quite close to where we were watching the whole battle. We quickly motored over. Richthofen had already gone back to the Front, after landing first, and shaking hands with the officer he had brought down. A bullet had pierced the officer's pocket, ruined a package of cigarettes, travelled on down through his sleeve, punctured his Sam Browne belt and gone on without injury. We looked over his coat, that might so easily have been his shroud.

Asking him to ride with us, we took him back to the flying field, where we picked up Richthofen and together went to the Casino for a good breakfast and friendly chat. I took moving pictures of the officer and Richthofen. Later I acquired a patch of the fabric from Richthofen's sixtieth victory. After a pleasant breakfast, we turned the prisoner over to headquarters, since it was against regulations to keep him for any length of time.

For several days we followed Richthofen's fights. Many of his victories were easy, especially when he attacked the clumsy two-seaters. His usual technique was to dive in their rear, zoom under the tail, and shoot them from very close range. By this time he had become a first class pilot and handled his plane with utmost skill. Seldom did he use more than a quarter of his ammunition on an enemy. Four hundred rounds were carried for each of the two guns. When pilots went from one combat to another, they usually fought until their ammunition was exhausted before returning home.

I think one of the reasons Richthofen survived so long was his ability to keep guarding himself while he attacked. Many other aces were shot down during a fight unexpectedly, as they were training their guns on an enemy pilot. Richthofen would fight very close to his wing men, and not until it was a real dogfight, with the whole air in confusion, would he release his formation to permit every pilot to shift for himself. He was an excellent teacher, and young pilots who showed exceptional skill and courage were sent to his *staffel* to get experience. At first they were taken along to observe the fighting from a distance, and forbidden to engage in combat at all during the first three flights. For it was found that many of the new pilots were killed in their first fight, before they had learned to be all eyes in every direction.

Immediately after each battle, Richthofen would gather his officers for conference and a discussion of the tactics. Occasionally he would censure pilots too aggressive, or too willing to pull away before the battle was over. He was perhaps not so much liked as admired, but the respect other pilots had for him was unbounded.

Proud though he was, the réclame of his feats gave him no particular pleasure. He was not interested in publicity, and though he received letters by the ton from all sorts of people, he cared little for fan mail. When he was around, parties were never wild, for the other pilots felt constrained in the presence of their chief.

Richthofen knew little or nothing about the technical details of airplanes. Unlike Boelcke and Immelmann, he was not even interested, except as it was necessary for him to know for his own safety and development.

While they were alive, we did our best to show the flyers a gay time. It was an open secret that all airplane manufacturers entertained lavishly while the pilots were on leave, and when the aces came to Berlin for the periodical competitions. Because of the popularity of the Fokker plane at the Front, many of the pilots on furlough preferred to make their headquarters with us at the Hotel Bristol. I had a deep admiration for them, and counted many as close friends. Some were so young, I felt almost paternal towards them, although I was only twenty-eight when the War ended.

It was a pleasure to keep open house for the pilots. Naturally it served our interests to hear them talk, discuss one plane and another, the latest tactics of the Allied-airmen, sketch their ideal of a combat ship. But what they wanted most, and what we tried to give them was gaiety, charm, diversion, the society of pretty girls, the kind of a good time they had been dreaming about during their nightmare stay at the Front. Berlin was full of girls eager to provide this companionship, for aviators in Germany as in every other country were the heroes of the hour, and the spirit was in the air to make these men happy before they returned to face death alone.

APPENDIX II:
DICTA BOELCKE

Oswald Boelcke (1891–1916) of the German Air Service was one of the first fighter pilots to develop the theory and tactics of aerial combat. His set rules of air fighting, the Dicta Boelcke, *became the basis of the training principles for German fighter pilots in the latter years of World War I and throughout World War II.*

1. Always try to secure an advantageous position before attacking. Climb before and during the approach in order to surprise the enemy from above and dive on him swiftly from the rear when the moment to attack is at hand. 2: Try to place yourself between the sun and the enemy. This puts the glare of the sun in the enemy's eyes and makes it difficult to see you and impossible for him to shoot with any accuracy. 3: Do not fire the machine guns until the enemy is within range and you have him squarely within your sights. 4: Attack when the enemy least expects it or when he is preoccupied with other duties such as observation, photography, or bombing. 5: Never turn your back and try to run away from an enemy fighter. If you are surprised by an attack on your tail, turn and face the

enemy with your guns. 6: Keep your eye on the enemy and do not let him deceive you with tricks. If your opponent appears damaged, follow him down until he crashes to be sure he is not faking. 7: Foolish acts of bravery only bring death. The *jasta* must fight as a unit with close teamwork between all pilots. The signals of the formation leader must be obeyed.

APPENDIX III:
FIGHTER ACES OF THE WORLD

A fighter "ace" is generally taken to be the victor in 5 and more aerial combats. Since 1914 more than 5000 fighter pilots have achieved ace status. Among the greatest are:

World War I

Germany/Austria-Hungary

Manfred von Richthofen (Germany) 80
Ernst Udet (Germany) 62
Erich Loewenhardt (Germany) 53
Werner Voss (Germany) 48
Fritz Rumey (Germany) 45
A selection of others:
Oswald Boelcke (Germany) 40
Lothar von Richthofen (Germany) 40
Godwin Brumowski (Aus) 35
Herman Goering (Ger) 22

Allies-France/Belgium, Great Britain, Italy, Russia, Canada, Australia, USA

René Fonck (Fra) 75
William A Bishop (Can) 72
Raymond Collishaw (Can) 62 [possibly 60]
Edward Mannock (GB) 61 [possibly 73]
James McCudden (GB) 57
Others:
Georges Guynemer (Fr) 54 [possibly 53]
A. Beauchamp-Proctor (SA) 54
Albert Ball (GB) 47 [possibly 44]
Francesco Baracca (Ita) 34
Willy Coppens (Bel) 37
Edward Rickenbacker (US) 26
SC Rosevear (US) 23
Alexander Kazakov (Russia) 17

Spanish Civil War

Joaquin Morato Y Castano (Spa) 40
Others:
Frank Tinker (US) 7 [possibly 8]
Stephan Suprun (USSR) 15
Werner Moelders (Ger) 15 [plus 101 WWII]

World War II

Axis Powers—Germany, Austria, Hungary, Rumania, Italy, Japan

Erich Hartman (Ger) 352
Gerhard Barkhorn (Ger) 301
Gunther Rall (Ger) 275
Otto Kittel (Ger) 267
Walter Nowotny (Ger) 258
Others:
Johannes Steinhoff (Ger) 176

Hans-Joachim Marseille (Ger) 158
Hiroyshi Nishizawa (Jap) c110
Adolf Galland (Ger) 104
Tetsuzo Iwamoto (Jap) 80
Constantine Cantacuzine (Rum) 60
Adriano Visconti (Ita) 26

Allies—France, Great Britain & Empire, USA, USSR

Ivan Kozuhedub (USSR) 62
Aleksandr I. Pokryshkin (USSR) 59
Richard Bong (US) 40
Mato Dubovak (Yugoslavia) 40
Thomas McGuire (US) 38
Others:
James E. Johnson (GB) 38 [possibly 36]
Pierre Clostermann (Fr) 36
Adolf "Sailor" Malan (South Africa) 35
Brendan E. Finucane (GB) 32
Clive Caldwell (Aus) 28
Douglas Bader (GB) 23

Korea

United Nations

Joseph McConnell (US) 16
James Jabara (US) 16
Manuel J. Fernandez (US) 14
George Davies (US) 14
Royal N. Baker (US) 13.5

North Korea & Allies

Nicolai V. Sutyagin (USSR) 22
Yevgeny G. Pepelyaev (USSR) 19
Alexandr Smortzkow (USSR) 15
LK Schukin (USSR) 15 [possibly 14]

Others:
Chszao Bao-tun (China) 9
Kam Den Dek (North Korea) 8

Vietnam

United Nations

Randy Cunningham (US) 5
Robin Olds (US) 5 [plus 12 WWII]

North Vietnam & Allies

Nguyen Toon (North Vietnam) 13
Nguyen Van Coc (North Vietnam) 9

For further information see, *inter alia*:
Above the Trenches, CF Shores et al, 1990; *Horrido!* T J
Constable & R F Toliver, 1968.
Fighter Pilot "Ace" List website:
(www.csd.uwo.ca/~pettypi/elevon/aces.html), Al Bowers
& David Lednicer, 1999.